In Hitler's Germany

ALSO BY BERNT ENGELMANN

Germany Without Jews

In Hitler's Germany

EVERYDAY LIFE
IN THE THIRD REICH

BERNT ENGELMANN

Translated from the German by
Krishna Winston

METHUEN LONDON

First published in Great Britain 1988
by Methuen London Ltd
11 New Fetter Lane, London EC4P 4EE

First published in English in the USA 1986
by Pantheon Books

Grateful acknowledgement is made to the McGraw-Hill Book Company
for permission to reprint and paraphrase material on the Lebensborn
from Marc Hillel and Clarissa Henry, *Of Pure Blood* (New York:
McGraw-Hill Book Co., 1977).

British Library Cataloguing in Publication Data

Engelmann, Bernt
In Hitler's Germany: everyday life in
the Third Reich.
1. Germany—Social life and customs—
20th century
I. Title   II. Bis alles in Scherben fällt.
III. Im Gleichschritt marsch. *English*
943.086′092′4   DD239

ISBN 0-413-17250-3

Typeset by Rowland Phototypesetting Ltd, Bury St Edmunds, Suffolk
Printed and bound in Great Britain by
Redwood Burn Ltd, Trowbridge, Wiltshire

Contents

Foreword

In reading Bernt Engelmann's book of revelations, I was haunted on almost every page by the reflections of Erich Lüth. I had visited the elderly German in Hamburg in 1967. The city had not been one of Hitler's favourites; he was wary of its spirit of independence. Nonetheless . . .

'Under Hitler, I have been a coward. Cowardice under a dictatorship is legitimate. You cannot be brave every day. I have tried to be courageous . . . You see, I belong to a nation which has always been rich in military heroes, but is underdeveloped in civil courage.'

Civil courage, and much more frequently the lack of it, are what this astonishing book is all about.

Though the experience was uniquely German (and Austrian, *vide* Waldheim), is the recurrence of it elsewhere, in a distinctly more benign style, so outrageous a thought?

Engelmann has taken a journey back in time, visiting places he had known as a child and young man. He looked up old acquaintances, rehashed old times, and found himself engaged in spontaneous conversations with others in cafés, shops, and hotel lobbies.

These were not war criminals nor heroes of the resistance; just your ordinary, comfortable-as-an-old-shoe people. What was everyday life like under Hitler? How was it on the job? How did conversations go in the family parlour? What do you most vividly remember?

Engelmann himself remembered, and was reminded by others, of a surprising number who behaved decently at no small risk: Aunt Annie Ney, the café owner, and Herr Desch, the fashionable tailor, who smuggled Jewish kids out of the country; the conservative Pastor Klötzel, who had confirmed the author in 1935, who had said yes to God and no to Hitler, who had died in a camp, and whose memorial service drew an unprecedented crowd of worshippers; the thunderous applause during a performance of Schiller's *Don Carlos* – 'Sire, grant us freedom of thought.'

Nonetheless . . .

It is Marga, a schoolgirl friend from Düsseldorf days, who most clearly represents the spirit of the times. Oh, with what delight she remembered her birthday of 3 March 1933. It was a week after the Reichstag fire. Engelmann was remembering the first wave of terror that week, the SS trucks roaring down the streets, dragging people out of apartments, and all that. Marga remembered and 'loved the constant marching and singing, with flags and bunting everywhere. All in all, we had a wonderful, carefree youth, didn't we?' And the unity of the German people, of course. Standing tall, no doubt.

As for Grete's mother, a gentle woman, who never knowingly harmed anyone, her love for the Führer was a love that passeth all understanding. When she eventually faced up to the truth of Buchenwald, she suffered a breakdown, though in her sufferings she blamed 'the riff-raff', not Hitler. He had nothing to do with it.

It was the press and radio that really set the tone. As early as 30 January 1933, when Hitler assumed the chancellorship and opposition was still strong, Radio Cologne said it all: 'Like a blazing fire, the news spreads across Germany. A million hearts are aflame. Rejoicing and gratitude pour forth.' What did you expect of young Marga and of Grete's mom?

It was so easy. Nobody was more surprised than Adolf Hitler himself.

It was the evil of banality as much as the banality of evil that was the challenge there and then. It may possibly be the challenge here and now. Bernt Engelmann's account is more than a memoir; it is a cautionary tale.

Studs Terkel

Introduction

When Adolf Hitler came to power in 1933, I was a schoolboy of twelve. I was twenty-four at the end of April 1945, shortly before the unconditional surrender of Hitler's 'Greater German' Wehrmacht, when General Patton's Third Army liberated me from the Dachau concentration camp.

Between these two events lay the twelve grimmest years in modern European history, years that saw a country with a highly developed cultural life and all the characteristics of an advanced civilisation revert to a barbarism beyond that of the darkest Middle Ages, which found its horrible climax in the Holocaust, the physical liquidation of the Jews of Europe. As this book shows, those years are reflected very differently in the memories of Germans who lived through them. Much depends on how each individual viewed the Nazi regime at the time and how he chose to respond to it: as a blindly loyal supporter; as an opportunistic fellow traveller who saw only his own gain; as a docile, apolitical citizen, who obeyed the authorities and did what he considered his duty; as one who kept quiet and shut his eyes but was 'privately against it all'; as an innocent victim; as someone who resisted the regime as best he could, cautiously and rather passively; or even as someone who repeatedly risked his life by resisting boldly and actively, like my 'Uncle Erich', Alias Major von Elken.

As luck would have it, I became aware of the political situation while I was still quite young. I knew where I stood, and even as a child participated in clandestine resistance to Hitler's lawless regime. My lively interest in what was going on can be ascribed to my immediate environment: my parents and relatives and their closest friends.

I had an excellent relationship with my father, who told the most marvellous stories when I was little. Later, when I had developed into a rather precocious youth, avid to learn and to understand the world, he answered all my questions patiently and thoroughly. He followed the politics of the Weimar Republic attentively, though from a distance. He was a staunch advocate of democracy to whom Nazism appeared as a dangerous sickness – he could only hope that the patient, Germany, would survive.

My mother was a hard-working, strong-minded woman. She manifested little interest in politics, but was quick to recognise practical steps that could be taken to assist the victims of an obviously inhuman policy.

From my father I learned to analyse things logically, from my mother to draw practical conclusions and to act on them. Both abilities were necessary, for when I was barely sixteen, my parents had me declared legally of age and transferred to me what was left of the family fortune, as well as the resources of relatives and friends, who by then had fled the country. My family was split up by the outbreak of the war. The plan had been to leave Germany by the autumn of 1939 and wait in England for the fall of Hitler. My father was already in London, but my mother and I were unable to join him.

I should acknowledge, also, the influence of my grandparents. My maternal grandfather was a remarkable man. He came from a very poor family with many children; most of its members were small farmers and tradesmen in the mountainous region of Silesia, one of the most impoverished parts of Germany. Like most children from that area in the nineteenth century, my grandfather got almost no formal schooling. At the age of five he was put to work as woodcarver. At fifteen he went to work building the railway, but later had the good fortune to be taken on as an apprentice cabinetmaker. When he was twenty-five, he moved to Berlin and took a job in a furniture factory. After three years he set up his own workshop, specialising in the restoration of valuable old pieces, and a few years later he established an antique business in the fashionable West End of Berlin.

This self-made man was also self-taught, and he acquired knowledge of many fields and enjoyed a great reputation as a licensed art appraiser. But even as a wealthy man he remained what he had become as a boy of seventeen working on the railway: a trade unionist, Social Democrat, and confirmed pacifist. He greeted the Nazis' propaganda with mockery and scorn. From my grandfather I received not only a sense for the value of fine old things, a receptivity to art, and a love of books, but also certain fundamental political views. It was he, the solid businessman with a house on the elegant Kurfürstendamm, who advised me when I was eleven to join Red Falcon, the organisation for the youngest members of the Socialist Workers' Youth.

Another great influence on me was my father's mother. This tiny person, not at all pretty but sharp-witted and splendidly educated, was the eldest daughter of Leopold Ullstein, who in 1887 founded a newspaper company that grew into the largest publishing house in Europe. Among the many books brought out by Ullstein was one that had previously been rejected by twelve other German publishers: Erich Maria Remarque's *All Quiet on the Western Front*, which achieved worldwide sales higher than any previous work of fiction.

The Ullstein family were Jewish, but like most of Berlin's upper-crust Jews, they had little use for their Jewishness. In Berlin one was enlightened, cosmopolitan, emancipated, liberal, tolerant, and uninterested in religion. Instead of religion one had education and culture, which were considered much more important than money.

Thanks to this faith in culture and cultivation, my grandmother was given an education far superior to that of most non-Jewish daughters of the upper classes in Germany. She studied languages and acquired an extensive knowledge of classical, European, and American literature.

In short, my grandmother was a walking encyclopaedia, a living history of literature, from whose brilliant conversation I learned more than from five years at three famous universities. My grandmother could impart the most detailed information without boring me for a second. In addition, and this was significant for my immunity to fascism, militarism, and reactionary politics, my grandmother implanted in me an ineradicable commitment to democracy. For in the Berlin of her youth, both the solid bourgeoisie and the unionised skilled workers were, for the most part, strictly opposed to the ruling Hohenzollern monarchy, to the sabre-rattling militarism that flourished under the Kaiser, to the prevailing imperialistic megalomania, and to the habit the conservative aristocracy had of regarding the leading government posts and the officers' corps as their special purview. Berlin's bourgeois – and among them, of course, the Ullstein family – were left-liberal in their politics, still filled with the spirit of the middle-class revolution of 1848, that first and unsuccessful attempt at establishing democracy in Germany. In the city parliament, Leopold Ullstein represented the bourgeois radical left, the Free Liberal or Progressive Party; he was one of those who sought a link between the bourgeoisie and the social-democratic Workers' Party.

With this sort of family background I might have been expected to resist the contagion of Nazi ideology, as well as the ultra-conservative nationalism that raged through Germany during my school years. Yet, as this book reveals, through the example of my uncle Karl, and more especially his wife and daughter, there existed even within my own family and its circle of friends widely diverging political opinions and positions. It was not uncommon for young people in Germany to reject their families' convictions and follow the Nazis, and many fathers and mothers, themselves strongly opposed to the Hitler regime, were denounced by their own children as 'enemies of the state' or even turned over to the Gestapo.

I attribute the fact that I never dreamed of yielding to the Nazis' propaganda and indoctrination not only to my origins, my education, my family and their friends, but also in great measure to the books these people gave me to read. With such guides as Jack London, B. Traven, Erich Kästner, Mark Twain, and Wilhelm Speyer for a start, and later on John Dos Passos, Upton Sinclair, Thomas Mann, Lion Feuchtwanger, Kurt Tucholsky (who became my favourite author), Robert Neumann (who wrote sparkling parodies of the Nazi writers' bathos), and the anti-war writers Erich Maria Remarque, Romain Rolland, and Arnold Zweig – with these, it was impossible for me to become a Nazi, or even a militarist. And when the books of most of these authors were banned and burned by the Nazis, I knew beyond any doubt that Hitler and his henchmen were my enemies; how else could they do such a thing to the books I loved?

My own bitter experiences during the Nazi years explain why I cannot agree with those intellectuals in present-day Germany who view the twelve years of Nazi domination as the 'work of sinister demons', as 'the product of a grim fate' for which no one can be held accountable. I am convinced that one must seek to understand the factors that made individuals and groups vulnerable to the lure of militarism and totalitarianism, and that one must continue to resist them whenever they appear in the world today. It is in the hope of contributing to such an understanding that I offer this book to the reader.

This account of life in Germany during the years of Nazi rule is based partly on my own memories and partly on discussions with others who lived through the period. I recorded their statements on tape, and most of these appear in the text with only minimal editing.

As I promised my informants, I have altered most names, places, and any other details that might reveal their identity. These small changes do not affect the truth of the interviews or the case histories.

All my informants' descriptions of actual happenings were carefully checked, and corrected where necessary, for it was only natural that recollections of events going back almost half a century should contain some factual errors. Numerical data, for example wages and prices, were checked against official statistics. For corroborating information, particularly on the general mood of the population, I consulted the reports of the Sicherheitsdienst (SD), or Security Service, as well as the 'Reports on Germany' issued by the German Social Democratic Party during the years 1934 to 1940.

This English-language version has been condensed from the two-volume original German edition.

Bernt Engelmann

Prelude: The End of the Republic

What the Nazis called the 'Third Reich' actually began for me eight months before Hitler and his collaborators seized power on 30 January 1933. 30 May 1932 was a Monday, I recall. When I arrived that morning at my secondary school in Berlin's Wilmersdorf section, I saw a large swastika flag waving from a little turret on top of the building.

Students and teachers were swarming around the playground, talking and gesticulating in great agitation. As I passed, I heard one of the older teacher snap at the janitor, 'Get up there and take that thing down! It's a disgrace! Don't just stand there gawping!'

The janitor, grinning insolently, replied that he couldn't find the key to the turret door. The principal was on the telephone with the superintendent of schools, who would have the last word on the incident. Several senior students who overheard the exchange laughed. 'Maybe Adolf Hitler's already the chancellor,' said one of them. 'Then the flag will have to stay up!'

'We'll see heads roll before long,' another remarked, and the janitor nodded approvingly. The teacher pretended he had not heard them and turned on his heel.

Suddenly silence fell over the playground. Everyone craned his neck, staring up at the roof, where a figure could be seen scrambling out of a dormer window. When they realised who the man on the roof was and what he meant to do, students and teachers broke into applause – just a few at first, then more and more of them. The boos and hissing that followed were drowned out by the clapping.

The man up there was Dr. Levy, our French teacher. We recognised him by the empty left sleeve of his jacket that fluttered in the breeze as he groped his way over the roof to the turret, climbed up the iron fire ladder, swung himself over the railing, and pulled down the swastika flag.

Dr. Levy led our second class period. All our hopes of his discussing the incident were dashed. The class followed its normal course: we worked on a new reading passage, and then Dr. Levy wrote out the irregular verbs on the blackboard. When the first board was filled, he pushed it up to reveal the other late panel underneath, where he meant to add the last few verbs. But two words were already written on the board, in large block letters: SALOPE JUIF!

These vocabulary words were unfamiliar to us. Dr. Levy, too, seemed perplexed at first. He simply stared at the board and shook his head. Then he turned to the class and asked, 'Did one of you write that? No? – I believe you. I wouldn't expect this sort of thing from any of you . . . Does anyone know what these words are supposed to mean? No? I thought not. Well, "salope" is a slang word that means figuratively something like "sow". The word is feminine in French, just as it is in German – "la salope" – and therefore the adjective should properly be "juive," not "juif". "Le juif" is the French word for "Jew," and "juif" means "Jewish". So what you see there on the board could be translated "Jewish sow". What is probably meant is "Jewish swine", but the person who dreamed up this insult for me is weak in French and couldn't even use the dictionary properly . . .'

Then he took the sponge, wiped away the word SALOPE, and replaced it with a new word. Now the phrase read MANCHOT JUIF. Manchot, we had learned from him was slang for a veteran who had lost an arm – as he had in 1917 at the Battle of Arras.

On this day, the Nazis were feeling cocky because they had just won an absolute majority in the regional elections in Oldenburg. Furthermore, Chancellor Brüning, from whom President Hindenburg had 'withdrawn his trust', had just resigned. Many people expected Hitler to succeed Brüning, although as recently as April almost two-thirds of all German voters had cast their ballots against him in the presidential election.

There were approximately forty Nazis among the 450 pupils in our school, and they seemed confident that their hour of victory had struck. They certainly behaved as if the Nazis were already in power on this particular Monday: raising their flag and insulting our only Jewish teacher turned out to be merely a prelude to their plans for the rest of the day.

During the midday break three pupils from the upper school, one in an SA* uniform, the two others in Hitler Youth uniforms, went to the

---

*SA (*Sturmabteilung*, or Storm Troops). Also called 'Brownshirts', the SA was the original main force of the Nazi militia, organised by Ernst Röhm. The organisation was later eclipsed by the elite SS (*Schutzstaffel*), also called 'blackshirts', commanded by Heinrich Himmler.

principal to register a complaint against Dr. Levy. Their dress constituted a deliberate provocation, for the government had recently banned the uniforms of all political paramilitary organisations. The principal should have called the police. Instead, he listened to the charges the three raised against Dr. Levy: as a Jew he had no right to become involved in 'German concerns', and moreover, he had dishonoured the flag of the 'movement'.

The principal promised a 'careful investigation' of the matter and suspended Dr. Levy 'until further notice'. News of this action spread through the school like wildfire. Most of the pupils were outraged, but the Nazis smirked with satisfaction.

Thus encouraged, they waited until noon, when school let out, and then began to hound their Jewish classmates. Their first victim was Philipp Löwenstein, a delicate, very pale boy of twelve. Four Hitler Youths from the middle school, all a head taller and considerably stronger than Philipp, attacked him on the Hohenzollerndamm and beat him brutally with their fists and their shoulder belts. He lay on the ground, writhing in pain, blood pouring from his nose and mouth. When a few classmates and I came running to his aid, the bullies beat a hasty retreat to the opposite side of the street. One of them shouted to us, 'If Hitler comes to power today, we'll string them all up, the Jewish swine!'

I arrived home late for lunch, and immediately asked my parents if it was true that Hitler would be named chancellor that day. I was much relieved to hear that the Nazis had rejoiced too soon. I then described to my parents the morning's events at school, recounting how our principal had allowed himself to be intimidated by the Hitler Youths.

'That's the sort of cowardice that will do in the Republic,' my father remarked, and my mother added that the atmosphere at the most recent parent-teacher evening had been rather ominous. The principal announced that he would proceed with 'utmost severity' against any politicisation of the school, but avoided saying anything against the Nazis. Some of his remarks directed against the other side, however, had been pretty strong, she said. 'You could almost tell by the tone of his voice that he was a Nazi sympathiser.'

Not long after these events we moved away from Berlin, and I went to a new school, where I found to my gratification that there were as yet no traces of the 'Third Reich'.

Almost fifty years have passed since then, and twelve of them, as it turned out, were in fact the 'Third Reich', the years of Nazi rule. Those years have marked my generation, destroying our hopes and surpassing our worst fears. And yet, one can meet, among the survivors of those years, some who seem to bear no trace at all of the greatest catastrophe of our time.

ONE

Shades of the Past

'I'm telling you, doctor, these endless negotiations are for the birds! They won't accomplish a thing! The only language the Russians understand is a show of strength! Backing down is a sign of weakness, and they'll take instant advantage of it. We have to convince them of our military superiority; there's just no other way!'

The place was Detmold, the year 1981. The man at the table next to mine in the restaurant of the town's best hotel spoke so loudly that I looked up from the newspaper I was reading. He was a tall man in his late sixties, with short-cropped hair and a healthy tan – an energetic upper-echelon managerial type. On the lapel of his dark blue blazer he wore a tiny Rotary pin.

'Just think, doctor: what if the Soviets were to attack us again. Economic sanctions and protests wouldn't do a bit of good. If you falter for a second, they'll swarm all over you. I know the Russians! Back in December 1943, west of Kiev, outside Zhitomir, when I was just a young fellow . . .'

As he launched into his war stories, I did a quick calculation: in 1943–44, when the Soviet troops began their great counteroffensive, encircling and wearing down one German army after another, this man at the next table must have been about thirty – old enough, at any rate, to know that the war in the east had started with a *German* attack, first on Poland, then on the Soviet Union. He must have known who swarmed over whom.

Soon he was telling his companion – who several times turned toward me with an embarrassed look – that he had been 'a tank driver with the Adolf Hitler division of the Waffen-SS', and that he had volunteered for service on the Eastern Front. I could not help thinking that Hitler had spoken the same way about Russia, using similar expressions: 'Strike ruthlessly', 'no sign of weakness', 'the struggle for the triumph of the German people', 'political necessity'.

I had decided to visit Detmold, in the state of Lippe, because it was here that Hitler's National Socialist German Workers' Party (NSDAP) had won a decisive regional victory on 15 January 1933.

That election, marked by an unprecedented campaign of rallies, marches, and propaganda, had proven crucial for Hitler's seizure of power just two weeks later. I was particularly curious to hear how that time was remembered now.

The grey-haired Rotarian at the next table was still going strong: 'Oh, you don't know what you're talking about, doctor! Back then we hadn't the slightest doubt about the rightness of our cause or the certainty of our ultimate victory. That's what we grew up with – at home, in school, and in the Hitler Youth. I was a member even before '33. In fact, that almost got me kicked out of school just before the university entrance exam . . .'

He laughed heartily and explained that his family had had to draw on all its connections to make sure he got off with only a warning. His 'youthful idealism' was accepted as a mitigating circumstance.

'Of course, we saw ourselves chiefly as a bulwark against the Red Peril. Don't forget, doctor, there was a Bolshevik coup in the offing! Remember, we had six million unemployed in 1932. We small manufacturers would have been the first to be strung up!'

The other man raised an objection. I could not hear what he said, but clearly he thought the businessman exaggerated the fears of Detmold's middle class. In any case, the businessman admitted that the Communists had not played much of a role in Detmold and that the majority of the population, especially in the countryside, had been 'nationalistic in its thinking'.

'Most of the civil servants and the majority of our own employees also had perfectly sound views,' he said. And, as if to prove the point, he reminded the doctor of Hitler's great electoral triumph in the region shortly before the seizure of power.

'Do you remember January the 15th 1933, doctor, or weren't you here yet?'

This time I could hear the other man's reply. He said that he had moved to Detmold only a few days before that date.

'So you didn't really know the town yet. But you must have seen the sea of flags, the cheering crowds, the tremendous enthusiasm. I'll never forget it myself. I've never seen so many ecstatic faces in my entire life. People were wild with joy . . . On the evening of January the 30th, when Hitler had finally been named chancellor, my father went down to the cellar and brought up our best bottles of wine. In the middle of the night he was still out on our balcony shouting, "Sieg Heil! Sieg Heil!" And my mother wept for joy. "To think that I should live to see this!" she said, "Now everything will be all right . . ." And you know, it was all handled quite correctly and with perfect discipline here in Detmold. You must remember that, don't you, doctor? They didn't harm a hair of anyone's head, not even later, or at least not to my knowledge . . .'

He broke off. Perhaps the other man said something that rubbed him the wrong way. But after a moment's pause the businessman continued in a slightly changed tone, 'Well, we've all become older and wiser. Though I sometimes wish our young people today had half the discipline we had and a bit more enthusiasm for the things that really count – you know what I mean . . .'

Then he beckoned to the waiter, paid, and rose from the table, explaining that he had to get back to the plant.

As soon as the grey-haired man left, his table partner moved to the seat he had just vacated. He was a small, portly gentleman in his mid-seventies with rosy cheeks and alert eyes behind sparkling glasses. He ordered a cup of coffee and promptly struck up a conversation with me.

After enquiring whether I was staying in Detmold or only passing through, and whether I had already seen the town, he said, 'Well, Detmold was not really as Nazi as the man at my table would have you think. Hitler's party did have its adherents here, but our little state of Lippe could hardly have been considered a stronghold of Nazism. And as far as Detmold itself goes, it was – as it essentially still is today – a decent small town. At that time it had only about 18,000 inhabitants. There was hardly any industry. The tourist brochures were quite right when they spoke of the "tranquillity and dignity of the former princely seat".'

He told me that he had been born in Anklam, in Pomerania, had studied medicine in Greifswald, and had come to Detmold in January 1933 to do his residency at the hospital. Later, he established a general practice in town.

'I know Detmold well,' he explained, 'and I can assure you that the state of Lippe had a strong democratic tradition before 1933. Until 1932 the Social Democrats were by far the strongest party in Lippe-Detmold.'

In fact, up to 1932 the Nazis had fewer than 3,000 followers in all of Lippe, fewer even than the Communists, and thus amounted to little more than a splinter party, without representation in the state parliament. But in the last parliamentary elections in Lippe-Detmold, on 15 January 1933, the popularity of the Nazi Party increased dramatically, and they captured almost 40 percent of the votes.

'But,' the old man added, 'you must realise that these elections were a matter of life or death for the Nazis, and that they went all out to win them.'

During the worldwide depression which began in 1929 and deepened steadily until 1932, increasing poverty and mass unemployment made more and more voters receptive to the Nazis' slogans – 'The Needs of the People Before the Needs of the Individual', 'Work and Bread for all', 'Down with the Tyranny of Investment Capital'. Some voters mistakenly believed that the NSDAP was truly a national-socialist party, and supported it for that reason. The lowest strata of the middle class yielded particularly large numbers of people ready to bow down before the 'strong man' who promised every person what he wanted to hear and blamed the Jews for all of Germany's troubles.

In July 1932, elections for the Reichstag were held. Hitler's party drew more votes than ever before from the army of unemployed lower-level white-collar workers, small farmers on the verge of bankruptcy, and tradesmen. But after these elections, the NSDAP's popularity fell off again. When new elections were held in November 1932 the Nazis suffered serious reverses throughout the country. The situation was critical for them. Voters were abandoning the party, and, worst of all for Hitler, the Nazis' financial backers in banking and industry were unwilling to keep on paying.

'So the Nazis put on one last, desperate effort, summoning all their resources to make a good showing in the regional parliamentary elections in Lippe, elections which in themselves had little significance,' the old gentleman continued. 'If they had sustained another reverse here, then the people who financed the Nazis would have written them off once and for all. Then the Party would most likely have broken up, and then . . .'

He made a gesture that seemed to suggest that we Germans would have been spared the 'Third Reich', and Europe the Second World War.

'In those few days at the end of 1932 and the beginning of 1933 Germany was teetering on the razor's edge, and that's why the regional elections in Lippe suddenly became so crucial. Hitler and Goebbels launched the greatest propaganda campaign that Germany had ever experienced in connection with an election, or has experienced since.

'Believe me, when I arrived as a young doctor in Detmold in January 1933 and saw all the pre-election goings-on, I wanted to turn around and go right back where I had come from. What a storm burst over Lippe-Detmold during that period! The Nazi leadership threw their last reserves of money and propaganda into the struggle, brought in speakers, agitators, newspaper reporters, and agents from all over Germany, and prepared for a massive assault on the voters of Lippe, who numbered barely 100,000. Several thousand SA and SS troops were rushed to the area.

'Just think,' the old man continued, 'within the space of only ten days, from January the 4th to January the 14th, our little state had to submit to 900 events staged by the Nazis! Ninety Party speakers were sent in. Hitler himself spoke at sixteen major rallies. The local Nazi newspaper, the *Lippe Courier*, carried special inserts and supplements every day, and columns of SS troops shouting slogans marched through the villages and towns from morning till night. In every market square an SA band or a troupe of Nazi minstrels played marches for hours on end, and dozens of cars equipped with loud-speakers drove through the state.'

He paused for a moment and looked at me triumphantly.

'And why am I telling you all this? Well, because in spite of these unprecedented efforts, when the fifteenth of January arrived, more than 60 percent of the voters still voted against the Nazis! The democratic parties, from the Social Democrats to the Conservatives, won almost 50,000 votes in Lippe; and the Communists got 11,000. Hitler's party did manage to gain 39,000 votes, just 6000 more, incidentally, than in the November Reichstag elections. Yet the Nazis managed to create the impression that the current was once more running in their favour. All the newspapers devoted their headlines to the "Victory of the Hitler Party".

'Hitler had achieved what he wanted: the appearance that the Nazi Party had gained new strength and had become the leading party in Lippe. And with that the scales tipped in favour of the Nazis, and two weeks later Hiter was named chancellor by Hindenburg.'

'And what was the payoff for Lippe-Detmold?' I asked. 'Hitler must have been very grateful to its voters.'

The old man shook his head. 'It wasn't a question of gratitude: on the contrary. Our little state lost its autonomy, which it had been so proud of. Along with a number of other small states it was placed under the dictatorial rule of a Statthalter, a governor-general. The newly elected state parliament was sent home and disbanded. Of course, the people had anticipated nothing of the kind on January the 30th, when they celebrated Hitler's move into the Berlin chancellery. In any event, the only ones cheering were the Nazis' supporters; the "silent majority", almost two-thirds of the population around here, had nothing to celebrate and simply stayed home that day.'

He fell silent and seemed to want to end the conversation, but I asked him, 'Do you still remember that thirtieth of January?'

'Of course,' he said, after a moment's reflection, 'I remember it very clearly. I had been in Detmold only four weeks and was working at the hospital. As a resident I had night duty in the emergency room. I still remember the head nurse telling me with great excitement that Hitler had become chancellor. "Isn't it wonderful?" she said. "Now everything's sure to improve!" I just laughed. I had no interest in politics. Later, during our tea break, I recalled that my father, a schoolteacher, had said that if Hitler came to power we would surely have war before long. I felt that was an exaggeration; and besides, the idea of war didn't terrify me, for as a doctor I would be fairly safe, or so I imagined. Doctors stayed home or worked in military hospitals. I wasn't particularly worried about the Nazis . . .'

'Did the situation strike you in any way as hopeful?'

He considered carefully before answering. Finally he said, 'Well, at the time I did wonder whether Hitler's seizure of power might not prove helpful to me. In medical school my fellow students were often complaining that opportunities for doctors were getting worse every year, because Germany had so many doctors. But if Hitler came to power he would "eliminate" our Jewish competition, and then we "Aryans" could have a profitable practice . . .'

He glanced at me, expecting a reaction. But when I said nothing, he continued: 'Of course that was nonsense – in 1932 and '33 there were about 50,000 licensed physicians in all of Germany, not even half the number we have today in the Federal Republic alone. But many viewed the mere 10,000 Jewish doctors as a serious threat to our profession. People were envious of the Jews because they attracted more patients and because so many of the most distinguished physicians were Jewish. For someone like me, a civil servant's son without independent means, the prospects for setting up in private practice were not exactly rosy . . .'

He broke off, but before I could respond, he added hastily, 'Please don't misunderstand! At home we had Jewish neighbours with whom we got along splendidly; and whenever one of us was sick my parents would call our old Jewish family doctor, Dr. Marcuse. No, I wasn't prejudiced! Besides, when the Nazis promised to "eliminate" the Jewish competition, I pictured something quite harmless, perhaps a temporary limit on the licensing of Jewish doctors or something of that nature . . . But perhaps I was just fooling myself, because in fact it wasn't hard to guess what the Nazis really had in mind.'

'What do you mean?'

'Well, I was scared of the Nazis. They had such a brutal manner, a
penchant for violence, and that bloodthirsty way of expressing themselves. On the evening of January the 30th when I was on duty in the
emergency room I got a taste of what was in store for anyone who
resisted them. I had my hands full with all the injured people who
were brought in – Communists, members of the socialist organisations, several Jewish shopkeepers, the administrator of the co-
operative society. They had been beaten up by SA men, drunk with
victory. And then the instigations to violence in the newspapers! The
most vicious of the attacks were directed against Fechenbach, editor of
the Social Democratic *People's Press*. Does the name mean anything
to you?'

Felix Fechenbach had been the closest collaborator of Kurt Eisner,
the first prime minister of Bavaria after the Marxist revolution that
occurred there in 1918. The socialist Eisner was very popular among
Munich's workers but fiercely hated by the right-wing extremists. He
was murdered in February 1919, after which the political right began
to close in on Fechenbach. In 1922 Fechenbach was sentenced to
eleven years in jail for alleged treason. The man was clearly innocent.
Two years later, public indignation resulted in a pardon, and he was
released.

'I had no idea Fechenbach was in Detmold,' I said. 'Did you know
him personally?'

'Yes, I treated him once. You know, of course, that Fechenbach was
viewed by the Nazis as a mortal enemy because of his courageous
stance against them. For weeks the *Lippe Courier* waged a downright
murderous campaign against the "Jewish traitor to the people", as they
labelled Fechenbach. Then, about four or five weeks after the Nazis'
seizure of power, he was attacked on the street in broad daylight and
beaten up. I can still see him lying on the stretcher. He could barely
speak, but he forced his swollen, bloody lips to smile and said, "I just
had a slight run-in with the Nazis, doctor. They don't like me, and the
feeling is mutual." He was a very brave man.'

'And what became of him?'

'After I treated him for his injuries, I asked whether I should get in
touch with his family. He said he had already moved his wife and two
children to safety out of Detmold right after January the 30th. I asked
him why he himself hadn't left, and he replied, "You may think it
stupid of me, doctor, but I can't just run away from the situation. The
workers here trust me, and I wouldn't want them to think I was
cowardly and disloyal." Upon his release from the hospital Herr
Fechenbach was taken into "protective custody" by the Nazis, in order

to "protect him from the rage of the German people", as the news-paper put it. I can still recall the photo in the *Lippe News* which showed him walking between auxiliary policemen in SA and SS uniforms. On the same page were pictures of the Volkshaus, which the Nazis had occupied, and of SA guards in front of a Jewish shoe store. The caption read, "Action-filled street scenes in Detmold", or something of the sort.'

'You might almost call that objective reporting.'

'Well, the *Lippe News* was a middle-class paper and rather restrained. Sometimes you could even read disapproval between the lines. The Nazi paper, on the other hand, wrote openly about the "final reckoning", saying that this was only the beginning.'

'And Fechenbach was sent to a concentration camp?'

'At first they put him in the Detmold jail, but soon afterwards a note appeared in the local papers to the effect that he had been "shot during an escape attempt", while being transferred to a concentration camp. But there wasn't the slightest doubt he had been murdered. No one said anything out loud, but people whispered to one another that the whole business was unspeakable.'

By the summer of 1933 most Germans were adjusting to the new circumstances, at least outwardly. Hardly anyone dared to criticise the numerous violations of the law by the Nazis. Many former supporters of the democratic parties joined the NSDAP purely out of fear. Businessmen and civil servants were particularly quick to follow the new drummer.

'Like most people, I took the path of least resistance,' the old man admitted. 'I said "Heil Hitler!" like a good boy when it seemed called for and joined the National Socialist Physicians' Association and a few of the many other Nazi organisations besides – like the National Socialist People's Welfare, the Reich Air Raid Defence League, and so on – but only as a dues-paying member. Our head physician, who was a devoted Nazi, almost persuaded me to apply for admission to the SS as a battalion doctor. Fortunately I was a few centimetres too short for the SS, and not blond enough. I acted as though I were terribly disappointed . . .'

'So you were actually opposed to the regime?'

'To be honest with you, I wasn't really against the Nazis at that particular time. I often found their methods appalling – their total disregard for the law, and the brutality with which they terrorised innocent people. But then too I was afraid of getting myself into political hot water. I avoided all conversations about politics and kept my mouth shut. The truth is, all that business about the "unity of the

German people" and the "national rebirth", the sense of new vitality and purpose in 1933 – that really impressed me. And I thought it was high time something was done about the massive unemployment. The Winter Aid* campaign was a fine thing. To my mind, no measure could be considered excessive when it was a question of eliminating poverty and bringing about stability. At the time I didn't realise that most of it was simply propaganda; and as for the many unpleasant side effects, I told myself they were none of my business. After all, I wasn't Jewish, nor was I a Social Democrat, nor a Communist. So I kept quiet and consoled myself with the thought that this must be a passing phase. I dare say most people felt as I did.'

He finished his cup of coffee and ended the conversation as abruptly as he had begun it. He paid his bill, let the waiter help him into his overcoat, wished me a pleasant stay, and left the restaurant.

'Will there be anything else, sir?' the waiter asked as he cleared the next table. He and I were alone in the restaurant. 'We stay open until three this afternoon,' he said, 'I'd be glad to bring you another cup of coffee.'

When he brought it, he lingered by the table. 'In January '33 I was an apprentice waiter here, in my third year.' He gestured with his chin toward a table that was partly hidden from the rest of the dining area by a wooden partition. 'In that alcove there,' he said, 'you could always find the men in the brown shirts: Pommerenke, managing editor of the *Lippe Courier*, Dr. Schröder from the Kreisleiter's office, Sturm-führer Segler . . .' He named a few others, and then he went on to describe an incident he remembered as if it had taken place yesterday.

About three weeks after the seizure of power, in February 1933, Pommerenke and Segler had had a little too much to drink, and they called the apprentice waiter to their table and ordered him to take a note to one of the other guests, the distinguished lawyer Rosenbaum. As they handed him the slip of paper, he could not help seeing the words, 'Get out, filthy Jew!' He was horrified, the waiter told me, but he was afraid to disobey.

When Rosenbaum received the note, he jumped up, beetred, and shouted, 'I served at the front! Was wounded twice, at Ypres and Verdun! I'm an officer in the reserves and have an Iron Cross First and Second Class! I shouldn't have to put up with such abuse!' The lawyer showed the note to some of the other guests, but they all turned away in embarrassment and remained silent. Suddenly it became so quiet

---

*Winter Aid was a relief fund financed by street collections, wage deductions, and other 'voluntary' contributions.

that you could hear the rattling of the pots and pans out in the kitchen.

'Then Sturmführer Segler bawled into the stillness: "Get out of here, you Jewish pig! Or do we have to show you the way out?" and Pommerenke brayed with laughter. Rosenbaum clenched his fists and began to tremble all over. I thought something terrible was about to happen, but then he just turned around, laid money on the table, and hurried out without another word. He was a good customer and always left a very nice tip . . . But that evening he left a twenty-mark note on the table. That was of course far too much, for his bill amounted to just over three marks. When I gave the banknote to the headwaiter, he said, "Run after him and bring him his change." But by the time I got ouside, he was out of sight. You realise of course that sixteen marks was a great deal of money in those days – it was almost exactly what my father received in weekly unemployment compensation, with a family of four.'

The young waiter wanted to give the extra money to his mother, but she insisted that he deliver it to Rosenbaum at his home early the next morning. She explained to her son that the lawyer would probably soon need the money more than she did.

Shortly after six the next morning, he rang the bell at the lawyer's apartment. It was a long time before he heard anyone stir. He was about to leave when the door opened. Herr Rosenbaum stood there, fully dressed, in hat and coat. He looked very pale, and on his coat he had pinned a broad ribbon with his war decorations.

'He stared at me, and I had to explain who I was and why I was there. Then he recognised me, put down the suitcase he was holding, and leaned against the doorframe. He had probably been expecting the auxiliary police; it was known that they always arrived very early to avoid creating a stir. I handed him the money. He wanted to give me a mark, but I refused to take it. When I told the headwaiter the whole story, he said, "It makes one ashamed to be a German." I'll never forget him saying that.'

I had finished my coffee some time ago, and it was nearly closing time.

'By the way,' the waiter said as I was paying, 'one thing that man at the table next to you said was true. He said we've all become older and wiser. You see, he was the one back in March 1933 who had my father taken into so-called protective custody. He had just turned twenty-one and liked to throw his weight around because he was the boss's son. Shortly before Christmas in 1932, he went parading through his father's factory in his SS uniform and threw my father out for "insubordination and disturbing the peace in the plant". My father had worked there for twelve years, and his only crime was that he refused to wash the young man's sports car. "Just wait, you Communist scum," he told my father, "you'll pay for this!" Well, now the man's older and wiser, as he says himself, and tomorrow he has important clients from Israel coming. He's reserved the best table and ordered a fine spread . . .'

I paid and went out to take a look at the 'tranquillity and dignity' of Detmold.

TWO

The Beginning of the Third Reich

As I strolled through Detmold's lovely old quarter, I tried to imagine how it would have looked back in January 1933. Pretty much the same as elsewhere in Germany, I thought, not very different from my own town.

I tried to remember what the onset of the Third Reich had been like. I was twelve. In June 1932 my parents had moved to Düsseldorf, and I had adjusted quickly. In my new school there was a rule against discussing current politics, even in the upper grades. When Hitler was named chancellor, our school took no notice.

But at home that day, as I was eating lunch with my parents and my cousin Lilly, who was visiting from Berlin, my father suddenly went into the next room to listen to the midday news broadcast, in spite of my mother's reproachful look. When he came back to the table, all his good humour had vanished, leaving him stony-faced.

We asked him what was wrong, whether some accident or catastrophe had occurred. He replied simply, 'Yes,' and added after a pause, 'Hitler has been named chancellor of the Reich.'

I do not recall exactly what was said after that, or indeed whether anyone said anything. But I can still see my cousin's horrified expression. She was married to a Jewish doctor whose practice was located in Neukölln, a working-class district of Berlin. 'I must get back to Berlin at once,' she whispered.

Although I was still rather young to understand the connection, I sensed at once what my cousin was afraid of. My experiences at school shortly before we left Berlin had made an indelible impression on me. And now my father's apocalyptic predictions of a few days earlier added to my fears: 'They will destroy everything,' he said, 'law, order, civilisation, everything we value. They will be a more dreadful scourge than we can even begin to imagine. As soon as Hitler gets into the government – which God forbid – he'll start rearming and preparing for a new war. He might need four or five years, and then it'll be about the same number of years before our poor country is utterly smashed . . .

'But before the Nazis fall from power, we may see ten or twelve or even more years pass,' he said in conclusion, 'years of unparalleled terror for anyone who opposes the Nazis, especially for those Hitler will make his scapegoats, chief among them the Jews.'

I asked whether there was nothing that could be done to prevent the Nazis from coming to power. My father replied, 'Maybe, but only if all the others stop fighting among themselves for a change and unite to prevent the calamity.'

That didn't sound very promising, but my father's words came as a confirmation that I had done well to join the socialist workers' youth organisation, called the Red Falcon, back in early 1932, while we were still in Berlin. As a middle-class boy and a student at a university-preparatory school, I was rather out of place in the largely working-class organisation. Only one of my schoolmates ever knew of my membership, and he approved of it, even envied me for it. But he had been forced to drop out of school because his father, a writer and known union activist, had been fired from his job. After that we lost contact with each other.

As a Red Falcon I had already had some experience with the Nazis in Düsseldorf. A group of us used to distribute anti-fascist pamphlets on the Hindenburgwall, near the government unemployment bureau, where many unemployed workers congregated. It was just before Christmas 1932, for I clearly recall street hawkers with Christmas trees and the unemployed trying to warm up at the little stoves belonging to the hawkers. There was a brisk black market trade in tobacco smuggled from Holland, cigarette papers, chocolate, and sometimes even cheap Japanese bicycles. Here and there brown-shirted SA men moved among the unemployed, trying to recruit the younger men. They promised warm meals from their field kitchens and coupons good for brand-new brown boots of real leather.

Our pamphleting was directed against these SA recruiters. Most of the unemployed workers agreed with our leaflets, which warned against the 'brown Pied Pipers' and called for solidarity in the fight against the Nazis. Many encouraged us to keep up the good work, and when the SA men noticed what we were up to and threatened to beat us up, there were always a few men who stepped forward and forced the brownshirts to leave us in peace.

But one day we were making our way home through the Palace Gardens when we suddenly found ourselves face to face with the enemy. SA men and Hitler Youths appeared out of nowhere, just ahead of us. They were all far bigger and stronger than we were. Our leader, after all, was only fifteen. Yet we didn't fear a confrontation. We were quite cheerful, prepared to defend ourselves vigorously.

But then we noticed that the biggest of the Hitler Youths was holding a yellow leather-covered object with a bouncing steel ball at the end, about the size of a ping-pong ball. And suddenly we also noticed the brass knuckles on the hands of the others. They glowed faintly in the dim light of the street lamps. One of the two SA men had a horse-whip.

Seeing all that, we thought it wisest to melt into the bushes and run home as fast as we could. We were better runners than our pursuers in their high boots, and soon managed to shake them off.

At our next Red Falcon meeting we discussed whether we should arm ourselves. Most of the boys agreed with the group leader that it was simply not appropriate for us to fit ourselves out like highwaymen with brass knuckles or bludgeons. Our weapons were our superior arguments and the solidarity of all anti-fascists. As one of the youngest, I listened to the discussion without comment, but I had serious doubts about our not defending ourselves. In any case I knew what my father and other adults meant when they spoke of a reign of terror that would descend on us if Hitler and his Nazis succeeded in seizing power.

And now, by noon on that thirtieth of January 1933 Hitler and his SA had attained their goal. When we listened to the radio again that evening, I heard the voice of a new announcer. It was entirely different from the ones I was familiar with: no longer calm and objective, but full of a fanatic fervour. Hearing it, I remembered my encounter in the Palace Gardens. I remembered the glint of the brass knuckles and the menacing bludgeon in the hand of the Hitler Youth.

'Like a blazing fire, the news spreads across Germany: Adolf Hitler is chancellor of the Reich! A million hearts are aflame. Rejoicing and gratitude pour forth . . .'

Many years later, when the Third Reich was a thing of the past, I dug around in the archives of the Cologne broadcasting station and found the very text read by the announcer that evening of January 30. As I perused it, I felt the same amazement and disgust that had filled me as a twelve-year-old boy.

There it was, in black and white, and the announcer had spoken the text as an overwhelmed eyewitness might describe the finish of the Monaco Grand Prix auto race:

'A procession of thousands of blazing torches is streaming up Wilhelmstrasse . . . They have marched through the Brandenburg Gate, the brown columns of the SA, victors in a long and arduous struggle, a struggle that claimed many victims. The banners glow blood-red, and against a white ground bristles the swastika, symbol of the rising sun! A glorious, an inspiring sight!

'And now – yes, it is! At this moment we hear from the south the thud of marching feet. It is the divisions of the Stahlhelm. The crowd listens with bated breath, the torches sway . . . Everywhere torches, torches, torches, and cheering people! A hundred thousand voices shout joyously, 'Sieg Heil! Heil Hitler!' into the night!

'And there, at his window, high above the cheering throngs and the sea of flaming torches stands Reich President von Hindenburg, the venerable field marshal and victor of Tannenberg. He stands erect, stirred to the depths by this great moment. And next door in the Reich Chancellery, the Führer – *yes, it is the Führer*! There he stands with his ministers, Adolf Hitler . . . the unknown soldier of the World War, the unyielding warrior, the standard-bearer of *freedom* . . . !

'His eyes gaze out into the distance. Surely he is thinking now of the long years of struggle, thinking of those who fell for the Movement, of the long march and its privations – and *now* – *yes! yes!* a thundering chorus swells up toward the young chancellor from a hundred thousand voices – the German anthem! From the shores of the Maas to the banks of the Memel . . . *Deutschland, Deutschland, über alles!* . . .

'Like a prayer it rises toward the heavens, like a hymn of gratitude and rejoicing! And *now: Yes! Yes!* Now the crowd strikes up the fighting song of the Nationalist Socialist Movement, the Horst Wessel Song!

'With one accord, as far as the eye can see, a hundred thousand arms are raised in the German Salute . . . The billowing crowd salutes the Führer with faith and gratitude, and at the same time honours the unforgotten victims of the struggle, comrades shot by the Red Front and the forces of reaction . . . Yea, truly they are marching in spirit among the ranks!

'Many there are in that crowd who furtively wipe the tears from their eyes, tears of gratitude and rejoicing! *Hail to you, our Führer, hail to the German Fatherland!* sing their hearts; and the little old grandmother there in the crowd on the sidewalk speaks what they are all feeling, all the men and women down there, and also the stalwart men of the SA and SS, marching past in long columns beneath the swastika banner: *Thank you, Almighty God, for letting us live to see this day!*'

As I strolled through Detmold's Rose Garden and recalled that day, I found myself thinking about something else that had happened at home on the evening of 30 January.

I was just getting ready for bed after the radio broadcast, when the telephone rang. It was Fräulein Bonse, a lady we had known only a short while. She worked for an institute that organised summer courses for secondary-school and university students, as well as foreign study and academic exchange programmes. May parents had met her through mutual acquaintances, and she had visited us a few times to discuss my participating in a German-English exchange programme. But on that evening Fräulein Bonse called for another reason.

She wanted me to run with a message to someone who lived in our neighbourhood and had no telephone; in an hour he would be picked up by car, and he should therefore make preparations for leaving as quickly as possible.

'And will he know what it's about?' I asked.

She hesitated a moment, and then she said, 'Please tell him it's very urgent. He has to be in Roermond before midnight.'

The man to whom I brought this message was a sculptor. He was in his studio working when I arrived. I recalled having seen him on the street a few times, and also recalled that there had been a red flag hanging out of his window a few weeks earlier, shortly before the last Reichstag elections.

He listened calmly to the message and did not even seem especially surprised. He merely asked, 'Is there really such a rush?'

'There must be,' I replied, 'otherwise she wouldn't have made a point of saying it was *very* urgent.'

At that he nodded. When he saw me to the door, he pressed my hand firmly and said, 'Thank you. And please give Fräulein Bonse my thanks. Tell her I hope she doesn't have any difficulties with the good Lord on my account.'

As I was on my way home, it dawned on me that Roermond was not even in Germany but already over the border in nearby Holland. I also realised that Fräulein Bonse, a good Catholic, who, according to my father, worked closely with Dr. Klausener, the leader of Catholic Action,* must have arranged for the sculptor to flee to Holland, where the Nazis could not get at him.

---

*Catholic Action, called for by Pope Pius XI in 1931, was a movement of 'lay participation in the apostolic mission of the Church'. In Germany, the Catholic Action was known to oppose Nazism.

The next morning I told my parents what I thought. 'So that's what it was all about,' my mother said. She had already been to the corner bakery, where she had heard the neighbours talking: very early that morning SS men had broken down the sculptor's door to arrest him, but he was gone. 'I hope no one saw you,' my mother said. And my father added, 'Fräulein Bonse must have access to excellent information – we should invite her over soon.' After a pause he continued: 'These are really very interesting times we're living in. I only wish they were a little less interesting . . .'

When I returned to my hotel in Detmold late at night, the lights were still on in the restaurant. I felt in the mood for a beer and would not have minded continuing my conversation with the friendly waiter. But he had gone off duty, so I drank my beer and went to bed.

Dancing Lessons and Torture Chambers

A few days after my visit to Detmold I bumped into an old school friend on a street in Düsseldorf. I was standing in front of a shop window when a handsome, very elegantly dressed older woman addressed me: 'Could it be? . . . Why, of course it's you!'

I recognised her at once. It was Marga, who as a girl belonged to the group of friends – Ali, Günter, Kulle, Susanne, and Ingrid – with whom I spent most of my time.

We decided to go to a café on the Königsallee for a cup of coffee, and on the way she filled me in on her life since we had left school. She had done her stint in the Labour Service,* then gone to Munich to study medicine, but she soon dropped out, and in 1939 she married an officer, who was killed during the war on the Eastern Front. She lived in Bavaria until 1949, when she moved back to Düsseldorf, where she had a nice income from her pension and the apartment houses she had inherited from her family.

No, she had not remarried, and her only child from her short marriage, a daughter, was married to a hotelkeeper in Switzerland.

We sat in the same café where we had sometimes met as students. It was not far from Corneliusplatz, which had been renamed Albert-Leo-Schlageterplatz at the time we knew each other – in honour of the early follower of Hitler who in 1923 had been shot by a French firing squad for sabotage in the occupied Rhineland. But only fanatical Nazis and bus conductors, whose job officially compelled them to, used the new name. We continued to call it Corneliusplatz, and always arranged to meet at the clock on the corner of Königsallee.

'Do you still remember the first time we all met there?' Marga asked. 'I even remember the date: it was Friday, March 3rd, 1933, my birthday. I had a new dress for my first dancing lesson – do you remember it?'

I made a wild guess and said, 'It was green, wasn't it?'

---

* Labour Service: work for boys of premilitary age, instituted by the Law of 26 June 1935.

I had guessed right. Green was Marga's favourite colour, and she wore green dresses whenever we went somewhere together.

'All kinds of things were happening that March the 3rd,' I remarked. 'It was the week after the Reichstag fire, and on Sunday, March 5th, crucial elections were due to take place.'

'That I don't remember at all,' Marga said, 'but in those days there were all kinds of excitement: marches, parades, the Führer's birthday, the Harvest Festival, the Day of National Labour, Strength through Joy,* the Winter Aid campaign, and we kept getting days off from school – that was the best part!'

'All that came much later,' I said. 'Have you forgotten what made such a deep impression on us that first week in March?'

I was referring to the first wave of terror that swept over Germany and claimed many victims in Düsseldorf. The constitution was meaningless by that time. SA and SS troops roared through the city in trucks, breaking into houses and apartments, driving their victims out into the streets, and dragging them to the cellars of buildings they had taken over, or to empty factories and warehouses. We witnessed such a scene ourselves.

'I just remember how thrilling it was,' Marga commented. 'People were electrified, and all they talked about was the "unity of the German people", and the "national uprising". I loved the constant marching and singing, with flags and bunting everywhere. I wanted to join the League of German Girls, [Bund deutscher Mädel – BDM] but my mother wouldn't let me . . . Anyway, since I didn't have that to occupy me, it was great to meet in town, and go to a café or a movie. Do you remember the time we saw *Mädchen in Uniform* in that crummy cinema out in a worker's district, in Gerresheim or Bilk?'

'It was in Bilk. We took the trolley – do you remember what we saw there?'

'I told you already: *Mädchen in Uniform*, with Dorothea Wieck. It was such a fantastic film, but you had to be over twenty-one to get in, and that's why we went to that cinema out in the suburbs, where they weren't so fussy.'

On our way home by trolley we had seen one of the lorries in which the SA transported people they had taken into 'protective custody'. Suddenly, one of the prisoners, a young man bleeding from a deep cut on his head, jumped from the lorry onto the running board of our

---

* Strength through Joy (*Kraft durch Freude*), an administrative programme concerned with the organisation of leisure time, provided entertainment, education, sports facilities, and collective holidays for workers.

moving trolley. People were just coming home from work and the trolley was crowded, but the passengers helped the man on and cleared a space for him. No one said anything, and it was suddenly very still in the bus. The conductor acted as though he had noticed nothing. Only one old woman took out a handkerchief, wiped the blood from the young man's face and said in a loud voice, 'It's a damned shame what those scoundrels think they can get away with!' No one contradicted her, and no one prevented the fugitive from getting off at the next stop, where he ducked into a dark doorway before the lorry, which was stuck in traffic, could catch up. I reminded Marga of this incident.

She laughed and said, 'Oh, yes, now I remember. I got into a lot of trouble with my father because of that. I was supposed to be home at seven in those days. That evening I was fifteen minutes late, and to excuse myself I told my parents the trolley had been delayed because someone had been trying to escape from the auxiliary police. My father had a fit when I told him the man actually got away. "Didn't anyone try to stop the Bolshevik?" he shouted, and he even wanted me to tell him which house the man slipped into, because he wanted to report it.'

'Was your father such an ardent Nazi?' I inquired.

'And how! You know he was an associate judge for the district court. He always claimed he would have been promoted long before if it hadn't been for the Catholics and the Jews. My mother, who was very Catholic and a good churchgoer, tried to persuade him to join the Catholic Centre Party. Instead he secretly joined the Nazis in 1932. When Hitler became chancellor he was beside himself with joy. "Now I'll be made presiding judge," he told my mother. "And who knows, maybe presiding judge of the higher regional court!" Then he proudly showed her his membership booklet. And do you know what happened? My mother burst into tears. Then she packed a suitcase and said she was leaving and wouldn't come back until he had dropped his membership.'

'And did he?'

'Of course not. After two or three days my mother came back – for the children's sake, she said. My father was very unhappy when she ran away, and almost cried when she came back, he was so moved and relieved. They celebrated their reconciliation with champagne, and my brother and I were allowed to stay up late and have a glass too. I guess my parents reached an unspoken agreement not to provoke each other. Father would always take off his Party badge before entering our apartment, and he refrained from praising the Third Reich and the Führer. Mother restrained herself too, and didn't say anything critical in his presence about what she called "the brown plague".'

'And that worked out all right?'

'Well, there were occasional quarrels: for instance, the day my father found a shopping bag from Alsberg's and scolded my mother for shopping in a Jewish store when she was the wife of a Party member and a district court presiding judge – he had received his promotion by then. Mother said she would do her shopping wherever she pleased. She went by prices and quality, not by baptismal certificates, Party membership booklets, or documents proving Aryan descent. Then my father begged her to consider the harm it would do him if she were seen entering or leaving a Jewish store. I don't know whether she gave in – probably not. But in any case by then there were fewer and fewer Jewish businesses. Most of them had to be sold by their owners – Aryanised, as it was called. And then, in the summer of 1934, my father no longer cared whether my mother did something the Party disapproved of. His enthusiasm for Hitler and the "national uprising" suddenly drained away. He seemed a changed person, and for a while he didn't say anything about politics.'

'What happened?'

'I didn't find out about it until a couple of years later, when I was already married. My father came to visit and one evening when we were sitting together, he told me. Our family had been vacationing in Munich that June of 1934. And on June 30th, just one day before we were supposed to go back to Düsseldorf, something awful happened . . .'

It was on this day that Hitler had his old guard liquidated: Ernst Röhm, supreme commander of the SA, the only friend with whom he used the intimate *du* form of address, as well as at least 150 high-ranking members of the SA were dragged out of their beds in the middle of the night and driven to their place of execution, where they were put up against a wall without explanation and shot. The victims also included the leader of Catholic Action, Erich Klausener, and Hitler's predecessor as chancellor, General Kurt von Schleicher, and his wife, as well as many others who were killed either for revenge or because they knew too much about Hitler's past and his private life. One of them was Hitler's most dangerous rival in the NSDAP, Gregor Strasser. Another was the priest Bernhard Stempfle, who had helped Hitler write *Mein Kampf.* In all, many hundreds, perhaps more than a thousand, were murdered between 30 June and 1 July. But in a speech before the Reichstag on 13 July Hitler announced that sixty-one persons had been shot, among them nineteen 'high-ranking SA members'; another thirteen had lost their lives 'while resisting arrest', and three had 'committed suicide', making a total of seventy-seven dead. Hitler also claimed that these killings had been a matter of 'national security', but it has since been established that there was no coup being planned by the SA.

The surprise action to wipe out all social-revolutionary elements and to settle a few old scores – the so-called Röhm Putsch – was intended to make the generals of the Reichswehr and the old-money power elite happy. In the course of the operation a few slip-ups occurred, and it was one of these that affected Marga's father so deeply as to transform his admiration for Hitler into silent revulsion.

On the evening of 30 June one of his friends, the music critic of a leading Munich daily, Dr. Wilhelm Schmid, was playing his cello while his wife cooked supper for their three young children. As soon as the children had eaten and gone to bed, the couple planned to meet Marga's parents at a little wine tavern in downtown Munich. But they never got there.

Toward seven-thirty their doorbell rang. Four SS men stalked into the apartment and ordered Dr. Schmid to come with them at once. They offered no explanation. Dr. Schmid was not even allowed to say good-bye to his wife and children. He who had never paid the slightest attention to politics went along without resisting. Two days later Frau Schmid received word from the police that her husband had had a 'fatal accident'. The body was released for burial, but the sealed casket was not to be opened.

For forty-eight hours Frau Schmid had tried desperately, with the help of Marga's parents and other friends, to discover the whereabouts of her husband. She then learned that her husband's arrest and execution – carried out without any investigation, or even a check of his identification papers – had been the result of mistaken identity. The SS men had been looking for an SA leader named Willi Schmidt, but he had already been located by another SS squad and shot. By way of comfort, the national head of the SS, Heinrich Himmler, offered her a rather large sum of money, which she rejected indignantly.

On the same day that Frau Schmid learned of the 'unintentional' execution of her husband, she read in the papers that the bloodbath of 30 June and 1 July had been declared 'legal' retroactively by the Reich cabinet, and that President von Hindenburg had 'congratulated the Führer and Reich Chancellor' on his 'courageous personal intervention' and had expressed his 'particular gratitude' to him.

'That was too much for my father,' Marga said. 'My brother and I didn't understand at the time what was wrong with him, and Mother couldn't explain. But Father's sudden disillusionment had other repercussions, which were mysterious but very welcome to us: for one thing, he stopped paying attention to when we got home. I was especially grateful for that on the afternoons when we had dancing lessons. Of course you were too young to go to those . . .'

I had started school than most, which explained why I was in the same class with Marga and the others, who were all older than I. They took dancing lessons in the late afternoon, and sometimes I would meet them afterward for a stroll around town. Once I was waiting for them downstairs, listening to the music floating out of the open window on the second floor; they were learning the foxtrot, the quickstep, and other dances condemned by the Nazis as 'Negroized music', which no doubt added to their popularity.

As I stood there, I saw Hedwig going by. I ran after her, and we greeted each other warmly. 'Do you have a moment?' she asked. 'I have to tell you something.'

We went into the ice cream parlour on the corner and found a table near the window that allowed me to keep an eye on the dancing school. Hedwig looked around with what we ironically called 'the German glance', to make sure no one could eavesdrop on us. Then she began to tell me what had happened to her husband, Fritz.

Hedwig had been employed in my parents' household for more than ten years. When she first came to work for us she was a shy seventeen-year-old girl from the country, very thin and pale. I was a little boy of just four, but I remember how much my mother and I liked Hedwig from the start, and she us, as it turned out. My father had reservations about her at first, because she insisted on addressing him as 'Mr. Engelmann, sir'. But after two weeks she gave up the obsequious 'sir' and then shook off her shyness along with her paleness and thinness. By the time we moved to Düsseldorf, she had become a plump young woman in her twenties and was like a member of the family. Soon after our move, she fell in love with a man about her own age, a very calm, reliable craftsman. When they married six months later, my parents and I were very happy for her, though we were sorry to lose her.

On this particular afternoon Hedwig, usually so cheerful, seemed full of despair and close to tears. When I was a child, and even later, Hedwig had always been there to comfort me. Now Hedwig looked to me for comfort. Her Fritz had been arrested by the Gestapo two weeks ago. Early in the morning, just as he was leaving for work, two agents had come and taken him away.

'Why didn't you tell us?' I asked.

'I didn't want to drag you into it,' Hedwig replied. 'Actually I shouldn't be telling you any of this. But I just have to talk to someone.'

She told me that Fritz, who I knew belonged to the now outlawed Communist Party, had been betrayed to the Gestapo by a former comrade – 'under torture', as Hedwig said.

'Torture?' I asked in disbelief. 'You mean they beat him until he talked?' I had heard rumours of such things, and also that prisoners had simply been executed, 'shot while attempting to escape', as it said in the newspapers; for a time you could read such items in the paper almost daily. Everyone knew what that phrase really meant.

But 'torture' meant something different to me: burning at the stake, the 'Spanish boot' from the Thirty Years' War, the 'Iron Maiden of Nuremberg' from the Middle Ages, thumbscrews, the rack. I could not believe that such things existed in the heart of Europe, in our city in the year 1934! Even the worst SA bullies could not be capable of such methods.

'First they squeezed him into an iron locker,' Hedwig said softly, making a great effort to suppress her agitation. Then she leaned over and whispered to me: 'He was jammed in there for twelve hours, until late in the evening. Then they came back and interrogated him. First they drove little pointed sticks under his nails, then they forced him . . .' As she continued, I felt so sick to my stomach that I had to run to the lavatory.

'I shouldn't have told you,' she said when I returned. 'I'm really sorry. Please don't tell anyone, not even your parents!'

I promised, but I pressed her for more details: 'Who was it they tortured into betraying Fritz? And how do you know all this?'

Then Hedwig told me the rest of the story. After the Communist Party was banned, her husband had remained in contact with his comrades, taking great precautions, of course. Fritz had not told her what kind of 'illegal work' he was engaged in, but some evenings he had driven to the Dutch border – 'probably to smuggle comrades abroad', Hedwig thought. 'It's better if you know nothing,' Fritz had said.

Three days before Fritz was taken away, his younger brother, an engine fitter, was arrested on the street by two Gestapo agents. They took him to Prinz-Georg-Strasse, where the Gestapo had quarters in a large building. There they gave him the 'special treatment' until he spilled all the information that they wanted on his brother.

'And now they'll torture Fritz the same way,' Hedwig whispered.

I held her hand in silence; I did not know what to say. But I still wondered how she had learned so much of the Gestapo's methods.

She shook her head and bit her lips. 'I can't tell you,' she said finally. 'You must try to understand. I heard it from someone who saw him and spoke with him afterwards. It's all true . . .'

After this, Hedwig came to see us often. One time she had just received a letter from her husband, from a concentration camp in Emsland. He wrote that he was all right, considering the circumstances. My mother promptly made up a parcel for him, which Hedwig was to mail, and they both wept . . . A year or two later Fritz was released. He even found a job again, and on one of the first Sundays after his return he came by, 'just to say hello, and thanks'. He was even more taciturn than before, and since we knew that former concentration camp inmates were not allowed to speak about their experiences, we did not press him.

'Did you notice,' my mother asked me after he had left, 'that his hair has turned completely grey?'

I debated whether I should tell Marga this story. While I had been dwelling on my own memories, she had prattled on – about the school ball, the clothes she had worn in those days, the popular songs and films of our youth.

'Do you remember the first time we went to the theatre by ourselves?' she asked. She was able to tell me the names of the actors, what friends we had bumped into during the intermission, and how impressed we had been when Schiller's Marquis Posa had said to King Philip of Spain, 'Sire, grant us freedom of thought!' and the audience had broken out in thunderous applause. But apparently she had no idea why they were applauding, and she was astonished when I explained that people had taken this opportunity as anonymous members of an audience to protest the Nazis' suppression of criticism. And those in power got the message. Schiller's *Don Carlos* was immediately removed from the repertory – on orders from Gauleiter Florian, we heard.

'Oh, so that's what that was all about,' Marga remarked, and trotted out some more memories. Several times she mentioned our mutual friend Susanne, who had had a crush on our tall, blond biology teacher and who one early summer evening had saved Kulle from drowning, when on a dare we jumped into the ice-cold Rhine. Marga recalled that one day in 1935 Susanne had suddenly left school . . .

The fact was that blue-eyed Susanne with the blond braids, who had recently been praised in our 'Racial Theory' class as a perfect example of the build and skull formation of the Nordic type, was abruptly expelled from school after being classified as one-hundred-percent Jewish in accordance with the Nuremberg Laws. Had Marga forgotten that? Apparently she had, and I refrained from mentioning it.

My thoughts drifted to Susanne, and how her parents had sent her to England, with the help of Fräulein Bonse and a Christian charitable organisation. I had accompanied Susanne to the station, where she was to take the train to Ostende. Her parents said good-bye to her at home. 'We don't like to be seen in town,' Susanne's mother said. 'We're so well known.' Both of Susanne's parents came from distinguished families and, before his forced 'retirement' in 1933, her father had belonged to the boards of directors of a number of civic and cultural organisations. But because they were non-Aryan that was all over now. Even the decorations that Susanne's father had received for courageous service in the World War could not help him.

Susanne told me later that she never saw her parents after that leave-taking. In 1942 they received orders to report the following morning with a maximum of fifty kilos of luggage to the livestock depot, for 'evacuation' to Poland. Knowing what awaited them, they took their own lives.

Was it possible that Marga was ignorant of this? She had been close to Susanne; was she perhaps embarrassed because of the way she had dropped Susanne shortly after she left school? 'Someone told me Susanne is still in England,' Marga was just saying. I said she was. 'If you're still in touch with her, please tell her I'd love to hear from her,' Marga said. 'We used to be such good friends.'

I promised to deliver the message.

After about an hour and a half we parted on Corneliusplatz by the old clock. 'It was lovely to see you after so many years,' Marga remarked. 'I really enjoyed talking about old times. There are so many things one forgets, and then suddenly it all comes back . . . All in all we had a wonderful, carefree youth, didn't we?'

FOUR

How We Were 'Brought into Line'

The evening after my encounter with Marga I went to visit Kulle, who lived not far from Düsseldorf. Kulle had become a wealthy man. He showed me around his new house, which was richly decorated with Baroque furniture from Aachen, Flemish genre paintings, and other rare and valuable items.

It was gratifying to see that our teachers had been wrong about Kulle: he had amounted to something after all. He was a full professor, dean, and head of a faculty of religion, the very subject that had caused him the most trouble when we were in school. I reminded him of that, and he laughed.

'You remember that I started out in a monastery school. And when the Nazis closed it down and clapped half a dozen of the monks into jail – for alleged currency smuggling and crimes against morality – I came back to Düsseldorf. My parents were very upset.'

Yes, I remembered. In 1933, right after Hitler obtained the concordat with the Vatican that he needed to polish up his tarnished international reputation, the Nazis launched their programme of 'bringing into line'* the Catholic youth organisations. Their next step was to ban countless Catholic publications. Then they shut down monastery schools and Catholic hospitals, and arrested thousands of priests, monks, and laymen in leading Church positions. The Nazi newspapers, especially the anti-Semitic and anticlerical *Stürmer* and the official SS newspaper, *Der schwarze Corps*, specialised in lurid portrayals of the unbridled decadence of the Catholic clergy.

'In the beginning I had an awful time in regular school,' Kulle remarked. 'I was lost, especially in the sciences. I had no chance to show off my strong points, like Church history, the lives of the saints, moral doctrine, and sacred music. And my parents complained about

*'Bringing into line' (from *Gleichschaltung*) was the Nazi policy that sought to reorganise all aspects of social and political life, and all institutions, in conformity with Nazi ideology.

the added expense of having me home. At the monastery school I had a scholarship.'

'Your parents were very religious, weren't they?'

Kulle laughed. 'Well,' he said, 'they came from the country, from the Lower Rhine. They went to church every Sunday and took Communion, and at home we said grace before every meal. But they sent me to a Catholic school only because my father didn't earn enough to send three sons to university-preparatory school and then on to university. So my father entrusted us to the Church and himself to the Catholic Centre Party, mostly because his supervisor at the Postal Service was big in the Centre Party. After Hitler came to power my father was very frightened. But he was immensely relieved after Hitler praised the churches as "the most important factors in the preservation of our identity as a people". He declared he placed great value on friendly relations with the Pope. But then in the process of "bringing into line", the Nazis abolished the Centre Party, as they did ever other party. Most of my father's influential friends in the Party were removed from their civil-service positions and replaced with loyal Nazis. When that happened, my father panicked and joined the NSDAP, fearing for his job and his promotions.'

'Were you really heartbroken when the Nazis closed down the monastery school? You didn't seem to mind being back in Düsseldorf.'

He laughed again. 'I was delighted – except for school. I loved being among real people again. It was such fun to stroll around down-town, admiring the pretty girls and the elegant women. The Nazis did me a real favour when they rescued me from that monastery.'

In fact, Kulle had been so stridently anticlerical that our group, especially Susanne and I, had at first regarded him with suspicion. Usually, only the wildest Nazis were so flamboyant in their opposition.

'I suppose I behaved like a fool for a while. But don't you think that was just a normal, healthy reaction?' Kulle asked.

'I'm sure it was,' I said. 'And you managed to stay out of the Hitler Youth, too.'

'Come now, don't make a resistance hero out of me,' Kulle broke in. 'I just stayed clear of things as much as I could. I wanted to enjoy my freedom – that's all. Later on, when I was in the Labour Service and then the Wehrmacht, one wasn't required to belong to any Nazi organisation. So it didn't take any particular skill on my part, and certainly not any heroism.'

Kulle was right. It wasn't terribly difficult to stay out of the Hitler Youth, even once you had been recruited. In May 1933 I myself had involuntarily become a member of the Jungvolk,* which had simply absorbed the nonpolitical youth group I belonged to. So I was in the organisation for several months, and as long as my old friends were there with me and we went about our activities in the usual way, it was even enjoyable. But when the Jungvolk leaders began to 'bring us into line', I realised the implications. Fortunately I was able to find an innocuous pretext for dropping out: I was going to England for several months. After that I managed to avoid such organisations without repercussions.

When we finished our tour of Kulle's house, he remarked, 'Recently I had an argument with someone who claimed that almost everyone of our generation was in the Hitler Youth. I pointed out that by 1938, when we graduated, the Hitler Youth had had five years in which to recruit, and that many of the youth organisations dissolved by the Nazis had been simply absorbed by the Hitler Youth, and yet the Hitler Youth, the Jungvolk, the League of German Girls, and the Young Girls combined had only about seven and a half million members. Those were the official numbers, and they were probably exaggerated.'

'True,' I said, 'but that seven and a half million must have been close to two-thirds of all the eligible young people.'

'Yes, but don't you see that this also means that more than a third of German young people were *not* involved in any Nazi organisation? And besides, quite a few who were members only paid dues and got out of performing their "duties" with a doctor's certificate or a letter from school saying they had academic problems and couldn't afford the time for extracurricular activities. And some simply didn't show up for duty. When you add it all up, you realise that many young Germans had nothing, or as little as possible, to do with the Nazi youth organisations.'

It was true that pressure to join did not increase until 1937. And it wasn't until 1939 that a law was passed requiring all young people to serve in the Hitler Youth, so our age group was not affected.

'Are you two trying to "come to terms" with your past?' Kulle's wife asked, as she and a friend, Grete, joined us by the fire in the living room. She was considerably younger than Kulle, and, as he told me later, her father had been a high-ranking SS officer whom the Yugoslavs had caught and hanged. Before her marriage to Kulle, she was his academic assistant.

'There's not much to come to terms with,' Kulle said. 'As I see it

Jungvolk: a division of the Hitler Youth for boys aged ten to fourteen.

there were only three types of real Nazis: first there were the members of the World War generation who couldn't accept the German defeat or the dissolution of the monarchy or the Weimar Republic – people who never found their way back into civilian life. Then there were those who felt they had got the short end of the stick: they were mostly from the lower middle class, and under the Nazis they became block wardens or Kreisleiter. That way they could throw their weight around and take out their frustrations on ordinary citizens, whom they terrorised. The third group consisted of the lumpenproletariat, who were too lazy to work, as well as rowdies and hoodlums. All the other members of the Nazi Party were either intimidated petty bourgeois or opportunists, and that last category included quite a few intellectuals and technocrats – they were especially dangerous . . .'

'You've left out one category,' put in Grete, who had said nothing up to this point. 'There were also those who believed in the Führer as a saviour and were hypnotised by him. My mother, for example. She never got any benefit from being one of the earliest members of the Nazi Party and of the Nazi Women's League, or at least no material benefit. They let her sit in the front row at Nazi events, and once she handed a bouquet to the Führer – that was the high point of her life. But they certainly put her to work, taking in membership dues, collecting contributions, running around to all the offices and agencies to find housing for large families, or for people who had been bombed out. She ran herself ragged! Every single moment she could spare from her household chores was devoted to some "project". She was convinced everything the Nazis did was right and essential, and she dismissed all the whispered rumours of atrocities as stupid, malicious gossip. But she never knowingly harmed anyone – she always wanted the best for people. In May of '45 her whole world collapsed. At the time – I was just sixteen – we had been evacuated to Fürstenfeldbruck. Mother was among those the Americans forced to tour nearby Dachau, and I had to go along. I'll never forget those heaps of emaciated corpses . . . Mother suffered a nervous breakdown. It took her a long time to recover.'

'And then?' Kulle asked. 'Did she still continue to believe in the Führer or was she cured? She must have known that the camps existed and that horrible crimes were committed there in the name of her Führer?'

Grete shook her head. 'No, nothing could shake her faith in Hitler. "I'm sure the Führer wouldn't have wanted *that*," she said later. Another of her articles of faith was: "True National Socialism was pure and decent!" She clung to that till she died, only three years ago.'

'And how did she reconcile the concentration camps with that belief?' Kulle wanted to know.

'She accepted the explanation they gave at the Party meetings,' Grete replied. 'It went something like this: The riff-raff have to be cleared off the streets! Repeat offenders, sex criminals, and the parasites on the Volk, like usurers or profiteers, will be reeducated in the camps to do honest work. They will taught discipline and cleanliness – and, of course, not a hair on anyone's head will be harmed.'

'That's what I heard at home, too, when I was ten or twelve,' Kulle's wife remarked. 'My parents spoke of the camps as having an important educational function. Of course, in my house there was more talk of "dangerous enemies of the state", and I also heard that they were dealt with severely.'

'But you must admit,' Kulle said, 'that no one could really claim afterward that he or she had not even known that such camps existed.'

He said this with palpable bitterness, and when I looked at him with raised eyebrows, he continued, 'Take my father, for instance. He was only a simple Party member, the kind who just went along out of fear. In 1945 he claimed he had never suspected that hundreds of thousands were thrown into concentration camps and tortured to death. And yet he always read the paper from front to back . . .'

'But were the papers allowed to report that so-and-so had been sent to a concentration camp?' his wife asked. 'I thought such things were shrouded in secrecy.'

'No,' I said, 'from the beginning of the "Third Reich" you could find something in the paper every day: "Enemy of the Volk Goes to Concentration Camp", or "Concentration Camp Inmates Treated Well". There were also photos showing prisoners who had been selected specially for their repellent appearance.'

'And besides,' Kulle continued, 'there was a familiar saying: "Hush! Watch out! You don't want to end up in a concentration camp!" If a person told a political joke or voiced even mild criticism of the Gauleiter's most recent measures, someone would be sure to whisper that warning. That was the key to the success of the "bringing into line" campaign: everyone was terrified of the Nazis' brutal methods. And precisely because most people had no clear idea of what went on in the camps, they were that much more afraid.'

'I'm sure your father knew the camps existed, even if he had no notion of what they were for,' his wife commented.

'I'm sure he did,' Kulle replied, 'but there was a good reason why he stubbornly refused to admit he had known anything about them.'

Then he told us the following story:

In the summer of 1935 Kulle's parents took their first holiday with the children. Kulle's father had received the hoped-for promotion, and with it, an increase in salary. So they had gone to the Eifel region for two weeks. Among the other guests at their hotel was a painter with whom Kulle's father drank a beer now and then, which led to some 'very interesting discussions', as he put it.

One morning toward the end of their stay the family had breakfast out in the garden. Kulle's father saw a newspaper lying on the table next to them, where the painter had been sitting. As the painter went into the pension, he called out, 'Good-bye! Have a fine day!' and threw Kulle's father a significant look.

Kulle's father fetched the newspaper and was about to settle down with it when a couple who had come only the previous day sat down at the next table. Kulle's parents politely said, 'Good morning,' to which the new guests replied loudly, 'Heil Hitler!' At that, Kulle's father hastily said, 'Heil Hitler!' and hoped he had repaired the damage.

But then, as he opened the newspaper and began to read it, Kulle's father shuddered and went pale. Only after some strenuous thought did he jump up, crumple the newspaper in ostentatious outrage, and then go over to the couple at the other table.

'Heil Hitler! Please pardon my intrusion, but something unspeakable has just happened – I simply must talk with you, Party member to Party member, as it were,' his family heard him say.

And then the two men – the other was an Untersturmführer in the SS, as it turned out – smoothed out the newspaper, examined it, and discussed it vehemently. 'An émigré propaganda rag, published in Paris by the Jew Georg Bernhard!' the SS man could be heard expostulating. Then Kulle's father came back to the breakfast table, visibly relieved, while the SS officer went into the hotel to make a telephone call. Ten minutes later the painter, who was about to set out for a walk, was seized by two Gestapo agents and taken away.

'We never heard what happened to the man,' Kulle said, 'and the next day we went home. Nothing more was ever said about the incident . . .'

'Do you really suppose your father had such a guilty conscience because of that one incident?' Kulle's wife asked. 'He was just protecting himself and his family; he had to assume that the SS officer could see that he was reading a seditious paper. And then *he* could have been arrested and maybe even sent to a concentration camp.'

'That's certainly true,' Kulle responded, 'but he could also have said that he found the paper lying somewhere – while he was walking in the woods, for instance . . .'

'Do you think the Gestapo would have swallowed that? It was morning, and he was supposed to have found a paper in the woods the afternoon before and kept it to read at breakfast?'

'You're right, of course,' Kulle admitted. 'He probably thought he had only two choices: to risk being caught with that forbidden paper, or to denounce the other man. He chose the lesser of two evils. Of course, for the painter it was the greatest evil of all – and for all of us, too, in the end, because that's exactly how the system of terror worked. If he had quietly put down the paper and waited to see how the man at the next table behaved, it's very likely nothing would have happened. But my father's nerves weren't steady. He wasn't the kind of person who denounced out of malice, just a timid man afraid to lose the civil-service position he had fought so hard for. And it was precisely because most Germans were timid in that way that the SS, the Gestapo, and the Security service had such an easy time with us. The main thing was that each individual knew or at least suspected how brutally and ruthlessly the regime dealt with anyone who refused to be "brought into line" or disobeyed any of the thousands of regulations and prohibitions. That's how a small minority succeeded in holding the great majority in check.'

FIVE

Who Were the Nazis?

Was it really only a small minority that terrorised the great majority of Germans? I tried to remember how many Nazis I had known of at school. Among my classmates in Düsseldorf very few were 'real' Nazis who firmly believed in the master-race and Lebensraum theories, the racial theories, and the propaganda. I'd say they made up at most 18 percent of the student body, but probably closer to 10 percent.

The Nazi share of the teaching staff was about the same. It's true that the principal and the senior teachers, as well as the younger ones who were just preparing for their certification exams, usually displayed a Party badge on their lapels, and they greeted people with the obligatory 'Heil Hitler!' and followed the Nazi guidelines in presenting their material. But none of the older and very few of the younger teachers were genuine Nazis. One teacher, who made a particular show of his fervent loyalty to Hitler, had a Jewish girlfriend, whom he probably hoped to protect in this fashion. Only the gym teacher, disliked by students and teachers alike, was a thorough Nazi.

But as I thought it over, I could not take too much comfort in the small representation of Nazis at my school. These university-preparatory secondary schools generally represented only the upper-middle and cultured middle class; in those days, the children of workers, farmers, white-collar workers, and lower-level civil servants – and that meant the majority of German youth – rarely attended such schools. In addition, my observation was restricted to one school, which was located in a predominantly Catholic city in the Rhineland and considered quite liberal.

So I tried to find some other way of determining whether the majority of my contemporaries were Nazis or not. I decided to examine some statistics. Just before Hitler seized power, at the end of 1932, the Hitler Youth had numbered about 100,000 members. By contrast there were about ten million young Germans who belonged to other youth organisations, including nationalistic organisations, religious organisations (Catholic, Protestant, and Jewish), and about 100 other groups of more than local significance. So before Hitler came to power the Hitler Youth had managed to attract no more than 1 percent of all the young people belonging to these organisations.

I had just come to the conclusion that Hitler Youth statistics from that period would not settle the issue when I ran into my friend Werner, who was almost exactly my own age and had long been a trade union activist. As we sat over a glass of beer, I asked him if there had been a lot of Nazis at his school.

'Well, I wasn't in university-prep; and I left school at fourteen. But in any case there was just a sprinkling of Nazis in Ludwigshafen before '33. We didn't even see any Hitler Youth uniforms in my school until after Hitler came to power. The boys who wore them then were mostly the sons of lower-echelon civil servants or white-collar workers. They were distinctly in the minority as long as I was in school, and they behaved more or less accordingly. But our homeroom teacher began to act more and more like a fanatical Nazi after '33. He never let me forget that my father was a Communist. I had to work extra hard on my homework and the compositions. Otherwise he would say, 'Well, with a family like that – no wonder you're lousy in German!' I wanted to strangle him every time he said that.'

'Was your father arrested?'

'Nothing happened to him while I was still in school. He worked for the National Railways, as the freight depot, and his fellow workers and supervisors had great respect for him. Other workers who had joined the SA would even warn him when a wave of arrests was in the offing. "Franz, the air's not so good today – maybe you'd better take some time off and go to see your relatives out in the country," they'd say. Then, instead of coming home after work, my father would take the train out to Ellerstadt, where his sister had a little farm. It was only a few kilometres away, and as a railway worker he could travel for free. One of the other workers would let my mother know, so she wouldn't worry. After the Reichstag fire at the end of February he had to lie low for several days, and my mother had me stop by the freight yard on my way to school to tell the foreman my father had come down with the flu. "Well, well," he said, "if that's the case he should be careful and not try to get up too soon," and then he wished my father a speedy recovery and gave me five pfennigs so I could buy myself ice cream. With that kind of support we managed to avoid problems until Easter 1935. Right after the holidays – I had just left school and had a few days until I began my apprenticeship – the Gestapo turned up early one morning – two leather-coated men with pistols in hand. We had a two-room apartment in the rear section of the housing complex, not exactly spacious for a family of five. The two Gestapo men turned the whole place upside down. They pulled out drawers and tore the beds apart. They even emptied the salt container onto the table and poked through the ashes in the stove, searching for something they could use to incriminate my father.'

'Did they find anything?'

Werner laughed. 'No, at least not what they were looking for. The books and pamphlets my father had collected and studied over the years were wrapped in waxed paper and buried under the woodpile, and those they didn't find, of course. So they merely confiscated a few books, like Franz Mehring's *Essays on German History*, a book I had already read with great interest when I was ten, and my favourite novel, Traven's *Treasure of the Sierra Madre*, and Heinrich Mann's *The Loyal Subject*. But they took my father away anyway. He was sentenced to two years' imprisonment for 'conspiracy to commit high treason' – certainly a mild sentence for the Nazis, which meant that they were unable to prove anything against him.'

'And what about you?'

'Until my father was released – in October of '38 – I had a really rough time. My mother received a tiny sum from the Welfare Bureau which didn't even cover the rent, and she took a job as a cleaning woman. The other children were still too young to earn anything, so I had a newspaper route early in the morning before work – that brought in a few marks that we desperately needed. After only a week I lost the apprenticeship my father had arranged for me, for "political unreliability". The owner of the business was a Nazi Kreisleiter, and he told me he didn't want the son of a "Communist traitor" as an apprentice. The Chamber of Commerce was so embarrassed by this harsh action against a fourteen-year-old that it promptly found me a new apprenticeship, in a model Nazi business, a printing plant, which mainly produced pictures of the Führer and printed materials for the Party. It called itself an "art manufacturing plant", and I was very happy to get work there.'

'But weren't the other employees all Nazis?'

'No, in fact, the other workers were anything but Nazis. Almost all of them were Social Democrats and union members, and they had a solidarity pact with each other. From the start they treated me very decently. "You've got to show them", they told me, and I realised that by "them" they meant the Nazis who had sent my father to jail. The master to whom I was apprenticed even gave me the day off once every six weeks when my mother and I were permitted to visit Father. We had twenty minutes to talk to him, with a guard always present. When I went back to the plant feeling pretty low after being at the prison, my master would try to cheer me up, saying "This won't go on forever. One of these days the whole nightmare will be over . . . Just be grateful your father's in good health and being treated decently – it could have been much worse!" I knew what he meant, because in March of '33 one of our fellow workers was in a concentration camp for a few weeks, and afterwards he suffered from constant pain and paralyzing depressions.'

'How did workers feel about the Third Reich? I mean in general, not just in your plant.'

'The workers in the printing trade were a pretty special case. Almost without exception they were skilled workers, unionised, and politically aware, not easily taken in. And they stuck together. The Nazis had much less trouble with the chemical industry, because there the workers were mostly unskilled and resented the minority of skilled workers. Of course if you look at the total picture, the working class gained nothing at all from Nazi rule: the unions were smashed right away, wage-scale autonomy was abolished. Instead, wages were set by the so-called Labour Trustees, who worked things out with management without consulting the workers. And the real income of workers and white-collar employees steadily declined, while income from capital investment and factory ownership increased sharply. "Increases not by hourly wage but through higher productivity" was the "iron law" Hitler proclaimed. In those days, when wages were based largely on units produced, that meant the workers could earn higher wages only by working faster and for longer hours.'

'Did they realise that? The propaganda claimed that everything was getting better and better . . .'

'That's true. In their public proclamations the Nazi leaders all declared their solidarity with the workers and portrayed themselves as their benefactors. But their actual policies were quite another story. There was the Law for the Organisation of National Labour of January 1934, which dubbed the entrepreneurs "leaders of industry" and the workers and salaried employees their "followers". According to the "Führer principle" the entrepreneurs were therefore "sole masters in their realms of activity", to whom their employees owed "absolute fealty". There was no longer such a thing as a works council, no youth representation, no forum for workers' participation. In cases of gross abuse the functionaries of the German Labour Front could intervene. But they confined themselves to issues like provision for rest rooms or locks on lockers; wages, production quotas, overtime, and deductions from pay were dictated from on high. And in 1935 they reintroduced employment booklets, such as workers had in Kaiser

Wilhelm's day. Without an employment booklet no one could get a job, and if an employer didn't want a worker to leave, he could refuse to return the worker's employment booklet.'

'Did anyone dare to protest?'

Werner thought for a moment. 'Not openly, because then the "factory leader" would have phoned the Gestapo, and half an hour later the ringleaders would have been behind bars. But there was passive resistance, and sometimes it was actually possible to get better working conditions that way, so long as all workers stuck together, which was seldom enough the case. Quite a few of them let the wool be pulled over their eyes, or they were bought. Do you remember the Nazis' incentives for loyalty – the "Strength through Joy" holidays and the promises of a "Volkswagen"?'

'As I recall, the Volkswagen hadn't even been built at that time. Wasn't that just another propaganda slogan : "For every member of the Volk a Volkswagen", and wasn't it Hitler himself who formulated that particular slogan?'

'You're right,' Werner replied. 'The Volkswagen was never produced during the Nazi years – but you could pay for one in advance. You'd even get a voucher with an order number once you paid three-quarters of the projected price. A lot of workers did it. They had five marks a month withheld from their pay, on top of taxes, deductions for social projects, dues for the Labour Front, the obligatory contribution to the National Socialist Welfare Agency, and a few pennies for the Winter Aid Project, for Strength through Joy, and various "voluntary" contributions. There wasn't much left in the pay envelope after that, and the Volkswagen turned out to be a mirage. Nobody ever got a car – or their money back . . .'

'Still, the elimination of unemployment must have made quiet an impression on the workers, since they were the ones most affected.'

'People let themselves be dazzled by that. It was the Nazis' main argument. Today we know for a fact what we only suspected back then: not until the autumn of 1936 was unemployment reduced to anything near a normal level. So it took almost four years, and during the same time, the other major industrialised countries had recovered from the Depression without resorting to terror, or drastic measures, or the massive war preparations that Germany used for getting the unemployed off the streets . . . And what kind of blessing was it for a man to exchange his unemployment compensation for the skimpy hourly wages he earned at backbreaking compulsory labour, often living far from his family in primitive barracks and eating field-kitchen slops? That's how the autobahns were built – the highway system, you know, was constructed for purely strategic purposes, like the West Wall.* And the entire public works programme was financed with freshly printed money, or, even worse, with drafts on the Reich Bank. Eventually we were going to have to pay the piper . . .'

We had one more beer and were about to leave when the proprietor, a broad-shouldered, rather stout man (of seventy-four, as he soon told us) came over to our table. He asked whether he could join us, and treated us both to his homemade brandy.

'We were just talking about the Nazi years, and whether most people were better or worse off. What do you think?'

'Well, you've asked the right man,' he said. 'In the beginning, I was the most enthusiastic Party member in this part of town, maybe in the whole city. I joined early in 1930. I wasn't in the restaurant business then – I had just taken over my father's store after he died suddenly. We sold electrical appliances and phonograph records. I was pinning all my hopes on the Nazis, because our business was on the verge of collapse. Hardly anyone came in to buy anything, and those who did bought on credit and paid in installments of a few pennies a week. We couldn't squeeze a living out of the store.'

'What did you think the Nazis would do for you?' Werner asked.

'They had a policy that sounded perfect,' the proprietor replied. 'They called it "breaking the tyranny of investment capital", which meant expropriating the department stores and renting out the space at low rates to small businessmen. That would have saved us, because it was the cheap light bulbs in Woolworth's and the popular records at rock-bottom prices in the department stores that were stealing our customers. How could we compete with Oppenheim Electric, with their big store downtown and two branches in the suburbs? It was a Jewish company, and it did such a large volume of business that it could buy cheap and spend a lot on advertising. And the Nazis promised they would get rid of our Jewish competition. But when it came down to it, that was the only promise they kept! The result was that one of Oppenheim's managers – a German – took over the business and renamed it Schmidt Electric; and the competition got even more cutthroat! The big department stores like Tietz's remained in existence, and there was no more talk of renting out the sales space to little guys like us!'

'But even so, you remained devoted to Hitler?' Werner asked.

'Well, my wife and I kept on hoping, but my mother nagged us

*West Wall: the fortifications along the Rhine, also called the Siegfried Line.

constantly: "When are we going to move?" she'd say. "I'm sure sales would increase if we were on the ground floor of Tietz's!" So I spoke to our Kreisleiter about it. First he told me to be patient and said we had to give the Führer time. All the important tasks couldn't be accomplished at once, just by waving a wand. Then in '34 I went to him again and said things couldn't go on this way; after all, I was one of the original Party members and had made great sacrifices for the movement. He advised me simply to close the store, or else to offer it to Schmid as another branch. He promised to make sure something better came my way.'

'Did you take his advice?' I asked.

'What choice did I have? We couldn't live on my gold Party badge. We were about to go bankrupt,' the man replied, and sighed. He refilled our glasses and continued: 'By October of '35 we had run through what little money the sale of the store brought, and I still had no source of income. But I had more than enough *work* to do; they had me taking in and recording Party dues and collecting for the National Socialist People's Welfare. I went door-to-door with our official Party paper, the *Völkischer Beobachter*, to line up subscribers, took part in all Party events, and served in the Ancient Combatants'* Honour Guard. I was especially busy on the first Sunday of every month, when all restaurants and private homes were supposed to serve only stew and donate the money saved to the Winter Aid. People made fun of me, calling me the "truffle hound". One time I went to collect the donation from Kuhbier the butcher. I heard his daughter call to him, "Papa, the truffle hound from the Winter Aid is here. What should I tell him?" I felt like a beggar, and the roast in their oven could be smelled halfway down the street. "Give him eighty pfennigs and two of those Drummer cigarettes," I heard Kuhbier say. "No one smokes those anyway . . ." Drummer cigarettes were produced for the SA by some clever manufacturer, and they were really vile . . . Anyway, by October 1935 I had had it up to here, and I told the Kreisleiter so. At first he wanted to give me the usual lecture – "The Party isn't a welfare agency", and so on – and tell me to be patient a while longer. But an idea occurred to him, and he asked me, "You don't have a police record, do you?" I told him I had been fined three times and sentenced twice to prison during the "Time of Struggle" for disobeying the ban on uniforms, for breach of the peace when we broke up a meeting of the other side, and for slandering my business rival, Oppenheim. Those were honourable

* Ancient Combatants: the *Alte Kämpfer*, 'old fighters', were early members of the Nazi Party.

penalties, the Kreisleiter assured me, and even qualified me as a "martyr for the movement". Then he asked whether I was still in the Church. My wife was still a Catholic, but I'd left the Church a while back, because of Church taxes, and now I was a "believer in God", as the Nazis put it. That was the deciding factor. "Excellent," the Kreisleiter said. "I'll see to it that you're put in charge of the canteen in the new SS barracks. I'll speak to the commandant's adjutant – he'll take care of it." And that's how I got into the restaurant business, and I've been in it ever since . . .'

We drained our glasses. 'So it was worth it for you,' Werner said as we were leaving, and the proprietor agreed.

As Werner and I walked to the underground station, he commented, 'Well, that was a typical "Ancient Combatant" story. I would venture to say that very few of those who joined the Party before 1933 got any farther than our canteen manager. The ones who really succeeded under the Nazis were the opportunists and the technocrats. The loyal truffle hounds were shoved aside when Hitler and his henchmen set about building their perfect police state.'

Early in 1935, barely two years after the seizure of power, the Nazi Party counted up exactly how many members it actually had – in contrast, that is, to the existing membership lists, which had risen to over four million, because those who died or left the Party remained on the rolls. It turned out that there were about two and a half million members, of whom a third were the so-called Ancient Combatants, who had joined before 30 January 1933. Of these 800,000, about 125,000 had joined before September 1930, when the Nazis scored their first big electoral victory. According to these figures, there is no question that most of them did not benefit much from joining early. Forty, maybe fifty thousand men and a few women profited – the 'golden pheasants', as the high-ranking Party functionaries were mockingly called, the people who occupied the most powerful positions in the government, the SS and police, and last but not least the *Reichssicherheitshauptamt* (RSHA), the heart of the terror apparatus, which in 1934 began to construct the perfect police state under the leadership of hardly more than two dozen SS leaders.

SIX

The Perfect Police State

The Third Reich was inaugurated with a wave of terror such as Germany had never before experienced. In the first weeks after Hitler came to power many more than 100,000 persons – mostly Communist and Social Democratic functionaries, prominent union officials, leftist and liberal intellectuals, and other opponents of the regime – were arrested, hauled away, tortured, and in many cases killed.

By such means the Nazi leadership precluded any attempts at resistance and intimidated the mass of the population. Over the next few years the leading Nazis set about legalising and bureaucratising the terror that was necessary for preserving their hold over Germany. This process began shortly after the Röhm Putsch – the bloodbath of 30 June–1 July 1934, when the SA leadership was almost completely wiped out, and the SS won autonomy as a reward for its services as a death squad. The SS promptly began to consolidate its position, forming closer links with the police system and establishing an 'order' that raised it above the tangle of competing jurisdictions. The first step was to dissolve the last of the 'private' concentration camps that individual SA leaders had set up. Unspeakable atrocities had been committed in them. Among the victims were anti-Nazi lawyers and journalists who, during the Weimar Republic, had earned the hatred of the SA leaders who ran the camps. But wealthy Jewish business-men with no involvement in politics had also been thrown into these private concentration camps. The SA leaders often blackmailed such victims' families, using the threat that the prisoners would suffer further mistreatment or death if the families did not pay up. A number of SA men had enriched themselves considerably in this fashion.

Toward the end of 1934 the SS leadership began to clamp down on such 'excesses', as they were called. But this hardly meant an end to arbitrary arrest and torture. A document composed by the comman-dant of Dachau, former police inspector Theodor Eicke, shows how the SS intended to arrange things. This set of regulations was made binding on all the camps in the Reich in 1934, when Eicke became inspector of concentration camps and commander of SS camp guards. Some of its articles read as follows:

§11: Any individual who discusses politics in the camp – at the work site, in the barracks, in the latrines or place of rest – for the purpose of inciting to rebellion, or makes inflammatory speeches, or meets with others for this purpose, or forms cliques, or loiters about, or collects true or untrue anecdotes in order to spread propaganda about atrocities in the concentration camp or its intallations, or receives such anecdotes in writing, buries them, passes them on to others, smuggles them out of the camp by secret code or other means, transmits them orally or in writing via released or transferred prisoners, conceals them in articles of clothing or other objects, throws them by means of stones, etc., over the camp walls, or drafts secret documents . . . will be hanged under revolutionary laws as an inciter to rebellion . . .

§12: Any individual who physically attacks a guard or an SS man, who refuses to obey or to work, who instigates others to do the same for the purpose of mutiny, who mutinously leaves a marching column or work site or urges others to do so, who hoots, shouts, taunts or makes speeches during a march, will be shot on the spot as a mutineer . . .

Fourteen days of strict arrest and twenty-five lashes at the beginning and end of the penalty period shall be the punishment for anyone who uses letters or other means of communication to make derogatory remarks about National Socialist leaders, the state and the government, its agencies and institutions, or glorifies Marxist or liberal leaders . . .

Theodor Eicke began his career as a policeman in Ludwigshafen, where my friend Werner grew up, and Werner was able to give me some details of this man's shady past. In the early 1920s Eicke was dismissed from the police force for his involvement in rightist-extremist political activities. By 1930 he had become leader of the Ludwigshafen SS battalion, and by 1931 head of the SS for the entire Rhineland-Palatinate. After 1933 his penchant for violence and his ruthless determination to rise within the SS almost cost him his future: he struck down a Gauleiter who got in his way, and for that he was sent to prison. There he began to rave and had to be put in a straitjacket. Under orders from the Reichsführer of the SS, Heinrich Himmler, he was sent to a hospital for psychiatric observation and might have languished there indefinitely had Himmler not discovered a use for this man who was at once unscrupulous, brutal, and blindly

loyal to him. Eicke played a major part in organising the Röhm Putsch
– it was Eicke who shot SA Chief of Staff Röhm.

A few days after the putsch, Eicke was put in charge of all the
concentration camps and promoted to the rank of SS Gruppenführer,
the equivalent of a general, with almost unlimited power over tens of
thousands of prisoners. The punishments he imposed included not
only hanging and shooting, lashes and weeks of solitary confinement in
the dark with only bread and water, but also techniques Eicke had
invented and tried out on his prisoners at Dachau. The most notorious
of these was the feared 'tree-hanging'.

The prisoner, who was being punished for something like smoking
in secret or going to the latrine without permission, would have his
hands bound at his back. Then he was hoisted up and suspended by
his hands from a nail driven into a tree or post. The body dangled
about six feet above the ground with all its weight on the wrists, which
were twisted back. The result was that the shoulders were gradually
wrenched out of their sockets, which was excruciatingly painful.
Prisoners who cried out were often further punished with a whipping.
Those who fainted were revived with cold water, and anyone who
survived this torture, which could last anywhere from thirty minutes
to an hour, was physically and mentally broken for life.

Despite newspaper accounts that portrayed the camps as 'ir-
reproachable', rumours about what was actually going on were rife in
Germany, especially by the fall and winter of 1934. Off-duty SS
guards often blurted out the truth after a few drinks in a bar; delivery
men bringing supplies to the SS kitchen in a camp might happen to
witness a prisoner being worked over; and the wives of the few married
members of the Death's Head SS sometimes failed to keep quiet about
the camp conditions their husbands described to them.

'In the winter of '34 to '35,' Werner told me, 'when I was barely
fourteen, the boys who lived in the front part of our building waylaid
me in the passage leading to the inner courtyard and shoved me into a
corner. They wanted me to explain why I wasn't in the Hitler Youth.
"Because I don't want to be," I said. They laughed, and one of them,
two years older than I, said spitefully, "That's a lie. They won't let you
in because your father's an enemy of the state. You watch out or you'll
end up in a concentration camp just like your father!" I knew he wasn't
in a concentration camp but a regular jail, and that he had actually
been tried and convicted, but I seized the opportunity to get them to
talk. I said, "Concentration camp? I thought they didn't exist, that
those were only horror stories." The boy replied promptly, "They
don't exist? My brother's with the Death's Head SS at Buchenwald.

That's where they send the destroyers of the Volk to get rid of them. They have some from Ludwigshafen, too: Mehlmann, the Communist, and old Landauer, the Jewish swine." I knew both men. Erwin Mehlmann was a friend of my father's; they later killed him. Old Landauer owned the haberdashery on Maxstrasse and always gave us candy when we were sent there to fetch something . . . "The Jew Landauer has to clean the latrines with a toothbrush," the boy continued, "and if he misses a spot, up he goes onto the sawhorse!" I asked what that was, and he explained: "They're strapped on, and then they get twenty-five lashes on their bare backsides, with a horsewhip. And then they get a bucket of cold water poured over their heads, and they have to say, 'Thank you, Corporal, sir, I promise to behave better.' My brother even whipped Landauer once!"

'I'll never forget the way he boasted about that,' Werner concluded. 'But after 1945, when the nightmare was over, they all acted as though they'd never heard of anything like that. Supposedly they hadn't even known such camps existed!'

In the first years after the war I heard many people claim that they had not known about the existence of the camps, much less what went on in them. I was sure they were lying – how could anyone who lived through the Third Reich not have known? But it was possible that people denied what they heard, refused to believe it, refused even to acknowledge that they had heard it. After all, the Nazis did everything they could to encourage such repression, from branding the rumours 'horror stories' to issuing orders that 'rumour-mongers' were to be reported to the Gestapo. It was extremely dangerous to repeat openly what one had learned about the camps. For the Gestapo worked hand in hand with the secret SD, the Security Service, which we started hearing about only toward the end of 1934.

For their Security Service, the Nazi leaders had taken pains to recruit persons who were neither members of the NSDAP nor known supporters of the regime. The SD had its spies within the Nazi Party and all its branches, and soon spread its net over the entire country. In its time it employed a good 100,000 part-time informants, who gathered information about anything and everything and reported it to the central office in Berlin. They prepared analyses of the general mood of the population, and spied on anyone who aroused suspicion by word or deed.

Soon no one dared to utter anything that might be construed as hostile to the regime or even critical of it, unless he was completely sure of everyone within earshot. And no one knew whether there might not be an SD spy among their close friends or even among their own family.

I myself had not even heard of the SD at the end of 1934 when my parents and I went to visit friends in Westphalia who owned the best hotel in town. I was almost fourteen, and my parents allowed me to stay up for New Year's Eve. Together with other friends of the innkeepers we ate at a large table in a corner of the dining room. After the late supper the adults danced to the music of a small band – waltzes, tangos, foxtrots. Soon the mood became quite exuberant, and at midnight people drank to each other, clinked glasses, and wished one another a Happy New Year. As people kissed, the lights in the room were switched off for a moment.

When the lights came back on, the noise suddenly died away. A heavy, wheezing man in a brown Party uniform with an extra-wide leather cross-strap and brown riding boots clambered up onto the podium to make a speech. Most of those present did not seem particularly delighted at this interruption of their celebration. The speaker's words were already somewhat slurred, and a few of the guests even laughed as he began to get tangled up in his long, bombastic nationalistic phrases. Others gestured or made faces to hush those who were laughing. Finally the man in the brown uniform concluded with an emphatic 'God save our Führer!'

'And us from him!' an elderly gentleman at our table had the temerity to comment softly, but loudly enough so that a few people stared at him in horror, as the music started up again.

Just a few days later, the incautious older gentleman, a lawyer highly respected in town, was arrested by the Gestapo. The local newspaper reported merely that he had been 'unmasked as a dangerous enemy of the state' and 'consigned to a concentration camp'.

Later, when my parents and I had returned home, we received a letter from the hotel owners informing us that 'the friend who had so suddenly fallen ill after New Year's Eve fortunately didn't have to suffer long'; the urn with his ashes had arrived from Esterwegen and had been 'buried in a private ceremony'. Since there was an infamous concentration camp near Esterwegen in the East Frisian Emsland region, my parents had no trouble deducing that the prisoner had been killed there.

My parents and their friends were shaken to realise that one careless remark could have led to such disastrous consequences. When we visited our friends later that year, they and my parents spent many hours trying to reason out who might have betrayed him.

They discussed the matter only in whispers, and with the gramophone playing. None of the help, they recalled, had been nearby when the attorney made his comment, so it had to have been one of the close acquaintances at the table. There was no one they could imagine capable of such a thing – certainly not Dr. Heinz, who was soon to marry their daughter. 'Out of the question!' said Uncle Franz, as I called the innkeeper. 'He's not even in the Party, he wouldn't do a thing like that. He's a university-educated man!' This was something Uncle Franz was particularly proud of.

Dr. Heinz, a medical student, had just passed his state examination and planned to become a military doctor. He was, as I myself had heard him say, 'thrilled by the new Germany, by the Movement, and by the great opportunities the Führer has opened up.' But he belonged neither to the Party nor to one of the Nazi militant oganisations, but only to the National Socialist German Student League.

'I checked with Kreisleiter Müllershagen,' Franz added, 'and he assured me this National Socialist Student Association is more or less compulsory; you have to belong to it if you want to avoid trouble at the university. In any case, he's finished with his studies now; and, he said, he'll soon resign from the Association and not be joining anything else. He wants to go into the military, and there no one asks whether you belong to the Party or the National Socialist Medical Association . . .'

But Franz was wrong. The fat Kreisleiter, the man who had delivered the New Year's address, had been misinformed: he confused the German Student League with the German Student Association. The latter was an organisation that the Nazis had 'brought into line' and made compulsory for university students.

The German Student League, however, to which Dr. Heinz belonged was a very different story. Membership was voluntary, but subject to a strict selection process. At most 5 per cent of all students could be admitted, according to the organisation's guidelines. Because the total number of students had fallen sharply since 1933, the League had only about three thousand members in all of Germany. It was intended, in the words of the Führer's deputy, Rudolf Hess, to serve as 'a sort of intellectual SS', bringing together the political elite of the Nazi Party at the universities. The League provided the training ground for future high functionaries, especially for the SD, the secret Security Service.

In short, the League was a particularly dangerous organisation, whose members went on to careers as civil servants, doctors, teachers, architects, lawyers, or other distinguished professionals, but at the same time secretly belonged to the SD and spied on their fellow Germans. Undoubtedly it was Dr. Heinz who turned in the elderly attorney.

But in the spring of 1935 we knew none of this. At most we had our suspicions, and every time a friend or acquaintance was visited by the Gestapo, and it emerged that the Gestapo possessed detailed knowledge of things they should have had no way of knowing, our fear of the almost omniscient secret police grew, along with our sense that we could not be too cautious or too suspicious.

One's first suspicions tended to light on people with whom there had been friction. There was that neighbour who had threatened to call the police when Frau Meinzerhagen beat her carpets in the courtyard during his afternoon nap. Might he have tried to get even by denouncing her to the Gestapo? How else would the Gestapo agents have known that after midnight the Meinzerhagens sometimes listened to 'nigger jazz' or 'horror stories about Germany' on foreign radio stations?

When they interrogated her, Frau Meinzerhagen explained that she had simply been trying out a new radio. As the widow of a soldier killed in the Great War she hadn't the slightest interest in foreign broadcasts! She got off with a stern warning, but from that time on she and all her close friends and relatives brooded over who might have denounced her. She and her daughter had been alone in the apartment, with the windows closed and the heavy drapes drawn. Maybe once or twice they had turned up the volume to hear something more clearly. Only their immediate neighbour could have known about it – perhaps he had drilled a hole in the wall. Or might a listening device have been planted in her telephone, which stood next to the radio?

Once this possibility had occurred to them, Frau Meinzerhagen and her close friends took to popping a thick tea cozy over the telephone whenever they discussed anything sensitive. But it was important to remember to remove the tea cozy when they were finished; otherwise, anyone coming into the apartment would have been suspicious.

The tea cozy was just one of many precautions people devised, most of them as ludicrous as they were ineffective. But the fear many people in Germany felt was real, and completely justified. For time and again, and at the most unexpected moment, the Gestapo struck.

The next victim among our acquaintances was the Protestant pastor of our parish.

My parents had continued to pay their church tax and their parish dues, and they also made a donation whenever some from the church came around collecting. But they took very little part in the life of the parish, and we seldom went to Sunday services. So it came as quite a surprise when in 1935 my parents advised me to enroll in classes in preparation for being confirmed. 'It's important to give the Church more support these days,' my father remarked. 'It's our last bastion against barbarism.'

My mother defined the issue in more specific terms: 'Pastor Klötzel has been very courageous in his sermons, speaking out against brutality and despotism, and especially against all this racial insanity. We really must give him our backing. We should all start going to church on Sundays for a change.'

So I went to confirmation classes, which were taught by Pastor Klötzel himself and proved much more interesting than I had expected. He had a knack for making the Bible and the catechism relevant to our times, being careful not to draw explicit parallels but making the connections clear enough so that only a complete dunce could fail to see them. Pastor Klötzel did not conceal his membership in the Pastors' Emergency League and the Confessing Church, and he flatly rejected the Religious Movement of German Christians created by the Nazis.

Established in 1932 by Nazi Protestants, this 'Religious Movement' was headed by an East Prussian military chaplain named Ludwig Müller. In September 1933 the Gestapo ruthlessly crushed the considerable resistance to his candidacy as Reich Bishop, after which the intimidated synod felt obliged to elect him. The 'Reibi', as he was mockingly known, had been delegated by Hitler to unite all the factions of German Protestantism into one Reich Church and to bring Protestants rigorously 'into line'. But a countermovement sprang up, calling itself the Confessing Church.

At a synod of the Confessing Church held in May 1934 in Wupper-tal-Barmen and at another meeting in November 1934 in Berlin, the assembled pastors announced that they alone were entitled to represent Germany's Evangelical Church. The Berlin pastor Martin Niemöller, originally an extremely conservative man who had been a U-boat commander in the First World War and as late as the summer of 1933 had loudly proclaimed his enthusiasm for the 'national reawakening', served from that November meeting on as the spokesman for the Confessing Church.

Of Germany's 17,000 pastors, barely 3,000 were so-called German Christians. About the same number belonged to the Confessing Church; but the large majority adopted a wait-and-see attitude. On the one hand, it took a great deal of courage to declare oneself openly opposed to the Nazification of the Church, to the racial theories and other anti-Christian teachings of the Nazis, and to their cult of the Führer – and that was what one had to do as a 'confessing' pastor. On the other hand, very few pastors had any desire to support the persecution of the Jews and the megalomania of the 'Germanic master race'.

Pastor Klötzel, who confirmed me in 1935, was by inclination a conservative, cautious, and thoughtful man. But in matters of conscience he was uncompromising. 'Everyone, even the most simple-minded, can tell right from wrong,' he would say. 'And when we see a flagrant worng committed, when we ourselves are expected to do wrong, even on high authority, then we must refuse and listen to God rather than men, for men may well be deluded.'

One late afternoon in May 1935, about two weeks after my confirmation, my mother and I ran into Pastor Klötzel on the street. We greeted him and chatted a bit. Then the pastor excused himself. He said he still had to call on a family that had suffered a great misfortune. Besides, he was not feeling well and feared he was coming down with the flu.

My mother urged him to take care of himself, as the evenings were still very chilly. Pastor Klötzel merely nodded and smiled. Then, as he was already on his way, he turned and said, 'Some day we'll see the sun shine again . . .'

The next day I heard on my way to school that the pastor had been 'picked up'. When I saw his son coming down the street, I ran to meet him. 'Is it true?' I asked. 'Yes,' he replied sadly, 'they came with a warrant for protective custody. For "misuse of the pulpit" . . . and he's in bad shape. They really shoved him into the vehicle, those filthy cowards!'

A few weeks later a memorial service was conducted for Pastor Klötzel in his own church; he had 'passed away' in the concentration camp. We had never seen the church so crowded, and several hundred people clustered outside the door. Inside the church I noticed many good Catholics, like Fräulein Bonse. I saw a woman whose husband was imprisoned for being a Communist functionary. Even my father, who had not been to church in years, had come this time.

A young vicar from the Pastors' Emergency League delivered the sermon. At the very end he began to sing in a powerful voice 'A Mighty Fortress Is Our God.' The organ joined in, and all those present, both inside and outside the church, raised their voices in Luther's great hymn.

Around this time and during the following months more than seven hundred pastors of the Confessing Church were arrested all over Germany by the Gestapo and thrown into concentration camps. By the end of 1937, almost a thousand more of the Confessing pastors were in the camps, and many of them died there. By then Reich Bishop Müller had forsaken his attempt to drive every german Protestant into his Reich Church of German Christians, and had resigned and disappeared from public life. But his efforts had the desired effect, for when Pastor Niemöller was put into the remand prison in Berlin-Moabit on 1 July 1937, the resistance of the Confessing Church was virtually finished. Later Niemöller was sentenced by a special court to a short prison term, equal to time served. But the Nazis had lost all respect for the judiciary, even for their own special courts. As he was leaving the courtroom, Pastor Niemöller was taken into protective custody. He was sent to the concentration camp at Sachsenhausen, and from there to Dachau, where he was finally liberated by Allied troops at the end of the war.

Around the time of Niemöller's second arrest the great majority of Protestant pastors still at large were forced to swear a personal oath of loyalty to the Führer. With that, the last stronghold of moral resistance had fallen.

SEVEN

The Misunderstood Poet

'It was a difficult time for all of us,' said Dr. Barsch, 'an ordeal. And then I found myself in even greater difficulties; and in 1942 I lost my entire library, including valuable manuscripts, in an air raid – an irreplaceable loss!'

Dr. Barsch, at eighty-five, was a handsome man with a great mane of white hair that made him resemble the famous German playwright Gerhart Hauptmann, a resemblance he cultivated. He had received me cordially and was more than willing to answer my questions.

'I welcome this opportunity to clarify matters and set the record straight. When one has the proper historical perspective and looks at the whole business in the right light, everything is quite different.'

We had a long conversation, exchanging memories from the years 1932 to 1937, when we were next-door neighbours. At the time, Dr. Barsch was in charge of the cultural section of a respected daily newspaper. He also wrote poetry and plays under a euphonious pseudonym.

My father had once thought highly of him. 'An interesting and talented man,' was his opinion of our neighbour. 'Some of his poems really are first-rate.' But on the tenth of May 1933, an article signed by Eberhard Barsch put an end to the conversations across the garden fence and the invitations to 'stop by for a glass of wine'. My father was reading the newspaper at the breakfast table when suddenly he crumpled it up with a vehemence I had never seen in him before. But then he smoothed out the paper and said, 'This document of shame should be preserved for posterity . . .'

The 'shame' of which my father spoke was the Nazis' book-burning, which Dr. Barsch had chosen to describe as a glorious occasion. On the evening of 10 May, book-burnings had taken place in front of the Humboldt University in Berlin and in many other university towns. The works of all Jewish authors were tossed into the flames, as were the writings of others who for one reason or another were abhorrent to the Nazis. The list of nearly twenty thousand writers included almost every important name in modern German letters. Only a few well-known writers were spared, but to make up for that, the works of numerous foreigners fed the bonfires, among them those of Upton Sinclair, H. G. Wells, Jack London, André Gide, Émile Zola, Marcel Proust, and many others. The list also contained the name of scientists like Albert Einstein and Sigmund Freud.

'This truly revolutionary act of self-purification,' Dr. Barsch wrote, 'has cast its flickering glow not only over the end of an era that was rotten to the core and is now definitively terminated, but also over the dawning of a new era, the national rebirth of our people. At last the German soul can find its own voice again. The purifying fire has put a stop to a creeping poison and corruption . . .'

This 'new era' celebrated by Dr. Barsch was inaugurated with a degree of cultural regimentation unknown in Europe since the days of Metternich. In the course of a few months everything connected with culture had been placed under the absolute control of the Reich Minister for the People's Enlightenment and Propaganda, Joseph Goebbels. On 22 September 1933, Goebbels crowned his work by creating a 'Reich Cultural Chamber', which he directed personally. The purpose of this chamber, he declared in a radio broadcast carried by all stations, was 'to unite all creative persons in a cultural uniformity of the mind'. According to the 'Führer principle', Goebbels explained, it was the Reich's responsibility not only to establish guidelines for intellectual and artistic development, but also to direct those professions that created culture, organising them and purging them of all 'degenerate' elements, and anything not in accord with National Socialist weltanschauung.

Seven individual chambers were set up to govern particular fields: the fine arts, music, theatre, literature, the press, broadcasting, and film.

Anyone active in these areas had to join the appropriate chamber and submit to its stipulations and guidelines. The chambers had the right to investigate their members' origins, since non-Aryans, especially persons of the Jewish faith, or with Jewish ancestors, were not admitted. In addition, anyone considered 'politically unreliable' was either not admitted or subject to expulsion at any time. Only those who were above suspicion could join and remain in a chamber. The others were not allowed to practise their professions in Germany and thus could not earn a living.

The result of these measures was that thousands of artists, writers, film and theatre directors, photographers, stage designers, editors, and others who worked for the press and the radio left Germany. And because most of the leading figures in German cultural life since the

First World War had been either 'non-Aryan' (or at least not 'purely Aryan') or were married to non-Aryans, Germany's hitherto vital culture became a wasteland of mediocrity.

Of course, the mass emigration of many recognised and successful artists and intellectuals proved beneficial for those who remained behind, so long as they were eligible for admission to the new chambers. In the absence of a better supply, the demand for their meagre talents rose.

I asked Barsch if he had hoped that his plays would finally be performed once the great 'purgation' of cultural life was completed. Perhaps that explained the zeal with which he supported the Nazis.

'Not at all!' he exclaimed energetically, without the slightest trace of embarrassment. 'You're utterly mistaken! My article on the book-burnings was something I was forced to write – that should have been obvious. I used the speech Goebbels gave in Berlin as a model, even repeating certain passages almost verbatim, adding a few strong adjectives here and there. I was hoping that the outrageousness of the exaggerations would make any attentive reader realise that here someone was writing under duress and against his own convictions in praise of something he despised from the bottom of his heart . . .'

'Who forced you to write that article?' I interjected, and he hastily added, 'Oh, I had reason to fear I would soon be removed from my post. The editor-in-chief had already been squeezed out to make room for an Ancient Combatant. The editor responsible for domestic politics had been fired on April the 1st. I was afraid I'd be next, and then I wouldn't have found any new job commensurate with my abilities. So I had to prove in a hurry that I wasn't the liberal intellectual the Nazis considered me. But to make it clear to my friends that I had written this only to save my job, I laid it on so thick that no one who knew me could seriously believe it was my real opinion. And in fact that's how many of my friends and acquaintances saw it. They supported me and urged me to stand fast and not let our cultural section fall into the hands of the Nazis. Do you understand the position I was in?'

I asked him how his article on the book-burnings was received by the new managing editors of his paper.

'They loved it,' he replied. 'They reacted just as I expected. Now I was their man, and the cultural section was saved. Of course,' he added, 'I had to make a few concessions, but I kept a good deal of autonomy and could slip in a number of things between the lines. Here and there I even managed to work in some sharp criticism. Do you remember my editorial on "Nationalist Kitsch"? Unfortunately the text perished, along with all my other valuable books and papers during the great air raid in 1942 . . . That column created quite a stir at the time. But no one could touch me, because at almost exactly the same time the *Schwarzes Korps*, the SS weekly, took a stand against the commercialisation of national symbols into kitsch . . .'

He paused, probably sensing my skepticism. 'You see, I had personal reasons as well for being extra cautious. But even so, I practised my own sort of resistance against the regime's misguided cultural policies. In the summer of 1937, for example, I ran a feature on "degenerate art" – with glorious reproductions of paintings by Chagall, Pechstein, Van Gogh, Gauguin, Cézanne, and Kokoschka on one page and on the facing page the worst examples of the Nazi leaders' bad taste. Of course in the text I had to present matters the other way around, but the pictures spoke for themselves, and there were many readers who wrote in, asking naively whether the paper hadn't switched the captions by mistake.' He giggled, obviously still proud of this bold stroke.

'May I ask, what *were* your personal reasons for being so cautious?'

He seemed to have anticipated my question, for he went to his desk and took out a large folio with 'My Ancestors' written on the outside. When he opened it up, the Barsch family tree was diagrammed over both sides.

'Interesting, isn't it?' he asked as he handed me the family tree. I skimmed over the many names and recognised one of them. 'Ah, you're descended from Schadow?'

He beamed. 'You put your finger right on the "sore point",' he said with obvious satisfaction.

Johann Gottfried Schadow, the Great German sculptor, married in 1785 the daughter of a Jewish jeweler from Vienna, Marianne Devidels. One of the children of this marriage was the renowned painter Friedrich Wilhelm von Schadow, who served as director of the Düsseldorf Academy of Art from 1827 to 1859. He was elevated to the nobility, and one of the main streets in Düsseldorf bore his name. It was not renamed during the Nazi period. A daughter of the painter was Eberhard Barsch's grandmother. Although in Nazi terms she would have been a 'person of mixed blood in the second degree', that would not have been a problem for her grandson, Dr. Barsch. The Nazis could not pursue their insistence on racial purity that far back without disqualifying everyone in the cultural realm. The only one-hundred-percent Jewish person in Barsch's family was Marianne Schadow, born long before 1800, and even according to the rigid guidelines of the 'SS Race and Settlement Central Agency' she did not count as an ancestor who could taint her great-great-grandson.

'We're also related to the Bendemanns,' Dr. Barsch put in.

That, as I happened to know, was even less of a problem. Eduard Bendemann, after whom another Düsseldorf street was named, was born in Berlin in 1811 into an old and respected Jewish family. He had himself baptised before he married Lida, a daughter of Schadow the sculptor, by his second, 'Aryan', wife. Bendemann, one of the most noted German painters of the nineteenth century, had then succeeded his brother-in-law, the younger Schadow, as director of the Düsseldorf Academy of Art.

But none of this had any bearing on Dr. Barsch's origins, since no blood relationship with the Bendemanns existed. The von Schadow and von Bendemann families in Düsseldorf had been related by marriage and by friendship, but even the wildest race fanatics among the Nazis could not have fashioned those connections into a noose to hand Dr. Barsch.

I said as much, but he brushed my objection aside: 'It's true that I was all right as far as the Nuremberg Laws were concerned, but what you don't know is that in 1933 I occasionally boasted to colleagues that I was descended from these great figures in German art history. For the cultural section of the paper that worked in my favour. An additional difficulty was that my wife's mother was born a Barnay – she was a daughter of the great actor and the founder of the German Stage Guild, Ludwig Barnay. I sometimes stressed this fact too, in my younger days. After all, I wanted directors to pay attention to my plays. But after 1933 I realised that Ludwig Barnay was also Jewish, and as his granddaughter my wife was classified from 1935 on as a "person of mixed Jewish blood in the second degree". . . . And that was very damaging to me.'

'I remember your wife only slightly', I said. 'Didn't you divorce her?'

'Yes, certainly,' Dr. Barsch replied, 'we separated in the autumn of '33 by mutual consent, before my admission to the Reich Press Chamber. We remained good friends, and fortunately nothing happened to her. But the divorce could not be avoided under those particular circumstances. Otherwise I could not have kept my department and would have been fired.'

'Is that a fact?'

'The publisher indicated that it would be wise for me to leave my wife – if I didn't, there might be too many difficulties, because of my prominent position. You know, they didn't wear kid gloves, those gentlemen from the Gestapo. And they were very intimate with the administration of the Reich Press and Literature Chambers.'

I could think of many men who during the twelve years of Nazi rule did not leave their quarter-, half-, or even all-Jewish wives, and who accepted the professional consequences. They often voluntarily moved from prominent positions to less important ones that did not necessitate their joining one of the chambers, and their superiors and fellow workers lent their tacit approval. Almost all of these men and their wives survived the Third Reich.

I changed the subject, inquiring whether Dr. Barsch had published much during the Nazi years in addition to his work on the cultural section of the paper.

He was very pleased to be able to talk about it. 'Yes, certainly, weren't you aware of that?' He went to the bookcase and came back with ten or twelve little softbound volumes, the paper already somewhat yellowed, as well as a thicker hardbound book, which he was about to put aside when the doorbell rang.

Before he went to the door he urged me to take a look at his volumes of poetry. As he left the room, he stuck the hardbound volume back into the bookcase.

I plucked it off the shelf and leafed through it. The book was called *Young Germany in the Third Reich.* It was an anthology, with contributions by many authors who came to prominence after the exodus of Germany's great writers and had fallen into complete oblivion since the end of the war: Hans Friedrich Blunck, Hans Zöberlin, Hertha Torriani-Seele, Heinrich Anacker. Two poems bore the pseudonym of our former neighbour Dr. Barsch. One poem was entitled 'Duty Is a Signpost', and the other 'Our Labour Service'. Dr. Barsch had the latter poem marked with a bookmark, and in the margin he had noted, 'On the occasion of the 1935 Party Rally – letter of appreciation from Reich Minister Dr. Goebbels.' The poem began with the lines:

> Deep in our souls
> Rests youthful might.
> We dig ditches and holes
> By passion's light.

Then came five other stanzas, and the last two read:

> Yet we are a part
> Of our Volk, of our time.
> If you've served with your heart
> You've known love in its prime.

The bare shoulders carry
The weather's brand.
We shall not tarry
To build a new land!

As I replaced the book on the shelf, I could not help wondering what the Bendemanns, the Schadows, and the Barnays, as well as the two million other Germans affected by the racial laws proclaimed at Nuremberg on 15 September 1935, would have thought of this cultural contribution, with which Dr. Barsch had seen fit to celebrate the codification of their persecution. Who had forced him to write that poem? Could bare necessity account for the zeal he had shown in placing himself on the side of the oppressors?

The Newspaper Editors' Law of October 1933 that mandated the bringing into line of the entire German press did indeed require that all editors and their spouses be citizens of the Reich and Aryans, and that they 'pledge themselves to uphold the National Socialist State'. Anyone involved with the press was obliged by law to 'exclude any material that might weaken the power of the German Reich internally or externally or the common will of the German Volk, or the German defence-preparedness, culture, or economy,' But no law required an editor to write sentimental hymns in praise of NSDAP rallies.

When Dr. Barsch returned to the room, I boldly asked him whether he hadn't been a Nazi believer, at least for a time, and if not, what had motivated him to go overboard in proving his loyalty to the regime. That little 'blot' on his family tree way back before 1800 could scarcely have been sufficient grounds; and by the end of 1933 he had already divorced his 'half-Jewish' wife.

'What more could they ask of you?'

'Listen, you were very young then. You can't possibly imagine the pressure we older people were under. think of being in constant fear of being taken away by the Gestapo and locked up in a concentration camp. I saw one of those camps once – not as a prisoner, thank God! It was a tour organised by the Reich Propaganda Ministry for several German and foreign journalists. It was dreadful – I'll never forget it! Of course they made sure that everything looked clean and orderly. But you could *sense* what went on there. When we asked prisoners how they were treated and they said well, we could practically smell their fear. I saw one person I knew, a sports reporter. Only a couple of weeks earlier I had been sitting in the bar across from the press building having a beer with him – and now he looked awful! Shaven head, frightened, aged by at least a year . . . The Gestapo had been after a friend of his, and he put the man up for a night and gave him money. That was sheer madness on his part, of course . . . but after that I often couldn't sleep nights, thinking something like that might happen to me. My wife still had a key to my apartment . . .'

EIGHT

Was There Really Nothing People Could Do?

Almost every one in the neighbourhood knew Annie Ney, whose bakery stood at the fork in the trolley-bus lines. Annie Ney's husband, the baker, was a true master of his trade and seldom emerged from the baking area. His wife presided over the bustling café, as well as the counter where cakes, tortes, pastries, and ice cream were sold. She had a friendly word for every customer, and even found time to chat with the regulars in the café. She liked to hear the latest about people's families and jobs, and was always ready to lend a helping hand.

My father spent half an hour at the café almost every afternoon. Usually he didn't bother to sit at one of the little marble-topped tables, but drank his coffee in the tiny office where Annie Ney took telephone calls and rested a bit, for she was 'no longer a young thing', as she would say, and had a bad hip that acted up now and then. In that little office my father and Annie Ney talked almost in whispers, and I gathered that these conversations, which certain other regulars often joined, amounted to a sort of political information exchange – and sometimes more. For 'Aunt Annie', as I called her, had all kinds of connections. People who rose to power and influence under the Nazis remembered that although she had criticised their politics, she had never left them high and dry if, at the end of the month, they didn't have enough to pay for a cup of coffee. Even the Gauleiter and the chief of police remained fond of her and respected her, although they knew perfectly well that Annie Ney had no love for the regime. But, after all, she was just an old lady who had trouble getting around and treated everyone with kindness and courtesy. They considered her harmless, and so, like a court jester, she enjoyed an amazing degree of freedom. She could say what she wished, even when she expressed firm though friendly criticism of the Nazis' practices, especially those directed against the Church.

I soon realised that the Nazis had completely misjudged Annie Ney. She knew that I knew, but that didn't trouble her. We had an unspoken understanding that we would draw on our mutual trust only when absolutely necessary, and even then we would speak calmly, almost casually, confining ourselves to the essentials.

'Here's your ice cream,' she might say, and I would notice that the helping was larger than usual, which meant she needed me for something. Then I would hang around the counter until she was free. 'Do you know the little Wolf girl, Ruth?' she asked me once. 'She's about your age, or maybe only fourteen,' she said, turning to serve a new customer.

The Wolfs were Jews whom I knew slightly. They came from Silesia or West Prussia. Ruth's father ran a little tailor's shop. I had heard from Rolf, one of my classmates, that hoodlums had thrown rocks through his shop windows that morning, torn clothes off the dummies and trampled them on the ground. 'They also stole bolts of cloth and tossed firecrackers into the drawers – the pigs,' Rolf had added in a low voice, even though he was in the Hitler Youth and usually found everything the Nazis did 'fantastic'.

As I was thinking about Annie Ney's question, I heard her saying under her breath to an older lady, 'The poor child had a terrible fright. She sleeps in the back of the shop, in the dressing room; they have only the one room, where they cook, sleep, live . . .' As I caught the sidelong glance she shot me, I realised they must be talking about Ruth.

'How is Fräulein Bonse these days?' Aunt Annie asked me a moment later, when the shop happened to be empty of customers. And brushing a few crumbs off the glass countertop with her hand, she added pensively, 'The girl hasn't learned any English in school; otherwise that would be a possibility . . .'

Just then another customer came in. 'Heil Hitler, Frau Ney, I'd like a nice big chocolate cake and a few Turks' heads, and maybe something else . . .'

'Good day to you, Herr Sturmbannführer – or is it Obersturmbannführer now?' I heard Aunt Annie saying, and thought it rather bold of her. 'Not yet? Well, it'll come before you know it, I'm sure. What did you say you wanted?'

She brought out the little tray and was busy arranging Turks' heads, raspberry tarts, eclairs, and elephants' ears as she remarked, 'It looks as though someone's having a birthday party, Herr Sturmbannführer. Is it yours? Well then, let me congratulate you and wish you all the best – especially a speedy promotion. May I? . . .' She filled a large snifter with brandy for the SS officer and a small one for herself, clinked glasses with him, and chattered away.

In the meantime I figured out that she intended to help Ruth Wolf, whom she presumably had never met, to leave the country. Aunt Annie probably wanted to know whether a girl who did not know English could take part in an exchange programme like the one through which I had recently spent eight weeks in England. She also seemed interested in hearing whether Fräulein Bonse could be approached about this case.

So after the Nazi officer left, I told her, 'Fräulein Bonse is just fine – thriving, in fact. Would you like her number?'

'No, I think it would be better if you called her up – she knows you. Please ask her if she would be so kind as to stop by for a cup of coffee, today if possible, or tomorrow bright and early. I'm in a bit of a hurry. And please tell her I would have come to her if I could leave the shop and didn't have such a hard time with stairs.' From this I deduced that Aunt Annie had already spoken to others about Fräulein Bonse. How else could she have known that Fräulein Bonse worked at home and could arrange her time as she wished, or that she lived in a fifth-floor apartment?

I telephoned Fräulein Bonse. She said she would visit Frau Ney in about an hour. She didn't even ask what it was about; apparently it was enough that Frau Ney was in a hurry to speak with her.

A few days later I dropped in on Aunt Annie and asked about her meeting with Fräulein Bonse. She was busy with a customer and merely nodded. Later she said to me, 'I haven't heard yet whether everything went smoothly.'

But a few weeks later, when I had almost forgotten the entire incident, Aunt Annie showed me a picture postcard from New York. 'I always wanted to go there myself,' she said, 'but only for a few days – I hear they don't have a single decent bakery, though it's hard to believe . . . By the way, you remember Ruth? She's there now, with her aunt and uncle. I hope her parents can follow her soon.'

I had a question, but several customers came in at that moment. Before Aunt Annie turned to them, she said under her breath, 'Fräulein Bonse has valuable connections with the Quakers – splendid people! What a pity they aren't Catholic!'

About two weeks after Aunt Annie's mysterious allusion to the Quakers – around the end of June 1935 – I happened to be in town with a friend. My mother had asked me to stop at Herr Desch's on the way home to pick up a suit for my father.

Herr Desch had an elegant tailoring establishment in a quiet side street off the Königsallee. He had been recommended to my father by Aunt Annie because he always did such an excellent job for her husband, who liked to dress like a fine gentleman when he left the bakery.

I didn't like Herr Desch. He was tall, lean, and almost oppressively elegant. He had a face like a carp, with cold, protruding eyes and thinning pale blond hair, which he wore meticulously parted. He had a curiously detached manner of speaking, except when he was discussing the quality of fabrics and the fit of his suits. To make things worse, he was a Supporting Member of the SS, and usually wore the SS insignia on his lapel.

I arrived just before the shop closed, but still had to wait because a high-ranking SS officer was fussing over his new dress uniform. With almost exaggerated courtesy Herr Desch assured him that the braid was placed exactly as it should be; he even pulled out a copy of the latest guidelines from the SS Central Office.

When the officer was finally persuaded and went into the dressing room to take off the uniform, Herr Desch turned to me and said in his usual quiet, detached voice, 'You're here for your father's suit, isn't that right? Why don't you go straight to the back room. Herr Wolf has it all pressed and will pack it up for you. I'll be with you as soon as I've closed up.'

The name Wolf didn't ring a bell for me until I saw the tailor in the back room. He was listening anxiously to hear whether the SS officer was still in the shop, and he reacted nervously when I asked him if he was Herr Wolf. Then it dawned on me: this must be Ruth's father!

'Did you have to give up your shop?' I asked him softly.

He nodded sadly. 'Perhaps my wife and I will be able to go to America soon,' he whispered. 'For the time being we're living here.' He gestured toward a door leading to the rear of the building. 'Herr Desch is a very good person. "You'll be safer here, Herr Wolf," he said, "and you won't have to pay rent." He really is a wonderful person, Herr Desch.'

I was speechless. Not until he had begun to pack up my father's suit did I pluck up my courage and say, 'Frau Ney showed me the beautiful postcard your daughter sent from New York. She told me the Quakers had helped.'

He was in the middle of laying out the suit with sheets of tissue paper, but when I mentioned the Quakers he started. 'Not so loud,' he whispered. 'That's nothing strangers should hear! Herr Desch doesn't want anyone to know what he's doing. He drove her to Basel in his own car – just imagine! Such a prominent businessman going to so much trouble for our little Ruth! He even . . .' he paused in embarrassment, for Herr Desch had just stepped into the room.

'I had to go to Basel on business, Herr Wolf, and there was plenty of room in the car,' he said, and it sounded as detached as ever. 'My wife was happy to have someone to talk to on the drive. I never talk when I'm at the wheel. So don't blow it out of proportion.'

Then he took the box with the suit, led me into the shop, and said, just before he unlocked the door to let me out, 'Will you be going to England again during your school vacation?'

'Yes, it's only ten days away.'

'Will you be taking the Channel steamer from Ostende to Dover?'

'Yes, just like last time.'

'Excellent,' he said. 'I assume Fräulein Bonse is familiar with all the details – the departure time for the train, the list of participants, and all the formalities?'

'She's the one who organises the whole thing.' I was amazed that he knew Fräulein Bonse, or at least her name. Had my father told him about her?

I was hesitating, wondering whether I could ask him what the connection was, when he inquired further, 'Isn't there a group going to France as well?'

'Yes, but there are more going to England. We all meet at the Central Station in Cologne, including those who are going to France. We stay together as far as Liège.'

'So it must be a fairly large group crossing the border at Aachen. How many do you think you'll be?'

'I would say between forty-five and fifty – maybe a few more.'

'That's splendid,' Herr Desch commented, and he sounded even more detached than usual. 'I imagine the border guards don't pay much attention to the group, or do they?'

'None at all. We have a single group ticket as far as Liège, and then each of the two groups has its own. Our chaperone shows the ticket to the conductor just once in Germany and once in Belgium, and the conductor counts to make sure the number on the ticket is right – that's all. We just have to stay in our compartments while that's going on.'

'And what about customs?'

'The officer collects our currency permits from the chaperone – each of us is allowed to take out fifty marks, and the border police count us to make sure that the number of passports is right. The whole thing takes less than five minutes. The guards get on at Aachen and have to leave the train at the next village. They don't take us very seriously. All they care about is whether the numbers are accurate.'

'That sounds perfect,' he said as he showed me out. 'I hope nothing has changed since the last time you went . . .'

Ten days later, when I joined the group at the Cologne station, I was not surprised to see that it was much larger than the previous year: about sixty-five boys and girls. I already knew some of them from an earlier trip, and others I had met at school. After we greeted each other and reported to our chaperone, we found the cars reserved for us and got settled in our compartments. As I looked out the window I spotted Herr Desch, whose luggage was being carried into a first-class car by a porter. As he passed, he looked up at me; his fish eyes remained expressionless as he nodded to me without a smile. On the lapel of his trenchcoat I noticed the SS insignia.

An hour and a half later, when we had crossed the border, and the customs officials, border police, and railroad guards had left the train – the checks had been as casual as I predicted – I saw Herr Desch out in the corridor. He was speaking with the student chaperone who was accompanying our group to London. She was handing him a little satchel containing passports and other papers.

In Liège sixteen boys and girls besides those who were to spend the next few weeks in France got off the train. The sixteen formed a separate party. A porter came along with a wagon on which I saw Herr Desch's suitcase, and soon Herr Desch himself appeared.

'Put your luggage on the wagon,' he said, 'and please hurry. Our train leaves in eight minutes. We don't have to change in Maastricht – our train goes directly to Rotterdam and will take us right to the harbour.'

He spoke in such a detached manner that the children stared at him with a combination of curiosity and anxiety. He seemed thoroughly indifferent. 'Please hurry,' he said again, and turned to go. He gave a distracted nod by way of farewell to the student who had handed him the passports and travel documents.

'Where are they going?' I asked the chaperone when Herr Desch's group was out of sight.

'Imagine,' she said, 'they're sailing to America! I had no idea. Fräulein Bonse told me only that a group of sixteen would be going on to Holland from Liège. I found that odd, because there's a direct train from Cologne. But the organisation that invited them wanted them to travel with us as far as Liège. It's called the Society of Friends, and the gentleman who just took over the group probably belongs to it too. It was certainly very nice of him to go to all that trouble. After he gets his group to their ship in Rotterdam, he's taking the night ferry from Hoek van Holland to Harwich. He's on his way to England to buy fabric. Oh, he asked me to give this to you – do you know him?'

I took the envelope she gave me and replied that my father had business dealing with him. Later I went into the washroom, bolted the door, and opened the envelope. Inside I found a message, as well as a smaller envelope, carefully sealed, and an English pound note. 'Please deliver the letter as soon as possible,' the message read, 'carfare enclosed.' The addressee, who had a German name, lived in the town in Yorkshire to which I was going. It would cost me at most an hour and sixpence in bus fare to carry out my mission, and I was certainly pleased at this addition to my skimpy travel funds.

Because of the currency restrictions – the Nazi leadership was pumping all available money into armaments and would release foreign currency solely for the purchase of essential raw materials – ordinary travellers were permitted to exchange only fifty, and later only ten marks. The export of German banknotes carried severe penalties, a formidable obstacle for any people who hoped to escape the terror in Germany by emigrating. Even if the Gestapo did allow an emigrant to leave the country, he could not take his savings; the controls were so tight that he usually arrived abroad with no more than ten marks in his pocket. The restrictions on valuables that might later be sold were also extremely rigid.

Yet Herr Desch seemed to have no currency problems. He had official authorisation to take out large sums of money to purchase fabric abroad. Might that be the reason he had become a Supporting Member of the SS, and a tailor specialising in dress uniforms of the finest English cloth?

In any case, I found out years later that by August 1939, when war broke out, Herr Desch had managed to get several hundred persons out of Germany, most of them children and young people from Jewish families. He provided them with some money and saw to it that they reached safety with relatives or his Quaker friends. Like Fräulein Bonse and Annie Ney, he had found his own answer to the question heard so often in those days: 'What can a person do?'

NINE

The Tightening of the Screws

'Shortly before Christmas in 1935 I decided to go skiing. The tension was building everywhere, and I thought this might be the last time I would see the Bavarian Alps . . .'

Mrs. Armstrong, a woman with a round, friendly face and silvery grey hair in a chic cut, was twenty years old in 1935. She was living in Cologne then, and had worked as a sound-editor at the radio station since just before Hitler came to power. Her maiden name was Margarete Nussbaum.

Grete, as she was known, had asked for ten days holiday and headed for the Alps. She received her first unpleasant surprise shortly after she reached her destination: 'At the station I got onto the bus, because the village where my parents' friends had a chalet didn't have its own railroad station. I looked out the bus window and saw the sunset. The broad, snow-covered meadows were bathed in scarlet – a magnificent sight. But at the entrance to the village a banner was suspended over the road. It said, "Jews enter at their own risk!" That put an end to the pleasure I had been feeling at being on holiday.'

For although no one at the Cologne radio station knew it yet, Grete was 'one-hundred-percent Jewish' according to the recently issued Nuremberg Laws. That meant that her German citizenship was void; indeed, she did not even have the legal status of a tourist in her native country. She was only 'tolerated' in the German Reich, and her civil rights were severely limited. Undoubtedly she would soon be removed from her job, with no chance of finding another in her field.

'I guess I'd been hoping that time would have stood still in that lovely Bavarian village. It was an illusion, of course,' Mrs. Armstrong continued. 'I had barely recovered from the first shock when I received another: at the Posthouse Hotel three signs were posted on the door to the dining room. The first said, '"Women with red talons and long trousers not admitted!" I was not wearing red nail polish, but I did have ski pants on. The second sign read, "The required greeting is Heil Hitler". The third said, "Dogs and Jews not allowed!" I turned on my heel, went up to my room without eating, and cried into my pillow for the better part of the night. My dream of finding a last bit of sanity and decency was shattered. It was not so much the signs themselves – I had seen similar ones in Hanover and Cologne; in fact the superintendent in my building had put up such signs as "Are there Germans in this house who do not display the flag on the Führer's Birthday?" and one which stated bluntly, "The Jews are our misfortune.' No, what threw me into such despair was the poisoning of this beautiful and idyllic spot.

'The next morning I took the train back to Cologne, without even having skied.' She paused for a moment, then shook her head. 'No, that's not quite how it happened. First I went to Hanover to see my parents. They were delighted to have me home for Christmas. But in spite of that we quarrelled, and that was awful!'

She sighed, then continued, 'This is hard to explain; would anyone nowadays be able to believe that my parents welcomed the Nuremberg Laws? They saw them as a sort of guarantee, or, as Hitler called it, "a definitive legal adjustment," which would make it possible for them to remain in their homeland, the homeland that meant so much to them. After three years of terrifying uncertainty and violence they felt great relief at seeing theings regularised.'

Grete's parents were not alone in this response to the new legislation. Many non-Aryans viewed the Nuremberg Laws as – at least – a bearable clarification. Of course they were offended by the blatant discrimination of such laws as the so-called 'Law for the Protection of German Blood', which forbade marriages and extramarital relationships between non-Aryans and Aryans under penalty of imprisonment, prohibited Jews from employing female household help 'of Aryan blood' if the employee in question was under forty-five, and made it illegal for Jews to 'display the flag of the Reich'. But because the Nuremberg Laws did not explicitly deprive Jews of the right to earn a living – except in the civil service or in jobs that required membership in one of the chambers – many Jews breathed a sigh of relief, assuming that the acts of random harassment would now cease. They hoped they would be spared further boycotts, attacks on their businesses, extortion of 'contributions', and arrests without cause, to say nothing of physical abuse and kidnappings.

Grete's father had been raised as a Protestant by parents who had converted from Judaism. He had served as an officer on the front lines in the First World War, and had earned a law degree. He was firmly convinced that he would now be free to continue managing the business he had inherited from his father, an export company that specialised in toolmaking equipment.

Grete's mother was the daughter of a wealthy notary who had married a Jewish banker's daughter. The Nuremberg Laws classified her as a 'a person of mixed blood in the first degree'. She owned two large office buildings in Hanover and several apartment houses, and had been afraid that her inherited property would be confiscated. The Nuremberg Laws contained no stipulations regarding non-Aryan property owners, so Grete's mother felt completely reassured. She even found she could keep her housekeeper of many years – the woman was over forty-five and therefore, in the eyes of the Nazi legislators, immune from 'miscegenation.' The gardener, too, who also served as chauffeur and butler, would be permitted to remain.

'My parents simply did not grasp what I meant when I told them I could no longer live in Germany,' Mrs. Armstrong explained. '"Where will you go – without any money?" my father asked; and my mother thought I must be depressed over an unhappy love affair. I tried to make it clear to them that I dreaded having to give up my profession. I enjoyed my work and found the people I worked with congenial. Most of them were obviously not Nazis, although that subject was taboo. One time a reporter brought in a tape recording of a visit the Führer had paid to our area. The background sounds on the tape made it clear how reserved the Rhinelanders had been in their welcome. After some discussion, the producer in charge of the broadcast said to me, "Fräulein Nussbaum, I'm sure you have some snippets of wild cheering tucked away. Would you just splice in a bit here and there so we don't find ourselves in trouble – but don't overdo it, all right?'

'No one at the broadcasting studio knew that I now belonged to the hundred-percent-Jewish category. But shortly before I left for vacation, Frau Jansen from the personnel department reminded me that I still had to provide documentation of my Aryan descent. "It's just a formality," she said, "but I do need your baptismal certificate before I can check you off. There are only five or six who still haven't brought them in, and I have to get my report to Berlin by January 31."

'The irony of it was that the only "evidence" the Nazis could depend on for enforcing their racial strictures came from the records of the very churches they were persecuting. A person could "prove" he was Aryan by demonstrating that his parents and grandparents had been baptised as children. Both of my parents had been, but my father's parents did not get baptised until just before they married, and the same was true of my mother's mother. To make things worse, the church records noted that my father's parents had "converted from the Mosaic faith to Christianity". In short, there was nothing to be done,

and I decided to hand in my resignation before the beginning of 1936.
Right after Christmas I wrote to the personnel office, saying I planned
to get married soon and therefore wished to be released from my
contract at the company's earliest convenience. This was my way of
avoiding the humiliating business of trying to prove Aryan descent.'

Since her parents did not support her plans for emigrating, Grete
remained in Cologne after sending her letter of resignation. She had
no one to talk to and no idea how to go about arranging to leave the
country. She knew only that she wanted to get out as soon as possible.

A girlfriend in Hanover advised her to work on her French or
English, preferably by taking a course abroad. The friend had given
Grete the address of the 'office' that organised exchange programmes.
'The woman who runs it is a very competent person, and I'm sure
she'll be able to help you. She's in Düsseldorf, and that's not far from
Cologne.'

As soon as she returned from Hanover, Grete took the train to
Düsseldorf, and that is how she met Fräulein Bonse. 'I trusted her at
once, perhaps because of her matter-of-fact manner,' Mrs. Armstrong
recalled. 'She offered me a cup of tea, asked a few polite but imper-
sonal questions about the courses I wanted to take, and then said
abruptly, "Listen, young lady, I don't really have anything for you,
since I usually deal with children and students. But if you have serious
urgent reasons, I'll try to help you. You may speak perfectly openly
with me – as you would have spoken with me three years ago, before
Herr Hitler became chancellor . . .'

'When I heard that, I poured out the whole story. Only once did she
interrupt me. She seemed quite alarmed: "For heaven's sake, child,
what if anyone discovers you've been working for three years in the
political department of the Cologne Broadcasting Company!" I explained that no one there knew about my Jewish origins and that I had
already resigned. But she seemed very worried, and with good reason,
as it turned out.'

Fräulein Bonse asked many more questions, took some notes, and
finally said she would need two or three days before she could tell
Grete anything final. In the meanwhile Grete should immediately
renew her passport, informing the passport office that she planned to
participate in an academic exchange programme and that it was urgent
that she have the extension promptly. Fräulein Bonse gave her the
name of an official at the Cologne police headquarters to whom she
should apply.

'Fräulein Bonse took down my telephone number, and three days
later she called me. It was very early in the morning; my landlady was

still asleep, but the telephone was in the hall, and I was just coming out of the bathroom when it rang.

'"I'm glad you're the one who answered," Fräulein Bonse said. "Something unpleasant has happened, but don't be afraid – just do as I tell you." She gave me precise instructions and told me to hurry. I was very nervous, but I forced myself to do as she had said. I packed a small suitcase with the bare necessities, as well as a few personal things I didn't want to leave behind, and wrote a note to my landlady, telling her not to worry – I had to leave unexpectedly for Munich because of a death in my family. I stuffed my house key, my postal savings book, my ID from the broadcasting company, and the few valuables I owned into my coat pocket and took the trolley to Cologne-Mühlheim, a suburb on the right bank of the Rhine.'

In Mühlheim she withdrew all her money from her postal savings account and deposited it into a postal checking account whose number Fräulein Bonse had given her. It was a largish sum, since she had cut short her holiday in Bavaria. By 8.15 she was on a train to Düsseldorf. She got off in the suburb of Benrath, and from there took a trolley to the Ney Café, where she meet Fräulein Bonse around 9.30.

'She seemed very relieved to see me come in. She even hugged me, but quickly resumed her usual cool manner. "The first thing now is to have breakfast; you can't wage war on an empty stomach," she said firmly, and that made me aware of the seriousness of the situation. Besides, it was an excellent piece of advice, one which I have followed ever since in critical situations.'

To Grete Nussbaum's surprise, Fräulein Bonse had in her possession the passport that Grete had turned in at the Cologne police headquaters only two days earlier; and the passport had been extended through January 1941.

'"It's a lucky thing," Fräulein Bonse told me, "that you handed in the passport immediately, because as a result I was warned that you were about to be arrested. The Gestapo agents have probably already gone to your house, to haul you in for interrogation."

'Fräulein Bonse thought that someone at the broadcasting station had become suspicious, probably because of my sudden resignation, and on checking my file had discovered that I had been hired just before Hitler's seizure of power, that I didn't belong to any Nazi organisations, had never documented my Aryan origins, and so on. "The person in question probably made inquiries about you and your family, perhaps through the police in Hanover – and then went straight to the Gestapo," she explained. "Well, anyway, everything has turned out all right, and you needn't be afraid. You're safe now."

'It struck me as odd,' Mrs. Armstrong continued, 'that I should be sitting here in this café, with only a little suitcase and no place to stay, barely an hour from Cologne, and that this should count as being safe. Then, to make matters worse, an SS officer came into the café, booming out "Heil Hitler!" to the proprietress, to whom I had paid no attention until then – and she replied amiably, "Good morning, Herr Obersturmführer!' He sat down at the table next to ours and ordered a cup of coffee. Fräulein Bonse laid her hand on my arm and began to discuss the purchases we had to make: underwear and stockings and a few warm clothes; also at least two pairs of shoes and a raincoat. At first I thought her chatter was all for the benefit of the black-uniformed officer, but then I realised she actually wanted to equip me for a long journey. "That will come to quite a bit of money," I said, "and I have only fifty marks on me." To my amazement, she said she had spoken to my mother on the telephone, and my mother had said I could choose whatever I liked "for my birthday". When the SS officer left, Fräulein Bonse said, "Now we'll take the bus to Krefeld and do our shopping there. I'll lend you the money, and your parents will pay me back." Then Frau Ney came over and shook hands with me. "Everything is taken care of, Fräulein Nussbaum," she said quietly. "Our delivery man will be in Krefeld toward three this afternoon – we have a lot of bakery orders to drop off there. He'll pick you up at the Ostwall and take you to the house of good friends, where you can stay a few days, and by Saturday at the latest you'll be in complete safety . . ." I didn't know what to say – I was trying to thank her and at the same time ask her why she was doing all this for a complete stranger. And she said – and I shall never forget this – "Because I don't want to be ashamed of myself when I come to stand before my God." And then she gave me a kiss, pressed my hand warmly, and saw us to the door.'

Everything happened exactly as planned, and by late afternoon Grete found herself at a beautiful old estate near the Dutch border. Two maids relieved her of her luggage, which had become quite substantial, and then the lady of the house invited her to tea, at which they were joined later by the lord of the estate, a baron.

'They didn't ask any questions,' Mrs. Armstrong recalled. 'They acted as though they had invited me, and spoke only of perfectly innocuous matters. Later the baroness took me up to my room and asked whether I needed anything. After supper, when I was suddenly overcome with exhaustion and asked to be excused, the baron said, "I wish you a good night. Under our roof you may feel perfectly safe. Tomorrow we'll decide on the next step. I understand you have a valid passport, but still it might be better to avoid the border checkpoint.

Late tomorrow afternoon the three of us can take a walk to St. Jakob – it's not even half an hour from here. My wife and I walk there once or twice a week. It's just over the border, in Holland. Your luggage will already be in Venlo, which is ten minutes from St. Jakob by trolley. The innkeeper at the Limburg Arms, directly on the market square, is informed and will have a room reserved for you. Early the next morning Father Vincent will come to see you. He'll handle the rest; he's a good man . . ." It was tremendously reassuring to have these kind strangers taking such care of me.'

And that was how Grete Nussbaum, now Mrs. Margaret Armstrong, literally walked away from the Third Reich one foggy afternoon in January 1936, strolling with her hosts over the 'green frontier' into neighbouring Holland, where no one was discriminated against for having grandparents who had been slow to get themselves baptised, and where she was safe from the Gestapo, who for two days had been searching for a 'camouflaged Jewess who had weaselled her way into the Cologne Broadcasting Company.'

The morning after her departure from her homeland, Father Vincent called on her at the hotel, drank a cup of coffee with her in the breakfast room, and handed her an envelope that contained a ticket to London, some money, a baggage receipt, and an invitation from the British Academic Exchange Service, which guaranteed her a six months' stay in England.

'That will gain you some time,' Father Vincent remarked. 'In half a year you'll be fluent in English, and then it should be possible to find a suitable job, perhaps even in broadcasting. By the way, your luggage has already been shipped; it will be waiting for you at Victoria Station.'

It was like a dream: she had been rescued from certain disaster by a network of strangers who took it for granted that people should help each other, and who had risked danger for her sake. She wondered if sheer luck had put her in the hands of some of the very few helpful and brave Germans. Or did Germany, which to all appearances had been completely 'brought into line', actually possess an invisible but active opposition? Four and a half decades after the events she described, she was not yet sure of the answer.

TEN

Resistance in Hamburg

I asked Werner to introduce me to resistance workers he had known in Hamburg, and so he arranged a meeting with Alma Stobbe. On the appointed day, we went to an old building in Hamburg-Altona and knocked on the door of a fourth-floor apartment.

'Hello there, Werner, how nice to see you again. Please come in!' These were her first words as she opened the door. But then she noticed me and instantly cooled; and it was not until Werner introduced me as a friend and colleague that she relaxed and offered me her hand, urging us to enter.

The apartment, which consisted of a living room, a kitchen alcove, and a small bedroom, was filled with the wonderful smell of freshly brewed coffee.

'I've been expecting you,' she said. 'Your card said around three, and here it is almost four!' As she spoke, she pointed to a picture postcard propped on a shelf above the stove, next to a bottle of cleaning fluid and a box of matches.

'Just like old times,' Werner said and grinned. Then he explained: 'Alma Stobbe's place used to be our mail drop. She was always ready for an unannounced visit from the Gestapo, otherwise she wouldn't be alive today . . .'

Alma Stobbe used to keep the picture postcards from Prague, Haderslev, or Stockholm with their coded messages for comrades in Hamburg in a place where she could burn them at the slightest sign of danger.

'Twice she got off scot-free, isn't that right, Alma?'

'Three times,' she corrected him.

Alma's hand shook as she poured coffee for us. She was an old woman with a wrinkled face and dim eyes. It was hard to imagine her as a young and energetic resistance fighter.

She took off her apron, set a plate with pieces of streusel cake on the table, and sat down with us. 'Three times they came in here and turned everything upside down and inside out. They even sifted through the salt box – it looked like Sodom and Gomorrah when they got done. But they couldn't find a thing, not a thing, and all they could do was go away empty-handed.' She made the observation matter-of-factly, but one could still feel her sense of triumph.

With a little prompting, she then told us about her life. As a seventeen-year-old worker she joined the German Communist Party in 1931. When the Depression and unemployment were at their worst, in 1932, she managed to recruit many of the other women who worked in her factory, and became a Red Union Opposition (RUO) cadre leader.

In the district known as Waterside, most of the approximately 28,000 members of the Red Union, which had ties with the Communist Party, also belonged to the Independent Union, which in turn was affiliated with the General German Federation of Unions. Thus the RUO had considerable influence in the Federation, which was led by right-wing Social Democrats. The Red Union had succeeded, at least to some extent, in creating a unified anti-fascist front, made up of workers, salaried employees, and the unemployed, whether Communists, Social Democrats, or unaffiliated.

When the Nazis came to power in January 1933, the RUO had to go underground long before the Social Democratic or Christian unions. No official ban was issued, but Party functionaries became the targets of police measures and brutal attacks by the SA and the SS.

By the spring of 1933, the Nazis' anti-labour campaign was intensifying from month to month, yet the Hamburg RUO leadership, working with twenty-one committees in different sections of the city, managed to keep a good 7,000 members together. An RUO newspaper appeared regularly and was distributed secretly; and every month dues were collected. Beginning in June 1933, the RUO cells in the plants began to contact individuals and groups from the recently banned unions of the General German Federation, and to involve them in their underground activities.

'I still have a sample of the *ICU*, the *Independent Class Unions* – that was the name of our illegal paper, which was always very well informed about conditions inside the factories,' Alma Stobbe said and fetched a yellowed mimeographed sheet from her dresser drawer. 'Whenever they raised the unit quota, lengthened the working day, or forced some other outrage on the comrades, you could read all about it in the *ICU* a few days later . . .'

'You kept something like that in your apartment?' Werner exclaimed.

Alma shook her head and laughed. 'No, no, my place was always clean. This is a copy the Gestapo stole from other comrades. Shortly after the war those of us who survived went to take a look at the bastards' headquarters, and I took this paper with me as a souvenir – and this too!'

She pulled another bundle of papers out of the drawer and handed them to Werner, who leafed through them.

'My goodness, this certainly is interesting,' he muttered. It was a Situation Report for the month of June 1934, written by a Hamburg police inspector and SA Standardführer named Richter.

'In February–March of last year,' the report said, 'several new personalities in the CP formed an alliance. The five men are: Walter Hochmuth, former member of the Citizens' Alliance, Bennies, Griegat, Gauert, and Grosse. These five men, all intelligent and resolute, succeeded in creating an underground Party apparatus within three months, an apparatus such as has not existed in Hamburg since the seizure of power . . .'

'That business about the CP is wrong,' Alma Stobbe remarked. 'All five of them were with us, the RUO. From the beginning we were strictly separate from the CP, so that if anything went wrong, only one organisation would be smashed, not both.'

'Displaying an astonishing degree of commitment,' the police report continued, 'as well as considerable resourcefulness, the five men managed to elude the intense efforts of the Gestapo, to strengthen their organisation, and, especially, to produce and distribute their illegal newspaper on a weekly basis. When we closed in on them about four weeks ago, even we had no idea of the dimensions of the organisation.'

'That was a nasty business when they nabbed those five comrades, and a lot of others, too. I'll never forget it, especially what happened to Albert Bennies: on July the 20th, after working underground for fourteen months and never having anything go wrong, he fell into the hands of the Gestapo. They took him to the cellar of City Hall and tortured him horribly . . . Albert stood firm and didn't betray a single comrade. But they found a postcard on him – a card I'd left for him two days earlier at our drop in the cemetery. It was from Copenhagen. They decoded the message and learned he was supposed to meet with someone on the Reeperbahn, in the Alcazar Club. They even knew the day and the time – the numbers were written under the stamp. The rendezvous was to be the next day at 10.00 A.M. So they took Bennies there – five fellows from the Gestapo, all in plain clothes and armed. Poor Albert had a walk ahead of them down the Reeperbahn toward the building where he was to meet the other comrades. They had taken off his handcuffs when they got to St. Pauli, so no one suspected. They almost succeeded – then they would have had not only the comrade from Copenhagen but also one from Hamburg-Harburg, from the Phoenix Rubber Plant. But Bennies didn't let them get away with it. Twenty paces before the Alcazar he began to yell at the top of his voice, "Watch out! The cops! Look out! Gestapo!" And then he threw himself in front of a passing bus. Of course there was a great commotion: everyone from the Reeperbahn rushed to the spot, and in the crowding and confusion the comrades escaped. Albert died on the way to the Harbour Hospital. They buried him on the sly, afraid there might be a mass demonstration, because all of Altona knew what had happened . . .'

When she had finished her story, she fetched glasses from her kitchen cupboard and poured us each a brandy. 'Here's to Albert Bennies,' she said softly, then downed her drink.

We learned from Alma Stobbe that in the summer of 1934 more than 800 members of the RUO in the Waterside district were convicted in almost sixty different criminal proceedings. Many of them were killed by the Gestapo during interrogation in the City Hall cellar or in the nearby Fuhlsbüttel concentration camp. The rest were sentenced to long prison terms. Many who had served out their sentences were rearrested immediately after their release and shipped off to concentration camps. The Jews among them – including Alma's close associate, Dagobert Biermann – were sent to Auschwitz years later, in 1941–42, and gassed.

'I met Dagobert Biermann in 1936,' Alma told us, 'when he came to see me about 'mailing' an important message to Copenhagen. We used to go to the fish market together on Sunday mornings, and then take a little walk along the Elbe. Biermann was a machinist at the shipyards and had managed to get jobs there for many of the comrades by claiming they were specialists needed for the work details, though some of them were hardly trained. In those years we had, for the most part, stopped our RUO work, and were cooperating closely with the underground union and resistance groups. The most important cause was the struggle in Spain, and as it turned out, the Franco-fascists received most of their supplies by way of Hamburg. Biermann had learned about huge arms shipments going to Spain from his brother-in-law, a barge captain, and he proceeded to organise a network of longshoremen and railroad workers to collect information about the transports for Spain.'

The centre of Biermann's clandestine news service was the widow Köpke's bar down by the harbour, where many sailors came and went. It became apparent not only that the quantity of armaments going to

Franco's side was huge, but also that Germany's own secret rearmament had reached immense proportions. Biermann and his associates soon found out, for instance, that the warships and fighter planes being built by Blohm & Voss of Hamburg were intended for the Wehrmacht, while rifle ammunition not stamped with the usual data about manufacturer, weapon type, and date was destined for Franco's troops.

For more than a year Dagobert Biermann and his friends, including Alma Stobbe, were able to smuggle this information abroad. But the group was destroyed by an informer planted by the Gestapo. 'One after another they were arrested,' Alma Stobbe told us, 'and each time I was sure I'd be next. But they didn't talk. Biermann got six years, and the others got long sentences, too. There was a Jewish lawyer, Michaelis, who belonged to the group, and him they executed because he had a university education and they assumed he was the ringleader . . .'

She went to her dresser again and after some rummaging brought us an old newspaper clipping.

'Look,' she said, 'they always talked about "red assassins", but everyone knew who the real assassins were. Michaelis, Biermann, all of them were murdered!' She wiped her eyes on her sleeve, then busied herself at the stove.

Werner read the clipping, then handed it to me without a word. 'Unbroken Red Trail of Assassination' was the headline, and then came the text: 'When Jews of the ilk of a Michaelis try to exonerate themselves by asserting that they belonged not to the Communist Party but to the intellectual realm of the League for Human Rights, it is important to realise that the League for Human Rights is nothing but a Communist so-called cultural organisation with despicable internationalist Bolshevist Jewish objectives . . .' The editorial concluded: 'International Judaism and the Comintern were equally interested in the victory of the reds in Spain. They hoped that such a victory would spark a treasonous uprising in Germany.'

It was true that thousands of Germans fought on the side of the Republicans in Spain against the forces of Franco, who enjoyed the support of Hitler and Mussolini. 'One hundred and twenty-three men joined the International Brigade from Hamburg alone,' Alma told us, 'mainly Communists, but also Social Democrats, union members, members of the Reichsbanner organisation, anarchists . . . Only about thirty of them returned alive.'

'They were sick of having to clench their fists in their pockets and submit to the brownshirts,' she explained. 'In Spain they could shoot back. But here in Hamburg we were fighting for Spain too!'

Alma described the longshoremen's resistance movement, which went into full force in the summer of 1936 when artillery pieces and shells disguised as ordinary freight were being loaded in Hamburg harbour for shipment to Franco's troops. Overnight, slogans appeared along the loading areas and on the planks of the docks: 'Long live the Spanish Republic!' 'No weapons for Franco!' Thousands of shipyard workers read them before the authorities could have them removed. The next day the early shift found new slogans: 'Down with Hitler and Franco!' 'Long live the freedom struggle of the Spanish people!' Stickers with the same or similar slogans appeared on the doors and windows of underground trains and buses, likewise on warehouses and factory gates, in the large shipyards and on the piers, even on all the beer bottles in cases delivered for the workers at Blohm & Voss.

In October 1936 the first acts of sabotage occurred. Five large crates labelled 'machine parts' – but actually containing brand-new field howitzers – were 'accidentally' sunk in the harbour. Two more crates were smashed on the wharf, and two officials supervising the loading were seriously injured. The Gestapo arrested several dockworkers but could not determine who was responsible.

In many large factories regular collections of money were undertaken, ostensibly to pay for a funeral wreath, an anniversary present, or the first week's household expenses traditionally given to the wife of a fellow worker when he married. The sums collected usually went to a fund for Republican Spain, as arranged in advance by those making the collection and those who contributed.

As the size of the weapon shipments from Hamburg increased, and as the first German soldiers were dispatched to Spain by Hitler in the so-called Condor Legion* the resistance formed intelligence units in all the German ports, and this network was even supported by some members of the Nazi-organised longshoremen's union. This 'signal service', which was especially strong in Hamburg, reported every movement of armaments from German habours, and abetted as much as possible the resistance counteractions, which included work stoppages by longshoremen and ships' crews.

'On the *Henrica* the entire crew refused to load the cargo,' Alma Stobbe recalled. 'The men announced they hadn't the slightest

---

* Condor Legion: code name for the regular German troops dispatched to fight in the Spanish Civil War on Franco's side, in all barely 6,000 soldiers, of whom about 450 died in battle.

intention of shipping cannon and planes to Spain to be used against the people there. But such an action was possible only because the overwhelming majority of the harbour workers were on our side . . .'

On the way home I asked Werner whether he knew how large the outlawed Communist Party had been in those days.

'At the end of 1934 there were still about 120,000 Party members, but half of them were in prisons and concentration camps. The Nazis had already executed at least 2,000 of the leading cadres. But the fact that so many Communists were still alive and at liberty was in large measure due to the support of former comrades who defected to the Nazis because they feared for their families, but remained loyal to us in their hearts. We called them "beefsteak Nazis", – brown on the outside but red inside. The Communists also got help from left-wing Social Democrats, and even from solid members of the middle class. The man who worked for Albert Bennies as editor of the illegal RUO newspaper made his office in a villa on Hamburg's elegant Rothenbaumchaussee. The people who gave him the space and let him hide in their house were a liberal upper-middle-class Hamburg family. They knew perfectly well that the Gestapo had been after him for months. They arranged things so that their 'house guest' – his name was Walter – never left the villa except for an evening stroll around the spacious grounds. They ran all his errands for him, and that included the risky undertaking of buying the stencils on which Walter typed his articles, and then delivering them to a cigar store downtown, where another comrade picked them up. The mimeograph machine was located in the cellar of a lending library on Lübecker Chaussee. The distributors came there regularly to fetch their packets. At a place like that the coming and going of people with heavy shopping bags or briefcases was not likely to arouse suspicion. Besides, most of those who came were women and children, who might say, 'I'm here for the romances you put aside for my grandmother,' and some of them even wore Hitler Youth or Jungvolk or League of German Girls uniforms and gave the German salute and said "Heil Hitler" as they entered. The disguise worked perfectly – otherwise the paper could never have been kept going as long as it was.'

'And what about those who picked up the papers, the children, for example – did they all know what was in the packets and what a risk they were taking?'

'Oh, yes,' Werner replied. 'The RUO never used people who weren't aware of what was at stake. Perhaps a few didn't know exactly what was in their packets, but at least they knew it was something strictly forbidden, that it was directed against the Nazis, and that they mustn't allow it to fall into the hands of the police at any cost. The parents impressed upon their children that they mustn't breathe a word to anyone about what went on in the lending library, because otherwise their fathers or older brothers might land in the Kolafu.'

'Kolafu? That's something I've never heard of.'

'It was the abbreviation comrades in Hamburg used for "Konzentrationslager Fuhlsbüttel", the concentration camp in the Hamburg suburb of Fuhlsbüttel, which was in existence until the end of 1935. Later there was a camp at Neuengamme, a little farther away.'

Then Werner spoke again of Walter and his refuge in the Hamburg villa. 'I don't think you would have encountered that sort of thing anywhere but in Hamburg,' he said, 'because that's where there was the strongest leftist opposition to Hitler. Remember, it was in Hamburg that Hitler had to swallow losing 25 percent of the vote in the 1934 "elections". Or to put it another way: in Hamburg, even the Nazis didn't dare to tamper with the election results too much, because they would've made themselves ridiculous. It was different in the Palatinate – there they could announce 97 percent support in the elections of 1934, and I estimate that about 70 percent of the voters actually voted for Hitler, about half of them out of more or less genuine conviction or simple stupidity, the rest out of fear. People knew that the Nazis would stop at nothing. Besides, they figured the results would be falsified in any case. In Ludwigshafen, where I was, most of the civil servants and shopkeepers were staunch supporters of Hitler, and among the workers and lower-level white-collar workers fear was the driving force. The majority of the middle-level and even more the upper-level white-collar workers at the big chemical companies were opportunists. In any case, in Ludwigshafen it would have been unthinkable for the "better class of people" to take in a Communist on the run from the Gestapo, and keep him hidden in their villa for months.'

'You really think so?'

'Yes, I'm sure of it. My father and his comrades found support only among their own kind – fellow workers and activists – if that. And I believe that was true everywhere but in Hamburg. Even solid middle-class people who opposed the Nazis had no love for "the reds". They were dedicated conservatives or pious Catholics. Maybe there were a few liberals or members of the Confessing Church who would have hesitated to denounce a Communist, but they certainly wouldn't have helped him. They were too scared, to begin with. They didn't even dare to help the Jews.'

'No, you're mistaken there,' I said. 'There were quite a few people, even in the so-called better circles, who weren't afraid. I knew some successful business people who not only helped Jews and risked a great deal to do so, but also didn't shrink from working with Communists. What mattered to them was that they were doing something against the Nazis.'

I was thinking of a certain Friday afternoon early in March 1936 when the 'watchmaker' from Switzerland appeared at the Ney Café.

ELEVEN

A Visitor from Basel

It must have been Friday, 6 March 1936, for the next morning we received another of those weekend surprises which had become the hallmark of the Führer's strategy.

The first of these weekend surprises had come the previous year, on 6 March 1935, also a Saturday. In a long speech before the Reichstag, carried by all the broadcasting stations, Hitler announced the return of universal conscription, even as he asserted that he wanted 'nothing but peace'. The Reich government, he assured us, would 'never go beyond the preservation of German honour and the freedom of the Reich'. At school we had to assemble in the hall to listen to the voice crackling out of the loudspeaker.

We had the rest of the day off, and on the way home, Kulle said he thought war was inevitable, and I agreed, for surely England and France would not tolerate this breach of the Treaty of Versailles. But London and Paris didn't even react at first, and later they protested only mildly. My father felt sure that Hitler had chosen a Saturday for this surprise announcement because members of the Western governments often spent the weekend hunting or salmon fishing in the country, and were hard to summon back to the capital.

Since that time almost a year had passed, and at school there had been constant talk of 'premilitary training' and the necessity for bolstering the 'will to self-defence'. This meant that the curriculum was modified to include classic plays with a military theme, like Schiller's *Wallenstein's Camp* or Kleist's *Prince Friedrich of Homburg*. It also meant that on Fridays we got two extra hours of physical education, which were supposed to serve as preparation for military service. The importance of this training was underlined by the fact that it was supervised not by our gym teacher but by our form master. His name was Dr. Konen, but among ourselves we called him 'Koko' because when he put his head on one side and looked at a pupil quizzically over his glasses, he looked like an old parrot.

We gathered in the dressing room next to the gym every Friday at

3 P.M., and while we were changing, Koko ran through the formalities that the Board of Education prescribed. We paid little attention, as he informed us without great conviction that we had come not 'for fun' but 'in service to the Fatherland' to improve our physical fitness as future soldiers in the new Wehrmacht, and to strengthen our muscles along with our 'will to self-defence'.

Depending on the weather, we either played two thirty-minute soccer games outdoors or stayed in the gym and played handball. Koko, who was not a Nazi and didn't give a damn about premilitary training, left us completely to our own devices. He usually brought along something to read, sometimes the *Berlin Illustrated Weekly*, which came out on Thursday and which he saved to get him through this irksome double period. After we put in our time, we had to line up and report to him before getting dressed and going home. Koko released us with the prescribed German Salute, raising his right arm and with outstretched hand giving us the signal to go to the locker room. I was always amazed at the way he managed to keep the gesture ambiguous: was he giving the Nazi salute or merely stretching out his hand to dismiss the class?

On this particular Friday we played soccer. I was hot, and on the way home I dropped in at the Ney Café for ice cream. I was still chatting with Aunt Annie when a man entered whom neither she nor I recognised.

He was a man in his mid-forties, short and very sturdy-looking. He wore a heavy grey topcoat, an elegant grey Homburg, dark grey kid gloves, and shiny black boots with grey spats. A furled black umbrella hung over his arm, and he carried an old-fashioned leather briefcase. Without the briefcase you might have taken him for a man going to the races; all that was missing was a pair of binoculars.

He stood in the doorway, and gazed around. Then he went up to Aunt Annie, politely tipped his hat, and asked her, 'Pardon me, are you perhaps Frau Anna Ney?'

When she replied that she was, the first trace of a smile appeared on his rigid features. 'Oh, but I'm glad to hear that,' he said, and it struck me that he spoke like the announcer for the Swiss National Broadcasting Company whose news broadcast my father listened to every evening. 'It is very good that I find you here. My name is Sprüngli. I have come here from Basel and am to bring you greetings from your brother. He is well.'

Aunt Annie, who had been quite guarded at first, now greeted Herr Sprüngli in a most friendly fashion. She invited him to sit down, brought him coffee and pastry, made enquiries about her brother, whom she had not seen in four years, and then asked 'Are you just passing through?'

'Yes, to be sure. In fact, I have interrupted my journey only to convey these greetings and to see about your pendulum clock. Your brother said it was a very valuable clock with a particularly lovely chime, made by Ernest Borel of Geneva. I happen to be a watchmaker, and I know this type of clock well – or have you already had it repaired?'

'No,' Aunt Annie replied with some hesitation.

'Well, then, perhaps my visit comes at an opportune time for you,' Herr Sprüngli said. 'Your brother told me the clock in question was in your little country house in Meerbusch, not far from here. Is that right?'

'About twenty minutes by trolley. Did my brother give you any other message for me, Herr Sprüngli?'

'No, or rather, of course he also asked me to give his regards to your husband. He said, "Don't forget to say hello to 'Greybeard' for me and ask him whether he still wears the necktie I gave him for his birthday, the dark blue one with the little silver crowns."' He looked at Aunt Annie solemnly, with a silent question in his eyes. She now struck me as decidedly nervous.

I was sure I noticed these nuances only because I was watching the two from close up and listening very carefully, while the other guests in the café were busy talking to each other and paid no attention to them.

The reason for my lively interest was a remark Aunt Annie had made some time earlier while discussing the brutal way the Gestapo treated Communists. Her husband Werner, whom she sometimes called 'Greybeard' because of his prematurely greyed hair, had described how a Communist worker of his acquaintance had been abused by the Gestapo.

'I'm against Communism,' Aunt Annie had remarked. 'I think people should believe in God and respect every religion. I'm also in favour of private property, at least when you've earned something yourself. But today I would help any Communist who was running from the Nazis – after all, our Jupp's a Communist. Thank goodness he went to Switzerland when he did!'

'Our Jupp,' I knew, meant her brother Josef, who lived in Basel. She had often mentioned him before without saying anything about his politics. I put the pieces together and deduced that there must be something serious behind this seemingly innocent chat with Herr Sprüngli.

Obviously, the 'watchmaker' first had to identify himself to Frau Ney by referring to several details of her private life that no outsider could have known about, such as the make of the clock on the dresser in her little house in Meerbusch. The clock, by the way, was not in need of repair. I had heard it striking the previous Sunday and had checked the time against my pocket watch.

As the conversation progressed, it appeared I had been right to suspect the man had not come merely to bring greetings. When Aunt Annie enquired whether he was in a hurry, Herr Sprüngli replied, 'Well, in a sense I am in quite a hurry. But I could allow a couple of days in my schedule. Such a repair, you know, is not child's play . . .'

By now, Aunt Annie – and I, too – realised that Herr Sprüngli was looking for a temporary safe refuge in her cottage outside the city, which was usually empty during the week.

'I shall certainly be finished by the middle of next week,' Herr Sprüngli added, and I saw Aunt Annie give him a searching look, leaning toward him and gazing over her glasses directly into his eyes. I recalled that she once said she could always tell a spy by the eyes.

Apparently Herr Sprüngli passed the test, for she leaned back, took a deep breath, and said, 'All right, then, but didn't my brother say something about his *favourite café*?' She spoke the last words with a little extra emphasis, and Herr Sprüngli replied promptly, 'Yes, certainly, your brother said he dreamt recently that it had palm trees overhead.'

'Well, then, everything's all right,' Aunt Annie said, and stood up. 'The trolley leaves in twelve minutes,' she said after glancing at the clock above the door to her little office. 'Let me pack a few things for you, Herr Sprüngli,' she said in her usual friendly way. 'On Sunday after Mass my husband and I will come out for lunch.' And to me she said, as she bustled toward the kitchen in the back, 'Could you spare a moment? I have something I want you to do for me.'

'Of course,' I called after her. 'I'm in no hurry.'

As Herr Sprüngli slowly ate his cake and poured himself more coffee from the little silver pot, I tried to think why Jupp's dream to which Herr Sprüngli had alluded seemed so familiar. It was clearly only a password arranged between brother and sister.

Suddenly I remembered: it was from a poem by Erich Kästner:

> I dreamt last night that my favourite café
> was on an island with palm trees overhead.
> Myself, I always sleep in my own bed,
> but dreams like to roam far away.

At home I had not only *Emil and the Detectives* and Kästner's other children's books but also his *Poetry for Everyday Use*. These volumes, which had appeared before 1933, were on the bookshelf next to the desk. Of course, from the outside they no longer looked like books by Kästner. I had covered them neatly in blue waxed paper and pasted on the proper octagonal labels, on which I had written in my best old German script, 'Algebra VIa', 'Racial Theory', and 'Medieval History'.

On my shelves were quite a few of these disguised books, which had been banned by the Nazis and were publicly burned on 10 May 1933, to the cheers of people like Dr. Barsch. Gradually they had wandered from my father's big bookcase to my shelves, after we had transformed them outwardly into old schoolbooks. Tucholsky's book *Deutschland, Deutschland über alles*, with collages by John Heartfield, became *German Geography*; Erich Maria Remarque's *All Quiet on the Western Front* was labelled *Sowing and Harvesting*; and George Grosz's *The Face of the Ruling Class* turned into *Diercke's Physical School Atlas*.

Since there were too many books for my shelves, some of them were taken up to the attic in a laundry basket. While transferring them, my mother always took care to cover the top layer with real old schoolbooks. She also tacked an index card to the old trunk up in the attic, making the disguise complete with the label 'schoolbooks'.

But I had saved many items from the attic, in co-operation with my parents, who of course did not want to have to climb up to the attic every time they wanted to read one of their favourite books. Thus Erich Kästner's poetry remained in my room, and I already knew many of the poems by heart. I was pleased to have recognised the passwords that Aunt Annie and Herr Sprüngli had used to be absolutely sure they were safe with one another.

After five minutes Aunt Annie returned from the kitchen with a basket of food, including ground coffee, cigarettes, and sweets, which she handed to me. 'Could you take this to our cottage in Meerbusch and accompany my brother's friend there, since he doesn't know the way?'

'I'd be glad to, Aunt Annie,' I said, and added in a low voice, 'Tell him I'll get into the second car and he should get into the first car just before the trolley starts. He should get out in Meerbusch and continue along the path parallel to the tracks. I'll catch up with him. Where are the keys to the house? I'll show him around.'

I enjoyed seeing Aunt Annie taken aback for a moment. But she quickly regained her composure, smiled, and said only, 'The keys are

in the basket. And hurry, the streetcar will be leaving in a moment –
and don't try to be smarter than you are . . .'

I had the satisfaction of seeing that Herr Sprüngli followed my
suggestions to the letter. He got into the first car just as the trolley
started up, while I watched from the rear platform to see whether
anyone was shadowing him.

During the short trip to Meerbusch, I wondered why he was here.
To judge by his accent he was a genuine Swiss. Why had he come here
from Switzerland, where he was safe from the Gestapo? Perhaps he
was a courier – I had heard of such things. I had even read in the
newspaper once that 'a courier of the Comintern from Moscow' had
been nabbed by the ever-watchful Gestapo, who had found on him
'instructions for fomenting a Bolshevist uprising and civil war'. But
Herr Sprüngli did not look as though he might incite people to civil
war, and his leather suitcase suggested more a country doctor than a
revolutionary. But of course it was easy to be mistaken about such
things.

What most preoccupied me was whether he was being followed.
What else could Herr Sprüngli have meant when he hinted that he was
in quite a hurry? On the other hand, he would hardly have come to the
Ney Café if he were not completely certain he had shaken off
any pursuers. I was still wondering about this when we arrived at
Meerbusch.

All the passengers got out and scattered in several directions. Herr
Sprüngli strolled calmly along the path next to the tracks, without
looking around for me. I waited behind to make sure he was not being
followed; then I broke into a trot and caught up with him.

'We turn left at that signpost,' I said after I had greeted him. 'It's the
first house after the turn.'

I led him in by the garden gate, which faced the tracks, so that none
of the neighbours could see us. Herr Sprüngli waited on the terrace
until I had gone around to the other side, opened the front door, and
let him in by the terrace door.

'The kitchen is this way,' I said and then showed him the bathroom,
the telephone, and the guest room. I unpacked the basket, and was
about to leave for home when he asked me, 'Tell me, might you
perhaps be able to see the Rhine bridges from your window?'

'No, we don't live along the Rhine.' Then I remembered Fräulein
Bonse. 'But Frau Ney knows someone who looks out directly on the
Upper Kassel Bridge.'

'Do you suppose Frau Ney could ask this person to glance out at the
bridge now and then tomorrow morning very early?'

I looked at him with surprise. 'Certainly. But what should she be looking out for?'

'For soldiers,' Herr Sprüngli said, 'troops marching in formation, military vehicles of all sorts, artillery – from about 5.00 A.M. on, I should think.'

'Is there going to be war?' I asked in alarm.

'There may be,' was Herr Sprüngli's only reply.

He looked over the house, made sure that the lights, the electric stove and the telephone were working, turned the radio on and off, and went out onto the terrace to inspect the antenna on the roof.

In the meantime my thoughts were racing. Finally I said, 'But we're in a demilitarised zone here on the left bank of the Rhine! My father said that if Hitler had the Wehrmacht march in, the French and the British would certainly stop them.'

'Let us hope so,' Herr Sprüngli said laconically.

After a pause he continued, 'It's not certain that there'll be war, but it's quite possible; and in any case, one must be prepared . . .'

I pondered his statement. I suspected that Fräulein Bonse would not be the only one watching the Rhine bridges early the next morning. Surely farther down the Rhine, in Uerdingen, Duisburg, and Wesel, and farther up the Rhine, in Neuss, Cologne, Bonn, Remagen, Coblenz, Mainz, Ludwigshafen, and Karlsruhe, there would be other friends of Herr Sprüngli's keeping an eye on the Rhine bridges . . . Perhaps he was responsible only for a certain section of the river and would keep in touch by telephone with the other observers. And certainly he would need a means of staying in contact with his comrades abroad – perhaps a shortwave transmitter? Is that what he was carrying in his briefcase? I did not dare to ask him about it. I said good-bye, took the trolley back to the café, and told Aunt Annie what she was to discuss with Fräulein Bonse. She was very alarmed.

'Is there going to be war?' she asked anxiously.

'He says there may be,' I reported.

'Jesus, Mary, and Joseph!' Aunt Annie whispered.

When I went to bed that night I set the alarm clock for 5.00 A.M. By 5.30 the next morning I was already standing on the Lueg-Allee, which led straight from the Upper Kassel Rhine Bridge to the left bank of the Rhine. And, sure enough, the soldiers came along: first sharp-shooters on motorcycles leading the column, then infantry on foot – about five hundred of them – followed by a few military vehicles driven at a snail's pace, a military ambulance, and a field kitchen.

Only a few spectators stood on the sidewalks. An SA man suddenly burst out in enthusiasm, 'Heil Hitler!' but when he noticed that no one chimed in, he quickly fell silent.

In school everyone was discussing the sensational event. Most of the pupils thought it was 'great' that the formerly demilitarised area on the left bank of the Rhine would now have Wehrmacht garrisons too. Some looked sombre and said they hoped this wouldn't end badly.

After break we were sent to the hall to hear the Führer's speech on the radio. Hitler was speaking in the Kroll Opera in Berlin to the hastily summoned Reichstag:

'In the interest of a people's most basic right to secure its borders and preserve its ability for self-defence, the German government has from today onward restored unlimited sovereignty in the demilitarised zone of the Rhineland!'

After the speech the six hundred Nazi deputies shouted 'Heil! Heil! Heil!' for several minutes and stamped their feet on the floor.

Of the rest of the long speech I recall only one sentence: 'We make no territorial claims in Europe, and Germany will never break the peace!'

After that we were dismissed for the rest of the day.

On this and the following day there was great tension at home. My father sat by the radio, listening to both German and foreign news bulletins. On Sunday afternoon he remarked, 'The British government called an emergency session today – the first time that has happened on a Sunday in a hundred years! But they aren't taking action, and neither are the French. Yet this is their chance to put a stop to this Nazi nightmare at very little cost. Later on they'll be sorry they didn't act firmly now.'

Not until years later did I understand how right my father had been in his prediction. It turned out that Hitler had instructed the Wehrmacht to withdraw immediately and without a fight to the right bank of the Rhine if the French or the British intervened. Hitler himself knew perfectly well, as several of his ministers, generals, and collaborators later testified, that he was taking a huge risk in occupying the Rhineland. His interpreter Paul Schmidt had heard him say, 'Those forty-eight hours after we marched into the Rhineland were the most nerve-wracking of my life. If the French had moved into the Rhineland, we would have had to retreat with our tails between our legs, for our military forces would not have been adequate to withstand even moderate resistance. And a retreat on our part would have meant total collapse . . .' And at the Nuremberg war crimes trials General Jodl testified that the French border troops would have been sufficient to 'blow away' the weak Wehrmacht forces.

In short, everything hung in the balance that weekend. But when the Western powers failed to offer any resistance, Hitler reaped the triumph he had hoped for, and thereby achieved new popularity not only with his followers but also with the many who had become disillusioned with his leadership. For in the winter of 1935–36, the level of discontent in large segments of the population had risen dramatically, mainly as a result of increasing prices and stepped-up work quotas.

On the Monday after the troops marched into the Rhineland I stopped by after school to see Aunt Annie.

'How's your guest?' I asked.

'He's gone already,' she replied.

Three weeks later, after unprecedented propaganda efforts, the Nazi leadership staged new 'elections'. The right to vote was declared an obligation to vote, and only the Nazi slate of candidates was presented. The ballot was cleverly tied to a referendum in which the voter had to indicate whether he or she supported the 'restoration of the German people's honour' as it had been achieved by the Führer through the occupation of the Rhineland.

For this election the Nazi Party and its many auxiliary organisations exerted more direct pressure on voters than ever before. In factories, tenants' organisations, offices, and even schools, the same slogans were heard over and over again for three weeks: 'No one must miss this election!' 'Every vote for the Führer!' 'Any one who does not vote for Hitler is a traitor to the Volk!'

On Sunday, March 29, 1936, shortly before midnight, Reich Propaganda Minister Goebbels triumphantly announced the election results: 'Ninety-nine percent of all Germans have voted for Adolf Hitler and the NSDAP!'

No one in Germany was surprised. Everyone had felt the pressure; everyone knew about the harassment, manipulation, and falsification at the polling stations.

An entire nation had bowed to a system of terror.

TWELVE

The Führer is Always Right!

Shortly after Easter in 1936 I was allowed to go alone to Berlin to visit the many friends and relatives we still had there. The trip was full of surprises, for very little had remained as I remembered. Three years of Nazi rule had wrought a complete transformation.

Several strange episodes occurred during the long train ride. I found a window seat in a compartment occupied only by two men who talked quietly and paid no attention to me. As I gathered from their conversation, they were autobahn workers who had just been home for Easter. They spoke of the backbreaking work to which they were returning, of the wretched housing and bad food.

In Duisburg a woman of about thirty joined us in the compartment. She wore her hair in two braids coiled above her ears, and on the lapel of her tailored suit was a large badge of the National Socialist Women's League. She greeted us with a cheery 'Heil Hitler!' and sat down. The two workers echoed the Nazi greeting mechanically and continued their conversation, which by this time had grown somewhat louder and more emphatic.

I said in English, 'Good morning', and added with a marked British accent, 'Guten Morgen' – a little trick I had successfully practised several times since my return from Yorkshire the previous summer. Pretending to be British was a good protective device, since at the time foreigners, especially the British, were honoured visitors whose approval the Nazis were eager to secure.

She gave me a friendly smile, as I had expected, and then buried herself in her illustrated *Völkischer Beobachter*. But after just a few minutes she let the paper sink to her lap, gazed sternly at the two workers, and remarked, 'Is this whining really necessary? And in the presence of a young foreigner? You should be grateful that you have work and thank the Führer for getting rid of unemployment!'

The two workers stared at her in consternation. Then the older of the two said quietly, 'Listen here, young woman: we work outdoors in all kinds of weather, shovelling dirt for 51 pfennigs an hour. Then there are the deductions and the voluntary contributions they take out automatically, and 15 pfennigs a day for a straw mattress in a drafty wooden barracks, and 35 pfennigs for what they ladle out of a cauldron and call dinner – slop you wouldn't touch, I guarantee it! Six months ago we were still getting 66 pfennigs an hour, and now they're pushing us harder and harder.'

'Let it go, Karl,' the younger one said, but his friend forged ahead.

'I'm trained as a printer. In the summer of '33 I lost my job. I collected unemployment until the spring of '34 – and that was a lot better than what I'm doing now. At least I was home, with my family, and now and then I could pick up some odd jobs, or I could work in the garden. Now I'm in compulsory service, with ten days' holiday a year! That's enough to do a man in, I'm telling you!'

'Forget it, Karl,' the younger one intervened again, 'the lady isn't interested.'

'But she should be,' the older one continued, undeterred. 'Listen, at the beginning of '33 there were over 6 million unemployed, and now there's only 2 million – that much is true. But it's also true that at the beginning of '33 I was still earning good money in my own trade and was home – and now we work ourselves to the bone and the wages keep going down – it's 16 marks net per week now. The whole thing stinks, and somebody's got to say it!'

The woman remained silent for a while. What he said had clearly affected her. But she soon felt compelled to reply, chiefly for the benefit of the 'young foreigner' in the compartment: 'You can't expect that the misery brought about by fourteen years of mismanagement will be cured in the twinkling of an eye! But now people have hope. They're off the streets, and Germany is strong and powerful again. We've regained our honour – that's the main thing! In three years Adolf Hitler has accomplished miracles, and from year to year things are getting better. Maybe next year you can take a holiday with your family on Madeira with Strength through Joy . . . You must have *faith* in the Führer!'

'Yes, yes,' the older worker said with resignation as his friend gave him an imploring look. But then he added softly, 'Madeira! I'd rather be sitting in my grape arbour after work!'

The two workers had to change in Dortmund. Other people came into the compartment, and the Women's League lady greeted them with her cheery 'Heil Hitler!' and even those who had come in saying 'Good day' quickly echoed the Nazi greeting.

She got off in Hamm, but before she left the compartment she asked me where I was headed. 'To Berlin,' I said, in my English-accented German. 'Ah, to Berlin, the capital of the Reich! That will certainly be wonderful and very interesting for you. In a few months the Olympic Games will be starting – then the whole world will see what our Führer Adolf Hitler has achieved!'

Then she gave me her illustrated *Beobachter*, trumpeted 'Heil Hitler!' and added in English, 'Good-bye! Have a nice trip!'

At the Zoological Garden Station Uncle Karl and Aunt Elsbeth, my mother's sister, were waiting for me. To my horror, Uncle Karl was wearing a Party badge and Aunt Elsbeth a Women's League pin. I made an effort not to show how startled I was, and we greeted each other heartily.

'You must be terribly hungry,' was Aunt Elsbeth's first thought, 'but I've saved you some lunch: veal roast with sour cream gravy, mixed vegetables, and of course, my lemon meringue.' She was known for her cooking, and would heap our plates with food for fear we might leave the table hungry. I always found her exceptionally warm and generous.

Uncle Karl, whose placid temperament and dry humour I remembered fondly, teased me in his old way, asking whether the 'provincial village' I came from even had its own railway station yet – for Düsseldorf was a name that conjured up a five-mile hike to the nearest station.

Except for the swastika badges they both wore, everything seemed like old times.

At supper, where the sheer quantity of food exceeded all my expectations, I enquired about my cousins, both of whom were still in school when I saw them last.

'Fritz usually comes on Sundays, when he's off duty,' Aunt Elsbeth told me proudly. 'He's doing very well, and he expects to be promoted next week, on the Führer's Birthday. He's earned it, too – our Fritz is so conscientious and enthusiastic! You know of course that he's in the Hitler Guard . . .'

I had had no idea that this cousin, who was four years older than I and so quiet that my parents thought him 'somewhat limited', had even gone near the SS. And now I had a cousin in the Adolf Hitler Guard!

'Fantastic,' I said, in genuine amazement. 'And how's Gudrun? What's she doing?'

Cousin Gudrun, I learned, still lived with her parents, but usually did not get home until late.

'She works terribly hard at the office,' Aunt Elsbeth explained. 'It's often eight or nine before she's finished, and then her bosses usually invite her out to dinner – recently it was at Horcher's! After that they drive her home.'

I wondered what office she was working at. I had heard from my parents that Horcher's was one of the most elegant and expensive restaurants in Berlin. But before I had a chance to ask any more questions, Uncle Karl said he had to hurry to his meeting: everyone from the block warden up was expected to appear. Dr. Goebbels himself, as Gauleiter of Berlin, would be speaking – primarily about the 29 March elections, where there had been some slip-ups.

'What sort of slip-ups?' I asked. 'Didn't 99 per cent vote yes?'

'That's just it,' he said as he put on his overcoat.

'In all the voting districts it was exactly 99 per cent,' Aunt Elsbeth explained. 'That doesn't look good. It doesn't make a very convincing impression abroad . . .' She sounded troubled. 'In Friedrichshagen fifteen voting centres out of twenty had exactly as many votes cast as there were registered voters, and in the other five it was just one vote off.'

'But that's perfect,' I said, 'after all, the slogan was "No one must miss this election!" How can you complain when every single voter turns out?'

She gave me a puzzled look. 'Oh well,' she said finally, and changed the subject, 'Uncle Karl has too many evening meetings. It would have been nice if he'd been able to play something for us this evening – some Schubert, maybe.'

Uncle Karl was a good pianist, but I wasn't sorry to miss a musical evening. I was more interested in why Uncle Karl was going to a meeting for 'everyone from the block warden up'. What sort of a post had he allowed the Nazis to talk him into? Aunt Elsbeth always complained that her husband had too many evening meetings. In the old days they were connected with his lodge, for Uncle Karl had been an active Freemason besides belonging to a chess club, a singing society, the district social welfare committee, and the board of directors of an orphanage. He held several honorary positions and was forever being summoned to meetings. As proud as Aunt Elsbeth was of his activities, she would have preferred him to be home more often.

I remembered my mother saying, 'Karl's too good-natured. If someone says "Karl, we need you," he always takes on the extra chore.' Perhaps that explained his attendance at Nazi meetings.

But the following afternoon I visited Aunt Martha, my mother's unmarried sister in Steglitz, and asked her whether she could explain why Uncle Karl and Aunt Elsbeth had suddenly become Nazis, at least to all appearances. She sighed deeply and replied, "They really believe in it. Not long ago Elsbeth told me, "We mustn't ever doubt the Führer – the Führer is always right!" She's the most kindhearted woman in the world, but she has no more brains than a chicken, and her son, my dear nephew Fritz, is even worse.'

'What about Uncle Karl?'

'With him it's a bit more complicated,' Aunt Martha explained. 'He never took any interest in politics, but then in March or April of '33 he got caught up in it in spite of himself. The lodge, which meant so much to him, was closed by the police, and Freemasonry was suddenly suspect. Then a few days later, some SA men roughed him up on the Kurfürstendamm because he looks so Jewish. It was at the corner of Fasanenstrasse, not far from the synagogue. An SA man knocked his hat off his head and struck him in the face. After that, Karl was afraid, and he began to think of all the terrible things that could happen to his family, and to the store.'

Uncle Karl was a licensed art expert, specialising in porcelain, glass, and ceramics, and he also ran a little shop, filled with very valuable old glass and antique porcelain. I could imagine Uncle Karl's terror at the thought that the Hitler Youth and SA might hurl stones through his windows.

'Now he has a large sign in the window saying "German-owned business",' Aunt Martha continued. 'Of course his customers used to be almost exclusively Jewish – the types in power now tend not to appreciate old faïence and Venetian glass . . .'

'And what exactly is Gudrun up to?' I asked, as I was taking leave of Aunt Martha, to meet my cousin Lilly for lunch.

'Gudrun? I don't really know. She's working in some new government agency, but Karl and Elsbeth won't talk about it. They're very secretive. All I know is that she's often brought home at night in a big car, and the driver wears an SS uniform . . .'

My cousin Lilly lived in a new apartment building in the working-class district of Neukölln, which, before 1933, had the largest percentage of Communist voters in the entire city. On the fence along the railway tracks one could still read the faded slogan, 'Neukölln: Red Forever!'

Lilly was married to Martin, a tall, strikingly handsome man whom I liked a great deal. He came from a small town in West Prussia, had studied medicine in Berlin and done his residency under a famous internist. To the chagrin of his family he had then established a practice in Neukölln instead of on the chic Kurfürstendamm.

Martin was Jewish, and I was afraid I would find his practice failing and Martin and Lilly depressed. Instead, the waiting room was jammed when I went to see them, and some of the patients even spilled out into the little entryway. Lilly welcomed me with an apology: 'I'm afraid it'll be a while before we can eat. Today's another one of those days when we can barely catch our breath.'

When we finally sat down, Martin told me, 'The practice is going better than ever. If I had more room, I could easily take in two associates. And the things the patients say! They tell me everything – they want to talk about things they don't dare to mention anywhere else, not at work, not in a bar, sometimes not even at home.'

Martin had recently lost his right to collect state health insurance reimbursements, and had assumed he would have to close his practice, which served almost exclusively needy patients. But, on the contrary, the number of patients had not dwindled at all. To be sure, most of the patients could hardly pay, because they were living on meagre unemployment benefits or welfare, or could not spare anything from their low wages. But often they paid in kind: some fruit, a few heads of lettuce or a cucumber from the garden, a couple of jars of turnip preserves, maybe even a pigeon or a chicken. Others offered to perform services as plumbers, electricians, or carpenters.

'It's going splendidly,' Martin commented. 'Yesterday there was even an SA man in to see me.' The man had waited during the evening hours until all the other patients were gone, and Martin was about to close up. 'There was nothing wrong with him, really,' Martin said. 'His throat was a little inflamed, probably from shouting "Heil" so much. All he wanted was a chance to talk – about the last elections and how he had been directed to check off "Yes" on over five hundred ballots, and about the injustice he said was being committed against the Jews. "I have nothing against you, I want you to know that," he said as he was leaving, and then he saluted, said "Heil Hitler!" and left, after putting three marks on my desk for the treatment. That was the largest sum I had taken in all week.'

Then Lilly and Martin told me they were preparing to emigrate. 'We have to get out while we can,' Martin said, and he sounded sad. 'Next year or the year after there'll be war. I know all about the secret rearming – my patients who are working are almost all in armaments factories. At the electrical equipment plant in Treptow they're working two shifts, and that'll soon increase to three – all their deliveries go to the armed forces. And the Communists here have told me that a new military airport is being built near Erkner. Every worker is in compulsory service and has to swear an oath to the Führer. They're getting five marks a day, working ten hours with fixed quotas – and Sundays. By the time war breaks out, it'll be too late for us. We have to get out, and it's such a shame, because we like it here, and the practice is doing so well!'

That afternoon I also met Bobbi, a former schoolmate who had joined the Red Falcon with me. He was wearing a Hitler Youth badge.

'So, how long have you been with that outfit?' I asked.

'For a long time – I joined in May of '33. My father's a civil servant, you know, and besides, I love it. There's a terrific group spirit, and at Whitsuntide we're going camping. You really should join – we're all part of one big family now, and the Führer has worked miracles . . .'

'Yes,' I said, 'I know. He's eliminated unemployment and built the autobahn.'

'And that march into the Rhineland – that's where you live now, isn't it? Those people must be so proud that the Führer has given them back their honour!'

'Why, of course!' I replied.

THIRTEEN

Getting By

More than forty years passed before I saw Bobbi again – it was in the Munich Ratskeller, where he occupied the place of honour at a large table with elegantly dressed men and women. Only a few stray locks of his chestnut brown curly mop remained, and he had grown rather heavy and short of breath. But his laugh, his gestures, and his voice had not changed.

I asked the waiter to bring him my card, on which I had written 'Bobbi?' He promptly made his way over to my table. After we greeted one another, I learned he had been in the 'West' since 1949, that he was doing well as senior partner in a large Frankfurt law firm. He explained that he had just delivered an address – in memory of those who died in the Resistance.

He noticed my astonishment and hastened to explain. His father, a civil servant in a high position, had reactivated his status as first lieutenant in 1936, the year of the Olympic Games, and had risen during the war to the rank of major general. He was involved in the assassination plot of 20 July 1944, and the Nazis condemned him to death and executed him at the prison in Berlin-Plötzensee.

'It came as a terrible shock to me,' Bobbi said. 'My whole world collapsed. I was a young first lieutenant at the time, serving on the Eastern Front. When my commanding officer informed me that my father had been executed for plotting against the Führer, I thought he was out of his mind. My father – a dedicated National Socialist and a model officer – it was unbelievable. Why would he have gone over to the opposition? We owed the Führer everything!' He used the term *Führer* without a trace of irony.

Bobbi described his own successful military career, and the comfortable life his family had enjoyed as a result of his father's rapid advancement. 'We had a lovely villa in Berlin-Zehlendorf, servants, a chauffeur, orderlies . . . My mother was delighted to have the entrée into Berlin high society that she had always longed for – invitations to receptions, balls, elegant dinners. My older sister had married an embassy councillor in the Foreign Office, and I was engaged – don't laugh – to the daughter of a judge of the People's Supreme Court. When I was on home leave and went to visit her, my future mother-in-law would warn us not to make so much noise playing our dance records: "Hush, children, Papa can't work when you make such a racket. He still has a dozen death sentences to sign tonight." Of course the engagement was broken off – a good thing, too, I must say in retrospect . . .'

'But Bobbi,' I interrupted, 'if you were involved in the campaigns in Poland and Russia, you must have seen with your own eyes what was going on. Didn't that help you understand your father's actions?'

'Well, of course, what they did to the Jews was revolting. But we were told over and over again that it was a necessary evil – and by the way, I'm sure my father knew nothing about it. After all, he was just a paper-pusher, and he dealt with entirely different matters. No, I must admit, at the time I had no idea we had fallen into the hands of criminals. I didn't realise that until much later, after it was all over . . .'

Then he told me how helpful it had been after the war to be the son of a victim of Nazism. He received a scholarship, and his brother-in-law was taken into the new Foreign Office in Bonn and then even into the Federal Chancellery, his honorary rank in the SS completely cancelled out by the fact that his father-in-law had been executed by the Nazis. This connection with the federal government also proved very beneficial to Bobbi's law practice.

'Would you mind telling me why you joined the Red Falcon with me in '32?' I asked somewhat later, as we talked about school days.

Bobbi laughed. 'Actually it was all because of you,' he said. 'If my parents had found out, I'd have gotten a good beating. Oh, well, that was just a phase, though I must say I enjoyed parts of it – the summer solstice celebration, for instance.'

'I think you're confusing the Falcon with the Jungvolk.'

'That may be – it's all so long ago . . .'

As we said good-bye late that evening, Bobbi said, 'I almost forgot – I was supposed to say hello to you for a lady who was at my table earlier. Her name is Marga, and she said you two were friends in school, and that she ran into you in Düsseldorf recently. She wanted to talk with you, but had to hurry to make her train. She came just for the ceremony and had to get back.'

I was astonished to hear that Marga had come to a ceremony in memory of the victims of the Twentieth of July.

'You mean to say you didn't know?' Bobbi asked. 'She's the widow of one of the executed officers. It's odd she didn't tell you that.

Though for a long time she tried to keep it secret, even from her daughter. Her husband was adjutant to one of the chief conspirators, and he was among the first to be executed.'

'When we ran into each other after all those years we talked mainly about our school days. She told me that her husband was an officer and fell on the Eastern Front.'

'Is that so?'

I did not reply, but I decided to ask Marga about all this as soon as I had a chance.

A few weeks later I was in Düsseldorf and called up Marga. She invited me to lunch.

She lived near the zoo, in a lovely house built in the twenties. 'My father bought the house when he finally became regional court presiding judge,' Marga explained. 'That was at the end of 1938, just after I got engaged. So we celebrated our wedding here in April '39. We were lucky the house survived the bombing – I really love it. I loved it from the very beginning.'

I knew the house. Before Marga's father bought it, it belonged to the grandparents of our mutual friend Susanne, whose grandfather had also been presiding judge of the higher regional court, until the Nazis ousted him in 1933. Before Susanne left for England, she and I had visited her grandparents here several times.

I wondered, was it possible Marga knew nothing of the connection? When I mentioned the former owners, she responded, 'Well, that may be. At any rate, Father got the house at a very good price.' She laughed. 'Come, I'll show you around – we have time before lunch.'

As she showed me the house, I noticed the elegant and expensive decor. Over sherry, I asked if she lived alone.

'Yes, except for Fräulein Marquardt, my housekeeper. Of course we always keep a room ready for my daughter – she comes to see me every two or three months. We also have a Spanish maid . . .'

Before Fräulein Marquardt came to summon us to lunch, I broached another matter: 'Tell me, you must have married very young. We finished school early in '38, and then we all had to go into the Labour Service . . .'

'Yes, that's true, and it was during the harvest season that I met my husband. We were working on his father's estate in Pomerania. After that I went to Munich to study medicine because he was garrisoned nearby, and we formally celebrated our engagement on November the 9th. That was the happiest day of my life! My father threw a banquet for us at the Breidenbach Hotel – it was fabulous!'

'How unfortunate you had to pick that day of all days for your engagement party!'

She looked at me with raised eyebrows.

'I mean,' I said, 'that was Kristallnacht.* The night of the 9th of November 1938 was the beginning of Germany's worst pogrom.'

'Oh yes, I remember,' Marga said. 'When we left the banquet that night, the streets were littered with broken glass. And of course I had on delicate evening slippers, and a floor-length gown. Father said it was a disgrace that the crews hadn't cleaned up the streets yet . . .'

The Spanish maid served the hors d'oeuvres, and Marga changed the subject, telling me about her grandchildren in Switzerland, her son-in-law's hotel, and how he had arranged for her to get this 'pearl of a girl from Estremadura.' She recalled how easy it had been to get servants during the war, when she was an officer's wife, and talked about the splendid apartment they had in Striegau right after their marriage. 'It had everything – I didn't need my trousseau at all!'

'I imagine it belonged to a Jewish family that was thrown out just before you came.'

'That's right,' Marga replied. 'And I remember I got into a lot of trouble right after we arrived because I let a little girl into the apartment. I found her standing at the door, and she asked so timidly whether she could come in and fetch her diary, which had been left behind. Of course I let the poor thing in. But when I told my husband later, he made a huge fuss. He said everything in the place was the property of the Wehrmacht, and what did I think I was doing, letting a Jew into the house. It was our first quarrel.'

'So your husband was a real Nazi?'

'Oh, no, not a bit! He was a professional officer, but not in the slightest interested in politics. He just didn't want trouble with the Kreisleiter.'

She continued to reminisce about her experiences as an officer's wife; it was remarkable how little she had been touched by the war. After 1941, when she had her baby, she had been living in the Bavarian countryside, at a holiday home that belonged to relatives. Here she was spared the constant air raids and even the food shortages from which almost everyone else suffered.

Her husband was seriously wounded, and in 1944 after a long hospitalisation he was assigned to Berlin as adjutant to an officer in the

Kristallnacht, or the Night of Broken Glass, was a Nazi-organised pogrom, perpetrated against the Jewish communities of Germany on the night of 9 November 1938.

supreme command of the Wehrmacht. At that point she might have moved to Berlin, but she insisted on remaining in Bavaria with her young daughter. 'I saw him for the last time in '44 at Whitsuntide. He had changed a great deal.'

'You mentioned he was killed on the Eastern Front.'

'Yes, well . . . ' She must have remembered that I had talked with Bobbi in Munich, so now she told the truth. 'Please don't misunderstand,' she said, 'I always made a point of saying he had fallen in combat – and in a sense it was true. At the time I thought it would be better if the people in the village, and especially my daughter, believed I was the widow of an officer killed in action. It didn't make much difference to me – I already accepted the fact that he wouldn't be coming back. And in any case, we had grown apart . . .'

'Did the Gestapo leave you in peace?'

'Yes, I was lucky. They called me in for questioning, but everything went well. I must say they were very considerate and assured me that I wouldn't suffer any consequences. And they didn't bother me after that. Of course, it may have helped that I was having a little affair with a very important man . . . I met him in Munich. Whenever he came down to inspect the SS training academy in Bad Tölz, he would drop in to see me.'

Something told me that the place of that inspector of the SS training academies was taken after the war by a captain or major in the US military government.

Marga rattled on. It was amazing to me that she had such an excellent memory for everything that had given her pleasure, and no memory at all for unpleasant matters such as Kristallnacht. And as she talked about her Uncle Hubert, who had predicted at her engagement party that her path would always be strewn with roses, and cousin Jürgen, and Aunt Mimi, and so many other friends and relatives, it occurred to me that there was one name she had completely suppressed: that of her husband, executed in 1944 at Plötzensee Prison in Berlin.

FOURTEEN

From the Anschluss to the
Night of Broken Glass

'I believe that it was God's will to send a boy forth from this land to the Reich, to let him grow to manhood, to raise him to be Führer of the nation, that he might lead his homeland into the Reich. There is a higher Providence, and we are nothing but its tools . . .'

It was just weeks before my graduation, and this was the last speech by the Führer which we were forced to listen to over the radio in our school hall. It announced the 'long-awaited reunion of Austria with its true home', as Hitler described the forcible annexation of Austria. The Führer, a native of Lower Austria who had formulated his ideas of conquest while down and out in Vienna, where he held odd jobs in construction, sold postcards, and lived in a homeless men's shelter, flew into ecstasy on the occasion of his triumphant return. He thought of himself as God's emissary, but he did not neglect to castigate his defeated opponent, Austrian Federal Chancellor Kurt von Schuschnigg, as a 'false, wretched liar', an 'insane, deluded man'.

Von Schuschnigg had called for a plebiscite on 13 March 1938, in which it was generally expected that Austrians would vote overwhelmingly for continued independence; but Hitler preferred to trust to 'God's will' – in the form of the Wehrmacht – and moved swiftly to occupy the entire country. On the heels of the army came the Gestapo, the SS Death's Head squads, and many other 'special units' for terror and propaganda, which would 'bring into line' the Austrian cities and provinces.

The Viennese Nazis were even more brutal than the Germans, according to observers. William Shirer, then in Vienna, described what he saw as an orgy of sadism. Jews were rounded up to scour von Schuschnigg's election slogans off the walls of buildings, while crowds gathered to taunt them. Others were forced to clean public lavatories or the toilets in the SA and SS headquarters. Tens of thousands of Jews were jailed, their property stolen or confiscated. The Christian opposition was destroyed when Vienna's Cardinal Innitzer issued a statement welcoming the Nazis and urging Austrian Catholics to support them. When Hitler finally staged his own election in Austria and Germany on 10 April 1938, after the campaign of terror and intimidation, the annexation of Austria was made official.

By the time that unhappy 10 April arrived, my classmates and I had already graduated from school and been in the Labour Service for ten days. We were scattered throughout Germany, no two of us in the same camp, and we had already received our pay for the first ten-day period: two and a half marks.

'You are about to partake of a great experience,' a high-ranking officer in the Labour Service assured us before we boarded our trains in Düsseldorf, 'the experience of oneness with the Volk, the experience of physical labour out in the fresh air, working toward a common goal, the experience of the true meaning of blood and soil . . .'

The commander of our camp delivered a similarly bombastic speech soon after we exchanged our civilian clothes for earth-brown uniforms with swastika armbands and were equipped with factory-new glittering spades.

'And note this,' he had said in conclusion, 'here you are all equal, whether the sons of counts or bankers, or simple factory or agricultural workers, for that is the National Socialist unity of the Volk!'

Of course, it turned out that some were more equal than others, for a moment later the command rang out: 'Gradjits step forward!'

There were only two *gymnasium* graduates among almost three hundred Labour Service inductees, a near-sighted boy named Peter and I. Because of his thick horn-rimmed glasses, Peter got the nickname 'Professer', while I remained simply 'Gradjit'. We were called by these names for the next six months by the camp commander, Oberfeldmeister Kamesaska, a gaunt Lithuanian with a hooked nose and thin lips, whose chest bristled with decorations.

'I want you two no-goods – the gradjit and the professer – to report to me first thing tomorrow morning. I have a special assignment for you.'

The next morning, while the others marched off singing, with picks, shovels, and axes to clear stumps from a huge area devastated by a forest fire, Peter and I presented ourselves for our special assignment. To our surprise, Oberfeldmeister Kamesaska first asked us whether we could read maps and handle a tape measure. We assured him we could, already envisaging ourselves surveying the entire cleared area and recording it on a General Staff map. But it turned out he had a more pressing task for us: surveying and marking the terrain and calculating the materials required for the construction of a bicycle path.

The path was supposed to lead in a straight line from the camp to the camp commander's house, a distance of about half an hour's walk, and then on to the nearest station of the local railway, another two hours' walk. The terrain consisted largely of heath and sand, with occasional clusters of trees. Our camp was located, I should explain, in a desolate section of Mecklenburg Province.

'I want this bicycle path done right. How long will you no-goods need for the measuring and calculations?' Oberfeldmeister Kamesaska wanted to know.

Peter replied promptly, 'That will take several weeks, sir, if it's to be done right.'

He nodded, and thus we spent the next few months planning a bicycle path exactly 13.333 kilometers in length. It led (on paper of course) in almost a straight line from the camp to the railway station, curving only to avoid a swampy area, and it was to have a solid base of gravel and a macadam surface, and was to be bordered with yellow and blue pansies, planted one meter from the edges of the path; these we included in our drawings.

It was a lovely, restful summer for Peter and me. Most of the time we lay in a concealed spot, surrounded by our equipment. At the beginning we did not dare to go swimming, for now and then Oberfeldmeister Kamesaska would dispatch a Labour Service leader to check on our progress. But we soon learned how to handle these snoops – usually one bottle of pilsner for each eye they closed proved sufficient.

In this fashion we became experts on the meagre flora and the rich fauna of Mecklenburg, particularly the swamp and water birds. Peter already knew a good deal; he intended to study zoology and write his dissertation on the kingfisher.

When the planning for the bicycle path could be dragged out no longer, Kamesaska wanted to assign us to survey the vast burned-over area. But the 'professer' persuaded the Oberfeldmeister that we should design a lighting system for the bicycle path, since his house and the camp would soon be hooked up to an electrical grid. Thus we managed to spend the rest of our six-month stint measuring and planning – and swimming.

When I met Peter again after many years, he had hardly changed. His temples had greyed, his face was wrinkled, and although he was not tanned as he had been that summer of '38, in his keen eyes one could still discern the scamp who had recommended lighting for the bicycle path.

It was the summer of 1981 when we bumped into each other in Marburg. He had come to give a lecture there, and we discovered we were staying at the same hotel. Peter had become an architect, not a zoologist, but he had recently become a real 'professor', having received an honorary degree.

'You see, Kamesaska sized you up right.'

'And I him,' Peter replied. 'He was your typical old mercenary: useless in times of peace, lazy and brutal.'

'Kamesaska was perfect, at least for our purposes,' I objected. 'We ought to be grateful to him.'

'And to his deputy – do you remember him? Feldmeister Wondraschek, the noble Aryan, the tall rangy one who used brilliantine by the pound? He must have been a pimp in civilian life. Whenever he came to check on us, just a couple of bottles of pilsner would persuade him to submit a "very fabourable" report on our "untiring efforts".'

This Wondraschek was the one responsible for the 'ideological instruction' that was considered so important that even we bicycle-path surveyors had to attend it. But it was given only during drenching rains. We called Wondraschek the 'noble Aryan' because his pet obsession was the superiority of the Aryan race. He considered the 'Nordic' to be that race's most outstanding type, and liked to point to Oberfeldmeister Kamesaska, that much-decorated veteran of service in the Baltic and the Free Corps, and to himself as elite examples.

'Heroic types like us,' he would say, contrasting Kamesaska and the other noble Aryans with subhuman Jewish types – the 'Semitic-Bolshevist financiers', the 'Einsteins and Mandelstamms'. He knew Einstein from his manual as the 'relativity Jew', but he must once have had a bitter confrontation with some Herr Mandelstamm, from which he had come away the loser, for he always repeated this name in his ideological harangues.

'The other member of that merry threesome was Unterfeldmeister Perkuleit,' Peter recalled, 'that malicious bowlegged dwarf with the Hitler mustache. Wondraschek certainly couldn't describe him as a "Nordic hero", that sneaky informer . . .'

I remembered him only vaguely, but Peter reminded me that a Labour Service man from Berlin-Gesundbrunnen had warned us against Perkuleit, telling us that before he joined the Labour Service, Perkuleit had been a spy in the factory where he was a warehouse supervisor, and had denounced several workers to the Gestapo.

'Yes,' I said, 'people like Wondraschek and Perkuleit made it easy for Hitler, Göring, and Goebbels to stage Kristallnacht . . .'

'Well, that's only partly true,' Peter commented. 'The ones who carried it out were certainly types like that. But neither a Wondraschek nor a Perkuleit nor even a Kamesaska would have been capable of *planning* that "spontaneous outburst of the people's rage", and setting it in motion throughout the Reich with such precision. The organising took people of quite another calibre. Do you remember my cousin Klaus-Günter?'

I stared at him with astonishment. What connection could there possibly be between Peter's cousin and the pogrom of 9 November 1938?

I remembered that Klaus-Günter visited us once for a couple of hours in our camp in Mecklenburg, and drove us to Neustrelitz, where he treated us to coffee and pastry. He also played host to us two or three times in Berlin, where we were allowed to go most weekends on leave. Klaus-Günter was a tall, pale blond man from Hamburg, then in his late twenties, who wore elegant custom-made suits and cultivated a smooth manner. He had studied law, and I recalled vaguely that he spoke often of his 'firm', which seemed to be working him very hard.

The second time we saw him in Berlin, he was with a colleague from the 'firm', and this colleague's companion, to my great surprise, turned out to be my cousin Gudrun. I remarked at the 'fantastic coincidence' and greeted Gudrun warmly, but Peter's cousin said something to the effect that he and his 'firm' left nothing to coincidence. 'Otherwise we would have gone bankrupt long ago,' he added with a laugh.

The five of us went to an elegant *café dansant* on the Kurfürstendamm, and where Peter and I excused ourselves at around nine o'clock to make our way back to camp, Peter's cousin kindly placed a car at our disposal. So we were able to stay later, and then a chauffeur drove us to Neustrelitz, just in time for the last train.

'My cousin's "firm",' Peter explained, 'was the Reichssicherheitshauptamt, the Reich Central Bureau for Security. Klaus-Günter worked directly under Reinhard Heydrich. And Heydrich, who was head of the SD and the Gestapo and the entire police organisation, was the one who organised Kristallnacht. He and his colleagues worked everything out to the smallest detail – my cousin told me that the attack on the secretary of the German embassy in Paris merely provided the pretext for an operation that had been in the planning for some time.'

On 7 November 1938, a Jewish refugee in Paris named Herschel

Grynspan shot the secretary of the German embassy staff, Ernst von Rath, in revenge for what was being done to Jews in Germany. Grynspan's parents had been among thousands of Jews living in Germany who were herded into boxcars for deportation to Poland.

The assassination prompted the Nazi leadership to launch the planned 'operation' on 9 November, following the annual ceremonies that commemorated those killed in Hitler's failed Munich putsch of 1923. On 8 November, last-minute preparations were made in the RSHA. Orders then went out by telegraph to all the Gestapo and SD headquarters. Among the instructions were the following: 'Only such measures may be employed as will not endanger German lives or property – for example, synagogues may be burned only when there is no risk that fire will spread to neighbouring structures. Jewish stores and dwellings may be destroyed, but not plundered . . . The police must not interfere with the demonstrations that will occur . . . Only as many Jews – particularly wealthy ones – should be arrested as can be accommodated in available jails. After completion of the arrests contact should promptly be established with the appropriate concentration camp to provide for immediate transfer of the Jews . . .'

In every city and town throughout the Greater German Reich, special-duty squads were formed. The Gestapo provided them with lists of all Jewish private dwellings, shops, homes, schools, and other institutions. The SA and SS units as well as the local Hitler Youth units received instructions to identify those of their members who could be expected to perform well in the planned operation. After the official ceremonies on 9 November, they were to report in civilian dress to previously designated bases. The National Socialist Vehicular Corps had orders to provide vehicles and drivers, as well as trucks for transporting the prisoners. The fire departments had to supply axes, picks, and other tools suitable for demolition, and assign a few 'reliable' officers to instruct the arsonists and prevent the fires from spreading.

In the course of the day, more and more Nazi functionaries and civil servants were informed of the plan. Only the mass of the population – allegedly thirsting for revenge and ready to leap into action – knew as little about what was afoot as the victims themselves. The Jews had received orders three weeks earlier to turn all weapons in to the police – on threat of severest penalties. The Reichssicherheitshauptamt had taken this precaution to make resistance to the pogrom impossible.

The planners and their closest collaborators, among them Peter's cousin Klaus-Günter and my cousin Gudrun, had even designed a form on which local Gestapo and SD officials had only to fill in the blanks with appropriate figures for such categories as: dwellings destroyed, stores destroyed, other destruction, estimated property damage, synagogues burned, synagogues completely demolished, deaths, injuries, arrests, male Jews delivered to concentration camp, and other incidents.

'When did your cousin tell you about all this?' I asked Peter.

'About six weeks later. We went skiing for Christmas vacation, and Klaus-Günter joined us for a few days. In the evening we sat around talking – five or six cousins, my parents, and I – and the subject of Kristallnacht came up. Everyone but Klaus-Günter expressed shock and disgust. My father found it particularly outrageous that they had burned and demolished synagogues. I said something about the unspeakable crudeness and cowardice of those bands of thugs who attacked old people living alone and families with small children . . .'

'Did you witness that sort of thing yourself?'

'Sure,' Peter said, 'I was coming home late that evening when I saw several thugs beating a man until he collapsed. They dragged him onto the trolleybus tracks and left him there. A policeman who happened to come by helped me carry him to the Elizabeth Hospital. He was an old man with white hair – a lawyer, I think. On the way back I saw a woman with two small children, with coats over their nightclothes. They were in a state of utter terror. "Why are they beating us?" the woman screamed. "We haven't done anything!" I offered to take them home with me, but she wanted to return to her apartment to look for her husband.

'When I described these incidents, my cousin Klaus-Günter said, "What are you making such a fuss about! These things are trivial. You have to perceive the larger historical context and accept the idea of political necessity! When we annexed Austria and the Sudetenland, we picked up almost half a million more Jews – and they're nothing but parasites! One decisive stroke is preferable to a hundred-year struggle. Besides, these Jews have thick hides. Some of them still don't realise that this was an ultimatum . . ." Then he boasted of how magnificently the operation had been organised, and praised Hermann Göring for having the brilliant inspiration that the Jews themselves should pay for the property damage. "Now they have to come up with a billion marks! We're going to keep the rich Jews in concentration camps until they cough up the money. Just think – a billion! That will come in handy. It'll pay for the West Wall!! Now do you understand how valuable it was?"'

'And what become of Klaus-Günter?' I asked.

'Oh, he survived the war. The Americans gave him a long prison sentence, but by 1950 he was out. He even draws a fat pension, because toward the end of the war he was promoted to general in the Waffen-SS. I have no contact with him.'

'After the war did you ever discuss his "firm" and the things he was involved in?'

'Yes,' said Peter, 'but you're mistaken if you think he might have seen the light or felt guilty. I ran into him in the early sixties – it just happened to be a November the 9th, and I reminded him. He wasn't the slightest bit embarrassed. "I didn't harm a hair on anyone's head," he said, "and none of us believed in that racial nonsense anyway. We were just little cogs in a huge machine – important cogs, true, but on the whole we did nothing different from any general staff officer . . ." He told me that he's now a director of a large industrial enterprise, and remarked, "People with technical expertise are always needed." And I'm afraid he was right.'

There was a pause in the conversation while each of us pursued his thoughts.

Then Peter continued, 'Imagine, he showed me an old-fashioned gold cigarette case shortly before his chauffeur came for him. "The woman to whom this belonged was someone I got an exit visa for – it almost cost me my life," he told me. "You see, we weren't monsters." I looked at the cover, which had the words engraved, "In memory of Lieutenant Helmut Lilienfeld," or something like that, and then his date of birth, his regiment, and the day on which he fell "for his beloved Fatherland". That just about finished me off.'

'I'm surprised he kept the case and showed it to you.'

'No – I'm convinced that Klaus-Günter thinks of himself as not only competent and hardworking, but even decent and kindhearted. I suppose that's why he always has the cigarette case on him – as a piece of evidence, so to speak. After all, he didn't save the woman's life because of the gold cigarette case. He could have simply kept it and shipped her off to Auschwitz. No, there were other reasons: first of all, this was not an anonymous victim, but a living human beng standing before him. Somehow the woman had managed to get in to see him. And then she showed him the cigarette case that had belonged to her dead husband, to prove that she was a war widow. Then he helped her, and he kept the case only to have a memento of his own decency.'

'Well, maybe,' I remarked dubiously.

'Definitely,' Peter said. 'I know him. Types like my cousin can cold-bloodedly murder tens of thousands – from their desks, issuing orders on official stationery in standard memorandum form; and they take great pride in their efficiency. But don't think for a moment

Klaus-Günter would have been capable of beating an old man unconscious and dragging him onto the trolley bus tracks, or attacking women and children and driving them into the streets. I'm sure he would have found it extremely difficult even to smash up an apartment or plunder a synagogue. He knew how to issue orders, but he and his ilk left it to the rabble to carry them out. You'll always find people willing to lend themselves to any atrocity anywhere. And in those years the gangsters and murderers were given a free rein. On Kristallnacht the police had orders to protect the criminals and not worry about the victims. The patrolman who helped me carry the old man to the hospital was terrified that he might be punished. Thousands of SA, SS, and Vehicular Corps men – all pretence of law enforcement abandoned – became accomplices to the squads of attackers. Even Hitler Youths were delegated to plunder synagogues and desecrate Jewish cemeteries.'

'Some of them must have enjoyed it, don't you think?'

He dismissed the suggestion with a wave of his hand. 'That's not the point. None of it would have taken place if it hadn't been ordered from "on high", if there hadn't been experts, most of them with university educations, organising everything so that the "operation" could be carried out with split-second timing throughout the Reich. The young men in the Sicherheitshauptamt didn't get their hands dirty. They sat in their offices and dealt with issues of "political necessity". They dictated telegraph messages and signed lists and special orders – like Klaus-Günter.'

'And girls like my cousin Gudrun, from solid middle-class families, assisted them. They sat there with their chic hairdos and pretty white blouses and typed neat lists of the victims – an important service for *Führer, Volk, und Vaterland*.'

FIFTEEN

Katrina with the Golden Hair

That night, after my conversation with Peter, I slept badly. We had laughed a lot, recalling our time in the Labour Service, had parted in good spirits, and agreed to get together again. But once in bed I was haunted by memories of Kristallnacht: the sound of axe-blows, splintering wood, shrill cries, a gramophone's absurd accompaniment . . .

My parents had moved to a smaller apartment while I was in Mecklenburg doing my Labour Service. We now lived on the fourth floor of a new building in the northern part of Düsseldorf. On the evening of 9 November 1938, my mother and I were home alone. I had been released only a few days earlier, and in three weeks I was due to report to the Luftwaffe. We were talking about that, and laughing about how Peter and I had managed to spend our six months planning a bicycle path, complete with flowers and electrical lighting.

She went to bed early, but I stayed up reading. I was planning to listen to the BBC news at eleven o'clock. But things turned out differently.

At first I paid no attention to the dull thuds that seemed to be coming from the wall. When I heard them again, I put aside my book and went out into the hall. When I opened the door to the stairwell, I could clearly hear the sound of axe-blows, and wood splintering, and broken glass tinkling.

A woman, pale and frightened, stepped out of the apartment next to ours. 'For heaven's sake, they can't do that,' she whispered.

I asked her what she meant, and she hesitated before telling me in a low voice: 'There are Jews on the ground floor.'

I ran down the stairs. On the landing above the ground floor I paused, for now I could see what was going on. The door to one of the apartments stood open. Glass from a large mirror in the hall lay in thousands of shards on the floor, and a chest of drawers had been hacked to pieces. I heard a cupboard full of dishes and glassware fall over with a crash. More axe-blows followed. Bits of wood, feathers from pillows and comforters, and scraps of cloth came flying out into the stairwell. And above this racket a gramophone was blaring a hit tune:

> At Katrina's with the golden hair
> The boys and girls are dancing there
> At Katrina's in the Golden Goose
> The boys kiss the girls and then let loose . . .

I heard a scream, then another – of a child shrieking in terror. The music rattled on. I hesitated for a moment and glanced up the stairs, hoping to see someone who would go with me. But I saw only our upstairs neighbour leaning over the banister.

'Call the police!' I called up to her, but she shook her head.

'The police are right outside,' she replied, but only just loud enough for me to hear.

Then I caught sight of my mother. She had come out in her bathrobe and was standing on the second-floor landing, in a state of great agitation. 'What are you waiting for?' she asked me. 'Are you scared to go in?'

'No,' I lied.

'All right then, come on!' She started down the stairs.

'Wait – you stay there!' I shouted, and ran down the last few steps. Inside the apartment wardrobes had been pushed over and smashed, furniture had been broken into kindling, easy chairs and pillows had been slit open, curtains hung in ribbons, and everywhere lay heaps of broken glass and porcelain. From one of the rooms the gramophone music was still blaring

> . . . in the Golden Goose
> The boys kiss the girls . . .

A young man in high brown boots, riding breeches, and a turtle-neck jersey was stuffing a silver candelabra into a bag. A second was stabbing a kitchen knife into a large oil painting that hung at a crazy angle on the wall.

'Are you out of your skulls, you idiots?' I heard myself shouting. Fortunately they were hardly older than I, only seventeen or eighteen, and I had the advantage of surprise, for with all the racket they had not heard me come in. They jumped at the loudness of my 'Labour Service' shout. The boy in the turtleneck quickly put down the silver candelabra and looked at me apprehensively. The other one stopped his slashing and called out, 'Squad leader, someone is here!'

The music broke off, a door flew open, and from the bedroom came a fellow in his mid-twenties, tall and broad-shouldered, in a blue mechanic's jacket, one hand tucked casually into his trouser pocket.

'So what do you want?' he asked, taking a step toward me. Behind him I spotted for a fraction of a second a terrified face, and then someone darted past us to the apartment door.

'You in charge here?' I asked in my best Kamesaska tone, and without waiting for his answer I continued, 'This man here is to report tomorrow to your unit commander, along with that candelabra! We'll see what happens next. And do me the favour of cutting out the racket. You're through here, right?'

I had the satisfaction of noting that he had taken his hand out of his pocket and remained at a respectful distance. He glanced around and said, 'That's correct, we're finished here. What's the story with the candelabra?'

'You can ask the man yourself – and don't forget to report it!' Then I turned and stalked out. Instead of going upstairs, I went out into the street.

Outside, a policeman was trying to disperse some passers-by who had stopped and were whispering excitedly to each other. I mingled with the group and withdrew a few paces with them, keeping my eye on the door to our building.

After two or three minutes, the broad-shouldered squad leader and the two boys came out. They crossed the street to a lorry and said something to the driver, who turned on the headlights and started the engine. They got in and the lorry roared off.

Now the small crowd began to grumble more audibly: 'It's a disgrace! The police just stand by and do nothing! Disgusting!'

I hurried back to the house. Since I had no key with me, I had to ring the bell – one long and three short, to let my mother know who it was.

'What are you doing here?' the policeman demanded. I heard the buzzer and pushed the door open.

'Why didn't you ask the thugs who just came out what *they* were doing here,' I replied, and the people standing around murmured their agreement.

The policeman just turned back to the crowd and barked, 'Get out of here! Go on, move it!'

Before I went upstairs I took another look at the devastated apartment. Slivers of glass and porcelain crunched underfoot. In the foyer beneath the frame of the smashed mirror, the silver candelabra lay amid the remains of the bureau. I picked it up and hid it in the overturned kitchen cupboard with the broken porcelain.

When I had made sure no one was in the apartment, I hurried upstairs.

My mother was standing in the doorway. 'Where were you?' she asked, as though I had dawdled on my way home from school. 'I've tried twice to call Fräulein Bonse, but there's no answer,' she continued.

'Try Aunt Annie, she might be with her,' I suggested, and then realised that someone else was in the room. 'Who's this?'

'It's their daughter. She's hardly more than a child. I've given her valerian drops and a sleeping pill – I hope she'll be able to get some rest. But that's not the most important thing right now. Her parents should be coming home any moment, and her mother has a bad heart. You have to warn them and tell them the girl is here with us.'

'But I don't even know them. How am I supposed to recognise them –'

'The father is fairly tall,' she interrupted me. 'He has a slight stoop and is wearing a grey felt hat and a grey overcoat. The woman is quite a bit shorter and somewhat plump . . .'

I had no trouble recognising them. They were barely a block from the house when I approached them. 'Please don't go into your apartment,' I said, after I had greeted them politely and introduced myself. 'Let's walk down Fischerstrasse a way . . .'

'But I must get home,' the woman screamed. 'Our daughter –'

'Don't worry about your daughter. She can spend the night with us. My mother is looking after her.'

We walked along Fischerstrasse, past the old cemetery. Bit by bit I informed them of what had happened. The woman wept; the man tried to comfort her, and then, having regained his compsure, said, 'The furniture's not important. This happened to us before, when we had the shop in Hilden. We wanted to emigrate to America soon anyway, before the end of the year.' Then something occurred to him, and he asked worriedly, 'Nothing happened to the painting, I hope. I put all the money we had into it. It's "degenerate art" – *that* you're allowed to take with you. We want to sell it over there and use the money to make a new start.'

'What does it look like?'

He described the painting, and I knew at once which one he meant.

'It's a Chagall,' he said.

'It's damaged,' I said cautiously, 'but I'm sure it can be repaired. I'll take it upstairs to make sure no one walks off with it.' And then I asked whether they knew anyone they might stay with for that night and possibly the next. 'Otherwise you'll have to move in with us, too,' I added, though I was reluctant to let them walk past their devastated apartment.

'Only the friends we were just visiting, but they've certainly gone to bed already,' the man replied.

I asked whether they were Aryans, and whether they had a telephone. When the man answered both questions affirmatively, I found a telephone booth and called them, explaining the situation. The friends said to come at once.

'I'll go with you,' I said. 'It's not far.'

We had to make a number of detours, for we came upon several blocks where people were clustering around, obviously watching the same kind of destruction I had just witnessed. But at last we reached our destination. The couple's friends embraced them wordlessly.

On my way home I saw something happening on Fischerstrasse: a house on the corner showed lights in many windows, and people all around were looking up. Noise and screams were coming from an upper story. Then a shot rang out, and broken glass came smashing down onto the sidewalk. Another shot, and someone tumbled out of a window and landed with a thud on the pavement.

Passers-by and people from the surrounding houses ran to look. A police van and several ambulances drove up. A man standing next to me said, 'That was Dr. Lichtenstein, the ophthalmologist.' He pointed to the dead man on the street and added, with palpable satisfaction, 'He put up a good fight. There's supposed to be another man dead inside, and another seriously wounded . . .'

Two ambulance attendants were just carrying an injured person to one of the ambulances. Then they brought out a body covered with a sheet.

'I'd like to see that happen to all of these damn thugs,' the man next to me said softly, but not so softly that some of the others could not hear him. No one protested.

Back home, I fetched the painting from the apartment and hid it under my bed. Then I set out again, this time with my bicycle. On Sternstrasse I braked just in time to avoid an entire X-ray machine that came hurtling out of a second-floor window. A heat lamp hit the side-walk with a loud crash, and all sorts of instruments came raining down after it.

From Sternstrasse I bicycled into the centre of town. All the Jewish stores with which I was familiar presented the same picture: smashed windows, vandalised interiors, the goods plundered or tossed out onto the street – it seemed to have made no difference whether they were stockings or fur coats.

Some distance away I saw the glow of fire against the sky. It was the Kasernenstrasse synagogue, which had fallen victim to 'a spontaneous outbreak of the people's rage', as we heard over the radio the next day. In actuality, the 'people', of whom only a few were abroad at this late hour, were horrified at this act of barbarism. The police and firemen stood by without lifting a finger. A fat Kreisleiter in a brown uniform was stomping about nervously, shouting at bystanders, 'Get out of here! What are you staring for? There's nothing to get excited about!'

On my way home I saw several lone pedestrians or couples lugging suitcases and bags and trying to hide in dark entryways as I passed. I couldn't tell whether they were Jews fleeing, or looters who had snatched up valuables they found in the street.

On Steinstrasse I encountered a woman with a little child. The woman cowered against the wall of a building when she caught sight of my bicycle headlight, but the child jerked away from her and began to cry.

I stopped and asked whether I could help. She gave me a look full of hate, and pulled the child close to her.

'We've had plenty of help this evening,' she said bitterly. 'Please leave us alone and . . .'

She broke off as loud male voices could be heard approaching.

I came up close to her and whispered, 'Don't be afraid.' I put my arm around her; she was completely rigid. The child was quiet now, huddled in the shadows. Four men in high boots and civilian clothes passed us, talking and laughing loudly.

'I'm taking the day off tomorrow,' one of them said. 'I've put in a hard night.'

The others laughed raucously. One of them yelled a coarse remark at us, whom they took for a pair of lovers; and they laughed again but didn't stop. A few minutes later they were out of sight, and the street was quiet once more.

'Thank you,' the woman said as I took my arm from her shoulder. 'Excuse me for thinking that you . . .'

'Do you have a place to stay?'

'Not any more.'

'Come along, then. I may know a place where you'll be safe.' We were right around the corner from Herr Desch's shop. He lived above the shop, so I took the woman and child there.

At the door I had to light a match, for it was pitch-dark. I found his nameplate and rang the bell, touching it for only a second. Almost instantly I heard his businesslike voice, 'Is someone there?' I stepped back two paces and looked up at the dark windows. There was no one to be seen.

'It's me, Herr Desch,' I said quietly, 'Bernt Engelmann. I'm sorry to disturb you so late.'

After a short pause we heard him say, in a tone he reserved for his customers, 'Oh, I see, it's about the uniform. It's really very late . . . but that doesn't matter, I'm still up. Just a moment, if you please.'

When he opened the house door, he was dressed very properly, as always. Certainly he had not been in bed, although it was almost 2.30 in the morning. His fishlike face remained expressionless when he saw the woman and child. He merely nodded, asked us in, and carefully locked the door behind us.

'It's a bit crowded,' He said in his normal voice, and showed us into the shop. In the workroom, in the pressing room, and even between the fabric racks in the back of the shop people were sitting or lying. Some had fallen asleep, others were talking in low voices. Some were still so much in shock that they did not even look up as we entered.

'In the kitchenette over there you'll find hot tea and milk,' Herr Desch told the woman with the child, 'and in the room behind it there's still some space. That should do for now, and tomorrow . . . we'll have to see. I'll come and talk to you in a moment.'

He led me into the darkened showroom. In the pale light shining from the half-opened workroom door I glimpsed an SS officer's uniform on a dummy.

'The injured ones are upstairs in our apartment, with my wife and Fräulein Bonse,' he said softly. 'The doctor has been here already. I still have no idea what to do with all these people. There are too many of them – someone is bound to notice.'

'How about Aunt Annie?'

'She's not feeling well; she had a heart seizure.'

'I'll go out to see her tomorrow. I hope she'll be all right – I know she's had problems with her heart. I was thinking of her delivery van. Maybe we could use it . . .'

'Yes, that's a good idea. I'll ask Fräulein Bonse which of her acquaintances along the Lower Rhine and in the Eifel region like pastry.' He accompanied me to the door, let me out, and locked it quietly behind me.

When I arrived home toward three o'clock everything was still. My mother woke me shortly after eight. 'We have to go down and fetch a few things – otherwise the girl will have nothing to put on.'

As we went downstairs we heard hammering. At the door to the wrecked apartment stood Frau Kannegiesser, who owned the building and lived on the second floor. A carpenter and his helper were busy removing the remains of the old door and replacing it with a new one.

'Perhaps,' my mother suggested to the carpenter, 'you could have a look around and see what's repairable?'

'Sure,' he replied. 'I've already looked – it's a mess in there. What a disgrace. It makes you ashamed to be a German.'

Frau Kannegiesser nodded without a word and wiped tears from her eyes.

'We're just going in to fetch a few things,' my mother said. 'The little one has nothing to wear.'

But instead of just fetching clothes, the two women began to tidy up. My mother directed me to stand the kitchen cupboard up; one of the carpenter helped me. Frau Kannegiesser went upstairs to fetch pails and brooms and dustpans, and they worked for over an hour, sweeping up the broken glass and splintered wood. Finally, my mother gathered up some clothes for the girl, who, as I had learned from Frau Kannegiesser in the meantime, was called Ruth.

Two other women from the building came to help with the cleanup, and when we got upstairs, the woman who lived on our floor came out and asked, 'Is there any way I can help down there?'

'Certainly,' my mother replied, 'there's still plenty to do.' When the woman was out of earshot, she whispered to me, 'Her husband is a government official and a staunch Nazi. He always greets you with "Heil Hitler!" It will do her good to see what her husband's friends in the Party are up to.'

An hour later I took the trolley bus into town and from there to Meerbusch to visit Aunt Annie. Everywhere I saw distraught, saddened, or indignant faces. An older man sitting in a seat reserved for handicapped veterans stared out at a devastated shoe store and remarked so loudly that everyone could hear him. 'Once upon a time looters were shot; now the police protect them. That's what Germany's come to. The country we risked our lives for!'

No one contradicted him.

At Luegplatz a woman wearing a large Nazi Women's League brooch got on. She must have sensed the hostility of the other passengers, for as we passed a destroyed fabric store, she said to the woman sitting next to her, 'They shouldn't have done that. I'm sure the Führer doesn't approve.' The other woman turned away without replying, and someone snickered.

When I arrived at Aunt Annie's, she received me at the door with the solemn words, 'We Germans will pay dearly for what was done to the Jews last night. Our churches, our houses, and our stores will be destroyed. You can be sure of that.'

She said she was feeling better, and besides, she had so much to do. Herr Desch had already telephoned. The driver of the delivery van had his instructions.

'My huband is worried about his cream tarts,' she said, and laughed. 'He has a great many to deliver in the next few days.' Then she added, seriously, 'They all have to get out of the country. They're no longer safe in Germany.'

I told her what had happened in our building, and mentioned Ruth.

'Did they – did those fellows do anything to her?'

'No, I got there just in time.'

'She can't stay with you,' she said, after brief reflection. 'In a house with ten apartments that sort of thing will get around, and someone might report it to the Gestapo. Bring her to me. She'll be safe here for the time being, and I can use some help right now.'

'All right,' I said, feeling greatly relieved. 'I'll bring her late this afternoon.'

SIXTEEN

Are You Familiar with Buchenwald?

'You must be out of your mind,' Kulle said when I told him shortly after graduation that I had volunteered for the Luftwaffe. 'Why can't you wait until they call up our age group?'

I tried to explain why my decision made sense: First, *gymnasium* graduates who volunteered had to serve only twelve months – by the autumn of 1939 I would be finished. Second, as a volunteer I could choose the type of weaponry in which I'd be trained and the base where I'd be stationed. I had chosen a small town in Westphalia where friends of my parents had a hotel. From there I could get home for weekends in two and a half hours.

But the most important reason was that my parents were planning to leave Germany. In October of 1938 my father had gone to England to investigate the possibilities. The official reason for the move was that he would be representing a German export company. The suspicions of the police and the foreign currency office, which would have to authorise any transfers of funds, could be disarmed most effectively if I, an only son, proved the family's 'national loyalty' by volunteering for military service. As soon as I was discharged, I could go to university wherever I liked. I had already applied for a scholarship at an English university.

'I still think you're out of your mind,' Kulle said. 'War might break out any day now . . .'

That was an important consideration. The country was rearming at a fantastic rate. Göring's slogan was 'Guns, not butter', and all the large factories were busy turning out artillery pieces and machine guns, while butter was rationed and only to be had for coupons. Along the border, from southern Baden to Aachen, construction was under way on the West Wall, a gigantic fortification for which thousands of workers had been pressed into compulsory service.

In September 1938 war anxiety grew dramatically as Hitler seemed determined to attack Czechoslovakia. The British prime minister, Neville Chamberlain, came to Germany twice, trying to mediate. No one could predict whether the French and the British would attack

Germany from the west when the anticipated German march on Czechoslovakia materialised. The Czechs had already mobilised, but soon realised that Paris and London were not prepared to act on their defence pact with Prague. Although France did begin to mobilise sixty-five divisions, and the British fleet was put on standby alert, the governments of these two powers seemed more inclined to let Hitler swallow up the Sudetenland than to risk another world war.

In the last days of September, the anxiety had reached such a pitch throughout Europe – but especially in Germany – that people breathed a great sigh of relief when an agreement was reached on the night of 29–30 September among the governments of Germany, England, France, and Italy. To be sure, the Munich agreement strengthened Hitler's position: Paris and London had abandoned Czechoslovakia, and on 1 October, German troops marched into the Sudetenland. But most people thought that war had been averted, and some even believed Hitler when he declared again that he now had no further territorial ambitions in Europe.

My father, who was usually more skeptical, calculated that peace would last at least another two years. His English friends had assured him of it. Not until England had completely built up its armaments would a confrontation with Hitler come about.

That prediction had been the decisive one for me. Two years from now, I thought, I will have long since finished my military service, and will be a student – and not in Germany.

So, early one day toward the end of November, I set out for the town where I was to be garrisoned. I planned to spend the night with my parents' friends at the hotel.

Uncle Franz, as I called him, had changed. 'Hitler's not doing such a bad job,' he said to me. 'Of course a lot of it was bluff, but he actually did what he promised. Look, we have Austria now; and even the Sudetenland is German again – and without a war. Pretty good, eh?'

He was also delighted that the town had a military garrison once more. It was very good for business.

His wife, Aunt Käthe, however, didn't seem so cheerful. As soon as Uncle Franz had left to look after the restaurant and the bar she confided to me, 'I don't know what to do – I think I've made a terrible mistake. Franz doesn't know, and for God's sake don't breathe a word in his presence – he's changed so much recently . . .'

Her 'terrible mistake', I learned, was that she had taken in a Jewish businessman from a nearby town. 'It's just for a few days,' she said in a low voice. 'He arrived yesterday afternoon while Franz was away in Bielefeld. I've known him a long time – a very decent man – and I couldn't bring myself to turn him away. He's just waiting for his passport so he can go to Sweden. His wife and son are already there. After that horrible night a few weeks ago they arrested him, and I think they had him in a concentration camp – it's a miracle he got out alive.'

I asked her why she was so worried. After all, she could put up any guest she wished.

'Oh, no,' she said, and sighed deeply. 'Since last week it's illegal for us to allow any Jews into the hotel – even into the restaurant! We're in dreadful trouble if anyone recognises him.'

'Where is the man supposed to go? He probably has nowhere . . .'

'That's exactly it,' Aunt Käthe confirmed. 'His factory has been Aryanised, his apartment confiscated. They even took away his car. They forced him to donate it to the Winter Aid.'

'So what will you do? You can't put him out in the street!'

'No,' she said, 'but he can't stay either. But I have an idea. We have to do it right away, because by ten o'clock Franz is usually through in the restaurant.'

She proposed that I spend the night in their hunting cabin rather than in the hotel. There was a shortage of rooms, so her husband wouldn't be surprised at her putting me up elsewhere. Of course, I was to take the illegal guest with me. Käthe would provide plenty of food and drink, and drive us out to the cabin.

I knew the cabin. It was only twenty minutes' drive from the hotel, and sat on a lovely slope of the Weser Range, with a view of the river.

'I'll pick you up tomorrow morning,' she said, 'and at the same time I can bring Herr Kahn his mail, in case any comes for him. Maybe his passport will be here tomorrow. Then I can take him straight to the station.' She looked tremendously relieved when I agreed to her plan, for she said she was afraid to leave Herr Kahn alone in the cabin after what he had been through.

Thus, I came to spend the night before the beginning of my military service in the company of a man who had just been released from a concentration camp.

Herr Kahn was a short, somewhat pudgy man with thinning hair in his late forties. He must have lost a good deal of weight, for his suit looked baggy on him. I could see in his face that he was a cheerful man with a sense of humour, but he seemed still to be under the cloud of his recent experience.

Over supper he began to tell me about it: during Kristallnacht his apartment was looted and ransacked. Fortunately he had already sold everything of value in order to pay the property levy, without which his family would not have been allowed to emigrate. But the following morning he was arrested by two Gestapo agents. They put him on a truck, with about a dozen other Jewish men, and drove to Bielefeld. After sitting for a long time in a waiting room, he and the others were called and forced to sign a document without having time to read it. Toward midday they were taken to the railway station.

'They marched us onto the platform five abreast, and then down a stairway and through a tunnel to another platform. All along the way young SS men beat us with leather whips. Some of us were badly injured. In the end they didn't take us to a train but hauled us away in a lorry – to Buchenwald. Are you familiar with Buchenwald?'

I said I had heard of it – it was a concentration camp near Weimar. 'Yes,' said Herr Kahn by way of confirmation, 'not far from the Weimar of Goethe and Schillar.'

In all, about twelve thousand Jewish men were delivered to Buchenwald after the Night of Broken Glass. They were housed in large barracks, some of which were still unfinished.

'There were about six thousand of us crowded into one barracks, which didn't have a floor yet – it was just damp clay. We had bare planks for beds, no mattresses, no blankets, no light. The latrines were unspeakable. And in the middle of the first night, just when things had quieted down a little, we were suddenly blinded by flashlights, and about a dozen men were taken at random and dragged away by the SS men. We heard them screaming horribly outside, and they never came back.'

This happened again the two following nights, and the prisoners were so terrified that they crept into the farthest corners of the barracks. 'Some of them began to rave and had to be tied down. You can't imagine what those nights did to us. It was pure hell.'

Herr Kahn continued: 'On the third morning we were lined up in front of the barracks – it was the first time we had been let out – and an Unterführer inspected the rows. Everyone with a visible injury was asked how he had come by it. The first few answered truthfully that they had been mishandled in Bielefeld by the SS. At that the guards whipped them until they said they had inflicted the wounds on themselves. All day they kept us in a state of terror with such treatment. Not until the fourth day did things get a little better.'

At that point they were assigned to completed barracks, where they had a little more room, and from then on they were allowed to use the money they had with them to buy eating utensils, food, and warm clothing. The doctors among them were able to buy medicines for the many sick and injured.

In contrast to the other prisoners, they did not have to work. They had to appear for roll call morning and night; otherwise they were left to their own devices. But the roll calls sometimes lasted several hours, and the old men in particular suffered horribly from being on their feet so long in the cold. Many of them simply dropped and died.

'On the twentieth day my name was called at the morning roll call, along with the names of about three hundred others. We were to be released. They took us to the prisoner barbers, who shaved us and cut our hair. And then we were examined by an SS doctor. Anyone who had wounds or bruises had to report that he incurred them before his arrest. Then a higher SS officer came to lecture us and say that he hoped we had been rehabilitated, and if we wished to prove it, we now had an opportunity to give generously to the Winter Aid. They led us past the collection boxes, and the SS man watched to make sure we all contributed. After that we had to turn in the eating utensils we had bought, and for each set of tin flatware we had to pay a 'use charge' of three marks. Then the sale of 'tickets' began, and anyone without money had to fall out to the right. The others were ordered to collect enough money among themselves to buy tickets for the rest. We were told that no one would leave until each had a ticket. When that had been taken care of, we got another lecture: we were warned not to say a word about what we had experienced in the camp, otherwise we would be brought back to the camp and then we could be sure of never getting out alive.'

Herr Kahn stopped talking, took a deep breath, and looked around the cabin. 'Why have I been telling you all this? I simply have to talk about it; I want people to know about it and to tell others. No one in this country should be able to say he knows nothing about it!'

He was terribly agitated.

I fetched a bottle of cognac from the basket of provisions Aunt Käthe had given us, and poured him a glass. When he had calmed down a little, he continued his story.

'By the time all the formalities were taken care of and those of us to be released were lined up near the gate, it was eight o'clock at night. We had eaten nothing since morning, and after fourteen hours of waiting we were exhausted from the tension.

'An old man – he was about eighty – asked the guards at the gate for a ride of some sort, because he couldn't walk the eight kilometres to the station in Weimar. The SS man laughed and said he'd call a taxi, but the old man would have to pay for the call. The old man gave him three marks and asked him to call several taxis, because others wouldn't have the strength for the long walk either. But the guard made each man give him money. He collected six hundred marks.'

Herr Kahn talked on for a long time. He kept coming back to those first nights in the camp, when they lay squeezed into the half-finished barracks, trembling as the death commandos chose their victims.

During the night, I was awakened several times by his loud groans. One time he shouted, 'Don't hit me!' He didn't sleep quietly until almost morning.

Toward nine o'clock we heard an automobile. Herr Kahn was terrified. 'Where can I hide?' he whispered to me. Then we saw that it was Aunt Käthe.

'Your passport, Herr Kahn! Your passport just arrived!' she called out as she ran toward us.

He was incredulous. His hands shook as he opened the thick envelope. The passport contained the longed-for exit visa, which required him to leave Germany that very day.

'The train to Hamburg with a connection to Copenhagen leaves Bielefeld shortly after eleven,' Aunt Käthe told him. 'I'll take you to the station.' She seemed very happy.

'No, please!' Herr Kahn said. 'Not to the station in Bielefeld – I don't think I could stand it . . .'

Aunt Käthe was surprised. She wanted to reply, but bit her tongue, and only said, 'As you wish, Herr Kahn.'

'Just let us pack our things, Aunt Käthe,' I said, 'and then we can drop Herr Kahn off at a taxi stand.'

'Yes,' Herr Kahn agreed, 'that would be very kind. I'll catch the train in Herford.'

Five minutes later we had tidied up everything and packed our few belongings. Herr Kahn was already at the door in his hat and coat, his suitcase in hand.

'Look at this,' he said, and reached into his breast pocket. 'See how my fatherland makes sure I'll always remember it, even when I'm abroad.'

He showed me the passport. On the first page, next to the emblem with the swastika that had replaced the imperial eagle, the passport office had stamped a large J.

SEVENTEEN

Moving Towards War

'But do you recall the texture shortage in '38 and '39?' Werner asked me one day as we talked about the food shortages that had resulted from the 'guns, not butter' policy.

'Not very clearly,' I said. 'I remember people complaining, and there was that joke about the "German Forest" brand suits you could buy: in the spring they began to swell, and in the autumn they changed colour . . .'

'For workers and lower-level white-collar employees that shortage became very acute,' Werner remarked. 'Before the push for rearmament, you could buy a decent wool suit off the rack for about 35 marks. By 1938 you had to spend at least 50 for a suit, which looked like wool in the store window but not when you got it home. Those suits crackled like paper, and they hung on you like a sack. My father wore his good Sunday suit for four years; the new one he bought in 1938 was ready for the dustbin in almost no time. Only if you had about 150 marks to spare could you get anything halfway decent.'

I found myself thinking of Herr Desch, who had stocked his fabric racks just in time with bolts of the finest English woolens. At Christmas in 1938 I went to see him on my first home leave after four weeks of military service.

He asked how I found it in the Luftwaffe. I told him it was tolerable, that they had assigned me to radio communications, and I hoped the rest of my tour of duty could be spent peacefully at a communications post. By the end of November 1939 I would be able to lay aside my uniform. His long face remained expressionless.

'Let's hope your gamble pays off,' he said. Then after assuring me I was very fortunate to have been assigned to communications – that it was by far the most useful thing to learn in the armed forces – he insisted on making me a dark blue dress uniform of the finest gabardine, something only he still had in stock. Later on, he said, I could remove the collar patches and the braid and have the buttons changed, and then I would have an elegant civilian suit for any occasion, one which would last for years. As he praised the fabric he assumed an animated tone, and before I could get a word in edgewise he was taking measurements.

'But Herr Desch, it will be much too expensive,' I objected.

At that he muttered something about 'a special price for a friend', and that we would work out an 'arrangement' whereby I could pay it off in installments. Then he asked how often I could expect furloughs.

'Basic training will last two months, and during that time I should be able to get home every other weekend. And I might get an extra day now and then if I do very well at target practice. When I start my radio training, I'll have every weekend free.'

'Excellent,' said Herr Desch in his usual indifferent tone. 'Perhaps you could tutor Fräulein Bonse when you're home.' And noticing my astonishment, he added in a low voice, 'She's interested in learning to operate a ham radio, you see.'

That explains how I came to have a custom-made dark blue Luftwaffe dress uniform, which I later transformed for civilian wear. It served me well for over a decade, until I could no longer fit into it. That also explains how in mid-January 1939 I began to tutor Fräulein Bonse in radio communications.

Although we never spoke of it, I suspected that she or one of her close friends had a small short-wave transmitter for radio contact with Holland. A mini-transmitter could reach that far – we were only about 50 kilometres from the border as the crow flies. And if the transmitter was operated only once a week, and at different times and perhaps even from different locations, it could never have been detected by Nazi radio surveillance.

Fräulein Bonse learned the Morse code very quickly, and soon achieved a speed on the practice keyboard that surpassed my own. She excelled in transmitting technique, and I taught her a relatively simple, constantly changing code that was almost impossible to break when used for short texts. It was based on a twenty-stanza poem by Heinrich Heine, 'The Pilgrimage to Kevlaar'. The first line of each stanza served as the coding basis for one day, and after twenty days you began again with the second line of each stanza.

Fräulein Bonse also made remarkable progress in encoding and decoding. As a teacher I was very pleased with her – though my friends wondered why I would spend two precious hours of every free Sunday in the company of this cool, brisk lady in her mid-forties. When they teased me, I explained that these hours were devoted to practising English conversation. After all, I expected to be studying at an English university starting in December 1939 – to which my friend Kulle remarked skeptically, '*If* you're lucky: I can practically *smell* war in the air.'

When I reminded Werner of this period, he said, 'Yes, I was also sure we'd have war by the spring of '39. Things got awfully tense in January, when Hitler demanded that Poland cede the corridor – Posen and West Prussia – and allow Danzig to be reunited with the Reich. And then, of course, there was Czechoslovakia, remember?'

I remembered. It was on a Sunday, 13 March, that I returned to my garrison after spending the weekend in Düsseldorf. I was surprised to find that everyone was still up and about although it was almost midnight.

'We march out of here at 0045 hours,' was the news that greeted me at my barracks, 'in full battle dress and with live ammunition – for a "mob" drill. Didn't they tell you to get back here immediately?'

I hadn't been at home to receive the telegram. My parents were in England, so instead of spending the night in the empty apartment, I stayed at Kulle's house.

Now I saw my friends' grave faces. The older ones especially were in low spirits.

'"Mob" drill means mobilisation,' one of them commented, 'and that means there'll probably be war.'

No one showed a shred of enthusiasm.

We drove that night in a long convoy to our 'mob positions' on the western edge of the Thuringian Forest. There we waited all day Monday for further orders. At about 6.00 P.M., word arrived: 'Back to garrison – the drill is completed.' There was a general sigh of relief, the tension dissolved, and in our radio car, a comfortable Horch eight-cylinder sedan (the ancestor of the Audi), we listened to civilian radio stations to learn what was happening.

Starting Monday morning at 6:00 A.M. units of the Wehrmacht had moved into Czechoslovakia, encountering no resistance. They occupied the entire country, and now Hitler had arrived in Prague to announce, 'Czechoslovakia has ceased to exist'. Its people were henceforth under the 'protection of the Reich'.

Later we heard his own voice in our earphones. With audible triumph he declared, 'In accordance with the law of self-preservation, the German Reich is determined to intervene decisively to restore the basis of a rational order in Central Europe and to make appropriate arrangements. For in its thousand-year historical development the Reich has already proven that it alone is called to accomplish this task, thanks to both the greatness and the special characteristics of the German people . . .'

A week after the Wehrmacht marched in, the Nazis established the 'protectorate of Bohemia and Moravia' in the place of the former Czechoslovakia, and concluded a pact with Rumania that reserved all of that country's raw materials for Germany.

'Yes, things did look critical for a time,' I agreed with Werner. 'But once again, Hitler's gamble paid off; the major powers merely issued protests.'

'Maybe so,' Werner said, 'but after the liquidation of Czechoslovakia England and France did finally seem to wake up to the fact that Hitler's promises and peace-loving statements were a pack of lies, and that their accommodations and concessions had only made him greedier. We ordinary folk – my parents, some of their friends and comrades, and even I – saw it all quite clearly from the start. But I only wish we had had a good network of loyal allies like yours, people like that tailor, or the lady with the shortwave set, or the baker's wife who smuggled people over the "green border" to Holland. We couldn't trust even our closest relatives. So many people let themselves be bought. A package of butter or a good sausage, real coffee beans or bacon from the National Socialist People's Welfare, warm coats for the children from the Winter Aid, or the prospect of a job that brought in a few more pfennigs – that was enough to soften many of them up. Wages were shrinking in the spring of '39, and the work day got longer, and anyone who wanted to change jobs needed official authorisation – it was almost slavery. And people were really hungry.'

'And you think that's why people lost their will to resist and to stand by each other?'

'I think so, yes. And then there was the constant bombardment of Nazi propaganda – and the constant fear of spies and the Gestapo. That broke down a lot of people. Only a broad alliance joining Christians and conservatives and Communists would have given us the strength to resist. But such an alliance never existed – or only in exceptional cases like yours, where you were pretty much safe from spies.'

I thought this over. Perhaps Werner was right. But were we really so safe from spies? Once, I recalled, I came within a hair of confiding in someone I considered absolutely reliable, but who had long since gone over to the other side.

EIGHTEEN

On Your Guard! The Enemy is Listening!

Shortly after Easter in 1939 I submitted a request for a special leave. The reasons I gave were: 'grandparents' golden wedding anniversary; grandfather's seventy-fifth birthday; cousin's wedding.'

In view of such an accumulation of authorised grounds for leave, my request was granted without further ado. Erwin, head of my communications unit, signed my application and checked off 'urgently recommended', adding that I was the only male grandchild of my grandparents, who in actuality had both been dead for many years, and would be best man for my cousin, who had no intention of marrying. Erwin noted in the margin of the application in green pencil, 'certification of registry office available upon request', and then personally carried the application to the office and smuggled it into the basket marked 'Company Commander'.

'You have to make like the Führer,' Erwin remarked. 'You mustn't stop at one brazen lie – you've got to pile them on thick.' Erwin came from Wuppertal, was a trained electrician, and had no fondness for Hitler. His father, a Social Democrat, had been in 'protective custody' in 1933, in the infamous Kemna private concentration camp, where all ten of his fingers had been broken and crushed.

Erwin did not pry into my reasons for being in such a hurry to get to Berlin. 'You two have a good time, and say hello to her for me,' was all he said.

Early Friday morning I was called to the office to pick up my leave authorisation, which was valid for Saturday, Sunday, and Monday. At noon Erwin said, 'Actually, you could leave today. You're not supposed to go till after work, but this afternoon we're driving to Bielefeld for a communications drill, and we'll drop you off at the station. We'll manage all right without you. There's a train at 2.30.'

Thus I gained an extra half-day of leave, and we set out in our radio car – Erwin, I, and the driver Barczustowski, a passionate Nazi who was nevertheless happy to co-operate because Erwin had granted him permission to visit his girlfriend after dropping me off. From his position near Bielefeld, Erwin planned to broadcast a few Q-groups –

'technical difficulties, breaking off radio contact' – and then find a shady spot in the hills for an afternoon nap.

Shortly after 3.00 I was sitting on the train bound for Berlin. On the way to Bielefeld I changed into my fine dress uniform made by Herr Desch. As the landscape flashed by, I thought over the events that led up to this trip.

That Wednesday evening I had spoken by telephone with my mother, recently returned from London. Our decision to move to England was now firm – provided Hitler did not throw a monkey wrench into our plans. It was clear that if he started a war by the fall, there could be no hope of my being released from the Luftwaffe.

Fräulein Bonse believed that war would begin soon. The previous Sunday I was arguing that with Czechoslovakia, the Nazis' hunger for territory should be satisfied: they already had Austria and the Sudetenland from the previous year, and the recently acquired Memel. Fräulein Bonse disagreed. Hitler, she said, was a gambler, and like a gambler was counting on his run of good luck. He wouldn't stop while he was ahead. He was in a positive frenzy to stake everything on one card again.

'But the West Wall is nowhere near finished,' I objected. 'They're working on it feverishly, but the fortifications certainly won't be ready before next year.'

Fräulein Bonse thought this was the only factor that offered any hope. But if Hitler was determined to go to war this year, he would have to do so by September at the latest, right after the harvest. And if he had that in mind, the preparations must already be in full swing, and people in key positions would know about them.

'You're going to Berlin soon,' she said. 'Don't you have any friends or relatives in the government or the SS? It's terribly important to get accurate information, and as soon as possible, if only for your own plans. Give it some thought.'

After giving it some thought, I conceived a plan that was at least worth a try.

But my chief reason for going to Berlin was entirely different. The day of my conversation with Fräulein Bonse, Herr Desch had asked me to find a contact in Berlin's Jewish community as quickly as possible, 'preserving the strictest discretion, of course'. Berlin had more Jews remaining than any other German city. Many had moved there from towns and smaller cities only recently, because they felt safer in a large city. Herr Desch's friends planned to help a considerable number of them go to the United States before the end of the summer. A Dutch ship would be sailing to New York from Rotterdam around the beginning of August. They wanted the leaders of the Berlin Jewish community to choose about 225 candidates for this rescue mission.

'The people in question must be brought from Berlin to the Rhineland and from here over the green border,' Herr Desch explained. But the most important step now was to find a reliable middleman, who could get word to the Jewish community leaders, and who would be trusted by them. Herr Desch himself had been informed of the plan only a few days earlier and his attempts to find a middleman had thus far proved unsuccessful.

'I spoke with your mother,' he said, 'and she told me your father has a childhood friend in Berlin whom you know well, too – a certain Herr Elkan.'

'Of course, Uncle Erich. He's a lawyer and notary. What about him?'

'According to my information,' Herr Desch said, sounding even more detached than usual, 'this gentleman belongs to the governing council of the Jewish community'.

'That's surprising,' I said. 'I went to school with his son, and he didn't have to take religion, because his parents didn't belong to any faith. I thought they were in Sweden now. They left in '33 when Uncle Erich had to give up his practice.'

'Perhaps,' Herr Desch commented, 'Herr Elkan rejoined the community after the persecution began. In any case, he seems to be the right man for us, and since you know each other well, there should be no problem. It's extremely urgent . . .'

He then gave me detailed instructions, which I memorised, since I did not want to risk having anything in writing.

On my way back to the garrison it occurred to me that I might be able to find an even better contact within the Jewish community. A friend of mine, Heinz Elsässer, had visited my mother only a few days earlier and had been very sorry to miss me. We had grown up together in Berlin, going to the same kindergarten, playing in the street and in the city park, and even attending the same school for a time. Shortly before I left Berlin we met again in the Red Falcon. But since our move to the Rhineland I had not seen him.

Heinz's father was the cantor at the New Synagogue on Oranienburger Strasse. His mother, a large, imposing woman, came from Bad Tölz and still spoke Bavarian dialect. She had converted to Judaism when she married, so Heinz would be classified as 'one-hundred-percent Jewish' under the Nuremberg Laws. I had the address Heinz had left with my mother, and I planned to stop by to see him. He lived with his parents in the eastern part of the city. If his father was still a cantor, I thought, it would be a simple matter to establish the desired contact through him, and I decided to go to the Elsässers' right away.

When I arrived at the Zoo Station shortly before eight o'clock, I called Aunt Elsbeth to tell her I was in Berlin and would be getting to her place around eleven. She was delighted to hear I was coming, and said she would not mind waiting up for me. She wouldn't be in bed anyway, since Uncle Karl had his course for air raid wardens that evening, and my cousin Gudrun would not be home until late. She promised to have something nice for me to eat.

I took a train to the Silesian Station in the east of the city. I felt as though I were no longer in the Berlin I knew. It was a grim area, and the people looked worn, pale, and preoccupied. Many of the women seemed only now to be getting out of work. I got directions to the street where the Elsässers lived. The building was one of many sprawling, dingy apartment complexes. An elderly man in house slippers was sitting on a kitchen chair at the entrance to the rear section of the complex. In spite of the warm weather he was wearing a sweater, with a Party badge pinned to it. 'Where to?' he asked, as I walked past him. I put my finger to my lip, winked, and said without stopping, 'That's between me and the lady . . .' Among the eighty parties who lived in the building there must have been a few young women who would qualify as candidates for my attentions.

Although it was still light outside, it was so dark on the stairs that I had to turn on the feeble light. On the third floor I found the apartment. Frau Elsässer opened the door, but shrank back when she saw my uniform.

'Don't you recognise me, Frau Elsässer?'

'Holy Saints!' she exclaimed, and then assured me that she was happy to see me again. Unfortunately, Heinz was not home, and her husband was still at the synagogue, though he would be back soon, since the Sabbath was beginning.

I had forgotten that it was Friday evening. She asked me to stay to eat with them, but I said my aunt was expecting me. Then I gave her the telephone number and asked whether Heinz could call me early the next morning.

She hesitated. 'I don't know whether he'll be home today,' she said finally. It seemed to make her uncomfortable to tell me this.

'That's all right,' I said. 'Just so long as he calls me as soon as he can. I'd like to arrange to meet him tomorrow.' Then it occurred to me that it would not be so easy to find a place where Heinz, a 'one-hundred-percent Jew', could meet me, a soldier in uniform. 'Maybe at the central post office on Spandauer Strasse', I continued. Frau Elsässer looked at me in surprise, and I added hastily, 'But we can settle that later, the main thing is that he call me as soon as possible.'

'I'll tell him when I see him,' his mother said. She seemed troubled. 'It's not about anything bad, I hope?'

'Not at all,' I reassured her, and said good-bye.

'God be with thee,' she said in her Bavarian dialect, trying to smile, 'and *Gut Shabbas*.'

Instead of going back to the Silesian Station I walked in the opposite direction and came upon the Jannowitz Bridge municipal railway station within a few minutes. As I went up the stairs to the platform, I bumped into a young woman who was hurrying in the opposite direction. 'Whoops!' she exclaimed and was about to hurry on, when she stopped short. 'Don't I know you? You're . . . of course! You're Bernt! My goodness, what a surprise!'

It was Ulla. I hadn't seen her for years. She had been our group leader in Red Falcon, and I had liked her very much. We gave each other a big hug as people pushed past us toward the platform. I suggested that she come with me as far as Alexanderplatz and go to a café.

'I'd love to, but let me run home first – I look a mess. Can we make it in an hour or so?' She named a café where we would meet.

She came a little late. She had put on a pretty summer dress and spruced herself up, but I could see how tired and drawn she was.

'They're really pushing us at the plant,' she told me, 'ten or ten-and-a-half hours every day. And I have to be up at five in the morning, so I can't stay long.'

'Where are you working?'

'At the electrical equipment plant in the S-division. S for secret. They have us working so hard you'd think the war was starting next week. My brother works in Wittenau, north of the city, at a branch of Düren Metals where all they make is airplane parts. They're even worse off than we are. They're up to twelve hours a day now, and they're constantly being forced to increase their output – all for 35 marks a week. And half of that gets deducted for dues, food, and contributions. I make 24 marks a week, but I take home only 15. You can't live on that. If we didn't have the garden, we'd starve.'

'I'll come and see you on Sunday,' I said. 'If you have time and are in the mood, we can go somewhere together. I have a lot to tell you – and who knows when we'll see each other again. At Christmas, when I'm discharged, I plant to get out, to England.'

'I hope you make it,' Ulla replied. 'My brother heard his department head saying war would begin by September at the latest. But maybe you'll be lucky. It's really unbearable here – it's enough to make you sick!'

She spoke these last words loudly and a man at the next table craned his neck in our direction, obviously trying to hear our conversation.

'Come,' I said, 'let's go,' and added in a low voice, 'you should be more careful!' I walked her to the station.

On the way she asked me, 'What were you doing in our part of town, if I may ask?'

'I wanted to see Heinz, Heinz Elsässer, but he wasn't home. Maybe I'll get together with him tomorrow. You remember him, don't you? He was in our group – what's the matter?'

She had stopped dead in her tracks and was staring at me. 'When was the last time you saw Heinz?' she asked.

I told her I had been out of touch with him for years. 'But ten days ago he turned up in Düsseldorf looking for me. He left his address, and since I have something to take care of here, which he might be able to help with, I thought . . .'

'I wouldn't, if I were you,' Ulla said, and then fell silent. She seemed to be wondering whether or not to tell me something. We had already reached the station when she made up her mind. 'Listen, I can't prove it, but I'm quite sure Heinz is a spy for the Gestapo,' she whispered so softly that I could barely hear her. 'Last year he was in a concentration camp for six weeks after Kristallnacht, and since they let him out the strangest things have been happening. He goes snooping everywhere, and after he's been in a place there's often a raid. Someone warned me to watch out for him, and just in time, because two days later I ran into him, by chance – or so it seemed. He asked all kinds of questions about my brother – whether he was still in touch with his old friends, that sort of thing. I suppose he wanted to find out whether Max was still involved with the comrades. I put him on the wrong track. "Max is cured," I told him, "he's in the SA now." When he heard that, he took off. So watch out for him!'

'Don't worry, I will! I'm lucky I ran into you.'

We arranged to meet again on Sunday, and then I took the train to Charlottenburg. It was exactly eleven when I reached Aunt Elsbeth's door.

She greeted me warmly, admired my fine uniform, and said it was certainly a good thing that thanks to the Führer we had a strong Luftwaffe – otherwise the Poles might have attacked Berlin by now. Then she brought me a plate with slices of cold roast and potato salad, and asked whether I would like a beer. She described all the work she had to do for the Nazi Women's League, the Winter Aid, and the Nazi People's Welfare.

'Unfortunately there's still so much poverty,' she said, 'although the Führer has done miracles in getting rid of unemployment.'

Soon Uncle Karl arrived, exhausted from the heat and the strenuous air raid wardens' course. He drank a glass of beer with me and then remarked, 'The Gauleiter said we were on the verge of a great test of our strength. What do you suppose he meant by that? I hope it doesn't mean we'll be at war soon.'

'I certainly hope not,' I agreed. He soon went off to bed, very sombre and reflective, not at all in his usual jocular mood.

Aunt Elsbeth waited until he was out of the room. Then she said softly, 'He's so troubled, especially since he found out I returned the ship tickets.' She noticed I looked perplexed. 'Our silver wedding anniversary will be in September,' she explained, 'and I thought Karl would really enjoy a holiday. I reserved a cabin on the *Wilhelm Gustloff* for a cruise to Madeira in September. It's supposed to be a beautiful ship.' There 'Strength through Joy' trips were in great demand, and the tickets must have been very hard to obtain.

'Why did you return them?' I asked.

After a moment's hesitation she confided, 'Well, I'll tell you, but you mustn't breathe a word to anyone, because you never know where such information ends up – the enemy is listening everywhere! Gudrun told me this a week ago in absolute confidence: the *Gustloff* isn't going to Madeira in September, because it'll be needed elsewhere – as a troop transport.'

'So that means there will be war by September?'

'Sh! Not so loud! Gudrun knows there will be. She works for an SS Gruppenführer – they're seeing each other, too – and he told her . . .' She stopped and looked nervously toward the door. 'Here comes Gudrun. Not a word!'

Through the open window we could hear a car door closing, and a male voice saying, 'Well, Heil Hitler, darling!' Then the car sped off, and a minute later my cousin Gudrun appeared, her eyes glowing, her face radiant.

'Mother, Mother, we're engaged!' she exclaimed. 'And on Sunday Horst-Eberhard will come by at eleven to speak with you – isn't it fantastic?'

Then she caught sight of me, and we greeted each other warmly.

'Congratulations!' I said. 'I'll leave you alone. I'm sure you have a lot to talk about. Good night.'

The next morning after breakfast I called up Uncle Erich. He was happy to hear I wanted to visit him, and enquired after my parents. 'But what brings you to Berlin?'

'I asked for a special leave to come here,' I said. 'I have something important to discuss with you – if it's true you're counsel for a certain organisation . . .'

There was a pause, and I could imagine his astonished face. No doubt he was thinking hard and twirling his moustache. 'Yes, that's what I am,' he confirmed in a markedly different tone of voice. I could tell he was reluctant to say more.

'Listen,' he said suddenly, 'we'd better meet somewhere in town – I just remembered that today's Saturday, and Frau Malzan, who looks after my place for me, won't be coming in. When she doesn't pick up after me, it's not very presentable. Do you remember where we met last time?'

'Yes,' I answered somewhat hesitantly, because I did not recall exactly where it had been. That meeting had taken place years before.

'All right, let's say we meet there for tea this afternoon around four. Does that suit you? Splendid. And tell me, are you still in the service of the Fatherland?'

Now all became clear, and I said with much relief, 'Yes, of course. I'm in uniform, and I'm looking forward to the lovely view – there's only one such view in Berlin, isn't that true?'

The place he had chosen, whose name he had only hinted at, in case our conversation was being listened to, was the large Fatherland Café, which on a Saturday afternoon would surely be crowded. It was located directly on Potsdamer Platz, where five of Berlin's busiest arteries converged, and was a favourite of visitors from the provinces.

It was four on the dot when I entered the tearoom, which was as crowded as I had expected. After a moment I caught sight of Uncle Erich, sitting alone at a table by the window. He stood up and gave me a friendly nod. As I went over to him, a waitress came toward me, balancing two trays at once and smiling at me. 'The major is expecting you,' she remarked as she passed. Fortunately she failed to notice my astonishment. Uncle Erich did have a sort of military air, though I could not pinpoint what accounted for it. Perhaps it was the close-cropped grey hair, which made his broad face appear even more angular, or the trimmed moustache, which had been bushier in earlier years, or his emphatically erect carriage, or the cut of his light grey suit. In any case, I greeted him in strict military style. I quickly took off my cap, clamped it under my left arm, removed my right glove, and with a proper bow grasped the hand he extended to me.

He took me by the shoulders, gave me a brief hug, and whispered as he did so, 'Please excuse the play-acting.' Then he stepped back a pace, looked me up and down, taking in the fine fit of my dress uniform, nodded with satisfaction, and urged me to be seated.

I handed my white cap and my white kid gloves to the waitress, who had come to take my order.

'Excellent pastry here,' Uncle Erich informed me in the clipped style and casual accent of the Prussian officer class. 'Recommend the poppyseed cake.' He spoke fairly loudly, and you would think he had spent most of his life in the officers' casinos of the famous old Prussian regiments.

Then the orchestra began to play. The first piece was 'Blood-red Roses', the second 'Beautiful Gigolo', and the third was the current hit 'Bel Ami'. While the music filled the air, I told him what I had learned from Herr Desch.

'It might be possible to save two hundred people during the next few weeks,' I concluded, explaining that the governing council of the Berlin Jewish community had only to make the selection and arrange transportation to the Rhineland. All the rest would be taken care of by the 'friends'.

He listened very attentively. During the short pauses between musical numbers he would remark in a voice that could be heard at the neighbouring tables, 'Cigarette, m'boy?' or 'Was out for a gallop through the Tiergarten this morning with another officer from the regiment – keeps you fit' or 'Must take you to the new show at the Admiral – superb!'

He explained that the governing council of the Berlin Jewish community, at whose disposal he had placed himself as an unofficial consultant, had received general information about the planned rescue mission and had already chosen the émigrés – about 180 boys and girls between sixteen and twenty-one, who wanted to go to America and had taken language and trades courses, and another sixty children from an orphanage that was destroyed during Kristallnacht, along with the orphanage staff and several other persons in particular danger. They had been waiting only for the precise details.

'So you've come to the right man,' he said softly. 'And the transportation to the Rhineland is all arranged.' During the last ten days of July a large moving van with a trailer would deliver the emigrants to the destinations in the Rhineland that Herr Desch had chosen. The van would make the trip by night over the course of four or five days. All that remained was to find someone in the Rhineland who could notify the people in Berlin before departure that everything was ready.

'The person who'll do that is a lady,' I said. 'You might want to take down her number.'

'Bel ami, bel ami, bel ami!' The music was coming to an end, and in the five minutes during which the musicians paused for refreshments, Uncle Erich remained silent, clearly thinking very hard.

'Do you have a request, major?' the violinist inquired as he came over to our table. Uncle Erich, lost in thought, gave him a cordial nod. 'Something by Linke, perhaps? That'd be colossal,' he drawled, brushing his hand over his moustache.

'Some day I may need to ask you and your friends for help,' he said in a low voice, as the music began again. 'I'm in the process of establishing a second identity, Major Erich von Elken, retired. I even have a second apartment, in a little pension by the Botanical Gardens – just in case. Fortunately I still have some money, and very steady nerves. Come what may, I have no intention of letting myself be treated like vermin by these scoundrels. I feel like a swindler, but it's only in self-defence.'

I realised that such role-playing must be taking a great toll on this dignified, respected lawyer. 'We'll be at war in a few weeks, Uncle Erich – by the beginning of September at the latest. Shouldn't one . . . wouldn't it be better to simply disappear, while there's still time?'

He looked at me. 'You may be right, but when one is brought up as we were, one stays as long as he's needed . . .'

I did not know what he meant by 'we' – perhaps his generation, or the old, established Jewish families of Berlin – but I secretly hoped that this 'we' included me.

That evening I telephoned Herr Desch as arranged.

'How's the merchandise?' he asked.

'You'll be getting your material – even a bit more. The quota has been increased, all very carefully selected merchandise. The shipping's arranged too.'

'Well, that's splendid. But I really need that shipment urgently. The customers are pressuring me. One of them wants everything ready before the manoeuvres ball; another wants his order filled this month, because the party season is about to begin around here. Can it be sent off by next week?'

I understood that the situation must have changed. Apparently manoeuvres were planned which could jeopardise the whole operation.

'I'll see to it right away. I'd better start back early. I'll stop by to see you tomorrow as soon as I get there.'

Fortunately I reached Uncle Erich by telephone at his old apartment on Lietzenburger Strasse. He agreed at once to start the emigrants moving the following Monday. 'The sooner the better,' he said. 'We're happy to be able to clear out our warehouse.'

The next morning, right after breakfast, I took the railway to the Jannowitz Bridge Station to say good-bye to Ulla, for I now intended to depart after lunch and spend the rest of my special leave in Düsseldorf.

She was very surprised to see me there so early. I stayed only a few minutes, for I could tell I was in her way. She had just put on a large pot of laundry to boil, and was sitting at the kitchen table with a pile of clothes to mend and socks to darn.

'Sunday is the only day I get,' she said apologetically.

I explained to her that I had to leave earlier than I had originally planned and had come to say good-bye.

'Did everything work out all right?' he asked.

'Yes, and thank God without any help from Heinz.'

'Did he call you already? No? If you happen to run into him, please be careful. Basically he's not a bad person,' she added thoughtfully, 'but I'm sure they gave him the full treatment and threatened to do it again if he didn't keep up a steady flow of information.'

'Are you sure of that?'

She did not answer, but the look on her face was enough. As she saw me to the door, she said, 'Take good care of yourself – things are getting more and more dangerous. And if you happen to be in Berlin again, come by to see us.'

Shortly before noon I was back at Aunt Elsbeth and Uncle Karl's. Their future son-in-law, the SS Gruppenführer, had just left, and they were still in a dither from the great honour that had been bestowed on them. Aunt Elsbeth was hoping he would stay to lunch, and had been busy in the kitchen since early morning. But the Gruppenführer had excused himself, pleading urgent business, and he and Gudrun had driven straight back to the 'office', although it was Sunday. Aunt Elsbeth described to me the marvellous black Horch which had waited for him in front of the building, with a uniformed chauffeur *and* an adjutant.

I pretended to be properly impressed and then asked whether anyone had called for me.

'Oh, yes,' Aunt Elsbeth said, 'I almost forgot. A friend of yours – Heinz was the only name he gave. I told him you had to leave early. He wanted to know which train you were taking – maybe he'll come to see you off.'

I got to the station a few minutes early, went in by the entrance near the luggage area, and from a distance watched the stairs leading up to the long-distance trains. Heinz was near the barrier looking out for me. I could not spot anyone who looked as though he were shadowing Heinz. So I went over to him, and we greeted each other. He looked pale, and seemed very edgy.

He said he would walk me to the platform, where the train was just pulling in. As we climbed the stairs he asked his first question: 'Did you see any of our old friends? Anyone from the group?'

'I was visiting relatives – my cousin just got engaged.'

'Didn't you see anyone else? My mother mentioned you said you had something very important to discuss with my father. What was it about?'

I had found an empty compartment, and he came in with me, saying, 'I'll ride with you as far as the Charlottenburg local stop. That'll give us a chance to talk a little.'

'Why are you spying on people, Heinz?' I asked.

His eyes widened and he turned even paler. 'What makes you think that? Who have you –' he began very indignantly, and then suddenly broke down. With a sob he gripped my arm tightly. 'You have no idea!' he said almost tonelessly, 'You don't know what they did to me . . . and what they threaten to do . . .' Tears streamed down his face, and he made no attempt to wipe them away.

'Why don't you just get out of here, Heinz?'

'Because then . . . then . . .' he began, and I saw the despair in his eyes, 'then they'll haul my mother in.'

I knew how much she meant to him, and suddenly I felt tremendous pity for Heinz.

The train pulled out of the station. In a few minutes it would be stopping at the Charlottenburg Station; that was all the time I had to persuade him to leave Berlin, not just for his own sake, but also for the sake of the many people whose lives he would destroy.

'When do you have to report back?'

He was still sobbing. With a terrified look he said, 'Next Saturday. It's always on Saturday. Why? What are you thinking of?'

'You're coming home with me – I don't want to hear any but's. I can promise that your parents will be able to follow within the week, and by next Saturday all of you will be over the border and in safety. You have to do it. There won't be another chance.'

'You're crazy! I can't – I don't even have enough money for a ticket.'

He protested a bit more, but I caught a glimmer of hope in his eyes.

'You take my military ticket. A lot of soldiers travel in civilian dress on Sunday leave. I'll handle the conductor somehow.'

The train had a three-minute stop in Charlottenburg. Before it pulled out of the station I had persuaded him to come along.

Right outside our compartment window was a large billboard with a poster, still wet with the glue with which it had just been mounted: 'Be on your guard in conversations! The enemy is listening!' The picture showed soldiers and civilians at a tavern table, and behind them the looming black outline of an eavesdropper.

The door to our compartment banged open and a mother with two little girls and a private in the Luftwaffe joined us. The private at once opened the window and leaned out.

The train began to move.

The private bawled, 'Stop! Don't go yet! Karl! Egon! Where the hell are you?'

We were already pulling out of the station, and the train was picking up speed. The private closed the window and sat down next to me.

'Damn!' he said, 'My two friends didn't make it, and I have their tickets.'

'Take it easy,' I calmed him, 'they'll be fine. Anyway, I could use one of those tickets – I don't know what happened to mine.'

NINETEEN

The Beginning of the End

'When is the Führer going to act?' Uncle Franz asked. 'The martyr-dom of the Germans in Poland is intolerable!'

I was having supper with him and Aunt Käthe. This last week in August their hotel had no guests at all, and even the restaurant was empty. Some of the regulars preferred to be outdoors in the hot weather, while others sat at home, glued to their radios for further bulletins. The Nazis' propaganda against Poland had turned into overt agitation. The negotiations among the British, the French, and the Russians over common guarantees for Poland had run aground. People spoke openly of the day when Hitler would strike. The newspaper carried headlines like 'Warsaw Threatens Bombardment of Danzig; Incredible Proof of Polish Megalomania', or 'Three German Passenger Planes Shot at by Poles; German Families Flee Polish Monsters; Flames devour German Farmhouses in Corridor'.

'What I simply don't understand is why the Führer got mixed up with the Bolshevists,' Uncle Franz continued.

Two days earlier, on 23 August, Hitler had announced the sign-ing of the German-Soviet non-aggression pact. The news had the impact of a bomb. Neither the Nazis nor their opponents could understand how the pact had come about or what it implied – aside from the fact that Hitler now had a free hand to do as he liked with the Poles. But was that enough to justify entering into a treaty with the Communists? Old-line conservatives as well as many Nazi stalwarts were profoundly shocked by Hitler's strategy.

'This can't possibly turn out well,' Uncle Franz remarked.

While Uncle Franz went on, the telephone rang, and Aunt Käthe said it was for me. I had arranged for Herr Desch to call me there, since I could not receive calls at my barracks. 'The merchandise has arrived,' he told me, 'and your friend Heinz and his parents are well.'

That meant they had reached New York! My great relief at the success of the rescue mission was mixed with a touch of envy.

'How about leave on Sunday!' Herr Desch enquired in his usual indifferent tone.

'That may not work out. We're sitting here with our bags packed, ready to hit the road.'

'Is that so? Well, that may change yet. Have you been listening to the news?'

When I returned to the table, I found out what Herr Desch had been referring to. The radio had just announced that Great Britain had concluded a mutual assistance pact with Poland.

'That's all we need!' Uncle Franz exclaimed indignantly. 'Now our English friends have gone over to the enemy, and *we're* allied with the Bolshevists.'

That evening in the barracks Erwin told me that the 'mob drill' had been postponed. We had been scheduled to move out the following night. 'Adolf got cold feet,' Erwin commented.

But the shock of British guarantees for Poland did not last long. The next morning, Saturday, 26 August 1939, the three of us were sitting in our communications car – Erwin, the fanatic Nazi Barczustowski, and I – listening to the news bulletins on all the stations that came in. The British, and even Mussolini and the Pope, were trying to find a peaceful solution to the conflict over Poland, we heard.

'I hope they succeed,' Barczustowski said in a subdued voice. But by evening it had become clear that all the European powers, including Fascist Italy and England, now allied with Poland, had merely been scrambling to keep themselves out of war. We realised that Hitler would now pounce.

At 11.00 P.M. we had just gone to bed when the sirens began to wail. Shortly before midnight the division was ready to move out.

'Now the Polacks' goose is cooked,' Barczustowski gloated. 'Next week we'll be in Warsaw, and then it'll be on to the east. The German people need Lebensraum . . .'

'Shut your trap!' Erwin shouted. 'You'll end up in front of a court-martial, Barczustowski, for giving away military secrets!' Then he ripped open the envelope that contained our marching orders, read them, and grinned. 'Listen to this, folks!'

Barczustowski and I – Erwin's communications crew – and the motorcycle courier Pliechelko, gathered around him.

'Our unit is to move to a forward position, which we must reach by 3.30 A.M. tomorrow. Until further notice there will be an absolute radio blackout. The headlights must be equipped with shields. Pliechelko is to ride five hundred metres ahead of the communications car and secure dangerous intersections. March speed: 50 kilometres per hour. Any questions?'

'Where are we headed?' Pliechelko asked.

'First we go to Paderborn, and then we follow the Reich highway west to . . .'

'West?'

'Don't interrupt, Barczustowski! West to Ratingen. There we proceed westward again. Our "mob" position is in Kaiserswerth, on the Rhine, eight kilometres north of Düsseldorf. And then the Polish goose will be cooked, eh, Barczustowski?'

From Sunday, 27 August, to Thursday, 31 August, 1939, our radio unit spent a quiet but very tense week at a little hotel on the Rhine, where we were billeted.

Since a radio blackout had been ordered, we had nothing to do but listen to news bulletins from morning till night. Now and then Pliechelko rode his motorcycle to the nearby staff headquarters or into town on various official errands, such as procuring a particular brand of aftershave lotion for the company commander or clothespins for the field kitchen.

I of course went along with Pliechelko to 'guide' him, as Erwin put it, since I knew my way around Düsseldorf. That meant that, in spite of all leaves being cancelled, I got to see everyone again, my mother, Aunt Annie, Fräulein Bonse, and Herr Desch. This time they were all certain that full-scale war was imminent.

And indeed, on the morning of Friday, 1 September, Hitler's decision was broadcast: 'And so I have determined to speak with Poland in the same language Poland has been using toward us for months now . . . My love of peace and my boundless patience must not be mistaken for weakness or cowardice . . . Since early this morning at 5.45, fire is being returned, and from now on each bomb will be answered with a bomb!'

I rode into town with Pliechelko. No crowds had gathered. We saw no trace of rejoicing, certainly none of the wild enthusiasm that Germans had shown when war broke out in August 1914. Here and there small groups of people clustered around the newsstands, talking quietly among themselves, depressed and anxious. No one waved to us soldiers or pressed bouquets into our hands, as they did in 1914.

'They don't believe it yet,' Pliechelko said. 'They probably thought everything would turn out all right this time, too.'

Then he wheeled the motorcycle around and we rode back to Kaiserswerth.

TWENTY

Wartime

'Oh, yes, I remember perfectly what it was like, back in the autumn of 1939, right after the war broke out . . . All the women in the neighbourhood and at work felt so worried and frightened. And the men who were still at home didn't say much, even the fascist Labour Front fellows, who usually liked to talk big. I was terrified for my boy, Georgie. He was with the infantry, and they sent him straight to the front, to Poland . . .'

Anna Neuber, a tall, gaunt woman with wispy white hair, was, she told me, 'as old as this century.' She showed me an old photo of herself and her son, both of them big, strong people, she in a white blouse and dark skirt, he in his army uniform. He looked about twenty.

Now Frau Neuber was living on a tiny retirement pension in a suburb of Munich, earning a little extra doing errands for the housebound residents of St. Martin's Home for the Aged, and by tending a few graves in the nearby cemetery.

'Luckily I hadn't been called up for compulsory service yet,' Frau Neuber said. 'I had a regular job at the *Munich Daily News*, as a packer on the night shift. We got to see the paper right off the press, and I remember what a shock it was to read the headline that night of the first of September, '39: "Heavy Fighting in Gleiwitz" – that's where my Georgie was! Out of the blue the Poles had begun firing on us and had even seized the radio transmitter . . .'

Apparently she still believed the Nazi version, that 'out of the blue' Polish partisans had swarmed over the border at several points, fired on Germans, and stormed the Gleiwitz transmitter.

It was long after the war that the truth finally came out. On 17 August 1939, at the urging of Reinhard Heydrich, head of the Security Service, Hitler ordered the director of military intelligence, Admiral Canaris, to procure two hundred and fifty Polish uniforms, Polish weapons, and military paybooks for use in a 'special SS operation'. On the afternoon of 31 August 1939, SS Sturmbannführer Alfred Naujoks received his orders: he and his 'Poles' (SS men from Upper Silesia wearing Polish uniforms, carrying Polish weapons, and trained to obey commands in Polish) were to launch 'operations' culminating in the attack on the German transmitter in Gleiwitz.

There the fake Poles fired shots in all directions, herded the staff into the cellar and locked them in, interrupted the broadcast with inflammatory speeches in Polish, and then made a quick getaway. Since Heydrich felt that 'physical evidence is essential for the foreign press and German propaganda purposes', actual bodies were placed at the scene of the 'attack' – prisoners from a concentration camp, who had been dressed in Polish uniforms and killed by injection shortly before the beginning of the operation. The SS referred to them cynically as 'canned goods'. Only one dead 'Pole' was dropped off at Gleiwitz – there would have been little resistance by the unarmed staff of the transmitter. The other corpses were deposited near the customs house at Hochlinden and by a forester's lodge close to the order, where similar scenes had been staged, provoking fire from the German side. Thus barely nine hours before the scheduled beginning of the attack on Poland the SD manufactured reasons for German 'retaliation', reasons subsequently publicised by the German and foreign press.

Even though Frau Anna Neuber still believed the old story of German 'retaliation', if it had been up to her, she said, there would have been no war, if only for the sake of her boy and all the others.

'The second week of September,' she recalled, 'about ten or twelve days after the beginning of the war, the first obituaries with Iron Crosses began to appear in the paper – saying the boys had fallen "For the Führer, the Volk, the Reich." I was so worried about Georgie I didn't get a single night's sleep.

'While I was scanning the death notices, the other women always read the official announcements first, checking the latest food allocations. I never managed to get by with my ration stamps. What I needed most were fat and sugar, so I traded points from my clothing allowance for stamps for cooking fat. Some of the girls wanted a stylish bathing suit or a new brassiere rather than food. Often the ones who had family out in the country could spare some of their fat rations. On Sundays someone from home might bring a piece of bacon or a jar of lard. I didn't have anyone to give me such things. I guess I could have traded my tobacco rations for some margarine, but I needed the couple of cigarettes they let women have for the packages I sent to my boy. Most of my sugar stamps went for that too – now and then you could get a chocolate bar or other sweets, and my Georgie had a sweet tooth . . .'

Rationing had been imposed on 28 August 1939, four days before the outbreak of war. It affected all the basic necessities – bread and other baked goods, flour, potatoes, cereals, meat and sausage, sugar, jam, cooking fat, nuts, cheese, tea, coffee, even coffee substitutes, soap, washing powder, coal and charcoal, textiles, and countless other items, notably shoes and leather.

These goods were now available only in limited quantities and only in return for government ration stamps or special entitlement forms. For tobacco, there were special smokers' cards, marked *M* for men, *W* for women – and women received only half the ration granted to men. And that was regarded as quite a concession, considering the Nazi slogan 'A German woman does not smoke!' But with all the groceries in short supply and women frustrated by shortages, long waits in line, and speed-ups at work, the government felt obliged to let them have a few cigarettes by way of consolation.

'I didn't really mind that meat and butter were almost impossible to find,' Frau Neuber told me, 'since I could hardly afford them anyway. But margarine was scarce, too; that was where we really felt the shortages. I didn't care though, because by October the war in Poland was over and my boy had got out alive. At Christmas in '39 he came home on leave for the first time. I rounded up all the extra rations I could. I gave the butcher's wife eighteen points from my clothing card so she could buy herself a nightgown, and in return she let me have a nice roast. Besides, Georgie brought some things with him from Poland – canned sausages and lard, and even a goose! That was the best Christmas I can remember. And we had some hope that peace would come soon. Hitler had mentioned it himself . . .'

She smiled as she spoke, but suddenly she turned very grave. A thought had cast a pall over her happy memories of her son's home-coming and the Polish goose. 'I noticed right away that Georgie had something on his mind. Then on the day after Christmas he told me what it was.'

During the very first days of the war, Private Georg Neuber had been a witness to the cruelty of German SS and 'special operations units' toward the Polish people. Near Naklo his company saw about eighty Jews being murdered. In a village close to Bromberg they had found bodies of more than fifty young Poles in a schoolhouse. Not one of them was over twenty, and all had been shot in the neck. Soon after that, Georg's company stood by as about a hundred Poles, with priests among them, were shot as hostages on Bromberg's main square. Soldiers from Georg's company just barely escaped being assigned to those mass executions, but in the following weeks, Georg was obliged to witness a good deal more. Time and again, Jewish men, women, and even children were hauled away and 'liquidated', allegedly for sniping – but the same fate befell many Polish teachers, professors, and owners, engineers, and pastors.

'Georgie was terrified that they might make him take part in the executions,' Frau Neuber said. 'You have to understand that his father was also shot by soldiers – right here in Munich in 1919 – and he was completely innocent! They thought he belonged to Spartacus!'

Anton Neuber had been killed in the tumultuous days after the Reichswehr and the right-wing Freikorps put an end to the soviet republic that had been proclaimed by workers and intellectuals in Munich a few weeks earlier. Soldiers burst into the tavern where members of Neuber's Catholic Journeymen's club were gathered to discuss a play they planned to perform. Among the stripped and horribly mutilated bodies of the twenty-one club members found later in the cellar was that of Anton Neuber, the twenty-year-old father-to-be. The Catholic Journeymen had protested that they weren't Communists, but to no avail. Only six of them, knocked unconscious and seriously wounded, survived to tell what happened.

'I didn't want to have anything to do with politics after that,' the old woman said. 'I kept myself and the boy out of that whole business, and we always did exactly what we were told. That's why I warned my boy at Christmas in '39 never to protest, always to obey his superiors, no matter what, and to pray to God that he would never be forced to do anything that was wrong. Besides, I told him, the war'll be over soon. Things looked pretty hopeful when Poland was conquered and the West didn't lift a finger . . . If only there had been more to eat and we didn't have to work so hard – I never left the printing works before 3.00 A.M., and that was after doing housework and standing in line outside stores all day. And then the long walk home during the blackout – you weren't even allowed to use a torch! No, we weren't really at war during that winter of '39 to '40, but it wasn't peace either.'

I had heard almost the same words a few days earlier from an older man who had been an officer when the war began, a first lieutenant in charge of an infantry regiment. He, too, informed me at the outset that he had 'never paid attention to politics' and had 'stayed out of everything'. He had been 'only a soldier'. Nevertheless, this stout but still very energetic man with white hair had risen to the rank of lieutenant general by the end of the war. Now he was enjoying his retirement on a generous pension in his country house in Upper Bavaria.

In December 1939, Lieutenant Wolfgang Scholz and his regiment had been stationed west of Karlsruhe, guarding the West Wall. He was 'in despair', he told me, because along the entire 170-kilometre front between Karlsruhe and Basel nothing was stirring – 'almost like in peacetime'.

'My gentlemen and I,' he said, referring to the officers of his regiment, 'had followed the blitzkrieg in Poland with envy – it took only eighteen days to achieve total victory, and decorations and promotions were to be had in plenty, whereas all we got was practice in sitting. During the second week of the war the French made a few inconsequential forays, just to reassure their Polish allies, but aside from that, the war for us consisted only of occasional small spy missions and a sprinkling of artillery fire. There was no way for my gentlemen and me to pick up any 'tinsel' for our chests, and we felt we deserved a turn.'

As he continued to describe the tedious 'sitzkrieg' on the Upper Rhine, I glanced around his comfortable living room. On the wall across from the picture window with its magnificent view of Alpine meadows and peaks, hung numerous hunting trophies. A photograph of Scholz stood on the mantelpiece. It showed him in a general's uniform, wearing the Knight's Cross and numerous other war decorations. So his wish for 'tinsel' had been fulfilled after all.

'We were prepared for the worst, that is, that peace might "break out", as we said in those days, without our ever making contact with the enemy. To add insult to injury, the propaganda boys sent us mountains of pamphlets we were supposed to shoot across to the enemy. "Frenchmen! Do you want to die for Danzig?" they said, and "We don't want war with you! Stay within your Maginot Line, and we'll stay within our West Wall."'

To his dismay, huge billboards had also been set up along the Palatine border and the right bank of the Rhine. They announced in letters visible from a considerable distance the peaceful intentions of the German leadership. From morning till night large loudspeakers bombarded the Maginot Line with French and German popular music, interrupted now and then by short appeals to the French soldiers not to view 'your German comrades' as the enemy.

'After the end of the Polish campaign the French withdrew the troops that had advanced three kilometres or so into German territory,' General Scholz recalled. 'It was then that we first realised what our peace propaganda had achieved. We had obviously made an impression on the French, and now they, too, wanted to demonstrate their peaceful intentions. As they withdrew, they left slogans on the walls of some of the evacuated villages along the border, defeatist slogans like "Down with war! Long live peace!" and so on. Along the Upper Rhine, near Breisach, French and German troops even

engaged in joint shooting practice, using a large straw-stuffed effigy of
the British prime minister, Chamberlain, which they had hoisted up
on a crane. It really was a *drôle de guerre*, as the French called it, a
peculiar war.'

On 6 October 1939, Hitler declared to the hastily summoned
Reichstag that he permanently withdrew his claim on the Saar region.
He asserted that his intentions toward France had always been
peaceable and that he had done everything in his power 'to rid the
German people of the notion that an unalterable tradition of enmity
existed between themselves and the French, and to inspire them
instead with respect for the great accomplishments of the French
people . . .'

He also asserted that peace with England had always been one
of his chief goals: 'I still believe that there can be true peace in Europe
and the world only when Germany and England reach an
understanding . . .'

'It was pure ingratiation,' General Scholz commented, 'but oddly
enough, neither Paris nor London responded.'

And then 'finally', preparations for a German attack on the Western
Front began. The troops on the West Wall were denied furloughs,
tank units arrived from Poland and took up positions on the right bank
of the Rhine, and Scholz and his 'gentlemen' had hopes that their turn
might come after all.

But the attack was repeatedly postponed, fourteen times in all,
either because Mussolini wanted another attempt to mediate, or
because weather conditions seemed unfavourable, or because
ammunition was lacking, or once, on 9 November 1939, because the
previous night a dynamite explosion had disrupted a celebration at
which Hitler and some of his oldest comrades were commemorating
their unsuccessful beer-hall putsch of 1923; seven of the Ancient
Combatants were killed and sixty-three wounded. Hitler himself
barely escaped the assassination attempt.

'Around New Year's we realised that nothing would happen before
May, at least not on the Western Front,' General Scholz continued.
'During the long wait, a negotiated peace might even be reached with
the Western powers; and the prospect depressed us. Please don't get
me wrong!' he added hastily, 'it was wartime, after all, and the
opportunity seemed too good to miss. Our victory over Poland and the
pact with the Soviet Union had left us with our rear safe, in contrast to
1914, when major forces were tied up in the East. Czechoslovakia had
already been taken care of, and there was no fear of attack from Italy or
the Balkans. So we could concentrate all our forces, most of them

already tested in battle, on the breakthrough in the West, where the enemy was demoralised and far inferior to us in battle strength. From the military point of view it would have been utter folly to let such an opportunity slip through our fingers!'

He then described the bitterness he had felt as a young lieutenant after the First World War, when the Treaty of Versailles required a reduction of the German armed forces to 100,000 men, leaving three out of four officers without a job. Even though the Reichswehr finally found a position for him, Scholz's prospects for promotion were almost nonexistent. Not until Hitler seized power did he recover a degree of optimism. 'And when the long-awaited moment arrived, and we were prepared down to the smallest detail, it was utterly maddening that my regiment and I couldn't be there, but instead had to spend month after month on a so-called front doing nothing!'

For Frau Neuber the new year brought very different worries:

'Right after New Year in 1940 I got a card from the labour bureau. I had to report there and was assigned to compulsory service. The girls felt very sorry for me when I resigned from the printing works, because I was being sent to work in a munitions factory. Instead of going to work late in the afternoon, I had to be at the factory – way out in Allach – at 6.00 A.M., which meant I had to leave the house before five to get there on time. The women had to work a twelve-hour shift, and when we came home, completely worn out, the shops were closing or had already closed, or if they were open, they had nothing left by the time we got there. And prices kept going up, even though the government said it had frozen prices and no one was supposed to profit from the war. The manufacturers and retailers managed to find more and more new ways to raise prices. Before the war you could buy margarine for 63 pfennigs a pound. Three months later, in the winter of '39 to '40, it cost 98 pfennigs! And I had to count every pfennig. In the printing works I earned 42 marks net in a week, but out in Allach, the women doing compulsory service all got only 35 marks; and 6.50 of that went on transportation, 4.90 for the cafeteria, and 90 pfennings a week for the Winter Aid. After I had paid my rent and bills I had barely one mark a day left for everything else – food, laundry, clothing, repairs. And I couldn't earn anything on the side, because in the evening I was just too tired to clean offices, as I'd done earlier. When I finally got home after shopping, I could have fallen asleep standing up. Luckily we didn't have night air raids that first year, or I probably would have collapsed; many women in our factory did later on. They couldn't take the pace, especially the older ones, and that wasn't surprising when you consider how badly we ate.'

She went on to describe the ordeal of working in the munitions factory, where the quotas kept going up. In February and March of 1940 the women often had to work overtime – ostensibly because a major offensive was pending on the Western Front. As the factory manager put it, 'Everyone has to work to the utmost for Führer, Volk, and Fatherland.'

'The factory manager was an evil fellow. He was always snooping around, and wouldn't let the women stop to catch their breath. He stood outside the rest room door with his watch in his hand: "You've been in there a minute and a half too long again, Frau Neuber! If that happens one more time, you'll have to work an extra hour." He was always chasing the younger women and giving them the easier jobs. That meant he had to drive the older women even harder. And he was always boasting that we had a model National Socialist plant and had to maintain the highest productivity. He constantly railed against the Jews, who he claimed had instigated the war to enslave Germany. I felt sorry for the Jews. They were even worse off than we were – the Kohns, who lived around the corner from us, lost their fabric store and had their apartment wrecked, and Marx, the watchmaker, committed suicide after they looted his shop. I saw it myself. There was nothing you could do. No one could help them . . . And you know, sometimes I still thought it would all be over soon, that Georgie would be on his way home. I believed it until 1943, when I heard that he had died in Russia.'

TWENTY-ONE

By the Shores of the North Sea

In February 1940, when Frau Neuber was working at the munitions factory and First Lieutenant Scholz was in his requisitioned villa in Karlsruhe, full of despair at not seeing combat, I was on the island of Sylt as a private in the Luftwaffe.

The post was monotonous and time passed slowly, weighing heavily on everyone. We all longed to get away from that bleak island, get rid of our uniforms, and go home to normal life.

Our communications unit now had two additions: the 'double doctor', a scientist with doctorates in two fields who had been called up in September along with other reservists, and a jolly Rhinelander whom we called Little Hans, although he was ten or twelve years older than us; he had a degree in meteorology. Except for Barczustowski, no one in our unit had any warm feelings for Nazis, and our commanding officer, Major Zobel, let us do pretty much as we liked. In civilian life he had engaged in behavioural research at a southern German university, and his assignment to our unit had resulted from a misunderstanding on the part of the Luftwaffe's personnel department: someone there thought behavioural research was a scientific speciality that could be helpful for radio monitoring and aircraft warning services.

We spent most of our time in Sylt at the Strand Café, drinking diluted beer, the only alcoholic beverage available, or at one of two other places open to the many navy, air force and Labour Service personnel stationed on the island – the restaurant in the City of Hamburg hotel and a fishermen's pub.

Before the war the City of Hamburg Hotel had been the 'best hotel in town'. Now it was the only hotel in town, for all other hotels and lodgings had been turned into troop billets. In the restaurant of the City of Hamburg you could eat well and expensively, without ration cards. For that reason officers were its main clientele. Noncommissioned officers and enlisted men seldom went there.

The fishermen's pub, which had no name, was tiny. No beer was served, only grog. If you got to know the owner well, he might give you Scotch whisky, but only after curfew, when just a few patrons with night passes were standing at the bar. The whisky was smuggled in from Rømø, a nearby Danish island. The owner, a grey-haired, taciturn Frisian, claimed it had 'washed up on shore'. He gave you whisky only after you had passed his test: you had to avoid drinking with him 'to the health of our beloved Führer'.

Erwin was the first to pass the test; he asserted that he would prefer to 'drink to the final victory'. Since that time we had been steady patrons. Every second evening we started out at the Strand Café, then moved to the fishermen's pub. We would have been there on the other evenings, too, but we had night duty. It was months since we had been allowed leave on the mainland, and there was really nothing else to do, except perhaps stay in quarters and go to bed.

One evening in February 1940 we were still at the Strand. Erwin, the 'double doctor', and I were playing chess. Whoever wasn't playing looked on or watched Inga, as did all the other fifty or sixty soldiers in the place. Blond Inga was the only female on the entire island as far as we knew, in any case the only woman we laid eyes on in six long winter months on Sylt. From week to week we found her increasingly desirable.

For her part, Inga had gradually relinquished her appointed duties. In the beginning she still actually served the patrons. Soon each man was fetching his own beer, and later bringing the empty bottles back to the crates and stacking the crates outdoors as they got filled up; eventually you had to wipe off the tables yourself, empty the ashtrays, and clear away the glasses. The much-admired Inga just went around and collected the money, though later on she had us bring it to her. In return she now and then played something on her accordion, mainly sailors' songs. Her repertory was small. She knew only half a dozen tunes, and Erwin claimed cynically that she merely pretended to be working the buttons and keys, that actually one of the guests played for her out of sight. Presumably she let him sweep the place out and rinse the glasses after everyone was gone.

It was almost 10.00 when Erwin checkmated the double doctor and suggested that we move to the fishermen's pub.

Inga was just singing the last verse of the song 'Where the North Sea waves lap the shores' when Little Hans came in and joined us.

'This evening I ran into someone who asked after you,' he remarked. 'He was in the restaurant of the City of Hamburg Hotel when I was having dinner there. The proprietor pointed me out to him as someone from the communications unit, and he asked whether I happened to know you. Here's his card – he said he'd expect you to stop by the hotel before 11.00 tonight. Otherwise you can see him there in the morning – he's staying till noon.'

I glanced at the buff-coloured business card which announced: 'H. Desch, Bespoke Tailoring, Finest Fabrics and Superior Workmanship.'

I hurried to the hotel, and immediately spotted Herr Desch in the restaurant. He was chatting with the proprietor, who was evidently amused about something. As I approached the table where they were sitting over a bottle of red wine, I heard the proprietor saying, 'Well, that's splendid! Would you like to take the measurements right away, Herr Desch? Or should we have another glass first?'

But when he caught sight of me in my uniform, an expression of consternation crossed his face. Herr Desch looked up, greeted me warmly, and reassured the proprietor, 'Don't worry, this is my nephew. No need to keep anything from him . . . Sit down, my boy. I'm sure my friend here can find a glass for you.'

I drew up a chair, calling Herr Desch 'Uncle Hubert' – it took me a moment to recall his first name – and hastened to assure him that his 'nephew' was just fine and that the sea air agreed with me. Then I just leaned back and absorbed the conversation; apparently the proprietor was to receive without coupons a suit 'of the best English worsted', and in return he would provide Herr Desch with several cases of vintage French wines.

As they talked, I wondered how Herr Desch could have gotten permission to enter this militarised zone, and why he had come to the island. Herr Desch explained when we were finally alone: 'One of my best customers urgently needed a new uniform. He was promoted to vice admiral and couldn't get away. So since I had business on the mainland nearby . . .' He concluded with a gesture that seemed to say, 'It's all so very simple!'

Of course it was patently absurd that a bespoke tailor from Düsseldorf should have business on the sparsely settled Frisian coast during stormy February weather, and in the middle of wartime, but Herr Desch showed not a flicker of embarrassment.

'Besides,' he continued after a brief pause, 'this was a good time to try to help your Uncle Erich with some problems he has been having.'

'Is anything wrong?' I asked.

'Don't be upset – the situation is under control, except that he'll have to give up his practice for good. And besides, he really needs a change of air. He's considering going back on active duty – after all, he's a major in the reserves – but a few matters still need to be cleared up.'

Now I had an idea of what was going on. The last time I had seen my honorary uncle, Erich Elkan, in Berlin before the outbreak of war, he was just beginning the process of going underground. He had already prepared a new identity for himself. The 'non-Aryan' lawyer and notary with a distinguished practice was metamorphosing into a retired major from a Potsdam regiment with a modest but suitable apartment in a quiet house near the Botanical Gardens.

If Uncle Erich now needed a 'change of air', that probably meant the Gestapo was on his trail and he had to get out of Berlin. But how could he disappear into the Wehrmacht?

'He's not really comfortable in Berlin, and I'm sure a use can be found for him – after all, these days they need every good officer they can get . . . I've been looking around here on Sylt – I've never seen so many staffs, commands, offices, headquarters, and units in one small place. Do people actually find their way through this maze?' Herr Desch wondered.

I agreed that the situation was quite confusing – even more than he might imagine. Each division had its own special assignments, and none bore any relation to the other. Still, I felt it would be risky to try to hide someone on Sylt. Aside from his lack of identification papers and military orders, it would be almost impossible for Uncle Erich to arrange lodgings, food, pay, and all the rest.

But Herr Desch interrupted me: 'And do you have a special assignment, too?'

'Yes, of course,' I replied, and told him what we did: our communications centre received all reports of planes entering the northern coast area. We maintained radio contact with the aircraft stations on Helgoland and Borkum and kept track of the course and the number of planes. When certain indications suggested the likelihood of an enemy attack, we would alert the appropriate flak batteries. We were responsible for the entire northern coastline as well as for Hamburg and Bremen.

Herr Desch seemed impressed. He questioned me about various details: how often we had to issue alerts; whether we also had responsibility for the civilian warning system that sounded the air-raid sirens; and whether Erwin and I, a noncommissioned officer and a private, actually made decisions on our own when we had watch duty?

I explained that so far we hadn't handled anything really serious. To be sure, we issued alerts every other night, but mostly because, according to military regulations, every member of the Wehrmacht on Sylt was entitled to 'combat duty supplements' for being on standby alert: one mark a day, a couple of cigarettes, twenty-five grams of real coffee beans, and sometimes chocolate or elderberry brandy. We arranged to sound the alarm about ten minutes before midnight, ending the alert twenty minutes later. Some coastal battery would promptly begin firing away like mad, so that, technically, the 'combat' extended over two days.

In January we had managed to get in twenty-seven days with combat supplements, and twice, the 'watchfulness of the coastal antiaircraft installations' had been praised in the report of the Wehrmacht High Command.

I went on to explain that the population was not affected by these alerts. The handful of civilians left on Sylt paid no attention to them, and only when larger numbers of enemy planes were approaching did we even have to telephone the air-raid warning centres on the mainland, and this had not yet occurred.

'Of course, if things get serious, it's up to our chief, Major Zobel, to make the decisions. But Major Zobel trust Erwin and me completely, and we haven't given him any cause for complaint.'

Her Desch encouraged me to tell him more about the delightfully unmilitary conditions on Sylt. When I mentioned the inn keeper who smuggled in whisky from Rømø, Herr Desch pricked up his ears. He wanted to know how far it was to Rømø, and how often the runs were made. He also enquired whether one could place civilian telephone calls from Sylt. Finally he said, 'I think Sylt may be the ideal spot for Major von Elken. I shall inform him right away. And perhaps you could ask the innkeeper whether your uncle might go along some time – to Rømø.'

TWENTY-TWO

Operation Weser

About a month after Herr Desch's visit, when I was just returning from overnight duty, I ran into Major Zobel in the corridor of our hotel. It was shortly after 6.00 A.M., and the major was wearing a short, red and white striped bathrobe over his nightshirt.

He answered my salute with a sleepy mumble and was about to vanish into his room when he paused and asked in a friendly way, stifling a yawn, 'Say – you're related to Major von Elken, isn't that right?'

Trying to conceal my surprise, I replied somewhat haltingly, 'Well, not directly, sir, but . . .'

'That doesn't matter, really. He sends you his best . . . What a nice person – I played chess with him last night . . .'

I knew now that Herr Desch had put his plan into effect, and as I was dropping off to sleep I decided to check at the City of Hamburg Hotel; I was certain he would be staying there.

After lunch I called the hotel, and asked tentatively whether Major von Elken was there. The switchboard operator replied at once, 'Of course, let me connect you with his office.'

Before I knew it, a familiar voice was saying in clipped military tones, 'Planning Bureau, Major von Elken speaking.'

I identified myself by rank and name, and Uncle Erich responded, 'Good to hear from you, lad; I was expecting you to call. I think we shouldn't get together right away. I need two or three days to get settled in here. But I'd like to invite you to dinner on my birthday, March the 27th. Will you be able to get away?'

I assured him I would. Only after I hung up did I recall that his birthday actually fell between Christmas and New Year's. So there must be another reason for the invitation. Presumably he wanted to hear from me whether it would prove possible for him to make his way from Sylt to neutral Denmark.

I had already spoken to the tavern keeper. Our conversation had been repeatedly interrupted by people stopping by for a drink, but in the end he had agreed to arrange things with a friend who had authorisation to fish the North Sea and did smuggling runs for him. Because it was an emergency, he promised the trip would cost nothing, and the fishing boat would take Uncle Erich to the Danish mainland – it was safer than Rømø.

During the 'birthday' dinner I conveyed this good news to Uncle Erich in seemingly innocuous scraps of conversation, and he seemed very pleased. Later Major Zobel and two other officers joined us; they greeted Uncle Erich like an old friend, congratulated him on his birthday, and were happy to share a bottle of champagne, which the hotel keeper had produced without a moment's hesitation. In spite of my fine dress uniform, I felt out of place with the officers, and took the first opportunity to get away.

I saw Uncle Erich several times before he left the island, but it was not until many years later that I learned from others what had forced him to flee Berlin and take on the role of a reactivated major on the island of Sylt.

After his collaboration with Herr Desch and others in getting the more than two hundred Jewish children and adolescents to the United States via Holland, Uncle Erich had to go underground at once; the Gestapo had learned of the operation, and was desperate to find its organiser.

But Lawyer Erich Elkan had vanished. His apartment on Lietzenburger Strasse stood vacant, except for a few empty wardrobes, an empty desk, and various pieces of furniture. In August, Herr Elkan had told the building superintendent he was going to Bad Gastein for a longish cure; he gave the man a nice tip and left a forwarding address for mail. At the end of September the superintendent received a card from Herr Elkan, postmarked New York, saying he had emigrated and was giving up the apartment; the superintendent could have for himself any furniture and household goods left behind.

Not until much later did the Gestapo realise that this postcard must have been mailed by someone else. In the meantime, Erich Elkan had registered with the police under the name of Erich von Elken, Major, retired. With his knowledge of legal forms and the authority he commanded as an officer, Uncle Erich had equipped himself with impressive false papers.

To discover what had happened to him next, I went to Berlin to retrace his steps. After some investigation, I found the apartment where Uncle Erich had established himself as Major von Elken. It was the large house that he had spoken of, near the Botanical Gardens. I was greeted there by Frau Gussi Hohlbaum, a small woman in her mid-sixties.

'Of course I remember him,' she said, after I introduced myself and explained the purpose of my visit. 'I was twenty-five at the time. Mother took in four or five long-term lodgers, older gentlemen, mostly high-ranking civil servants or professors. We never had any trouble with them, except in this one case. Major von Elken, or Herr Elkan, I should say, was our only officer. That is, he claimed to be one, and we had no reason to doubt him – he was so convincing!' She sighed, still smarting from the deception to which she and her mother had fallen prey.

Frau Hohlbaum showed me the room they had given him: 'It was our best room, with its own bath and a lovely terrace. Of course it was furnished differently then, except for the bookcase – that was already there and Major von Elken didn't mind keeping it in his room. It contained my late father's library, and the major asked if he could borrow a book now and then.'

I glanced at the titles of the books, neatly arranged in the massive oak piece from the Wilhelmine era: Hans Friedrich Blunck's *The Volk Awakens*, Hans Grimm's *Volk without Lebensraum*, Edwin Erich Dwinger's *We Summon Germany*, and many similar works. On a higher shelf I spotted Julius Streicher's *The Talmud Revolution and other Essays*, Alfred Rosenberg's *The Myth of the Twentieth Century*, Philipp Bouhler's *Battle for Germany*, and finally a luxury leatherbound edition of Hitler's *Mein Kampf*. Next to it I was surprised to see two slim volumes by Robert Hohlbaum: *Poems* and *Essays*.

'Father was a writer, you see,' Gussi Hohlbaum remarked with obvious pride. 'Unfortunately he died in an accident in 1938, while he was on tour doing readings – he was just becoming successful, as a playwright as well. It was a great blow to us, and Mother had to take in the lodgers to make ends meet.'

When I asked whether I might glance at her father's books, she hesitated for a moment, then told me to go ahead. Choosing several passages at random, I was taken aback to realise that Robert Hohlbaum had had one, and only one, theme: the greatness and glory of Adolf Hitler.

'You don't understand,' Frau Hohlbaum remarked, noticing my amazement. 'Nobody understands nowadays. But let me read to you what *I* wrote, back in November 1938, after my father's death. I've kept it all this time.'

She reached up to the top shelf and took down a thin book bound in coarse, light grey cloth. The front cover had a print of a swastika designed to look like the sun rising on the horizon. Gussi Hohlbaum lovingly dusted off the cover, opened the book and read aloud what she had written in old German script:

> For years it was my fondest wish to see the Führer. I knew his voice from the radio. I saw his picture every day – on Father's desk and on the wall next to my bed. I felt that if I could see him but once in reality I would be completely satisfied.
>
> But that was not true, for when I saw the Führer for the first time, in July 1936, in Munich, I felt as hundreds of thousands probably felt too:
>
> I wanted more; I wanted to see him from close up; I wanted to hear him speaking, to shake his hand. I so much wanted to tell him something, to thank him.
>
> But I would not have been able to say a word; like so many, young and old, in those days, I would only have wept.
>
> Berlin-Steglitz, 1 July 1938
>
> Gussi Hohlbaum

On the page opposite this entry was mounted a postcard-sized reproduction of a coloured lithograph by Hubert Lanzinger entitled 'The Standard-Bearer'. Beneath it, Gussi, who must have been twenty-three or twenty-four at the time, had copied in the same neat handwriting the words of the Führer:

> In good fortune or bad,
> in freedom or imprisonment,
> I remained true
> to my flag,
> which today has become the banner
> of the German Reich

'I suppose you, too, remained true to that flag?' I asked.

'Yes, to the bitter end . . . Of course later on we found out that mistakes had been made, that certain things happened that shouldn't have. But to this day I'm absolutely sure the Führer himself never wanted those things and probably didn't know about them. Göring and Himmler and a few others kept everything from him, and later they put the blame on him for all their mistakes and atrocities. And yet he really did accomplish the impossible! Millions of desperate people found new happiness, got decent jobs, and could face the future once more without fear. No one had to go hungry or freeze. The factories were working at capacity, the autobahns were being built, and Germany had the respect of the rest of the world – remember the 1936 Olympics! And even after the war broke out, the government went to a lot of trouble to make sure that a handful of unscrupulous types couldn't profit at the expense of the Volk. The government's welfare policies were exemplary . . . I myself worked for the National Socialist People's Welfare, as a volunteer, of course. We helped anyone in real need, even the families of Communists in protective custody. And at Christmas time we made up thousands of packages for the soldiers, each with a quarter pound of pfeffernüsse, a couple of apples, cookies and a bar of chocolate. We also arranged to take in soldiers who had no families to go home to. My family took one in – for two weeks at Christmas, and again at Easter in 1940.'

'Wasn't that during the time Herr Elkan was living with you?' I asked.

'Yes, we all celebrated Christmas together, and right after that there was Herr Elkan's fiftieth birthday. It started out very nice, but then Jochen – that was our soldier's name – began telling us about the campaign in Poland and the actions he had taken part in.'

'What branch of the service was he with?'

'He was with the SS special operations troops, and the trouble started when Jochen was describing the operations against the Jews. The troops had to be pretty tough, especially in Galicia. Major von Elken – I mean Herr Elkan – jumped up from his chair, jammed his monocle into his eye, and shouted at Jochen, "And you dare mention such things to a German officer! No decent soldier could commit such atrocities! They're fit only for marauders, and we know how those types are dealt with!" Jochen and I got up and left, and my mother tried to calm down Major on Elken – she of course took him for a real officer . . .'

Apparently Uncle Erich identified with his role so completely that he forgot to be as cautious as a 'non-Aryan' hiding from the Gestapo should have been, and instead vigorously defended the values of an officer of the old school.

Gussi Hohlbaum went on to tell me that it had not been until the end of April 1940, when the Gestapo came to the house, that she learned the truth about Major von Elken.

'That must have come as a shock to you,' I commented.

'We were flabbergasted! I would never have thought it possible – there was nothing about him like that . . . how shall I say it? He didn't look and didn't act like –'

'Like a Jew?'

'Well, yes,' she agreed after a moment's hesitation. 'At least not like the pictures I had seen. We didn't know any Jews, of course, although there were many in Berlin. Just once, in 1933, when I was seventeen, my father took my sister Grete and me to the eastern part of the city to see real Jews, in the Granary District. It horrified us that such people existed. The police were just conducting a raid – the types they rounded up! Lice-ridden, dressed in rags . . . Grete and I spent hours scrubbing ourselves when we got home . . . Of course there were other Jews around too. Dr. Wollenberg had his office next door to us, but he didn't look Jewish. I remember one time I hurt my hand, and I wanted to go to him to have it bandaged, but my father didn't want a Jew to touch me . . .'

I learned a lot from Frau Hohlbaum, but she couldn't tell me anything about Uncle Erich's escape from Berlin. So, still curious, I went to see her sister, Grete Weber.

'Yes, of course I remember Herr Elkan,' she said. 'I liked him very much, too, though his military posturing and his constant references to his "reg'ment" and fellow officers rubbed me the wrong way. But I must say I was tremendously impressed that time when he dressed down Gussi's SS man.'

She told me she had left Berlin shortly after Uncle Erich; her fiancé had been drafted and was serving in East Prussia, and she went to live with an aunt nearby, happy to get away from her mother and sister. 'It was largely thanks to my fiancé that I saw things differently than my family. He was the very opposite of a Nazi, though in truth he had more patience with my family than I did. You see, my father came from a small provincial town and wanted to study to be a teacher, but he didn't have the means to go to the university. He got a job as a sales assistant instead, for starvation wages, and when he joined the SA his Jewish employer fired him. From then on he hated the Jews and it became more and more of an obsession. And then after the seizure of power he suddenly achieved success as a writer. We moved to Berlin and bought that big house you saw. Father finally had a good income, and, even more important to him, recognition. He never realised that behind his back his friends in the Party made fun of his bombastic hymns to his beloved Führer.

'As for my sister, she was four years older, but my parents coddled her because she was frail and often ill. My father was constantly watching over her; he turned her into a complete sissy. I talked with Major von Elken about her one time. "As long as your sister remains so involved with the People's Welfare, you have to give her the benefit of the doubt – she doesn't know any better', he said; and I suppose he was right. He couldn't have known that Gussi of all people would prove his undoing.'

She noticed my astonished expression. 'So, she didn't tell you about that? Well, this is what happened. She couldn't stand having Major von Elken call her beloved Jochen a "marauder" and his military operations "atrocities", so at the end of January she mentioned the incident during a meeting at the Central Bureau for the People's Welfare. An outraged SS officer took down the name and address of the "Major", and a few days later turned up to "have a talk" with the famous Major von Elken. Fortunately I answered the door. I told the officer that Major von Elken had gone to Potsdam because of a death in his family. Actually he was in his room the whole time. The SS officer told me to inform Major von Elken that he should report to Gestapo headquarters on Prinz-Albrecht-Strasse as soon as he returned. When I spoke to him, without a word to my mother or sister, he took it very calmly. "I'll have to look for new quarters," he said, and the following day he left, with only a small suitcase, ostensibly to visit a sister in Küstrin.'

'Before he went, we had a brief chat. I asked him where he could go without having to worry about the Gestapo. "I'll have to go back into uniform," he said with a smile. "Then those fellows won't dare to lay a finger on me." A few days after he departed two men in leather coats came to take him in for questioning. My mother was all in a dither, and she reproached my sister bitterly when she found out it was she who had informed the SS of the incident on "Major von Elken's" birthday.'

I could not establish what Uncle Erich had done between the time he hastily vacated his room in the Hohlbaum house and the time he arrived on Sylt. I assume he tried to escape to Holland, with the assistance of our friends in Düsseldorf, only to find that the 'green border' was now too closely guarded. After that he and Herr Desch presumably settled on an escape through Denmark.

The date I had arranged with the innkeeper was 10 April 1940. As I returned from night watch on the morning of that day, I already knew that the plan must have failed. For in the early hours of the morning, 'Operation Weser' – the Wehrmacht's attack on Denmark and Norway – had gone into effect. The attack caught the Danes completely unawares. Their country was taken without a fight, and Esbjerg was swarming with German troops by the time Uncle Erich and the fisherman approached. With great presence of mind Uncle Erich put on the uniform he had already exchanged for civilian clothes, went ashore to look around, and then hurried back to Sylt with the terrified smuggler.

I ran into Uncle Erich around noon. He seemed very downcast. 'I'll stay around here a few more days. I must have a plausible reason for leaving. Perhaps I'll tell the other officers I've been transferred to Norway – then my sudden departure won't arouse suspicion.'

'How will you get away from here?' I asked.

'The same way I came – in uniform, with a first-class rail ticket, and with marching orders issued by the Düsseldorf garrison. Herr Desch has a good friend there. So I'll go back to Düsseldorf, and then we'll see . . .'

I asked him to give my regards to various people and advised him to get in touch with Aunt Annie. As I later found out, he spent several weeks at her cottage that summer.

'Did he ever get out? Did he survive the Nazi period?' Frau Weber asked, and was delighted to hear that he had. 'It would be awful to think that we – that my own sister should have him on her conscience. Naturally she had no idea who he was when she reported him, but when Major von Elken failed to return, the Gestapo probed further, and of course soon determined that he was in fact the lawyer they had been looking for.'

'How did your sister react when she found out?'

'She was outraged that a Jew should have taken us in that way. I think, though, that she played up her indignation because she was afraid her Jochen might leave her. Fortunately she never did find out whether her fears were justified; in the summer of 1940 Jochen was killed in an ambush by Polish partisans. It was awful for Gussi, because she was pregnant by him, and in her last months. One of Himmler's officers came to see her and suggested she go to an SS home near Bremen, where she could have the baby and recuperate under excellent medical supervision and care. The very next day an SS car and driver picked her up.'

'What sort of a home was it?' I asked.

For the first time Frau Weber did not answer immediately, and when she spoke, the subject seemed painful to her. 'Well, my sister had allowed herself to be recruited for the *Lebensborn*, or the "font of life" project – Himmler's "breeding place for the finest blood". She gave birth not only to Jochen's baby, but also to another one the following year. She probably would have had four or five more babies – that was the purpose of Lebensborn – but her health wasn't good. In 1941, after the second birth, they advised her to stay in the home to help take care of the other mothers. When she decided against that, she was transferred to an armaments factory in Prague.'

TWENTY-THREE

Lebensborn – 'In Thirty Years . . . Six Hundred More Regiments!'

The 'delivery and recuperation home', as Gussi Hohlbaum described to friends and family the place where she remained from the summer of 1940 to the end of 1941, belonged to the organisation known as Lebensborn. This organisation stood under the diret supervision of SS Reichsführer Heinrich Himmler.

Himmler, who had risen rapidly to become official head of security for the entire Reich, enjoyed so much power that he could carry out all sorts of personal schemes and indulge his wildest notions. Among these were the establishment of an SS research centre known as the 'Research and Teaching Institute of Ancestral Heritage', whose objective was to 'examine the geographic distribution, spirit, deeds, and heritage of Nordic Indo-European racial stock'; production of a supposedly miraculous mineral water; cultivation of certain roots, reputed to have remarkable medicinal powers; and also, the establishment of the Lebensborn, intended to serve as the 'nursery garden for Germanic blood', where a 'new superman type would be bred'. Himmler cherished the idea of applying some of his early experience in chicken breeding to human beings. He wanted to 'Nordicise' the nation, and the Lebensborn was to be the controlled environment in which this eugenics project was carried out.

The members of the Lebensborn Association, founded in December 1935, were exclusively SS and high-ranking police officers. The charter of the organisation called for 'giving shelter and care to expectant mothers of racially and biologically desirable stock, when careful examination of the mothers' family and that of the progenitors by the SS Central Bureau for Racial and Settlement Questions gives reason to expect that they will produce equally desirable offspring.' At the inauguration of Steinhöring, the model Lebensborn, Himmler announced, 'Sacred to us is every mother of good blood!'

The Lebensborn home to which Gussi Hohlbaum went was the Hohehorst Castle, which had been built in the late 1920s by two brothers from Bremen who, in 1930, were convicted of fraud. In 1938 the Lebensborn purchased the large estate – renamed 'Friesland' – for the ridiculously low sum of sixty thousand marks. Gradually nine other Lebensborn homes were established in Germany, most of them in similarly large, castlelike structures with spacious grounds. After the war broke out, more homes were set up in the occupied countries. They had complete administrative and financial autonomy, even maintaining their own registry offices, which issued birth certificates for children born in the homes; nothing in these documents gave the slightest indication that the children had been born out of wedlock. The mothers could choose whether to keep their children or to give them to the Lebensborn for adoption. The great majority of the mothers turned their children over to the SS, for most of those who bore children for the Reich were 'racially flawless' underage girls, who had concealed their pregnancies from their families. The fathers, whose names had to be recorded for purposes of documenting their 'racial qualifications', came almost exclusively from the ranks of the SS.

No expense was spared in furnishing and equipping the Lebensborn homes. The SS drew the money from a fund made up of confiscated Jewish holdings. In addition, one-fourth of the millions of marks taken from the Jews in 'compensation' for the damage of the Night of Broken Glass went to the Lebensborn.

The SS, however, found it more difficult to round up doctors, midwives, and nurses for the homes. The Red Cross refused any assistance, and the SS officers in charge of the Lebensborn had to resort to sending out letters to any Nazi organisations that might prove helpful. In the end, most of the personnel were recruited from among those young women who wanted to stay with their children or feared to return to their families.

There turned out to be no lack of mothers; on the one hand, Nazi ideology encouraged the bearing of as many children as possible, so long as they were 'Aryan' and 'from healthy stock'. On the other hand, the penalties for abortion had been drastically increased. According to one slogan, bearing children was something to which a woman was honour-bound. And the leaders of the League of German Girls proclaimed repeatedly that although the World War had left Germany with more women than men, and not every German girl could hope to find a husband, 'still, you can all become mothers!'

The result of such encouragement was a dramatic rise in the number of pregnancies; after the 1936 Party rally in Nuremberg, for example, a good thousand League girls, some of them very young, were pregnant, and many of them found refuge with the Lebensborn. And couples willing to adopt the babies were numerous within the upper ranks of the SS.

When begetting and bearing children came to be defined as a form of 'service to the Fatherland', a libidinous element crept into German life that presented a marked contrast to the Nazis' customary prudishness. Aware that the German public might not approve the goings-on in the Lebensborn homes, high Nazi officials invented elaborate rationalisations and euphemisms for Himmler's pet project.

For example, SS Oberführer Dr. Gregor Ebner asks in a letter, 'Is it really irresponsible when a woman who wishes to bear a child deliberately enters into relations with a man? On the contrary; I would argue that her action displays a profound sense of responsibility, and that such a woman . . . reveals great strength of character . . .' It was Dr. Ebner who expressed the view that 'thanks to the Lebensborn, in thirty years we shall have six hundred more regiments'.

Within the homes themselves the SS strove to maintain a chaste and disciplined atmosphere. The pregnant women were addressed only by their first names, like children. They were expected to clean their own rooms and keep them neat and tidy. Regular room and closet inspections took place. Visitors were discouraged. A newborn child would receive its name in a special 'Germanic ritual' ceremony: the baby was placed on a pillow before an altar covered with a swastika-emblazoned cloth; then, if it was a boy, he would be touched on the forehead with an SS 'dagger of honour' and initiated into the Black Order. For a girl, an SS leader would merely make a brief speech, and the 'ceremonial name-giving' would conclude with all those present joining in a song.

Those in charge of the Lebensborn homes considered an outward appearance of propriety so important that they called for an investigation when by chance two women pregnant by the same man turned up at the Kurmark home. SS guards maintained a strict watch over the homes, and only persons with special passes could gain admittance to the buildings or the grounds. This category included the staff, the Lebensborn heads, SS leaders on 'official business', concentration camp inmates working under guard on repairs or gardening, and sometimes groups of young girls brought in as potential recruits for staff.

Toward the end of the war the SS destroyed almost all documents pertaining to the Lebensborn. One document that survived is a summary of an address made to a group of nursing students who toured the model home, Steinhöring, in June 1940. The document gives us a glimpse of the kinds of arguments used to persuade these sixteen-to-eighteen-year-old girls to come and work in the homes:

Lebensborn – problem important for entire nation! Differences of opinion still prevalent. Something that provokes controversy not necessarily bad. See Time of Struggle! Justification through success. No difference between married and unmarried mothers. False morality! Extramarital relations tolerated so long as no pregnancy. But pregnancy the natural result of love relationship. . . . Great bloodletting in war – need for replacing lost lives – results more important than legality. . . . Woman surplus of more than 2 million! Even more with present war. Shortage of men also due to homosexuality: 1 million! Hence: 3 million too few men! Every man has his choice of five women. Likely to marry the most beautiful, the richest, the childless woman – the four others cannot marry – should they remain childless? So problem more serious: the existence or nonexistence of our people! Germany must again be land of children! Unwed girl without prospects must have right to motherhood – hence our struggle against defamation. . . . Is our work good or not? Good is what helps the people, bad what harms the people. The people: not only the living, also our ancestors and our descendants. Sacred to us is every mother of good blood!

What the recruiting campaign for the Lebensborn did not make clear was what was expected of the student nurses who served in the homes – caring for the pregnant women or bearing children themselves. In fact both were desired and encouraged, and it was mainly the student nurses working the homes that regularly became pregnant. A resolution by the Central Bureau for Racial and Settlement Questions dating from 1937 defined the young nurses' task as follows:

'The Lebensborn will bring them together with a man, not casually, but in full awareness that they are fulfilling a noble duty toward the nation.'

The girls chosen had to meet strict standards of quality established by the SS experts: they had to be of pure 'Aryan' ancestry as far back as 1750, at least 5′4″, blonde and blue-eyed, and fully convinced of the Nazi ideology and committed to the racial doctrine.

The student nurses and 'brown sisters' who, like Gussi Hohlbaum, were brought to the Friesland Home near Bremen to deliver their babies, came from Upper Bavaria, Tyrolia, and Styria for the most part. As the Lebensborn marriage registry indicates, they all had 'home addresses' in Munich – the same four addresses appear time after time. Marc Hillel and Clarissa Henry, two Americans who did research on the Lebensborn in the early 1970s (see *Of Pure Blood*), succeeded in discovering the particulars about only one of these addresses.

They found out that the house at 95 Ismaninger Strasse, an imposing villa shielded from the street by a high wall, had housed a casino for high SS officers during the year 1939–40. During this period Hans and Franziska S. lived next door, and thirty years later they were still there and could give some insight into what went on at that address.

'During the war,' Franziska reported, 'our neighbour was the Lebensborn. We didn't realise it at first, of course. A word too much or an indiscreet glance could have nasty consequences at that time . . .

'In spite of the constant fear, we were naturally curious, and every now and then risked a cautious look at the place. It was then that we saw the girls. A great many girls arrived there. They were all very big and blond, very Nordic, real Aryans, as the term was at the time. Those ladies were not our kind, they were not like our Bavarian women; in our part of the world women tend to be short and dark. They certainly didn't come from these parts . . .

'It took us a long time to put two and two together, but in the end we realised what was going on. The house was a kind of meeting place, an SS officers' club. Then we found out – how, it's difficult to say after all this time – that the girls came from all over the place, but were sent here by the Lebensborn head office in the Herzog-Max-Strasse . . . where the cinemas are. People said that it was there that they were picked.

'Whenever new ones arrived people used to say: "Look, there are some more new cows for our stud-bulls." I must say they were a lot of fine, strong young men. One could well imagine that a girl who got a bit tipsy, let us say, might well want to give a child to the Führer, as the saying was at the time, with those young men . . .

'So far as one could tell from their clothes and other details, the girls used to stay for several days, sometimes for several weeks. Then they vanished, and new ones arrived. The men changed, too, but not as often.'

The Nazis did not rely exclusively on these 'officers' clubs' for the mass production of 'noble Aryans'.

'I was a student nurse during the war,' reports Frau K., who is now over sixty. She had been trained at a Red Cross school in Berlin.

'One day all my girlfriends and I received orders to report to the Eastern Front,' she recalls, 'somewhere near Riga.' Only because her father had good connections was she exempted, which she regretted at the time. All the other draftees left for the front. Three of the girls with whom Frau K. was close friends stayed in touch with her and wrote regularly. 'They weren't sent to the front at all, but rather to SS quarters behind the lines to conceive children by the top officers.'

'I am firmly convinced that there was something fishy going on,' Frau K. commented. 'None of the three had any particular desire to bear a child – on the contrary. And they were not even all that dedicated to the Nazi ideology.' Her friends, all from solid middle-class families and 'jolly but not stupid', came home from Latvia pregnant. 'They were sent to a Lebensborn home near Würzburg, I don't know exactly where.' Finally Frau K. lost touch with her friends because she had married and moved to Bremen. 'I can still remember one of them especially well,' she concluded. 'She made fun of my wanting to get married; she always said she didn't want children.'

With the conquest of Denmark and Norway in April 1940, new possibilities of expansion opened up for the Lebensborn. SS Gruppenführer Wilhelm Radiess, commander of the Northern Sector, wrote a study for Himmler with the title, 'The SS for Greater Germany – with Sword and Cradle', in which he noted:

> It is highly desirable that German soldiers beget as many children as possible with Norwegian women, whether in or outside the wedlock. . . . The soldier in combat must be freed for all worries. The Reich Commissioner's Department will assume all costs incurred by mother and child . . .

Radiess's suggestions were well received and carried out with great success: with the express approval and encouragement of the occupation authorities, about 60,000 Norwegian women married German soldiers. And with a growing number of out-of-wedlock pregnancies, a series of Lebensborn homes were established in Norway. Children born there were turned over to 'politically reliable' German families for adoption; these children 'of pure Nordic stock' were in great demand.

On the other hand, the Lebensborn directors met with a total rebuff in Denmark; passive resistance to the German occupation proved obdurate. Homes established in Holland and Belgium likewise encountered major resistance, whereas the Lebensborn home set up near Paris experienced no serious difficulties. The more than 100,000 out-of-wedlock children born to French women and SS or Wehrmacht fathers, outside the framework of the Lebensborn, were considered 'of dubious racial value'. This was not so in the Channel Islands, where a special commission of the SS Bureau for Racial and Settlement

Questions determined that 'Norman blood is preserved in exemplary purity'.

Finally, there was the Moselland Lebensborn home in Luxembourg, intended primarily for the care of children abducted from Eastern Europe. For the SS did not stop at breeding new members of the master race; agents of the Racial and Settlement Bureau swarmed into Poland, the Baltic region, the Ukraine, Yugoslavia, Rumania, and Czechoslovakia, looking for children with physical characteristics suggestive of 'Aryan blood'. For the most part these were the children of executed partisans or hostages. When the Czech village of Lidice was levelled as a reprisal after the assassination of SS Obergruppenführer Reinhard Heydrich, thirteen children out of more than a hundred were allowed to survive – because they were blond.

For a full decade, from 1935 to 1945, SS Reichsführer Himmler pursued his *idée fixe* of breeding masses of 'pure Nordic types'. Determined, pedantic, and absolutely ruthless, he employed every conceivable means. He demanded reports on the milk production of the nursing mothers in the homes and gave prizes for those who established records; such quota-setting women received permission to spend another year at the Lebensborn. Himmler also wanted a special file set up for all mothers and fathers who had 'a Roman nose or the suggestion of one'.

'The Lebensborns were his hobby,' remarked Paula H., who served as a nurse in a Lebensborn home. As she spoke, she smiled gently, as if recalling a little quirk in an otherwise lovable and hard-working person. 'He had fantastic plans for them for the future . . .'

In the course of their research in the 1970s on the Lebensborn phenomenon, Hillel and Henry succeeded in tracking down some of the products of Himmler's massive genetic experiment. They found no appreciable differences in size or hair and eye colour between these people, now in their thirties, and contemporaries whose parents had not been selected for particular physical properties. Apparently Himmler's efforts were in vain.

TWENTY-FOUR

Hitler's Triumph

One day in mid-April 1940, Erwin and I were summoned by our regimental commander. Denmark had already been under German occupation for ten days, but heavy fighting continued in Norway. I thought nervously of Uncle Erich – I hadn't yet heard whether his planned removal from Sylt to the Rhineland had succeeded. But I reminded myself that the colonel would have had no reason to call in Erwin in connection with Uncle Erich.

'At ease,' Colonel Kessler ordered when we reported to him in his suite at the Miramar Hotel. He paced the room, gazed out the large window at the North Sea, glanced quizzically at us, and then began:

'So you are the two men on watch who have cost the Greater German Reich more than a million marks in the last two months . . .' To our relief, he did not sound terribly vexed. 'I certainly appreciate your vigilance and your unflagging zeal,' he continued, sarcastically. 'Not so much as one high-flying reconnaissance plane has escaped your notice. We've had an alert every night. All our batteries have already seen service. The consumption of ordnance has been not inconsiderable. Yet not a single plane has been shot down thus far . . . Did you wish to interrupt, Sergeant?'

'No, sir,' Erwin replied; he had in fact been about to speak, but stopped himself. 'It was just that something occurred to me.'

The colonel nodded encouragement, and Erwin took the opportunity: 'We've been able to fine-tune the aircraft reporting system, sir. The English pilots have been surprised at our total coverage of the northern coastline. Our fire power has impressed them, and caused them to alter their course. If I may say so, sir, that was the best possible result under the circumstances.'

He fell silent, slightly embarrassed after such an outburst of audacity.

'Is that all?' Colonel Kessler asked, feigning astonishment. 'I thought you would tell me that all those alerts helped get the troops used to combat conditions and kept the gunners in practice – not to mention the other benefits.' He gave us a searching look. We remained collected, and he continued: 'But all this has to stop! From now on, you may issue an alert only if you are sure that several – *more than two* – enemy planes are approaching. Is that clear? Dismissed!'

But before we had reached the door, the colonel called us back. 'They need one trained radio operator for service in Norway at the new aircraft warning centre in Drontheim. Work out whom we can spare and let Major Zobel know before the end of the week!'

Much relieved, we sent on our way. We knew it should have been Major Zobel's job to decide whom to send to Norway, but the colonel had apparently realised that Major Zobel could not be counted on. In recent weeks, he was even more distracted than usual, devoting all this attention to the migration of the Caspian terns, which had wintered in North Africa and were now returning to nest in the dunes of Sylt.

Erwin and I had little trouble deciding which man we could 'spare': Barczustowski was the only real candidate. If need arose, Erwin could drive the communications car himself, and besides, Barczustowski was becoming unbearable. England's and France's lack of action and the easy victory over Denmark had convinced him that the Führer had already achieved the 'final victory'. He saw himself as lord over thousands of Polish peasants, assigned as serfs to him, the loyal Party member from years back; or as an all-powerful district governor in the occupied territories, with a castle for his residence and a harem stocked with blond Polish girls and even blonder Norwegian girls . . .

If he had been content to bask in such fantasies we could have tolerated him; life on Sylt was so tedious that we welcomed any comic relief. But Barczustowski had begun to snoop around. Only the day before he had come to Erwin with an 'official report': a certain soldier had been telling 'horror stories' in the Strand Café, pure enemy propaganda, which he had picked up from a navy man who was boasting that he had heard it on the BBC.

Erwin gave Barczustowski a thorough dressing-down. He reprimanded him for addressing his superior with the familiar *du* when making an official report; he ordered him to put on his boots, for official business could not be transacted in sneakers; and finally, he told him his report consisted of sheer hearsay. In short, Erwin did what he could to prevent the sailor from being reported to higher authorities. But then he asked Barczustowski just what the 'horror stories' consisted of.

'The British claim to have sunk the heavy cruiser *Blücher* and the light cruiser *Karlsruhe* and ten of our newest destroyers,' Barczustowski told him truculently.

'Unfortunately that's all true,' Erwin replied. 'You'll read it tomorrow in the Wehrmacht Report.'

Barczustowski went away muttering, but it was clear to Erwin and me that we would not be able to squelch his little reports forever. So we told the major that we were reluctantly prepared to give him up.

Two weeks later, on 4 May 1940, our staff was ordered to leave the island that very night. At our first stop, in Rendsburg, a new driver joined us. Jens Kröger was twenty, and when we asked what he did in civilian life, he told us, 'I play percussion and bass and xylophone.' Erwin and I knew what this meant about his political orientation: jazz was taboo to the Nazis, and a jazz enthusiast was not likely to be a dedicated follower of Hitler.

'I volunteered for communications,' Jens Kröger told us later, 'because you can pick up concerts if you have a good enough receiver – maybe even Carnegie Hall.' Because his idol was Gene Krupa, we called him Krupa, and the nickname stuck. He was the proud owner of a portable phonograph and three dozen records that he had picked up in Denmark – the latest of Duke Ellington, Tommy Dorsey, Lionel Hampton, and of course, Gene Krupa. He turned out to be a good comrade and an excellent driver.

Three days later our communications unit received orders to move on to Broichweiden, northeast of Aachen. We stowed our gear, as well as such unauthorised items as the records and the phonograph, in our brand new eight-cylinder Horch, and set out, with very mixed feelings.

'This is it,' Erwin said. 'Tomorrow the western campaign begins, and there'll be nothing funny about the war from now on.'

And indeed, on 10 May 1940, the German Wehrmacht marched into the neutral Benelux countries and France.

Exactly a month and a day after our departure from Sylt, early in the morning of 5 June, our Horch came to a halt on a little square in St. Pol-sur-Mer, a village near Dunkirk in the most northerly part of France, close to the Belgian border.

'I hope this is the right place,' Krupa remarked, and yawned. He had been at the wheel all night, and we had been forced repeatedly to turn around and find new routes – bridges had been destroyed and roads flooded. Apparently the French had opened all the floodgates. 'If this turns out to be the wrong St. Pol *again* –'

'We'll just have to keep going until we find the right one,' Werner interrupted him.

'There must be at least a dozen,' Krupa mumbled, put his head down on the steering wheel, and fell asleep at once.

'Maybe Major Zobel meant St. Paul, not St. Pol – they're both pronounced the same,' the double doctor interjected. 'I can think of at least three St. Pauls . . .'

We had been on the road for almost three weeks, far from the rest of the staff and out of radio contact with our regiment. We hadn't seen any German troops in days, and at times suspected we might be in the rear of the French forces. Soon after we set out we saw an endless stream of fleeing civilians who, strangely enough, were moving in the same direction we were. Only with difficulty did we manage to get past them.

We saw a desperate father standing beside his overloaded Citröen. He had run out of gas, so we gave him twenty liters of our fuel, which he insisted on paying for. He took us for British soldiers; apparently the French were not familiar with our grey-blue Luftwaffe uniforms, whose tunics we wore with the collar open.

These wanderings through France had begun on 30 May, the day after we arrived in Tervuren, not far from Brussels. The Belgian capital was already occupied by the Germans, and Holland had capitulated five days earlier. A report came in over the radio to the effect that German tank divisions had reached Abbéville at the mouth of the Somme. With German troops at the Channel coast, the main forces of the French, the British, and the Belgians were now cut off from their depots and supply routes and in danger of encirclement. Unless French troops pressed forward from the south to cut off the German tank divisions in Abbéville, and link up with the main body of Allied forces, the campaign in the west would soon be decided in favour of the Wehrmacht.

Erwin reported the new tank positions to our commander and came back saying, 'Old Kessler's in a dither. He's consulting with Major Zobel, trying to work out how to get into some real action before the whole campaign fizzles on him! He has five more batteries under his command now, and I just heard him on the phone offering to provide flak protection to the tank divisions. Do you want to bet that in an hour at most . . .'

Sure enough, Major Zobel soon appeared and sat down with Erwin and me in the radio car. 'Well, our radio unit has a special assignment,' he sighed. 'You are to set out at once, without waiting for the others. You'll be on your own. You drive south on the road to Douai, via Mons and Valenciennes; and from Douai, work your way west. Try to establish contact with those tank divisions in forward positions, and don't worry about the other troops that will need protection from aerial attacks. Colonel Kessler's flank batteries will be coming along as fast as they can. In the meantime, you are to locate a suitable place for our communications staff. Pick up fuel and provisions along the way – I don't care how you go about it. Here's your pass from the commander.'

He gave Erwin a slip of paper covered with impressive stamps, lit a cigarette, and seemed ready to leave us. 'Is everything clear?' he asked.

Erwin shook his head. 'How are we supposed to find a staff headquarters, sir? Is that really up to us? And what should we do if we run into enemy troops?'

'Enemy contact is to be avoided at all costs,' Major Zobel explained, to our immense relief. 'And keep your radio transmissions to a minimum. Just inform the First Battery when you've reached your destination.'

'What destination?'

'Oh, yes, well, it's called St. Pol-*something*. You'll find it; it's right by the ocean; and there's got to be some little castle or resort hotel there that's suitable for headquarters, looking out over the ocean – you know what I mean. Now get going, so I can report to Colonel Kessler that you're on your way. I imagine we'll see each other in a week at most.'

The drive to Mons proved uneventful, but then we had to take our first detour, because the road to Valenciennes was under bombardment. We nevertheless managed to reach Amiens by the following morning, and remained there until late afternoon.

Amiens was the first town we saw that had been hit hard by the war. Numerous houses and all the bridges were damaged or destroyed, and the streets were pitted from the shelling. We walked through empty streets past houses with closed shutters. The only civilian we encountered was an old woman who stood in a doorway, staring at us in blank terror.

We finally located the newly established German supply depot on the edge of town. The staff sergeant who equipped us with rations and fuel pointed out the direction the German tanks had taken. 'Keep heading west, following the Somme,' he told us.

But we did not get far. After a few kilometres we were stopped by German military police. The officer examined our marching orders with suspicion. 'St. Pol? Where's that?' he asked.

'That's just what we'd like to know – it's supposed to be on the coast.' Erwin replied.

'Take charge of these prisoners first,' the police sergeant ordered us, gesturing with his chin toward the meadow beside the highway. There lay close to a thousand French soldiers – we had not noticed them before. Most of them were sleeping, in the shade of the bushes and trees. Others had taken off their shirts and were sunning themselves.

'Escort them to the reception camp – it's supposed to be at the airport, about six kilometres from here. The *capitaine* there, the one in the light blue cap, knows where it is. Hey, *capitaine*, have them form up!' and before we could protest, the military policeman roared off on his motorcycle.

We had no choice but to accompany the French soldiers. We swallowed hard when we noticed how many of them were still armed; Erwin and I had quietly got rid of our weapons a few weeks earlier, when we realised that our reservists – Krupa, Little Hans, and the double doctor – hadn't received guns when they joined us. But all the French soldiers I spoke with on the way were overjoyed that for them the war was over. They told me that the German tanks had surprised them as they marched north, confident they were far from the front lines.

When we delivered the prisoners three hours later, Erwin commented, 'Maybe they're not so wrong after all when they say they're better off than we are; for them the fighting's over, and they got through it alive. I tell you, I couldn't believe my eyes when they stacked up their guns and lit that fire under them. They really seemed to feel good about it.'

'Does anyone know which way we're supposed to be going?' Krupa broke in. 'I haven't the faintest idea how to get back to the main road.'

It turned out that none of us had been paying attention to where we were. The *capitaine* had marched on ahead, leading the column, while we followed, urging on the stragglers. Besides, darkness had fallen in the meantime.

'Let's try this road,' Erwin said. 'It seems to head more or less west. It'll take us back to the main road eventually.'

But instead we found ourselves zig-zagging all over the countryside, sleeping in barns, eating when we found a place open; the French money we had received for the gasoline certainly came in handy. A week passed before we found a complete set of maps for northwestern France at a petrol station, and by that time we were almost 600 kilometres away from the St. Pol we thought must be the right one.

No one stopped us along the way, nor did we see enemy troops. People were friendly in the villages, and apparently our presence aroused no suspicion. We really didn't see much sign of war, except for the long lines of vehicles in which people were fleeing south from the northern provinces.

Now, when we had finally arrived in St. Pol-sur-Mer, our first item of business was to procure a decent breakfast. Not far from where we had parked, a café was just opening. Erwin nodded to me to go and reconnoitre, since I was the only one who spoke enough French to make myself understood.

The proprietor seemed surprised when I politely asked whether we could have coffee and something to eat at this early hour. He removed the cigarette from his lower lip and looked me up and down, then said in a less than friendly tone, 'What, are you fellows still around?'

I didn't know what to say; we had just arrived in St. Pol, after all, so I smiled and offered him one of the cigarettes we had bought with our gasoline money. The proprietor accepted the cigarette, and as he lowered the awning and set out a few chairs, he said in a slightly more agreeable manner, 'I thought you Tommies had all left. They just said on the radio that the last of you were picked up by the boats – down there, where you see the fire . . .' He gestured with his chin in the direction of Dunkirk. I looked, and saw columns of black smoke, which the wind was carrying inland.

'How is it you haven't heard about the evacuation? They got out almost half a million men, including some of ours – twenty-five thousand of them yesterday alone. You should have seen it: launches, cutters, motorboats, excursion boats, even sailboats!'

'There are just five of us, and we'd like some breakfast,' I said. 'Coffee with or without milk, bread or croissants – would that be possible?'

Of course we knew all about what had taken place at Dunkirk; we listened to the news broadcasts. But we were alone here and needed to be careful. So I slipped a fifty-franc note out of my pocket and showed it to him.

'Sure,' he said. 'But you're stuck now – the evacuation is over. The Germans will be here by noon at the latest . . .'

'And would you happen to have any eggs?' I asked.

'Let me check. It'll be a few minutes until the baker gets here. You can sit outside here, but . . .' He looked me over carefully, saw that I was unarmed, and announced firmly, 'Don't bring your guns or there'll be no breakfast. I don't want any shooting around here.'

I was able to reassure him on that score.

After breakfast we set out to explore St. Pol and Dunkirk. We found signs of far heavier fighting than in Amiens: entire streets destroyed, bridges dynamited, oil tanks burning, heaps of abandoned, damaged and destroyed equipment. It was a depressing sight. Most of the city had been a battleground, and the civilian population had fled.

On the beaches and in the dunes north of Dunkirk thousands of light and heavy weapons lay in the sand, along with munitions crates, field kitchens, scattered cans of rations, and innumerable wrecks of British army trucks.

'Damn!' I exclaimed to Erwin, 'the entire British army went under here!'

Erwin shook his head vigorously. 'On the contrary! A miracle took place here! If the German tanks and stukas and navy had managed to surround the British here, shooting most of them, and taking the rest prisoner, then England wouldn't have any trained soldiers left. Instead the British seem to have rescued them all – and a lot of Frenchmen, too. Adolf can say good-bye to his blitzkrieg against England . . .'

He might have gone on, but at that moment we caught sight of the double doctor, who had stayed by the car and was now beckoning excitedly. 'The others have arrived,' he called out as soon as we were in earshot. 'I just spoke with Major Zobel. He's very proud of us! But we have to get moving again – south!'

TWENTY-FIVE

Death of the 'Sealion'

'Compared to us, you lived like lords in France,' said Werner, as we compared our experiences in the war. 'I was in the infantry along the West Wall and had to take part in reconnaissance operations. Three of my buddies were killed and two wounded. I was the only one in our squad to get out of it without a scratch.'

That was in early May 1940, and then all was quiet along the West Wall for almost a month. While the German tank divisions pushed through to the Channel and then swung south toward Paris, the troops along the French-German border from the Upper Rhine to the Palatinate were mired in the sitzkrieg again. Most of the French forces were holed up in the 'impregnable' Maginot Line fortifications.

'It was ghastly when the war finally did heat up there,' Werner said. 'With stukas and antitank grenades one French bunker after another was cracked, and then smoked out with hand grenades and flame-throwers. The troops inside never stood a chance . . . Fortunately I got out of it. While we were still dug in, a noncom next to me was hit by shrapnel. I heaved him onto my back and dragged him to the field hospital. He survived and was so grateful to me that he made sure I received the Iron Cross 2nd Class that was supposed to go to him, as well as ten days of special leave.'

On 14 June, the day Paris capitulated, Werner's regiment captured Verdun, which in the First World War had withstood all attacks. In 1916, 700,000 men had fallen there; and at a memorial service in 1936 the survivors from both sides had sworn never to shoot at one another again. This time Verdun fell quickly, and three days later the entire Maginot Line collapsed.

'On June the 21st, we heard that the French army had surrendered and a cease-fire was about to be declared,' Werner continued. 'God, were we happy! We thought the war was over.'

Werner's regiment spent the rest of the year near Amiens. 'Luckily, nothing was going on there.'

I looked at him in astonishment. 'You can't be serious!'

'No, really – nothing was happening. At least in our area everything was quiet. We were quartered in a school, and besides cleaning our weapons and peeling potatoes, there was nothing for us to do. In the evening we would sit in the "Soldiers' Home" and drink red wine for 30 pfennigs a glass. At first we were afraid to go to the cafés in town, because of the language barrier, but the population wasn't hostile at all. And from about September on, there was a military cinema that showed a new film every week – things like *Women Are Better Diplomats*, *The Glorious Night of the Ball*, or *Love, Love, and More Love*. But otherwise all that summer and autumn it was terribly boring.

'The only excitement came from our excursion to Paris – we toured the city in open trucks and then strolled around until midnight.' Paris made a tremendous impression on the soldiers. The city had suffered no destruction, and the cinemas, shops, theatres, restaurants, and night clubs were open and bustling. Supplies seemed plentiful, and if it had not been for all the Germans in uniform, one might have thought it was peacetime.

While Werner's unit was making an excursion to Paris, one of the most decisive confrontations of the war got under way, and neither the German people nor most of the German soldiers in France knew anything about it.

At the staff headquarters of the Kessler Group, a little castle in Caudebec-en-Caux, near Rouen, Erwin and I followed the events closely. It all began on 16 July with Hitler's strictly classified 'Führer's Directive No. 16', which called for the elimination of England as a base of operations against Germany, even if it meant occupying the island.

To Erwin's and my surprise, by the beginning of August there was hardly a sailor, dockworker, pub owner, or barge operator in France who had not already heard of the 'strictly classified' Operation Sealion, or *Lion Marin*, as they called it. The reason for this was that in the harbour towns along the Normandy coast, and also farther north, more and more boats were being collected, including motorised freighters and barges used on inland waterways. When we spent off-duty evenings in Rouen or Le Havre, the talk in the bars was about 'Monsieur Hitler's' planned landing of the Wehrmacht in England – over 250,000 soldiers would be brought ashore, and the conquest of England might be accomplished in a month or less.

These rumours astonished us, for we realised that in addition to troops and transport vessels at least three factors would be necessary: protection for the German flotilla against the far superior British fleet, German control of the skies above the Channel and southern England, and perfectly calm seas. As we knew better than most, there was no question of Germany's dominating the skies, at least for the present. And as for the weather, the waters of the Channel were always more or less choppy; that would make no difference to fishing boats and warships, but to flatbottomed barges and similar vessels it would mean certain doom.

Early in August we received our first official notification of Operation Sealion, from Major Zobel. He told us with great agitation that the Luftwaffe would be involved, starting on 5 August apparently he was one of the very few who had been completely unaware of the plan.

In fact 'aerial preparation' had been under way since 10 July, with the Luftwaffe attacking British convoys in the Channel, duelling with RAF fighter planes, and bombing harbours along England's southern coast. Erwin and I had kept abreast of these operations, but ever since the cease-fire in France, Major Zobel had been concentrating solely on certain species of birds that nested along the lower Seine, and on an attractive librarian at the Rouen public library, who had been providing him with books in his field.

On 15 August Major Zobel was roused from these peaceable pursuits by Colonel Kessler's demand for an immediate report on the operation against Britain. The major was immensely relieved to find that Erwin could tell him all he needed to know, though it wasn't good news.

That morning the Luftwaffe had attempted its first daytime raid, aimed against the Newcastle coal-mining district. The attack was intended to catch the British napping; Hitler's strategists had assumed that by attacking targets in the south at the same time as planes made for Newcastle they could keep the British fighter squadrons fully occupied.

But the Luftwaffe had a rude awakening: the British had been holding seven fighter squadrons in reserve near Newcastle, and before the Germans could get away, they lost about 30 Heinkel 111s out of a group of 100, each carrying a crew of four. As far as could be determined, the British suffered no losses.

In the south the British had shot down another 46 German planes. Some British aircraft were hit, but in most cases the pilots brought them in for emergency landings, or the crews bailed out and were rescued. When the German planes went down, the crews were either killed or taken prisoner.

Over the course of that week the British lost a total of 134 fighter planes, but the German losses amounted to at least twice, perhaps three times as many, for although quite a few heavily damaged

German planes limped back across the Channel, few were able to land safely.

During the last week in August and the first week in September 1940, the fighting intensified on both sides. The RAF flew nightly missions against German cities, bombing Berlin for the first time on 24 August. An average of 1,000 German planes attacked England by day, bombing military aerodromes, railway junctions, communications centres, harbours, industrial areas, and finally, the heart of London. For the first time the numerical superiority of the Luftwaffe began to make itself felt; the British defence capability was noticeably strained.

Still, the attack on Berlin on the night of 28 August had shaken the residents of that capital. Along with the bombs the British dropped leaflets saying, 'The war begun by Hitler will continue as long as Hitler is around!'

Göring had promised the people of Berlin that no enemy aircraft would ever penetrate the Reich, let alone bomb the capital. Now, as resentment against Göring mounted and morale plummeted – the people had been promised peace before winter – Hitler prepared a major speech for the Sports Palace on 4 September.

From the newsreels we could see how Hitler used the occasion to manipulate public opinion. He spoke before an audience consisting largely of National Socialist People's Welfare workers and nurses, and he focused on the two questions that most troubled these women: would England be defeated by Christmas, and what was being done to protect Berlin and the other major cities against British bombing attacks?

In response to the first question he said, 'If people in England today are curious and ask, "Well, why doesn't he come?" don't worry, he will!' The People's Welfare aides, the League of German Girls leaders, and the nurses squealed with laughter at this example of their Führer's humour.

Then Hitler spoke of the night raids, explaining that British bombers did not dare to fly over German territory by day, yet German planes flew raids against England in broad daylight. Germany had refrained from responding to the night raids on the assumption that the British would soon stop such nonsense, but 'Mr. Churchill took that as a sign of weakness on our part. You will understand if from now on we respond, night after night . . .'

When the storm of applause died down, Hitler continued: 'If the British air force drops two, three, or four kilograms of bombs, we will drop 200,000, 300,000, 400,000 or more kilos!' The audience went into a frenzy at this notion of overwhelming retaliation. Hitler basked for a moment in their approval, then continued, 'And if they declare they will stage massive attacks on our cities, we will *wipe out* their cities! We will spoil the fun of these night-flying pirates, so help us God!'

The audience leaped to their feet, shouting. Hitler calmed them, and concluded with the words, 'The hour will come when one of our nations collapses, and it will not be National Socialist Germany!'

And indeed on the evening of 7 September the first squadrons of German bombers flew over London to begin a major assault on the British capital, returning every night for a week. They inflicted tremendous property damage, killed or wounded thousands of civilians, but could not shake the determination of the English or halt their production. On the contrary, the Blitz, as they called it, merely stiffened British resolve.

Furthermore, the leaders of the German air war made a grave tactical error at this point. They called off the daytime attacks on southern England which had created such difficulties for the British in previous weeks. Now the Spitfire and Hurricane pilots had a much needed chance to rest.

When I relieved Erwin at 6.00 A.M. on 15 September 1940, all seemed quiet on both sides of the Channel. A few high-flying reconnaissance planes took off as usual to survey the previous night's damage in London.

But then around 11.30 the double doctor, who had been monitoring the receiver, gestured excitedly to the rest of us. 'Good God – this can't be real! They must be mad!' he exclaimed, and then reported in correct military style: 'In the Calais–Amiens–Le Havre sector with Dieppe as focal point 800 aircraft have taken off; heading north; probable target, London.'

At first nothing stirred on the British side, although the British must have been alerted. But that changed during the next fifteen minutes: one British fighter squadron after another scrambled and flew to meet the approaching German planes, intercepting them long before they reached London.

Neither the first great wave of German planes nor the next equally massive one even got near its target. With the exception of a few planes that changed course and approached at a high altitude to unload their bombs wherever they could, all the attackers were forced back, and the RAF fighters downed the heavy Heinkel 111s by the dozen.

Erwin kept a tally of the losses, and at the end of the day gave us a final result that far exceeded our estimates; British losses amounted to

26 Spitfires and Hurricanes, most of whose pilots bailed out safely over or near the coast. The Luftwaffe lost 183 aircraft – Heinkel 111s and Messerschmidt 109s. If one added the planes probably lost in crash landings, Reichsmarschall Göring ended the day with 200 fewer planes and 500 to 600 fewer men than he began it. The next morning Göring ordered the Luftwaffe in northern France and Belgium to cease all daytime attacks, 'until the British fighter arm has been completely destroyed – which,' he added boastfully, 'should be accomplished in four to five days.'

But from 15 September on, the British had the upper hand. They soon established aerial control over the Channel; and Hitler postponed Operation Sealion indefinitely, eventually giving up the plan altogether.

'September 15th may have been the turning point,' Werner remarked, 'but we in the infantry in northern France hadn't the faintest notion of what was going on. Of course I heard about the Battle of Britain later on, but back then, in Amiens, though we were so close to the action, all we got were the Wehrmacht Reports, and they had precious little to do with the truth.'

'Well, as far as the truth is concerned,' I said, and had to laugh as I thought of Erwin, 'we weren't so scrupulous ourselves. Erwin never admitted it, but his reports on German losses were generously rounded upward. When the individual squadrons accounted for their losses later, the British victory wasn't quite as overwhelming as he had claimed.'

Werner looked at me with surprise, and I hurried to explain the reasons for Erwin's behaviour:

'In 1933 the Nazis imprisoned his father as a Social Democrat and trade union officer. They tortured him so brutally that he never recovered; and his application for a disability pension was rejected on the grounds that his injuries were the result of an "accident outside of working hours. He petitioned Hermann Göring, who at the time was prime minister of Prussia, to order a police enquiry into the reasons for his disability and certify that he was entitled to the pension. The petition resulted in his being arrested again, and he wasn't released until he had signed a "voluntary" statement saying that he renounced all claims and "would never again appeal to the Prussian prime minister". Erwin's father died in the winter of 1939–40. He was forty-six years old.'

'If I'd had the opportunity then, I would have paid them back, too,' Werner commented. 'With pleasure. But I didn't get my chance till later. In 1940 I still had to be extra-cautious; my father finally found a job again, though it paid miserably, and he had to report regularly to the police. I had to be careful not to make trouble for him. Otherwise they would have locked him up again right away as a former Communist. That threat hung over the entire family. Everyone at home was terribly depressed; there was never enough to eat, there was no money, and after the collapse of France we felt sure the Nazis were here to stay. When I went home on leave, I spent most of the time with Aunt Alma in Hamburg. By then, Hamburg had air raids almost every night, and food supplies were low, but my aunt didn't let it get her down. "Listen to me, boy," she said. "Hitler cooks with water just like the rest of us, and when he's let off enough steam, his potatoes will burn – you mark my words!"

'She cheered me up. I gave her most of the stuff I brought home from France – coffee beans, butter, canned meat, cognac. Most of it she took down to a hiding place in the coal cellar. I used to joke that she just wanted to save it until I was gone, but she would flare up: "Don't joke – this stuff's not for me! There are people who really need it!" She never mentioned any names, but I knew that she meant people in hiding, comrades, and others who had to stay out of the clutches of the Gestapo.'

TWENTY-SIX

Clandestine Operations

For the Christmas of 1940 I was granted a twelve-day leave. I reached Düsseldorf early in the morning of 25 December and went straight to see Herr Desch. He greeted me cordially, and while I showered and changed my clothes, he made breakfast for us.

'I'm all by myself at the moment,' he explained. 'As you know, my wife is off taking the cure with your mother; and Frau Gerber, the housekeeper, has gone to see her husband and won't be back until after the holidays.'

In the code we used on the telephone and in correspondence, 'taking the cure' meant searching out new hiding places for fugitives, and as for Frau Gerber's husband, I knew he had received a long prison sentence for 'plotting high treason'.

'Do you still have anyone living downstairs?' I asked, recalling how Herr Desch had sheltered Jews in his shop.

But that, as I now learned, was no longer possible. For one thing, a new tenant had moved into the building, a suspicious, unsympathetic type. For another thing, Holland was no longer a refuge: the Wehrmacht had marched in the previous May.

'And the major?' I asked. 'I was expecting to find him here.'

Herr Desch told me that Uncle Erich had given up the role of Major von Elken and had returned to Berlin; he now lived just off the Kurfürstendamm, with a new name and new identification papers. In October, when he left, Uncle Erich had explained that he 'still had work to do'.

'You'll certainly look him up when you go to Berlin,' Herr Desch remarked. 'I only hope he exercises some caution. He's organising a new escape route. We're still in touch. Recently he sent a message asking whether I didn't know an innocent-looking young woman who enjoyed hiking and could take a vacation for a couple of weeks in southern Styria.'

'Is he thinking of the Yugoslav border?'

'Apparently. The young woman should speak some Slovenian, or a related language.'

'I think I might have someone,' I told him. 'And she gets around pretty well on skis, if that would be of any use. I'll ask her right now – I can get there in fifteen minutes by trolley bus.'

'That sounds excellent,' Herr Desch remarked after I had told him whom I had in mind. He provided me with a few more details of the assignment and then said, 'If you're back here by noon we can visit Frau Ney together in Meerbusch. We're invited to luncheon, and afterwards we'll have a little chat. Fräulein Bonse will be there too.'

Half an hour later I knocked at the door of Hedwig, my parents' former housekeeper. My visit did not surprise her, for she had written me a letter before Christmas urging me to come by if I were home on leave.

'Don't look at the mess,' she said. 'I had to get some sleep before I tackled the cleaning.' I knew from her letter that she was working in a munitions factory twelve hours a day, except Sundays, when she did all her housework and other chores. She looked pale and exhausted, much older than her twenty-nine years.

'I thought you were going to get a doctor's excuse and take some time off?'

'I did, but not until after the holidays! The People's Welfare was going to give out packages with a few sweets, a quarter-pound of cocoa, and a kilo of lard! I couldn't pass that up. But I've already talked to the doctor, and he's going to give me an excuse for ten days' sick leave, and on top of that I'll get some recuperation time. I'm really looking forward to not having to get up at five and spend the whole day on my feet cleaning those damned grenades.'

'You clean grenades?'

'Yes, the threads on the outside have to be cleaned with a wire brush and then oiled. We have a quota, of course, and the pace is murderous. The most tiring part is having to stand all the time, but perhaps they'll transfer me soon to the bullet division – there at least you can sit.'

'What do you plan to do with your vacation?' I asked.

'What *can* I do? Do you see me going to Garmisch for the winter sports, like some Kreisleiter's wife?'

'Why not? You need to recuperate, and you still ski, don't you?'

'I don't really know. The last time I had a chance was two years ago. I went with Fritz a few times. I did all right.'

I asked about Fritz, her husband. He was fine, she said. He was serving with an engineers' battalion in Posen, and had been home on leave in mid-November.

'So he should be due for a leave again soon,' I said.

She shook her head. 'No, he won't get off before February – they work them very hard.'

I then brought up my plan, which would give her a real vacation and at the same time help us find a safe route across the border into Yugoslavia. She worried about not knowing Slovenian, but I assured her that she would manage with Sorbish, her mother tongue, and with German, and that the important thing in dealing with people in the border area would be to let them know she was also of Slavic descent.

I also reassured her about the expenses for the trip: she would be given money for the train and for a modest hotel, as well as for any clothing and hiking shoes she might need.

'But what can I tell my neighbours and the other women at the plant? They know I can't afford a trip like this,' Hedwig protested.

'We've taken care of that too,' I said. 'Several wealthy businessmen are contributing two-week vacation trips through the Winter Aid Campaign for deserving munitions workers. One of these gentlemen – a good friend of mine – will bring you the train ticket and the gift certificates himself. He's a "sponsoring member of the SS", and the whole thing will be very convincing. Don't worry!'

'Wonderful!' Hedwig said, and gave me a big hug. 'The last thing I expected was a real vaction in the mountains! And you can be sure I'll find out what you need to know.'

At Aunt Annie's a simple lunch awaited us, even though it was Christmas Day. 'I don't want to get mixed up in the black market,' she said, when her husband remarked upon the tiny helpings of meat. Yet despite the slim rations before us, the entire group had a distinguished, even prosperous, appearance.

There was Aunt Annie, leaning on her cane and pouring coffee with her free hand, a dignified older woman with grey hair and a friendly face, a gold cross the only ornament on her silk dress. Her husband, master baker Ney, was wearing a custom-tailored Wehrmacht uniform, for he had been called up, though only as an auxiliary paymaster in the reserves stationed in Düsseldorf. On his chest he wore his decorations from the First World War. Fräulein Bonse, in a black suit and white blouse, looked more than ever like an instructor at an arts and crafts institute. She, too, wore a large gold cross; it hung from a fine chain around her neck. Herr Desch, who was talking with her, had replaced his customary SS badge with a tiny clip with decorations from the First World War.

To my surprise the 'watchmaker' from Basel was also present. But now he was dressed as a priest, and I was told that 'Monsignor Sprüngli' had come to distribute packages sent by people in Switzerland to prisoners of war, and planned to return home soon.

As we shook hands, Monsignor Sprüngli hesitated a moment; it had, after all, been four years since we met, and at the time I was still in short pants. He held my hand in his for a moment, looked intently at my Luftwaffe uniform, and then said in a friendly voice, with a hint of a twinkle in his eyes, 'Now I recognise you, my son! We may change our outward appearance, but our hearts remain the same, isn't that true?'

In the course of the afternoon we discussed not only the general situation but also the urgent necessity of finding new escape routes that could be used regularly.

'The German-Swiss border can hardly be crossed illegally any more,' Monsignor Sprüngli explained. 'Besides, the Swiss authorities are increasingly unwilling to take in refugees. You know that the *J* stamped on the passports of German Jews was introduced at the urging of Dr. Rothmund, head of the Swiss Immigration police. The Nazis adopted it enthusiastically, but it was a Swiss idea . . .'

'Switzerland is surrounded,' the monsignor continued after a pause. 'German tanks have been lined up along the French-Swiss border since summer, and to the south are the Italian Fascists.' He sighed. 'All in all, I think we have to count Switzerland out as a refuge for larger numbers of people. Only in very special individual cases can something still be done.'

'In four weeks,' Herr Desch reported, 'we will have definite information about the possibilities along the border with Yugoslavia. If small groups can get through regularly, my friends could arrange for them to go on to Salonika or Istanbul and from there, on neutral ships, to Central or South America. But we must act fast, for I hear from my sources that these routes could be cut off come spring.'

After we had also discussed the difficulties of escaping to Sweden, I asked whether any thought had been given to getting refugees into the unoccupied part of France, and from there through Spain to Lisbon. But that route, Fräulein Bonse explained, was being reserved for people forced to flee Holland, Belgium, and northern France as the German troops advanced. Most of these people had been interned by the Vichy government and were in danger of being turned over to the Nazis. Those who had escaped internment had gone into hiding. All efforts on their behalf were concentrated on obtaining French exit visas, American entry visas, and transportation.

When we parted, Aunt Annie pressed a thick envelope into my

hand. 'Don't let Greybeard see this,' she said; I knew that she kept secrets from him only when she went overboard in her generosity.

'I really don't need anything, Aunt Annie,' I protested, but she had already stuffed the enveloped into one of my jacket pockets. 'You're going to Berlin, aren't you?' she whispered. 'There are certainly people there who can make good use of these: travellers' coupons for lard, meat, and other food – they can be used anywhere – and a little money. Greybeard gives me the coupons for groceries, but I think we can manage perfectly well without.'

The next morning I took the train to Berlin. Uncle Karl picked me up at the station. He was alone and seemed gloomy. On his warm overcoat with the fur collar he was wearing the Party badge as well as a silver pin from the Reich Air Raid Defence League; under his coat, his jacket lapel sported the same arrangement of swastikas.

He saw me looking at this display and remarked apologetically, 'Well, I look so Jewish, you know . . . Gudrun had to prove Aryan ancestry back to 1750 before Horst-Eberhard could receive permission to marry her.'

'And did you really find nothing but Aryans?'

He nodded. 'Aunt Elsbeth isn't feeling well, otherwise she would have come along. The terror raids have affected her heart. Now the doctor absolutely forbids her to go up the five flights to the roof with wet mats and buckets of sand to do her fire watch.'

I pictured my overweight aunt standing guard in the attic at night in her helmet and gas mask, after a day spent running around for the Party, the National Socialist People's Welfare, and the Winter Aid – I almost burst out laughing.

'She'll have to stay in bed for at least ten days,' Uncle Karl continued, 'and you're going to stay with Gudrun, so she won't feel guilty about not cooking for you. Gudrun's expecting us for supper.'

I did not look forward to being put up by my cousin Gudrun and her husband, the SS Gruppenführer and police lieutenant general. Uncle Karl seemed to sense my reluctance, for he said, 'Horst-Eberhard is in Poland at the moment – they've given him a command there, and he won't be back until February. They have a beautiful house in Grunewald, and plenty of room.'

I could easily guess how the house in Grunewald had been obtained. But the main thing was that I would not have to see the Gruppenführer. And perhaps I might learn a few things from my cousin Gudrun, with whom I had been on good terms when we were younger.

The villa stood on a huge plot of wooded land. At the gate SS guards saluted when Uncle Karl showed his official identification. 'The private here is my nephew,' Uncle Karl explained, and they let me in without objection.

Once inside the gate we were received by another SS guard, who held two snarling German shepherds on a leash. 'Heil Hitler!' he said, 'I'll take you to the house. Please stay close behind me.'

Everything was pitch-dark because of the blackout. The door to the house was opened by a woman whose outline we could make out only dimly. Not until she shut the door did she turn on the light. She was a youngish woman in a simple dark blue smock, on which was sewn a cloth patch I had not seen before: it was a *P* on a yellow background.

She took us to the sitting room, and asked us to wait; the lady of the house would join us in a moment.

'Gudrun has Polish servants,' Uncle Karl explained. From his voice it was hard to tell whether he was proud of this fact or disapproved. 'Two maids and two girls for the kitchen; Horst-Eberhard sent them from Poland.'

He would have said more, but then Gudrun appeared, as blond, plump, and bubbly as I remembered her. She greeted us cordially and took us in to supper.

'You're so lucky!' she exclaimed to me. 'You're stationed in France where you can get anything – perfume, fancy lingerie, silk stockings, paté de foie gras, chocolates with liqueur filling, so many delicacies. All my husband sends me is bacon, lard, and geese. I used to love roast goose, but I'm sick of it now. Today we're having suckling pig, also from Poland. I hope you like it. And for an appetiser a little smoked salmon – is that all right?'

Gudrun went on and on. Uncle Karl seemed used to it, and concentrated on the excellent food. After supper he accepted a glass of cognac and then said good-bye. 'I shouldn't leave Aunt Elsbeth at home alone for so long,' he told me, 'and I want to get back before the alert.'

The evening continued as it had begun. Gudrun told me all about her wedding and the important SS officers who had been there, about the comfortable life she was leading, and the official duties she had, and about the boredom she was feeling with Horst-Eberhard on special assignment for four months.

'Why aren't you working?' I asked.

'I'd like to, but it's out of the question. I couldn't be a secretary any more, with Horst-Eberhard a general now.'

'What's he doing in Poland? Rebuilding the Polish police force?'

Gudrun laughed. 'Certainly not. The Government General, as it's called now, is just a sort of colony. The Poles are being trained to work for us. Horst-Eberhard told me the Führer wants to give the whole country to the SS as a present. Then they'll build fortresses, and every deserving SS leader will get his own estate and a few thousand Poles as workers. It sounds boring to me – I'd rather be in Berlin.'

She spoke enthusiastically about the good times one could have in Berlin, asked if I would take her out sometime, and want to listen to records with me. But I excused myself, saying I was tired from the long train trip.

Gudrun urged me to get a good night's sleep and told me I could ring for the maids whenever I got up. She summoned the young woman who had let us in and told her to take my bag upstairs. When I objected that I could do that perfectly well myself, Gudrun scolded me: 'You have to give these Polish girls a good workout. This is paradise for them, compared to what they're used to. So call them by their first names, and don't say please or thank you, and let them know who's boss.'

The next day I left the house long before Gudrun got up. By ten o'clock I was at the Rummelsburg Station, far from the centre of Berlin, where Herr Desch had told me I would meet Uncle Erich.

I hardly recognised him – he had changed so much since our last meeting. He looked like a delivery van driver. Instead of his monocle he wore cheap wire-rimmed spectacles, with one of the lenses held in place with adhesive tape. The carefully clipped moustache was gone; instead he wore several days' stubble. On his head, a grey wool cap with earflaps, and beneath his short, heavy jacket with a large oil spot on one sleeve was a dirty blue apron. He seemed to be absorbed in the *Völkischer Beobachter*.

I went up to him and said, 'Hello, Uncle Erich, nice to see you again!'

He put down the paper, looked at me over the top of his glasses, gave me a friendly smile, and greeted me in a broad working-class Berlin dialect. His new way of speaking was quite a departure from his former starched, regimental manner. I had never heard him speak Berlin dialect before, but he kept up a steady stream of it as we made our way to a nearby bar, which was not very full but very noisy. Two workers were engaged in a loud argument at the bar. The proprietor had the radio turned up so loud that the glasses rattled. It was the perfect place for Uncle Erich and me to talk.

'At the moment we have twenty-nine people hiding, with the Gestapo hot on their trail,' he told me in his normal voice. 'We have to get them out as soon as possible.'

I told him what I had learned at the Christmas Day meeting in Meerbusch and conveyed all the other information Herr Desch had given me, including our plans for reconnoitring southern Styria and the Balkans.

He listened attentively, expressing scepticism about certain points, and then remarked, 'The main difficulty is that the Styrian border is so far from Berlin. The railway stations and trains are closely guarded, and a traffic to and from Berlin has been cut way back and is often subject to checks. Even if we found a place to slip through the border into Yugoslavia and Herr Desch's friends had everything else organised, how would we get the people out of Berlin, at least as far as Dresden or Leipzig?'

'Is it easier getting out from there?'

'In Western Saxony there's an extensive local bus system that goes all the way into Thuringia. You have to change dozens of times, but you're safe from patrols. And every ten days there's a lorry with a trailer leaving Plauen for Austria, going to a branch factory near Graz. The driver is absolutely trustworthy, and he could easily take five or six people along every time. With a slight detour he could even drop them off at the Yugoslav border. I've just got to get these people out of here! It's much too dangerous, and can you imagine trying to sustain twenty-nine adults without ration cards?'

I thought of the envelope in my pocket. 'Here,' I said, 'this is from Aunt Annie. She sends her best!'

He looked around to make sure no one was observing us, then glanced into the envelope. 'My goodness, to think there are still people like Frau Ney! This'll keep the wolf from the door for a good three weeks.'

'Tell me,' I said, 'isn't it very difficult and terribly dangerous to maintain contact with so many people? You can't have them hidden in one building, can you?'

'No,' he said and slipped back into Berlin dialect, 'no problem – easy as stacking a bottle on a milk cart . . .' He was working as a milkman, he informed me with a grin. As he made his early morning rounds he was able to keep up his contacts unobtrusively.

We finished our beer and strolled a block or so together, arranging a way for Herr Desch to get a message to him as soon as the Yugoslavian escape route was worked out.

'I imagine that should be settled by January the 20th,' I told him. But I noticed that he was not listening. He was staring down from the bridge on which we were standing at a tugboat that was just pulling out of the East Port.

'By God,' he whispered, 'that could be our solution right there.' He gestured with his chin toward the tug and the heavy barge it was towing. I looked where he was pointing and read the name of the boat and its home port on its bow: *Walburga* – Dessau-Wallwitzport. 'Of course. On a boat like that they can go by way of the Spree and the Havel, and then by the Midland Canal to the Elbe, then upriver to Meissen or Dresden, and from there by bus to Plauen. I don't know why I didn't think of it earlier! I even know how it can be done – we'll get started right after New Year's.'

When we said good-bye at the station, he gave me the *Völkischer Beobachter*, 'so's you'll have somethin' to read on the train, boy,' he said loudly in dialect, and then added in a low voice, 'There's something in there for Herr Desch – you should read it too, so you know what's going on.'

Inside the newspaper I found five pages of onionskin paper with a single-spaced typed description of the 'sudden strikes' launched against the Jewish population. The report described the deportation in February 1940 of Jews from Stettin and Pomerania to eastern Poland.

'On 12 February 1940, the unsuspecting Jewish population of Stettin, about 1,200 persons, were deported to Lublin,' the report began. 'Between 3.00 and 4.00 A.M., SA and SS squads dragged entire Jewish familes out of their apartments and took them to the freight depot. The residents of the two Jewish old-age homes, among them men and women over eighty, were likewise deported. A piece of cardboard was hung around each prisoner's neck with name and deportation number . . . From Lublin the men, women, and children had to walk through deep snow to the villages of Piaski, Glusk, and Belcyce; it was – 20°C. This march lasted fourteen hours, and in the course of it, 72 out of the 1,200 deported persons perished. Most of them froze. Among them was a mother with her three-year-old child in her arms. The body of a five-year-old girl was also found . . . She had been visiting relatives in Stettin at the time of the deportation . . . Once in the three villages, the Jews were left to find their own lodgings in the overcrowded houses and cottages of the local Jews . . . Since food is in short supply, except for black bread, and the sanitary facilities are almost nonexistent, numerous persons have been dying daily . . . By 12 March the number of deaths had risen to 230 . . .'

The report also described in great detail the events of 22 and 23 October 1940, when, just as in Stettin, the Jewish population of Baden and the Rhineland-Palatinate was forced to 'relocate' with less than two hours' notice – sometimes only fifteen minutes – leaving behind all their possessions. Without prior warning and without the knowledge of the French authorities in the unoccupied area, the Jews were 'extradited' to France.

One of the women involved, Frau Else Liefmann, who later escaped abroad with French help, gave an account of this 'relocation'. She and her husband had been sitting at breakfast in the house they had occupied for almost fifty years. Soldiers burst in and ordered them to leave with only 100 marks in cash, and hand luggage. They were held until 2.00 A.M. the following day in the gymnasium of a school, then taken to France by train with an SS escort. The French border guards were told the Jews were expelled from Alsace-Lorraine. After a long journey they arrived at internment camps in southern France.

'Not Poland! How grateful we were for that!' Frau Liefmann wrote in her description of the beginning of the trip, when the prisoners realised the train was heading west over the Rhine.

That afternoon I went back to Grunewald to say good-bye to Gudrun, who was very disappointed to hear that I was leaving so soon. She assumed I was hurrying back to see a girl, and I said nothing to contradict her.

The next morning in Düsseldorf I again had breakfast with Herr Desch, and gave him the typed reports. 'I'll get these to Monsignor Sprüngli, and he'll take them back to Switzerland tomorrow,' Herr Desch said. 'We'll have them published there as quickly as possible, and also in other neutral countries. Perhaps it will do some good. After all, the Nazis are not yet completely indifferent to world opinion.'

I learned later that the deportations had indeed stopped around that time, but the reason is not clear. Probably it was less the reaction abroad than military necessity that prevented freight trains loaded with human beings from heading off to Poland during the next ten months. For before Christmas, on 18 December 1940, Hitler had already issued his Führer's Decree No. 21, ordering preparations for a surprise attack on the Soviet Union to take place by 15 May 1941.

TWENTY-SEVEN

'Carmen'

Upon my return from my Christmas leave, I found that a number of changes had occurred. Little Hans had been promoted to major on the basis of his civil service rank. He now had his own 'weather station' and was relieved of watch duty. In his place we had three new radio operators and an aviation cadet, whose political orientation we would have to feel out. In any case, this reinforcement of our unit meant that we could finally divide the twenty-four hours of the day into three equal watches, with the result that Erwin and I could have eight hours off together.

We used this time for excursions into Rouen or Le Havre. We soon made friends with a woman who ran a little restaurant on the edge of Rouen's badly destroyed Old City. She was a Basque, and because her last name, Ondarraitz, was difficult to pronounce, her neighbours and the patrons of her restaurant generally called her 'Marie la Basquaise'. One evening she turned to us for help; her only son, not yet eighteen, was about to be sent on a 'work detail' to Germany, and she was in despair.

We considered what we could do. It was obvious that a letter from his family doctor wouldn't do. Some German official department would have to certify that he was indispensable in Rouen. But which? I could not think which department we could appeal to.

But Erwin discovered in the fine print of the boy's call-up letter that anyone active in a public institution whose maintenance was of importance to the German military forces might become eligible for a dispensation. The certification of indispensability had to be signed by the regional commander or his deputy, and Erwin realised in a flash that our Major Zobel would gladly sign any request that came to him from the Rouen public library.

It even turned out that the charming librarian with whom Major Zobel was in love was distantly related by marriage to Marie la Basquaise, and within a day our major had signed the petition. From now on, young François spent two hours every afternoon hauling and dusting library books.

Around this time I received a postcard from Aunt Annie; she wrote that the 'charming major, ret.,' had moved to the Rhineland; 'our Hedwig's engagement party was a complete success – just imagine: thirty-one friends and relatives, but for the duration of the war we should not expect to repeat such celebrations.'

Then Aunt Annie added something that I could not at first decode: 'Herr Schneider would be very happy, though, if you were to get engaged. He certainly likes Carmen. Think it over.'

I did just that, and I came to the conclusion that Herr Schneider, that is, Herr Desch (*Schneider* is German for tailor) wanted to establish another escape route, since the rescue of the Jews from Berlin by way of the Yugoslav border could not be repeated. 'Carmen' must mean the border to Spain.

But how was I to go about working that out? Except for a few people in Rouen and Le Havre I had few contacts with the French population. The distance between our station in Normandy and the French-Spanish border was more than 800 kilometres and there were no official reasons for going to the Pyrenees.

I asked Erwin whether he had any ideas about ways of getting there.

'You're not planning on leaving us?' he asked.

'No, no, I'm just interested in that area. It's supposed to be so beautiful, and now that we occupy the whole coast as far as the Spanish border, it might be a good idea.'

Erwin thought for a moment, then shook his head. 'Well, I can't think how it might be done. And I can't give you any advice if you won't tell me what it's all about.' He seemed quite offended. Finally, I told him about the strikes against the Jews in Pomerania, Baden, and the Palatinate.

Once he knew what it was all about, he exclaimed, 'Well, that's entirely different. But why should you go to the Pyrenees yourself? Send people who know their way around there!' He then suggested asking Marie la Basquaise for help. 'You know – one hand washes the other . . .'

At the next opportunity I spoke with Madame Ondarraitz. She listened carefully and then commented, 'The border itself is no problem. Your people would just have to be good walkers; it's at least a two-hour hike over winding hilly paths. There would be no problem either with finding guides – my people all do a little smuggling. And the Basques on both sides of the border stick together; most of them are good Republicans and fought against Franco, and we haven't forgotten that Hitler levelled Guernica with his bombs four years ago. No, the problem is in getting to the border.'

She explained that any trip required an official pass; she herself had been unable to visit her aged mother because a pass was so difficult to obtain. 'But,' she added, 'it must be easier for you to get them.'

When I reported this conversation to Erwin, he promised to look around and see what could be done.

The next time we visited Madame Ondarraitz, she took us aside and said in a whisper, 'I've just received a letter from my sister. She says that in Gurs, not far from our town, there's an internment camp where many refugees from Germany, including many Jews, are being kept under miserable conditions. They're dying like flies from hunger and cold. I thought you should know about it – it might do something to your plans.'

This was the first I had heard of French camps for German refugees, and I was horrified. Forty years later I spoke with a friend who had been a prisoner in that camp and had escaped to the United States. Had he not escaped, he would have been turned over to the Gestapo in 1942.

My friend Ulrich had fled Germany in the thirties, and lived in Brussels until May 1940. From there he was evacuated to southern France, just in time to get away from the German troops marching into Belgium. He and several thousand other German refugees were shunted from one camp to another, until they ended up in unheated barracks in Gurs, in the Pyrenees.

I asked him what conditions in the camp were like.

Ulrich, a man inclined toward understatement, described them thus: 'The landscape around Gurs was beautiful, the food and sanitary conditions horrendous; and the death rate was enormous. When you came out of the barracks in the morning, you had to be careful to stay on the plank walks; otherwise you would sink up to your knees in swamp. The whole complex was built over a swamp, the barracks forming little islands. The prisoners were separated according to sex and origin, and you needed a pass to go from one island to the next. It was Lieutenant Guyot who handed out passes; he was one of a group of officers who tried to sabotage the harsh orders of the commandant, himself a faithful follower of the Vichy government, and to protect the interests of the prisoners. People like Guyot could be trusted.'

'Did any of you prisoners have money? Could you buy extra food?'

'My own funds were gone, and there was no way I could get to my account in Brussels. But some of the prisoners had money sewn into little bags under their shirts. Lieutenant Guyot and a few other officers tried to prevent inequities by getting a little more food for everyone, but it didn't work out.

'In March 1941 I received word that an American visa had been issued for me, one of the 'nonquota' visas occasionally granted at the intercession of the rescue organisations to persons at particular risk. My sister and a few friends who were already in the United States had obtained it for me, as well as money for the crossing and the required affidavit assuring that I would not become a burden on the American taxpayers.'

'So you were saved!'

'Not at all. In order to take advantage of my visa, I would first have had to be admitted to the emigrants' camp, Les Milles, located between Aix-en-Provence and Marseilles. Once released from there I would have to spend weeks running around Marseilles to get the necessary papers – and I had no money. Besides, I would have to get to Spain or Portugal; one could no longer leave from Marseilles.

'Emigration thus seemed impossible. In my despair I hit on a plan which in retrospect seems crazy, but at the time represented my only hope of getting out. It involved a wealthy fellow prisoner, Gerson, who was a compulsive gambler. He liked to bet on predictions of developments that would affect our fate. His terms always seemed remarkably generous, but few liked to bet against him, because his predictions seemed so likely to come true.'

'What did you bet on? I assume you won.'

'Well, I did. But I must explain first that in that camp we had lots of time for thinking. And during the long winter of 1941 I had done a good deal of thinking about what had occurred since Hitler's takeover. I suddenly perceived that Hitler's strikes against other countries were not mere flailing about; they followed a predictable pattern of motion – counterclockwise. In March 1938 Hitler annexed Austria; a year later, also in March, came the march into Prague. Half a year later Warsaw was captured, and in April 1940 Copenhagen and Oslo. Only a few weeks later German tanks rolled into Holland, Belgium, and France. If you plotted those attacks on the map, they formed an obvious circle, and it was also clear that the intervals between attacks were growing shorter and shorter. At the time I decided to make the wager, it was clear that Hitler's aggressive moves would continue. In February we already knew that two German divisions under General Rommel had gone to the assistance of the Italians, under attack by the British in Libya. If my analysis was correct, Hitler's next objective after the south would be the southeast, the Balkans.'

'Incredible! And that's what you bet on?'

'No, I was even bolder than that. I assumed that after a rapid conquest of Yugoslavia and Greece, which in fact occurred in April

1941, the next attack would be directed to the east, against Russia. That would complete the spiral. Before I proposed the bet to Gerson, I thought hard about possible timing. By now it was the end of March. The campaign in the southeast was still to come, though it might begin at any minute, to judge by the reports we were hearing.'

'Yes, I remember that,' I said. 'My friends were convinced from the beginning of February that the escape route through the Balkans might be cut off any day.'

'That campaign was predictable, but it was much more difficult to calculate the beginning of the attack on the Soviet Union. Finally I decided that Hitler would have to strike in the first half of '41, very soon after the Balkan conquest, because otherwise he could not hope to take Moscow before the onset of winter.'

'So that's what you bet on: the timing of the German attack on the Soviet Union.'

Ulrich nodded. 'That same evening I got Gerson involved in a political discussion. He agreed that it was only a matter of time before Hitler turned on the Soviet Union. But he thought it 'out of the question' that the attack might occur in 1941. I can still hear him laughing at my prediction that it would come before 1st July. But I certainly didn't mind the ridicule when he insisted on betting his eight hundred dollars against my one, just to prove me wrong. Lieutenant Guyot recorded the bet, and we signed by candlelight – there was no lighting in the barracks – in the presence of three witnesses. Everyone in the camp was talking about it.'

'And on the 22nd June you won.'

'Yes, the Gerson didn't hesitate for a moment to pay up. He congratulated me, and I think he wasn't sorry to have lost the bet. It seemed certain to us now that Hitler wouldn't be able to win the war he had started.'

'What did you do next?'

'Well, first I wrote to claim my visa; authorisation for it had arrived at the American consulate in Marseilles weeks earlier. To my great relief my application was accepted by return post, and I was released from Gurs and transferred to the emigration camp at Les Milles. After that, things moved fast. Once out of Gurs I discovered the existence of a committee that helped me collect all the papers I needed. By the 12th September, I was in New York. And before the year was out the Wehrmacht marched into the previously unoccupied section of France. Those who couldn't escape from the camps and hide out with French families fell into the hands of the Gestapo and were later sent to Auschwitz, where they were murdered.'

Meanwhile, the Pyrenees escape route was becoming more and more crucial. I received a postcard from Aunt Annie, saying that 'three particularly nice' – which meant particularly endangered – 'friends of Herr Schneider' were in Paris and absolutely had to get tickets for *Carmen*, which I assumed meant they needed to escape via Spain. After puzzling over the rest of the coded message, I figured out that I could make contact with them at the Hôtel Blanche in the Rue Banquier in Paris. The problem of the Pyrenees was now compounded by the problem of Paris. How to get there?

At that time, in spite of the war and the occupation, Paris still had a great deal to offer in the way of theatre, concerts, and nightclubs of all sorts, many of which stayed open all night. The city exercised such a fascination over all the occupation troops in northern France that the military had declared it off-limits. If you did not belong to a staff with headquarters in the city, you had to have a special authorisation, and those were very difficult to obtain. Erwin and I racked our brains to think how I might get around this obstacle. It seemed as though we had considered every option, and we would be forced to wait. But then luck turned our way.

On the afternoon of 10 May, Major Zobel stopped by. 'Everything all right?' he asked.

I reported to him on the 'extensive enemy activity, chiefly high-flying reconnaissance aircraft heading toward Reich territory,' but he paid no attention.

'Well, if everything's calm,' he said when I had finished, 'you can come with me. I have something to discuss with you.'

I turned the watch over to the double doctor and went with the major. It took a while for him to come to the point. Finally he said that since I spoke French so well, he would like me to make some purchases for him. He showed me a list several pages long in his rather angular handwriting. The items for the most part were women's clothing and underwear, and it immediately occurred to me that this was a unique opportunity to carry out the plan I had been nursing for weeks.

'I'm afraid, sir, we won't be able to find all these items here in the provinces,' I began.

Major Zobel interrupted me: 'Yes, yes, I know. You'll have to go to Paris. This will be an official errand, of course,' Major Zobel added, 'to the Luftwaffe communications depot in Belleville. You have to pick up a couple of cathode rods for us, or whatever they're called. I'll give you a special requisition for them, but never mind if they're not available. The other purchases are the main thing.'

I examined the list more closely, and it looked as thought I could easily find most of the items at the Galéries Lafayette or some other department store.

'How much time will you need? More than two days?' the major wanted to know.

I was expecting to have to go and come in one day, but now I remarked, 'It'll be a little tight, what with going and coming, sir, but I'll try to get it all done in two days.'

He promised to have the authorisations ready on the following day, and to let me take Krupa and the eight-cylinder Horch. He was in the right mood, so I asked him if he might get a travel pass for Madame Ondarraitz to go and see her mother, who was turning eighty. He remembered the name, and I reminded him of the connection with his librarian. The major promised to take care of the matter.

When I went back to tell Erwin of my twin triumphs, he whistled in admiration. 'Amazing! This seems to be our lucky day! Look what I've got here,' he said, and pulled out from under his jacket a number of stamped forms. 'Things are in total chaos in the orderly room,' he told me, lowering his voice so as not to be overheard. 'They have their hands full with the troops being transferred to Poland. I went to pick up the marching orders for the boys in our unit who are being shipped out. "Find them yourself, they're lying around here somewhere,' the guy in charge tells me. And while I'm looking, I noticed a pile of special travel passes signed by Colonel Kessler and ready to be filled out. I thought they might come in handy – in case someone wanted to go and have a look at the Pyrenees, for example.'

I stared at those precious forms with the impressive seal and the flourish that represented 'Kessler'. Beneath the signature was a little violet stamp that said 'Colonel and Group Commander'. 'That's exactly what we needed,' I said. 'Are there at least three of them?'

'Five,' Erwin said. 'You have to be prepared for all eventualities and think of yourself too . . . Come on, let's get over to Rouen to see Madame. We still have things to discuss, and there's no time to lose.'

Two days later in Paris, Krupa dropped me off near the Hôtel Blanche. The proprietress responded at once to Aunt Annie's password. I was directed to a room on the second floor, where I found three young men of about twenty, just my age. They were sturdy fellows, with a determined air about them. One of them kept his hand in his pocket, and I felt sure he had a gun. We soon established each other's trustworthiness, and I handed them the special passes.

'You have to fill them out in old German script, or with a typewriter, but not a French one. Do you know the script?'

The largest of the three, who was blond and tall enough to be an SS man, said, 'We went to school in Berlin until '36, so that's no problem.'

'Do you have uniforms?' I enquired.

'Not yet, but we will . . .'

I explained just how they should fill out the forms and told them they would be expected at a little hotel on Rue Othaz in Hendaye on the Spanish border. 'When you get there, ask the proprietor for Madame Ondarraitz, and then say "Marie la Basquaise from Rouen". She'll take care of the rest.'

Before I left, I asked them whether there was an active resistance movement now in Berlin.

The man who spoke for them hesitated for a moment, then said, 'Yes, there is. We're a small group, because most of the younger Jews left long ago, or they're in concentration camps. A few non-Jewish comrades from the Communist Workers' Youth Movement and from the Socialist Workers' Youth Movement are involved, and we have contact with a number of groups, but for the most part we're on our own.'

'Do you have weapons?'

He answered evasively, 'We confine ourselves to pamphleteering, especially in the factories –' he broke off and looked at his two comrades.

The one with the pistol in his pocket said, 'It's important to do something and not just wait to see what the others are going to do – do you see?'

I nodded, and he continued, 'If you ever want to link up with us, ask your Uncle Erich about "the Baum".'

Now the most important part of my mission was done. From the hotel I went to the Galéries Lafayette to start making the purchases for Major Zobel, and later met Krupa for lunch at a café on the Boulevard-St.-Michel, as we had agreed.

Krupa was pale and jittery. Not until we got to the café did he speak out: 'From the depot at Belleville I went to a barracks on the Place Balard, and as I was crossing the courtyard, not thinking a thing, I suddenly noticed a boy – he couldn't have been more than eighteen – tied to a post with his eyes blindfolded. Next to him was a rough pine coffin, and the officer who was about to have him shot was just pulling on white kid gloves. I was so horrified I turned and fled. As I got behind the wheel and was about to start up, I heard the shots. My hands were shaking so hard I couldn't drive. Finally a guard came by and asked what was wrong. He told me these executions take place almost every day and the boys being shot are all German soldiers, captured as deserters.'

Forty-one years later I discovered, quite by chance, the identity of the elegant captain in charge of those executions. The captain was none other than the writer Ernst Jünger, whose novel glorifying war, *Amidst Hail of Steel*, had been given to us to read in school as an example of 'heroic realism'.

In his book, *Un Allemand à Paris*, Gerhard Heller describes Jünger's feelings about the executions. The officer asserted he had tried to make them as humane as possible, yet on the other hand he had been 'interested in observing how a person reacts to death under such circumstances'. Heller suggested that such an interest had something slightly morbid about it, yet the officer insisted on characterising it as 'a higher form of curiosity'.

A few days after reading Heller's book, I learned that Ernst Jünger had just received the 1982 Goethe Prize from the city of Frankfurt.

TWENTY-EIGHT

'Hiwis' and Cockatoos

On 22 June 1941, we went to Madame Ondarraitz's restaurant to celebrate Little Hans's birthday. She had long since returned from Hendaye, with the news that the three young men from the Hôtel Blanche in Paris had safely reached Spain by way of the Pyrenees.

We had not yet begun our dinner when our motorcycle courier, Pliechelko, roared up to the restaurant. He let someone off and continued on his way. Krupa dashed in, and without waiting for any greeting, burst out: 'Listen! Since early this morning the Soviet Union has been under attack – along a 1,500-kilometre front, from the Baltic to the Black Sea. I just heard it on Channel 7.'

Channel 7 was the news service of the BBC which we regularly monitored. We asked Madame Ondarraitz to turn on her radio, and then we heard it for ourselves: the campaign against the Soviet Union was under way.

Little Hans, the meteorologist, was the first to speak: 'Three and a half months is all they have before winter sets in!'

Erwin observed that not even two years had passed since Hitler signed the non-aggression pact with the Soviet Union. 'And exactly a week ago,' he told us, 'I picked up a broadcast from Moscow. The word was that rumours about a war between Germany and the Soviet Union were "insane propaganda by the enemies of both countries".'

'And do you know who sent us the fuel for the tanks that are heading for Russia right now?' Krupa asked us. 'The Russians themselves! When I was home for Easter my father was on the telephone with some bigwig, and I heard him say that Soviet deliveries of petroleum, grain, manganese, and other metals needed for the war effort were way up in March, and this month we're getting 4,000 metric tons of rubber from them. He was laughing.'

'How does your father know all this?' Erwin asked. It was the first time we heard Krupa mention his father.

'He's big in the defence industry,' Krupa said with some embarrassment, 'in import-export, but for the last four years it's been mainly import, especially from the Soviet Union.'

Around midnight we listened to the news again, but no more details were available. The Wehrmacht high command and the Propaganda Ministry were silent, and the news blackout continued until the following weekend. Not until Sunday, 29 June did we receive the first 'special bulletins', carefully formulated for their effect as propaganda:

'The Wehrmacht High Command announces that in order to counter the danger threatening from the east, on 22nd June at 3.00 A.M. the German Wehrmacht thrust forward against the mighty advance of hostile forces. Luftwaffe squadrons swooped down in the early morning darkness upon the Soviet Russian foe. In spite of the enemy's numerical superiority, on 22nd June the Luftwaffe secured mastery of the skies in the east and demolished the Soviet Russian air force . . .'

The truth, as we learned some weeks later from pilots who participated in the raids, was that the Soviet aircraft had been parked on their aerodromes without camouflage or flak protection. That explained why close to three thousand aircraft could be destroyed on the ground. The Soviet leadership had considered a German attack out of the question, and was taken completely by surprise.

The next special bulletin cited the triumphs of the German ground forces, though, strangely enough, without any mention of particular towns or rivers. The third special bulletin contained more specifics. The double doctor listened carefully and afterward interpreted the report for us: 'They've been fighting for a week now, probably suffering heavy losses, and at this point they've taken Brest Litovsk, Vilna, Kovno, Dünaburg and now Lemberg – do you see what that means? It means they're still in Poland and Lithuania, and even if they push another 500 kilometers east, they'll still be only halfway to Moscow and Leningrad, and more than 2,000 kilometres from the Baku oilfields and the industrial centres at Sverdlovsk and Magnetogorsk.'

At the mention of Lemberg, the double doctor piped up, 'If the Ukrainian "Hiwis"* are used anywhere, it'll be in Lemberg.' That city was the centre of Ukrainian nationalist hatred of the Bolsheviks, the Poles, and the Jews. I learned a lot more about the actions of the Ukrainian Hiwis in Lemberg when, nineteen years later, in 1960, a certain Herr Grünbart came to see me. At the time, I was working as

---

* 'Hiwis' was short for *Hilfwillige*, the foreign volunteers in the Wehrmacht.

an editor for *Der Spiegel*, and I was used to having strangers come to me, often with remarkable stories.

Moritz Grünbart, a businessman from the Rhineland, told me he had been born in 1920 in Breslau, but had grown up in Lodz, in Poland, among Jews, Poles, Germans, and Ukrainians. After the Germans took Lodz in 1939, the Jewish Grünbart family had succeeded in fleeing from the Wehrmacht and the 'special units' that came in its wake. The family escaped to Kielce, about 130 kilometres south of Lodz. There they were confined to the ghetto the Germans had set up and subjected to the most terrible harassment. Hunger, poverty, and constant fear of death impelled nineteen-year-old Moritz Grünbart and two friends of the same age to flee the ghetto in the spring of 1941 and cross the demarcation line into Soviet-occupied Poland. He was immediately seized by Soviet border guards and, under suspicion of being a spy, thrown into the prison in the border town of Rawaruska and later transferred to the Brigittka Prison in Lemberg.

'I could have survived the war there. True, we had only bread and water, but at least we weren't constantly staring death in the face as in the ghetto of Kielce, where my parents and my six brothers had remained. I was a young fellow and wanted to live. It was better to be imprisoned as a spy by the Russians than to be a Jew under German control in a ghetto. My fellow prisoners were Poles, Ukrainians, Russians, and Jews; and most of the latter were Zionists.

'Before the war between Germany and Russia broke out, we prisoners already had an inkling of what was going on. The German Luftwaffe attacked targets in Lemberg, and the entire Brigittka Prison shook to its foundations. We noticed that the guards were getting more and more edgy. Night after night they came to get prisoners from the cells, mostly Ukrainians and Zionists. They never returned, and we heard they were shot.

'On the 24th or 25th June the Russians abandoned Lemberg. At first we were left to our own devices. As the Russians were retreating, we heard a lot of shooting. Later we learned that the Ukrainians in the town had shot at the Russian troops. But the Soviet departure was of short duration. That same day our guards were back, and then I heard that the Russians were taking revenge on the Ukrainians. I don't know how many of them they shot in the Brigittka Prison, but it must have been hundreds.

'Then the Russians withdrew for good, on the 27th or 28th June, I believe, and all was perfectly still in the prison and in the town. We all heaved a sigh of relief. That same day citizens of Lemberg – Jews and

Poles – came to the prison looking for relatives.* They broke open the doors and let all the prisoners out of the cells – Poles, Russians, Ukrainians, and Jews. A Jewish businessman who was looking for his relatives but couldn't find them took me home to his family. In those few days before the Germans arrived, life in the town seemed completely calm and normal. No one was afraid; we all felt liberated, especially those of us who had been in prison. We were wondering who would come to Lemberg next, the Germans or the Russians again. The Ukrainians, too, waited and watched.

'I like to recall those two or three days when Lemberg was left to itself. For the first time in many weeks I felt protected in the bosom of a family, even if it wasn't my own. The Jewish family that had taken me in really spoiled me. I also got to know the Ukrainian superintendent of their building, who tried to help me. He had, as he put it, some 'connections' with a Ukrainian nationalist organisation, and gave dark hints about announcements he had heard on the radio – that all Ukrainian men in Lemberg should hold themselves in readiness, for early tomorrow morning their brothers would arrive, serving in the Wehrmacht under German command. The superintendent, who apparently was much taken with me, advised me to find a very good hiding place. During the first days, and especially when Ukrainian soldiers in German uniforms marched into town, we could expect a bloodbath among the Jews of Lemberg. "An awful slaughter", was how he put it. I can still hear him saying those words.

'The next morning, which was the 30th June 1941, I went into hiding, together with the family that had taken such good care of me. While it was still dark, we took refuge in the cellar of the building across the street. The superintendent had shown me the place. Around 7.00 A.M. we heard the first sounds: hobnailed boots on the pavement, fists pounding on doors, then shots and screams. That continued with brief interruptions until late afternoon. When things quietened down and finally there was nothing more to be heard, I got impatient. Waiting in the cellar became unbearable to me.

'With two other young fellows I cautiously ventured out into the street. We realised immediately that we had left our hiding place too soon. Along the street stood Jewish men, women, and children, lined up and guarded by soldiers in German uniforms and civilians. One of the soldiers spotted us. He ordered us in Ukrainian to freeze. But we fled blindly into the next building, then up the stairs to the sixth floor,

---

*Of Lemberg's 316,000 inhabitants in 1939, half were Poles, almost 100,000 were Jews, and the rest were Ukrainians.

where we could go no farther. Soldiers and civilians who had run after us caught up with us and drove us with blows down the stairs and out onto the street. I begged the soldier who was beating me with the butt of his rifle to spare me. "I was a prisoner of the Russians, in the Brigittka," I shouted.

'Instead of listening, he beat me even harder and yelled at me. I was too bewildered to notice the details of his uniform, not that I would have known what they meant, except that it was a German uniform. I didn't know anything about stripes and insignia. But one thing was clear: in spite of his uniform, he was not a German but a Ukrainian. We Jews who had lived in Poland could recognise a Ukrainian as well as he could recognise us.

'All the Jews lined up on the street were now transported to Samastynov Prison, a small auxiliary prison for political prisoners, smaller than the Brigittka. We were escorted by the Ukrainians in uniform, as well as by civilians with yellow or yellow and blue armbands. These Ukrainians, however, were from Lemberg.

'On the way they beat us and shouted at us. Some of the prisoners were killed, some wounded. But things got even worse at the prison gate. Along the entry to the courtyard stood a double row of Ukrainians in German uniforms, with fixed bayonets. We were driven between the rows, while they stabbed at us and beat us – men, women, and children alike. Only a few survived the ordeal; the huge prison courtyard was strewn with bodies. As I later saw, some weren't dead yet. I myself miraculously survived. When I regained consciousness, I had enough strength left to drag myself to the fountain at the centre of the courtyard and wash myself. I had lost a great deal of blood and was very weak. But the water helped clear my head. I lay there very quietly and waited.

'When it was completely dark and everything was still, several Ukrainians in German uniforms arrived. They ordered the few survivors, including me, to load the dead and near-dear onto trucks. I remember that the men spoke with us very calmly and matter-of-factly. This whole horrible episode had not been the doing of wild, drunken soldiers. On the contrary, it seemed to me that everything had been crefully organised and ran with machinelike precision. As far as I know, the soldiers didn't plunder, or rape women; I kept my gold watch and my money through the whole time. They simply rounded up all the Jews they could get at and murdered them. I can't say how many died. I also can't say whether the same sort of thing went on in other parts of Lemberg.

'All I know is that I was driven out with the first lorryload of corpses. Outside the prison everything was quiet and very dark, and I was able to jump off the lorry and flee. I ran crazily through the town, trying to get as far away as possible from the mass murder. I ran until I couldn't run any more and thought I was fairly safe. I spent the night out on the street. Everything seemed quiet.

'I stayed in Lemberg for two more days, always hiding. I ran into several other Jews, who had escaped much the way I had. They told me that these operations supervised by Ukrainians in German uniforms continued during that time, though on a reduced scale. I myself didn't see any more of it.

'Not until the third day, after nightfall, did I dare to come out of my hiding place. I was obsessed with the idea of getting out of the town. With the money I still had, I paid someone to take me and two other survivors thirty or forty kilometres from Lemberg in his van. German troops had already reached the village we arrived at, but the atrocities seemed to have been less severe. I saw Jews standing in the market-place, speaking calmly with one another. The restaurants were open, and I went into one and had my first decent meal in days.

'A German family took me in and nursed me until I could set out again, heading back to the ghetto in Kielce, where my parents and brothers were. If I had to die, I thought, I didn't want to die alone, but with them.'

That was the story Moritz Grünbart told me in March of 1960. He later escaped other liquidations. While his entire family was murdered, he was sent as a forced labourer to an Upper Silesian armaments factory, because he was strong and healthy. Just before the war ended, he was shipped to a concentration camp, and finally sent west. On the way he was seriously wounded when an SS guard stabbed him with a bayonet, but shortly after that he was liberated by Soviet troops, taken to a hospital in Berlin in April 1945, and nursed back to health. In 1947 he moved to the Rhineland.

Little Hans and the double doctor already knew something about the Ukrainian 'Hiwi' battalions, though of course they could not guess what infamous role they were playing that day in 1941 when we sat around discussing the German advance into the Ukraine.

During the next days and weeks, we were more concerned with other questions: would the German campaign against the Soviet Union achieve its objectives before winter, and would the British attack the Germans in France to help take the pressure off the Russians?

It soon became apparent that a British attack along the French

Channel coast could not be expected. Great Britain had troubles of its own. The new Africa Corps under Rommel had advanced through the Libyan desert almost to the border of Egypt, threatening the Suez Canal, England's vital sea link with India. Under these circumstances the British had to be grateful that most of Germany's offensive forces were tied up in the Soviet campaign.

So things remained quiet on the Normandy coast during the summer and autumn of 1941. It was in these months that Erwin began to experiment privately. As a trained electrician and radio technician he accomplished in a relatively short time the task of building a wireless long-distance detonator that made it possible to radio-trigger explosives of any size or type.

'What in the world is that for?' I asked him. 'Don't you think the world already has more than enough devices for blowing up yourself and others?'

Erwin laughed. 'Oh, I just wanted to see if I could produce one of these. The Luftwaffe weapons development department already has something similar. I even know the code name for it: "Cockatoo" – I'll bet you're wondering how I found out . . .'

'And what do you intend to do with it?'

He hesitated. Finally he said, 'Well, if we actually conquer the Soviet Union before winter and perhaps also take the Suez Canal, I might possibly overcome my deep repugnance toward instruments of destruction . . .'

I was convinced Erwin would never use his homemade 'cockatoo', even if he had the chance to blow up the entire leadership of the Third Reich. His 'experimentation' was simply his way of overcoming the profound depression that seized us as each day brought fresh reports of Wehrmacht victories, and Hitler's empire seemed to be expanding unchecked, from the North Cape to Egypt, from the Pyrenees to the Sea of Azov.

Our training officer, super-Nazi Holzmann, who had recently been promoted to captain, announced in the 'morale' session he held every ten days, 'The final victory will be ours in six weeks at the least! Our enemies are already finished, and all that is left for our valiant army is a little mopping up. Once Russia lays down her arms, once bolshevism and Judaism are exterminated, England will capitulate, whether we take the Suez Canal from the Brits beforehand or not!'

After he had dismissed us with the promise that we would be home for Christmas, Erwin quietly remarked to me, 'Things have come to a standstill in Egypt, otherwise the Suez Canal wouldn't seem so unimportant all of a sudden. And, you know, by the 14th

September Napoleon was already in Moscow. I bet we'll hear next time that capturing the Soviet capital isn't the main thing after all . . .'

TWENTY-NINE

How the 'Final Victory' Turned into 'Wool-Gathering'

On 2 October 1941, the bulletin of the Wehrmacht high command reported, 'The final confrontation on the Eastern Front has begun.' The next day I set out for three weeks of home leave, the first part of which I was to spend in Berlin, since my mother had written she was 'taking the cure'. When I reached Berlin on the evening of 4 October, no one was waiting at the station for me.

I found Aunt Elsbeth at home, dressed in her fur coat and hat, just on the point of going out. She seemed all flustered, and said, 'I can't stay! The Führer is about to speak. That's why I couldn't come to meet you. Uncle Karl has gone on ahead. Just make yourself at home!' As she hurried to a waiting taxi, she called to me, 'I'll be back around ten. Your supper's on the stove!'

It was almost eleven before she returned, trembling with the excitement of having seen and heard the Führer from the eighth row. 'He's so wonderful!' she gushed. 'There's no one like him in the whole world!'

My uncle, usually calm and sensible, seemed almost as stirred. 'He convinced us completely,' he said. 'The Russians will be routed before winter, and then the war will be over, thank God!'

He led me to the large map on the wall where he had marked all the conquered territory. 'It's hard to believe what vast stretches we've captured in such a short time – and with relatively few casualties. The whole of Russia is open to German settlement now!'

'Is that so?' I asked skeptically. 'Soviet Russia is actually much larger than what you have here – it would extend way over to the big wardrobe if your map showed more than just the European part.'

'Listen, as soon as Moscow, Leningrad, and Stalingrad fall,' Uncle Karl lectured, 'the rest will collapse. It'll all be over in a week at most, I think.'

Aunt Elsbeth chimed in with accounts of how the postal clerk had refused to sell her military postcards and the butcher was unwilling to take ration stamps from her – on the grounds that the war would be over any day now.

She and my uncle explained eagerly how the Führer supported every point he made with facts and figures, proving for instance that England was on the verge of collapse.

'You must feel disappointed at times that you can't be in the thick of things,' Aunt Elsbeth remarked as I was going to bed.

Uncle Karl spared me the effort of replying by saying gruffly, 'Each person does his duty where he is needed: one as a bomber pilot, a U-boat captain, or an infantryman in a storm battalion, another at a radio post – or as a defender of the capital, like me.'

I spent the next few days looking up old friends. One of them was Ulla, whom I arranged to meet at a café on Friedrichsstrasse. She looked pale and strained, but tried hard not to show how weary she was. She told me that the pace and the pressure at work had increased since the last time I saw her, and that in spite of the ever-mounting quotas, the overlong work day, and the pitiful wages, there was just no way to organise resistance among the women.

'Half the workers simply haven't the courage to open their mouths. The other half seem intoxicated by all the victories and repeat whatever lies the propaganda men feed us. I can't stand this endless ranting and raving about the final victory and how it's just around the corner!'

I wanted to order her a drink, but the waiter shook his head. 'We're not serving now! And no more talking! In a moment the special bulletin's coming on!'

In accordance with a recent regulation, the radio in the café was on, turned up to top volume, and in a moment we heard the musical fanfares that preceded the special bulletin: 'Führer's headquarters. The High Command of the Wehrmacht announces that the final victory, heralded by the decisive battles in the east, is at hand!'

I had expected this bulletin to be greeted with cheers, but instead the men and women in the café sat there in silence, waiting for further announcements. But no details followed. At the tables people whispered about the special bulletin, but no one dared to voice skepticism out loud.

During the days that followed I observed an interesting shift of emphasis in the newspaper headlines:

11 October: Breakthrough in the East Broadened
12 October: Destruction of Soviet Armies Almost Complete

13 October: Battlefields of Vjazma and Briansk Now Far Behind
Front Lines
14 October: Movements in East Proceeding on Schedule
15 October: Combat in East Proceeds According to Plan

By 16 October, my last day in Berlin, there was no longer any
mention of the 'final victory'. Aunt Elsbeth and Uncle Karl appeared
much chastened when we sat down to our farewell breakfast.

'I don't understand it,' Uncle Karl said. 'Just last week the Führer
told us the Soviets had lost eight to ten million men, and he said, "No
army in the world can recover from such losses, not even the Russian
army!" And yet the battles go on and on.' He finished his tea and
pulled on his overcoat. 'I'm going to the Gauleiter's office. Perhaps
they'll tell me what's really going on.'

After he left, Aunt Elsbeth sighed and told me almost in a whisper,
'I spoke with Gudrun yesterday. Horst-Eberhard was home for the
weekend and told her what was happening on the Eastern Front – but I
haven't told Uncle Karl. He always gets so upset.'

The news she heard from Gudrun was that the Russian winter had
just set in, and that the German troops were wholly unprepared for it.
When the first snow fell on 4 October, most of the soldiers had only
light summer uniforms. Now they were freezing, and the cold weather
was affecting their equipment, too. Horst-Eberhard blamed the
generals, whom he called 'a bunch of arrogant cowards'.

Aunt Elsbeth told me all this with a troubled and embarrassed air.
As she was speaking, the doorbell rang, and when she went to open the
door, I heard someone say, 'Heil Hitler! I've brought you a copy of a
new poster.'

When Aunt Elsbeth returned, she showed me the poster, which
announced the recently launched collection of used woollen clothing
and rags. I read the rhymed text and examined the line drawings; both
were obviously intended to make a cheery impression, but clearly
more was at stake than finding a use for discarded textiles. Only now
was something being done – too little and too late – to equip the troops
for the savage Russian winter.

Aunt Elsbeth read the poster over my shoulder and realised its
implications. 'Those poor, poor boys!' she said. 'I'm sure the Führer
never intended this to happen!'

About ten years later I had the opportunity to discuss the Russian
campaign with Heinz Guderian, the general in charge of the tank
units, soon after his return from American captivity. Guderian

described the bitter confrontations between Hitler and his generals in the late autumn of 1941. The Führer rejected all of their warnings, insisting that they carry on with the offensive along the entire front.

'Hitler was convinced that the Soviet armed forces could no longer put up any real resistance. Before the onset of winter he wanted to capture not only Moscow but also Leningrad, Rostov in the south, the oil fields of Maykop on the northern edge of the Caucasus, and even Stalingrad on the Volga. When Field Marshal von Rundstedt tried to make Hitler understand that this would necessitate advancing east 600 kilometres beyond the Dnieper, Hitler replied that the Russians in the south were no longer capable of offering resistance.'

On 21 November 1941, von Rundstedt's troops actually did take Rostov. But five days later the Russians recaptured the city, and Rundstedt had to withdraw his army, which had come under attack from two sides. Hitler relieved him of his command and recalled him to Germany.

'At Rostov our sorrows began in earnest,' Guderian recalled. 'The handwriting was on the wall. Around Moscow, and even more, to the north, the winter storms let loose. The first great cold wave struck in early November.' Hitler had planned to have only one unit out of every five spend the winter in the defeated Soviet Union. As a result, four-fifths of the new troops had neither gear nor training for winter conditions.

'By the beginning of November,' Guderian told me, 'each regiment had already lost about 400 men to frostbite. The tanks could barely move; to get them started we had to light fires under the oil pans. Our automatic weapons jammed in the cold.'

Nevertheless, between 20 October and 30 November the troops charged with capturing Moscow had advanced another 30 kilometres toward the city. In their heated headquarters in East Prussia, Hitler and his advisers studied on their maps the 30 kilometres that remained, and continued to believe that the conquest of Moscow would be child's play. With Generals Hoepner and Hoth descending on Moscow from the north, Field Marshal General von Kluge's Fourth Army approaching from the west, and Guderian's Second Tank Division advancing from the south, it looked like a sure thing.

By 5 December Guderian knew the situation was hopeless. At –36°C his troops could barely move, and they were being attacked in the rear and on both flanks. 'I realised then that our attack on Moscow had failed. All our sacrifices and efforts had been in vain,' Guderian said.

But the worst had not yet come.

The next day something happened that no one in Germany would have thought possible: the Russians launched a fierce counterattack. Suddenly the emaciated, ragged workers' militiamen – among them quite a few women, children, and old men – were withdrawn, and the poorly equipped German soldiers found themselves facing fresh regular troops – a hundred divisions in all, almost as many as Germany had thrown into the original assault on the Soviet Union. Under the command of the previously unknown General Gyorgi Zhukov, they began the offensive along a 300-kilometre front with artillery attacks, covered from the air by numerous squadrons of the most modern planes. Their tanks rolled toward the Germans, followed by waves of new regiments, equipped and trained for the winter warfare.

This apparent miracle resulted largely from the efforts of one man, the journalist Richard Sorge, East Asian correspondent for the respected *Frankfurter Zeitung* and the German Press Bureau in Tokyo.

Born in 1895 near Baku, the son of a German engineer and his Russian wife, Sorge attended school in Berlin and then volunteered for service in the First World War. He later became a journalist, living from 1933 on in Japan, where he soon won the complete confidence of the German embassy staff, particularly the military attaché. He began to work for German military intelligence. No one suspected that he was also a high functionary of the Communist Party.

Dr. Sorge, who had joined the Party in 1919, established close ties with the Japanese leadership, and became good friends with the private secretary of Japanese Prime Minister Konoye. Between his German and his Japanese contacts, he always had access to excellent inside information.

In the spring of 1941 Sorge warned Moscow that the Germans were planning an attack, but the Soviet leadership disregarded his detailed reports on the tactics and timing of the impending attack. When the attack occurred just as he predicted, Sorge's reputation in Moscow soared. The next time Sorge conveyed important information from Tokyo, the leaders believed him and made his report the basis for action.

Sorge meanwhile discovered that the Japanese Imperial Council had passed a resolution, confirmed by the emperor, that Japan should remain neutral toward the Soviet Union while preparing an attack on the United States. Sorge transmitted to the Soviet leadership the exact text of the Japanese resolution that assured peace on the Soviet Union's eastern flank for the immediate future.

The Soviet high command thereupon withdrew their troops from

Siberia and the long border with China and Manchuria. All the armaments being produced in plants beyond the Urals were now shipped via the Transsiberian Railway to Moscow and the collecting points east of Moscow where the elite divisions from Siberia and the Far East were gathering. By early December the Russians were able to send seven excellently equipped armies and two cavalry corps against the Germans.

The blow came so quickly that the Wehrmacht never recovered. 'During the remaining bitter-cold weeks of December and on into January,' Guderian remembers, 'it looked as though the beaten and retreating German armies would dissolve and perish in the Russian snow like Napoleon's Grande Armée a hundred and thirty years earlier. There were quite a few critical moments when it would not have taken much. You can't imagine what our troops went through unless you've seen the endless stretches of snowy wastes, felt the icy wind cut through you as it blows the snow over every bump and hollow in the ground, driven hour after hour through no-man's land, weary and ill-nourished – and then encountered those well-fed, warmly dressed Siberians. It was only the bravery and the fighting spirit of the German soldiers that preserved them from a total debacle . . .'

Major General Guderian was relieved of his command by Hitler for ordering a retreat without authorisation from the Führer. General Hoepner was reduced in rank and discharged from the Wehrmacht for the same reason. General Count Hans von Sponek, forced to retreat with an entire division in the Crimea, was not only reduced in rank and arrested, but on Hitler's orders sentenced to death and executed. On 19 December Hitler sacked the commander-in-chief of the armed forces, Field Marshal General von Brauchitsch, and named himself as his successor.

With that, Hitler's triumph over his generals was complete. Now he held the offices of head of state, Reich chancellor, minister of war, supreme commander of the Wehrmacht, and commander-in-chief of the armed forces. His top officers were now mere pawns, forbidden to exercise independent judgment.

By the beginning of February the German troops had been pushed back 300 kilometres. More than 200,000 men had fallen, 46,000 were missing in action, and 725,000 had been wounded. Frostbite had accounted for another 110,000 casualties. The German allies – Hungary, Rumania, and Italy – had also suffered heavy losses.

Of course Aunt Elsbeth and I could not begin to guess the dimensions of the disaster as we examined that poster calling on German civilians to collect discarded woollen clothing and blankets. But Hitler himself seemed intent on destroying any illusions that Germany would win the war: on 11 December 1941, just a few days before the beginning of the Soviets' winter offensive, he convoked the Reichstag. In the wake of the Japanese attack on the American Pacific Fleet at Pearl Harbour, Hitler fulminated against President Roosevelt, whom he accused, together with his 'millionaire and Jewish backers', of being chiefly to blame for the war. Then he ranted on: 'It fills the German Volk, and, I believe, all decent people throughout the world, with profound satisfaction that the Japanese government, after years of negotiating with this swindler, has finally had enough of being subjected to scorn and indignities. The president of the United States may not understand why we are so gratified; in which case he merely shows his mental limitations. But we know that the aim of his entire struggle is to destroy one country after another. As far as the German Volk is concerned, it does not need alms from a Mr. Roosevelt or a Mr. Eden; it merely wants what is its right. And it will safeguard this right to life, even if a thousand Churchills or Roosevelts should conspire against it . . . I have therefore ordered today that the American diplomatic personnel have their passports returned to them . . .'

The rest of the Führer's speech was drowned out by the tumultuous applause of the members of the Reichstag, who had jumped up from their seats. The radio audience heard only later from the news broadcaster that the Greater German Reich was now at war with the United States.

But by this time I was back in France. Erwin, with whom I listened to the declaration of war over the radio, commented tersely, 'Well, now we're a whole lot closer to the final victory.'

'What do you think?' I asked. 'How long will it be before the Americans land on the coast here?'

Erwin didn't answer at once. Then he said in a low voice, 'Quite a while. Our Führer doesn't give a damn how many lives we lose in the pursuit of victory. Besides, the Americans have to do something first about our U-boats, because they can't transport an army so long as Germany controls the seas. They'll also need control of the skies. But our Luftwaffe is testing a device that may make that difficult. And I'm afraid the British haven't the slightest suspicion about that.'

But on this last point Erwin was mistaken, as became clear a few weeks later.

On the evening of 27 February 1942, Erwin, the double doctor, and I were celebrating Madame Ondarraitz's birthday at her restaurant. It was close to eleven when Krupa arrived to pick us up, but we didn't leave for another twenty minutes because our hostess urged Krupa to stay for a piece of apple cake, a glass of Calvados, and a cup of coffee. Erwin finally forced us to go. 'Something's in the air,' he insisted.

'It must be spring,' the double doctor commented, and indeed the air had a softness to it that night, and the moon was clear and bright.

When we reached our post, all was calm. 'Something's funny,' Erwin insisted. 'It's perfect flying weather, yet nothing's stirring.'

At that moment Dieppe, Fécamp, and Le Havre all reported a small formation of planes flying toward the coast. We were used to have British planes heading to Germany almost every night, but usually at such a high altitude that it was not worth alerting the coastal flak batteries. But this time the station at the Cap d'Antifer reported that the planes were coming in at an altitude of 50 metres. Then the radio connection broke off.

'Boy, they're flying in low this time!' Erwin exclaimed, and I saw him reach for the telephone to inform Colonel Kessler. But as he picked it up, the communications station at Fécamp reported, 'Enemy formation turning away on northerly course, distance 3,000 metres, altitude 150 metres.'

'Just listen to that!' Erwin commented, and asked the double doctor to try to make telephone contact with 'Caesar', the station at the Cap d'Antifer. When this proved impossible, Erwin called to wake our commander.

By the time Colonel Kessler, in his slippers, and with a nightshirt over his uniform trousers, joined us, we had more news for him. Between the Cap d'Antifer and the village of Bruneval parachutists had dropped from the low-flying planes. Then the planes had turned and headed back toward England. Now all telephone communications with the coast were cut, from Le Havre to Dieppe.

Colonel Kessler listened gravely to our report, then said, 'I'll take a drive over there,' and ordered Krupa to fill up the car's tank.

'You can make it in half an hour,' Erwin told Krupa. 'Report to us when you get there, so we'll know you arrived safely.'

Not until Krupa returned around 6.00 A.M. did we learn what had happened.

These British planes that the aircraft warning stations had not taken seriously suddenly swooped down over the Cap D'Antifer. The commandos who jumped out of the planes at barely 40 metres' altitude quickly swarmed over the Luftwaffe testing grounds near Bruneval. They shot the guards, using revolvers with silencers, forced their way into the barracks, seized the central telephone facility, and broke off all communications.

The squad quickly dismantled an apparatus that was being kept under special security, stowed all the transportable parts in rubber sacks, and destroyed the rest of the machine with a new kind of explosive. The explosion was a signal for all the commandos to retreat. With only a few losses they made their way down the steep cliffs to the beach, where they were picked up by two British speedboats, which raced off toward England.

'The entire operation took them ten or twelve minutes at most,' Krupa concluded. It was plain to see that he was impressed. 'And just imagine, the British took one of the top physicists who was experimenting with this device back with them! And all in the twinkling of an eye! By the time the colonel and I got there, the speedboats were almost home!'

'Do you have any idea what the device was?' Erwin wanted to know.

Krupa shook his head. 'No idea – something top secret. The boss mentioned a radio direction-finder. Can you make any sense out of that?'

Erwin thought for a moment. Then he surprised us by saying, 'Something tells me the Tommies accomplished more with this raid than with their victories in North Africa.'

We knew that Rommel's Africa Corps had lost almost half its officers and men in the border territory between Egypt and Libya, along with 386 tanks out of a total of 412. That meant Britain no longer had to fear losing the Suez Canal. It seemed absurd to compare such an important victory with the kidnapping of some radio-measuring device.

But, in fact, this English raid turned out to have enormous, possibly decisive, importance for the course of the war. The British were then experimenting with what their scientists and technicians called RADAR – for 'radio detecting and ranging'. Their success was already beginning to have an impact on the air war. But the Germans, too, had developed a radio-locating device. The original purpose of the British raid had been to find out how the German device functioned. When they examined the parts captured in the raid on Bruneval, British scientists discovered with considerable alarm that the Germans were already working with decimetre waves, which the British had just identified as the most suitable.

The British high command concluded that the Germans must be far ahead, and consequently redoubled their efforts. What the British did not realise was that the Germans had built only one experimental device that used decimetre waves – the very one at Bruneval. It had been judged unsatisfactory, and the Germans shifted their experiments to long waves. For that reason the German leadership did not consider the English raid particularly significant.

Not until half a year later, when the British high command staged a much larger raid at Dieppe, this time with many losses, to scout the German radar installations, did London finally learn the truth: the Germans were barking up the wrong tree, having thrown all their efforts into long waves.

Fourteen months after the commando raid at Bruneval, the British had developed their radar to the point where they could eliminate a major German threat, submarines, which had been decimating Britain's supply and troop ships. In May 1943 alone, the British sank 40 U-boats, whose commanders had thought it perfectly safe to surface under cover of darkness. Only now was it possible for the Allies to land troops, first in North Africa, then in Italy, and finally in France, as well as to supply the Soviet Union with weapons, munitions, and other equipment.

At the time, of course, we never imagined such developments. Only Erwin suspected the tremendous importance that radio detecting and ranging would have for the outcome of the war. But the Bruneval raid did not go entirely unnoticed. About two weeks later Colonel Kessler and all the other Luftwaffe commanders in northern France were summoned to Paris. Krupa drove the colonel to the city.

Late that night Krupa returned. 'Just think, I saw Reichmarschall Göring with my own eyes!' he exclaimed. 'He's even fatter than I imagined and he was wearing an ermine coat. He had on diamond and ruby rings, and his face was made up!'

Erwin wanted to know what had been discussed at this gathering of commanders. 'If Göring himself put in an appearance, it must have been something important,' he said.

'I know exactly why Göring came to Paris,' Krupa said with a grin. 'All the drivers were talking about it: he came to plunder museums and collections. Tapestries, rugs, antique furniture, and porcelains were hauled off by the crate. So far as I know, the conference with commanders was only a pretext. He's supposed to have warned the commanders that they must be more vigilant. He also handed out some decorations. Our old man got the German Cross in gold for his quick intervention and responsible action, and our aircraft warning centre also received a decoration.'

'How in the world?' Erwin asked.

'The colonel came back with an Iron Cross First Class for Major

Zobel!' We had to laugh; at the time of the raid on Bruneval the major had been on home leave.

'Well, I'm sure that'll mean a few days of special leave for those of us who actually were on watch that night,' Erwin remarked.

THIRTY

Clinging to Hope

'Those damned British,' my Uncle Karl said, 'are almost done for, thank goodness. It won't be more than a few weeks before they have to beg the Führer for peace. And that will mean the end of the terror attacks!'

His hopes were based, he told me, on the successes of the German U-boats in the Atlantic. In the month of February 1942 alone they had sunk more than seventy merchant marine vessels and tankers. Uncle Karl assured me the English had hardly any food, and their aircraft production had shrunk so much that the losses inflicted by our nightly raids could not be made up. Fuel for their planes was also in short supply, he said.

Uncle Karl smugly ticked off the territorial losses the British Commonwealth had suffered: in December 1941 Hong Kong fell to the Japanese, followed on 15 February 1942, by Singapore, once considered an impregnable fortress. This gave the Japanese control over Southeast Asia, the Indian Ocean, and the western Pacific. The Mediterranean had become a German-Italian lake. Only the island of Malta continued to withstand German air attacks, but would surely capitulate soon. In North Africa, Rommel had launched another offensive and would certainly soon gain control of all of Egypt and the Suez Canal.

'Without their colonies, and the constant flow of raw materials and foodstuffs, England will collapse,' Uncle Karl predicted. 'Then the British will surrender. And they'll be grateful when we take over the task of providing for them.

'Do you really think we'll have to feed the British?' I asked Uncle Karl.

It wasn't easy for him to answer. 'Well, we can't let them starve – after all, they're Anglo-Saxons, Nordic stock,' he said. 'But Churchill and all those responsible for the terror attacks on our cities will have their comeuppance first. That goes without saying!'

Since August 1940, when the British flew their first night bombing runs against Berlin, Uncle Karl's hatred for the British had been growing unchecked. By now he had missed so many nights of sleep that he was a nervous wreck. He pinned all his hopes on the impending collapse of England predicted by the Gauleiter's office.

It thus came as a dreadful blow to Uncle Karl when during the night of 30–31 May 1942 the British staged their largest raid yet: well over 1,000 aircraft bombarded not only Berlin, but also Cologne, the fifth largest city in Germany, for an hour and a half. The first squadrons dropped only fire bombs, the next squadrons explosive bombs, then came more attacks with incendiary bombs and phosphorus cannisters; at the end, the heaviest explosive bombs and aerial mines were dropped.

The centre of Cologne was reduced to rubble and smouldering ashes, and the surrounding parts of the city and the suburbs sustained heavy damage. Almost 20,000 apartments and more than 2,000 businesses were completely destroyed. Several hundred persons were killed, and over 5,000 were wounded.

The antiaircraft installations around Cologne proved useless against such massive fire power. Uncle Karl had been keeping track of enemy planes shot down, and calculating when the British would no longer be capable of mounting an attack. On this evening the small number of planes shot down disturbed him more than the fact that an enemy supposedly on its last legs could muster such a force.

Only long after the war did we learn that in May 1942 the main British bomber fleet consisted of barely 400 battle-ready planes. The more than 600 additional aircraft that flew the missions against Cologne and Berlin had been scraped together from the reserves, the repair hangars, and even from aviation schools. Some of these planes had never been flown before, some had wholly inexperienced crews flying with their instructors. If the Germans had been successful at shooting down a significant number of British planes that night, the RAF would have found itself without trainers, trainees, or reserves.

The plan worked, however, and the massive attacks proved much more effective than smaller ones. In the following days, weeks, and months further 'thousand-bomber attacks' were launched with varying success against Bremen, Frankfurt, and Essen, until such strikes against the residential sections of German cities became an almost daily trauma.

The first thousand-bomber attack on Cologne destroyed all of Uncle Karl's illusions. When he picked me up at the station in early June 1942, he seemed completed transformed. This time I had only one day to spend in Berlin – with my mother – and I had not planned to visit Uncle Karl and Aunt Elsbeth at all. It surprised me to see him there waiting for me.

'I rang your mother,' he explained, 'because I wanted to talk with you.' And then, when we had got away from the crowd in the station, he asked almost under his breath, 'How much longer do you think this infernal war can go on?'

When I looked at him with some astonishment, he added, 'Don't feel you have to beat around the bush – this is just between you and me. Your aunt still believes in the final victory, and I wouldn't want to upset her.'

'So you don't believe in it any more?'

He shook his head. His belief in the leadership and in its promise of a speedy final victory had given way to a profound skepticism.

I told him that my parents and I had felt certain from the very beginning that the Nazis would lose the war. I said 'Nazis' on purpose, but Uncle Karl did not contradict me. He said simply, 'The defeat will hit all of us,' and then continued, since I made no reply, 'the only question is how long this senseless bloodshed will continue. What do you think? And, by the way, how is your father?'

It was the first time since the outbreak of war that he had asked about my father, who had fortunately been abroad on business when the Gestapo came looking for him late in 1938, and had not returned.

'He's in Australia now,' I said. 'Under the circumstances he's doing well. We receive mail from him quite often through the Red Cross. I just hope the Japanese don't attack Australia. He said in his last letter that he hoped to be home in two years at most.'

Uncle Karl sighed. 'That's a long time – I just hope we live to see peace.'

I asked after Gudrun and her husband. Uncle Karl sighed again; perhaps he had realised that his daughter's marriage to an SS general might have disastrous consequences for him in case of a German defeat.

'She's here at the moment,' Uncle Karl said. 'Just for a few days, so her doctor can examine her again. If her pregnancy is going well, she'll spend the last months of it in Bad Tölz. Horst-Eberhard bought a country house there, so she can get away from the terror attacks. She'll take along the Polish servants and a trained nurse.'

He told me more about Gudrun, but I was hardly listening, for a sudden inspiration had come to me. When I could get a word in edgewise, I asked, 'Tell me Uncle Karl, doesn't a private nurse like that have a special kind of uniform? And does she have to give up clothing coupons for it?'

Uncle Karl looked at me with astonishment. 'Of course not – they get their uniforms like soldiers. But why do you ask?'

I summoned up all my courage and said, 'I need a complete nurse's outfit, Uncle Karl, and please don't ask me why. Can you get one for me by tomorrow? Size 12. It's for a good cause, and no one will ever know.'

He stared at me flabbergasted. He swallowed hard, then mumbled, 'All right. Sure – if it's important to you. Is ten in the morning early enough?'

I nodded, and he nervously changed the topic: 'Horst-Eberhard is completely beside himself over that business in Prague. He believes some of his commanding officer's duties will go to him, now.'

'Is Heydrich dead?'

'Yes, there was nothing they could do. Infection set in . . .'

I could not tell from Uncle Karl's expression how he felt about it, but the news was important to me, because it was a safe assumption that the Gestapo and the SS would take bloody revenge for the assassination of Reinhard Heydrich and would intensify their surveillance. The thirty-eight-year-old SS Obergruppenführer and police general Heydrich had been head of the Reichssicherheitschauptamt and deputy Reich protector of Bohemia and Moravia, as well as head of the SD and the Gestapo. He was the chief architect of everything those organisations had done in Germany and the occupied territories, including the atrocities committed by the 'special operations units' in Poland and the conquered Soviet territories. Since January of 1942, it later emerged, he had also been in charge of the 'Final Solution of the Jewish Question'.

Now two Czech army officers had provided a final solution of their own for Heydrich. The news of the assassination attempt had taken me by surprise, and it filled me with satisfaction to learn that Heydrich had succumbed to his wounds. I thought of Erwin back in Caudebec-en-Caux and his certain joy that the man responsible for his father's crippling had met his reward.

Uncle Karl interrupted my train of thought: 'Be careful what you say when your Aunt Elsbeth greets us in tears. She's just heard the news, and I'm sure she's very upset.'

I glanced at him from the side, but his face remained expressionless. I just hoped he would keep his promise and get me the things I had asked for. Then something else occurred to me, and I said, 'By the way, Uncle Karl, how would you and Aunt Elsbeth like to have a very nice dog? As I recall, you often spoke of wanting a dog.'

'Aunt Elsbeth does, but why just now, when food is getting so scarce? What kind of dog is it?'

'A wire-haired fox terrier – very sweet, and well brought up. A year and a half old, and completely housebroken.'

'Well, I'm not so sure . . .' Uncle Karl began, but I broke in quickly, 'I'll bring him by tomorrow, in exchange, you might say . . . Aunt Elsbeth will love him – his name is Maxi. If you don't take him, I'll have to have him put away. He has a ration card valid till next spring. All you'd have to do is get him a new licence.'

'Oh, all right,' Uncle Karl said. He probably guessed that Maxi had to be rescued, since barely three weeks earlier, on 15 May, all Jews still living in Germany had been forbidden to keep house pets of any kind. Heydrich had issued his ban simply for the purpose of harassment. I heard later that Heydrich had also been planning a ban on house plants; the last measure against the Jews to appear in the newspapers before Heydrich's assassination read as follows:

1. Jews compelled to wear the identifying patch (the Star of David) are hereby forbidden to make use of the services of hairdressers and barbers in salons, dwellings, etc.
2. Excepted from this prohibition are Jewish hairdressers and barbers . . .
3. Infractions will be punished by government police measures.

The next day I brought Maxi to Savignyplatz at 10.00 A.M. Uncle Karl, who was waiting for us at the appointed spot, took the dog in his arms, stroked him, and promised Maxi that he would be well taken care of. He seemed for the moment to have forgotten the uniform, but I then noticed a suitcase standing behind a park bench and felt reassured. A few minutes from now Frau Irene Herz, who was waiting for me in a room behind a tobacco shop on nearby Oranienburger Strasse, would be transformed into 'Nurse Maximiliane', and for the moment at least would be safe from further persecution.

Here is the story of Frau Herz, as she herself wrote it just before she left Germany in the early spring of 1945:

'I, Irene Herz, née Glogauer, was born on the 2nd June 1902, in Stettin. My parents owned a successful shoe shop. Through hard work they had become quite well-to-do. They owned the building the shop was in, and lived on the second floor. My father was respected in the town and belonged for years to the board of directors of the Jewish Cultural Community as well as to the Chamber of Commerce. He also served as a National Liberal Party member of the City Council.

'I was the youngest of five children. My eldest brother, who hoped to become a judge, volunteered for military service and was killed in 1914. My second-eldest brother succumbed to severe wounds on the front in 1917. My third brother was drafted in 1918 but was still in flying school when the war ended, after which he studied literature and drama in Berlin. My youngest brother had died as a child of diphtheria. So after the war, in which my father, too, had taken part since 1916, I was the only child at home, and my parents spoiled me terribly. I went to a fancy school for girls, and did not have to help in the shop where my parents worked from morning till night.

'In 1927, when I was twenty-four, I was visiting my brother Heinz in Berlin. Heinz was editor and theatre critic for a major newspaper. He had a good income and a wide circle of friends, to which he introduced me. Among his friends was Max Herz, who was just opening his medical practice. We liked each very much, and when Max proposed to me I accepted gladly. My parents, too, were happy, though they didn't like the idea of parting with me. In November 1927 we married in Berlin. It was a very fine wedding, and my father gave a speech I shall never forget. My husband, eight years older than I, had lost his left arm in the war, and he still suffered the effects of a bullet lodged in his lung. My father alluded to these handicaps in his speech. He said that I, as the daughter of a family that had made so many sacrifices for the Fatherland, would serve as the left arm for my husband, who had shown no less patriotism, and would prove a devoted support to him throughout his life. And that I did, until his early death. He died in 1932 of the delayed effects of his wounds, and so, ironically, he was spared much misery.

'Our brief marriage was happy. My husband's medical practice flourished, even during the depression. We had two children, a daughter, Hanni, born in 1928, and a son, Klaus, born in 1929. Our only sorrow was that our Hanni was not progressing in her mental development; this became unmistakable in my husband's last year. She was physically healthy and pretty as a picture, but none of the treatment we sought did any good. In 1940, when I was called up for compulsory service in a factory, I had to put the child in a home. Six weeks later I was notified she had died. I am certain they killed her, for around that time the parents of other Jewish children in the home received the same notification about their boys and girls.

'But 1933 had been the hardest year. Left without a husband, inexperienced in financial matters, with two small children, one of them retarded, I witnessed the collapse of the world as I had known it. Suddenly, whether we were religious Jews or only of Jewish origin, we no longer counted as Germans!

'My brother Heinz lost his job at the newspaper in Berlin, and was forbidden to work for any other paper. So he went to Vienna, where he managed to eke out an existence. He worked as a freelance critic and reviewer, and did some translating on the side. Upon the annexation of Austria, he was immediately dismissed, and then things went very badly for him. Every so often I sent him some money. But then in October 1939 a letter with money from me was returned, marked "addressee unknown". I learned from the Viennese Jewish Cultural Community that my brother had been "resettled" in the Government General [the official name for occupied Poland] and had suffered an "accident at work", from the effects of which he died in December 1939.

'Things went no better with our parents in Stettin. They, who had sacrificed two sons to the Fatherland, had a rude shock in 1933 when they found signs pasted onto the windows of their shop: "Germans! Do not buy from these Jewish traitors to the Volk!" That year my father sold the shoe shop, at a price far below its actual value. He hoped they could live on the proceeds and on rents from their building, lie low, and wait for better times. In November 1938, when my parents' apartment was completely smashed up in the Night of Broken Glass, my mother suffered a heart attack, from which she recovered only very slowly. My sixty-three-year-old father was dragged off to Sachsenhausen, where he lost his life. They beat him with dog whips because he had refused to say, "I am a filthy Jew who has no right to be in Germany". This I learned from someone who was imprisoned with my father and survived to return to Stettin.

'I wanted to go back to Stettin with my children, to be with my mother. But she herself and all our friends and acquaintances advised me very strongly against it, saying conditions were even worse there than in Berlin.

'In February 1940 my poor mother, who had not yet recovered from a bad case of influenza, was deported to Poland along with other Jews from Stettin. They came in the middle of the night and ordered her to get out of her apartment immediately. She was allowed to take only one suitcase with the bare necessities. Everything else had to stay behind. She had to "voluntarily" renounce any claim on the house in writing, and then she was taken to the goods station for "shipment". There she found herself together with all our other relatives who still lived in Stettin. Of the thirteen relatives there, the oldest was Mother's Aunt Selma, who was eighty-six, and the youngest were my father's niece, Hilde Löwenstein, and her two children, three-year-old Katja and six-month-old Michael.

'Each of the three hundred jews was given a piece of cardboard with his or her name and number to wear around the neck. They were all subjected to a thorough body-search, and all money, jewellery, even photos and little mementos, and any provisions they had brought along were taken from them. Before daybreak they had to get onto the train waiting to take them to Poland. I learned later from a lawyer, who had been a good friend of my father's and had been made trustee for the confiscated Jewish property, that my mother died the next day, while marching in bitter cold to a village near Lublin. In the next few weeks all the rest of my family perished there.

'At the time I was working in an electronics factory. I had been called up for compulsory work service, and had to wind wire on reels. The overseer, a staunch Nazi, treated me like a leper. When we were given our soup for lunch, all the others, including the Polish forced labourers, were allowed to eat at a table. I had to sit on the cellar steps. In the autumn of 1941 I was released, and found a job as a secretary at the Jewish Hospital on Auguststrasse. There I was given a room for myself and my son. I was even allowed to bring along our dog Maxi, whom little Klaus was very fond of. I owed this great improvement in my situation to one of the head physicians, a friend of my husband's.

'I lived there until the beginning of June 1942, and Klaus and I felt quite at home. There was a lot of work to do, and I soon learned to do much of it without supervision. My boss was considerate and kind. We got along very well with one another. He asked me one time why I had not emigrated while it was still possible. I told him the thought had never entered my mind. Where would I have gone?

'I had no relatives abroad, and no good friends. I would have been utterly helpless without money, without knowledge of foreign languages, without training in any profession. How would I have managed?

'I would not have wanted to emigrate to Palestine, either. My parents and my husband had always rejected Zionism. Since my marriage I had not participated in the activities of the Jewish community, not even for the High Holy Days. At home, we ate sausage, ham, and pork roast like any other German family, and my husband had office hours on Saturday. We felt only loosely connected with Judaism, and I could not conceive of living in Palestine, surrounded by religious Jews.

'My boss responded that there were nonreligious, socialist Zionists as well. I admitted that I had perhaps even greater prejudices against socialists. I knew, of course, that they were the only ones who had put up any resistance to Hitler and had suffered the direst persecution as a result, but I wanted nothing to do with the reds. My boss laughed and said I probably felt that way because I had been raised to be a patriotic German; perhaps I secretly admired and envied the non-Jewish anti-fascists. Unlike us Jews, the reds had only to give up their political beliefs, whereas neither baptism nor the most fervent dedication to the German people could help us.

'I have since given much thought to the matter, and have come to the conclusion that my boss was right. If I could have paid lip service to Hitler and thereby escaped all oppression and persecution, I think I would have done it. I dare say my parents and my brother Heinz, who worked for a German nationalist paper until 1933, would have done the same.

'Of course we viewed what had happened since Hitler's seizure of power as a national calamity and shame for Germany. We were affected doubly – as Germans, who were mortified by what was happening, and as Jews, who bore the brunt of it. That doubt load was actually more than one could bear, yet until the 2nd June 1942, I still hoped that things would improve for my Klaus and me.

'On that 2nd June, my fortieth birthday, I was supposed to run an urgent errand for my boss. Before 7.00 A.M. I had to go to an "Aryan" doctor in Lichterfelde to pick up a medication that we could not obtain otherwise. This former colleague of my boss sometimes helped us out in secret. I set out before 5.00 on my bicycle to get to Lichterfelde on time. We had been forbidden to use all public transportation since April of that year.

'On the way back I stopped in to visit my friend Lilo. I slipped into the building when no one was looking because I did not want to cause trouble for my friends with my Star of David. Lilo came from a Jewish family, but she was "privileged" because she was married to an "Aryan". She did not need to wear a star or mark her door.

'Lilo received me warmly. We celebrated my birthday with real coffee and fresh rolls, which gave me particular pleasure because these things were now forbidden to Jews – along with white bread, cake, wheat flour, eggs, meat, sausage, and whole milk.

'I did not set out for the hospital until 10.30. When I got there, it was almost 11.00. I put my bicycle in the cellar and was about to go upstairs when I remembered that I should go and buy a few cigarettes. At that time Jews still received ration cards for cigarettes; nine days later those too were taken away.

'Across the street was a little shop where I bought something almost every day, especially newspapers. We were forbidden to subscribe to newspapers or to buy them from street vendors or newsstands. But variety stores like Frau Brösicke's were not covered under the ordinance, so every day I bought the *Morning Post* there, but hid it under my coat as I crossed the street.

'When I entered the shop on this particular morning, Frau Brösicke stared at me as though I were a ghost. "My God, Frau Herz, you're still around!" she exclaimed in horror. Then I heard our little fox terrier Maxi barking. How did he happen to be over here?

'Terror gripped me, but my worst premonitions proved mild when Frau Brösicke told me what happened. Fortunately we were alone in the shop, and she locked the door and took me back into the little room where she lived. She told me that shortly after 6.00 that morning the Gestapo had "combed through" our hospital. About seventy persons, among them my eleven-year-old son Klaus and my boss and good friend, were driven away in trucks guarded by SS men. Klaus had just had time to give Maxi to Frau Brösicke and leave a message for me: he was already a man, and I shouldn't worry about him.

'My first impulse was to fetch my bicycle and set out to find my boy. I knew where the collection point was for the so-called evacuations. But Frau Brösicke held me back: "For God's sake, Frau Herz, don't go over there! They're still nosing around! And you can't do anything for the boy – they've gone already. The train left Berlin at 9.30."

'Everything began to swim before my eyes, and when I came to, I was lying on Frau Brösicke's sofa and she was giving me brandy. We debated what I could do. "You must get away, Frau Herz," Frau Brösicke insisted. "They called out your name several times, I'm positive. By now they must have a search warrant out for you. Isn't there someone who could take you in for a little while?" It was clear to me I could not ask Lilo for help. My only other close friend had moved to Düsseldorf years before. On her last visit to Berlin, about six months before this, she had said, "You can always come to me, Irene, if things get too hot here. I have room for you and your son."

'I asked Frau Brösicke to go to the post office to call my friend in Düsseldorf and explain my situation to her. It was my last hope, and I was sure something would go wrong. My friend was often away on trips, and perhaps we would not be able to reach her. But when Frau Brösicke returned, she said, to my great relief, "Everything's arranged, Frau Herz. Your friend's son is on leave at home. He'll come and fetch you tomorrow. In the meantime, stay here with me, and don't show your nose outdoors!"

'The next evening he appeared. Frau Brösicke let him in, and I was terrified at first when I saw his uniform. He stayed only twenty minutes, but he said, "Tomorrow this will all be over. I'll come to get you early, and we'll take Maxi along. My uncle will keep him, and he'll be well cared for. We'll take a taxi, first to Charlottenburg and then on the Friedrichstrasse Station. You'll change clothes in the ladies' room of the Central Hotel. You'll be travelling as a nurse."

'When I protested that I was not allowed to use a taxi or enter a hotel, he waved the objection aside. "That's over," he said, "From tomorrow on you're an Aryan. Don't forget to take off the star! By the way, I need two passport photos of you – would you happen to have any?"

'Fortunately I had two in my pocketbook from several years back, left over from when we were required to get new passports marked with a *J*. I asked him whether I didn't look very Jewish. He just laughed and said, "You're blond and have grey eyes. You really look more like someone from the old Prussian family. When you're dressed, they'll think you're an aristocratic head nurse. We're giving you a new name, with a "von" in it. And another thing: you were buried in rubble during an air raid and were injured. You've lost everything, and now you're on your way to visit friends in the country and recuperate. I'll bring gauze along tomorrow. The best thing would be for you to put your arm in a sling."

'Everything went according to plan, even though I was terribly nervous and probably acted rather strangely. When I opened the suitcase in the ladies' room, I found three brand-new nurse's uniforms, three aprons, three sets of underwear, stockings, shoes, a cap, and everything else I would need, including a nurse's pin with the red cross on it and an identification card with my own picture glued on and officially stamped. On the front was the official notation, "Duplicate issued for original lost in terror attack. Air Raid Defence Headquarters, Berlin." It was signed and stamped. That made me feel a little more secure, and my new name, Maximiliane von Anders, appealed to me.

'Nevertheless my heart pounded wildly when I went to the ticket counter and had to show my card for the first time. I thought it would be obvious to everyone that there was something fishy about it. But I had no trouble, either then or later on the train, when an SS patrol went from compartment to compartment between Postdam and Magdeburg, checking everyone. The men in black uniforms just glanced at me in passing, and the patrol leader even wished me a good journey.

'In late afternoon we arrived in Düsseldorf and were greeted on the platform by a gentleman in an elegant summer suit, with an SS badge on his lapel. I was alarmed, but my friend's son reassured me that this was Herr Desch, a good friend, and it was a lucky coincidence we had run into him. But in fact it was no coincidence, as I gathered from a hasty exchange between them. I heard the words "Gestapo raid" and "better not to go through the barricade". They must have noticed how frightened I was, because Herr Desch said, "Please don't be upset, Sister! You're going on by yourself to Krefeld – I'll see you to your train. The trip takes half an hour, and in Krefeld a lady will meet you, and all will be well. Here's your ticket." The ride to Krefeld passed uneventfully, and a friendly white-haired lady leaning on a cane greeted me as I got off the train. She said, "Welcome, Sister! I'm so glad you got here safely. I'm Frau Ney. Please let me take your arm – that looks better!" We made our way slowly to the barrier; from a distance I could see the SS guards, checking everyone carefully. A man in civilian clothes was standing nearby, keeping a close eye on the process. He looked to me like a Gestapo agent.

'"Stay calm, Sister, nothing will happen to us," Frau Ney murmured. She squeezed my arm slightly, and strangely enough I no longer felt any fear, even when one of the SS men commanded brusquely, "Heil Hitler! Identification check! Show your papers!" "Make it snappy!" barked the second SS man, who had a police dog on a leash. Frau Ney paid no attention to the two in their black uniforms. Without slowing down, she turned to the man in civilian clothes: "Good day, Herr Berger! Still on duty so late in the day? Would you please tell your young men that you know me – otherwise we'll miss our bus."

'The Gestapo agent nodded to the SS men, and they stepped aside. He wished Frau Ney a good recovery, to which to my amazement, she gave a friendly reply, "Thank you, I'm in good hands now. Sister von Anders has me doing some wonderful exercises." Then she seemed to remember something else, and she said, "Oh, and please tell your dear wife that she can come an hour later tomorrow, now that I have some help. We can make our own breakfast, right, Sister?"

'In half an hour we reached the Neys' country cottage in Meerbusch. Frau Ney showed me the pretty room on the second floor that was to be mine and said, "This is your home now. I hope you'll feel comfortable with us. At any rate you're safe here from Herr Berger and his men. He's a dangerous fellow, ambitious and brutal. I know because his wife has been helping me with the housework since my hip got so bad. You needn't worry about her – she's a decent woman, and very unhappy because her husband left the Church. He thought he would be promoted more rapidly as a 'believer in God', as they call it. He's still at quite a low rank, and they barely make ends meet on his salary. They have a son who's in university-preparatory school, and a daughter who's retarded." I could not help thinking of my own children, and tears came to my eyes. Frau Ney put her arm around me and said gently, "Go ahead and cry! You have every reason to be sad. But don't despair! God has protected you and will continue to protect you, because he has a task in mind for you." I asked her, "What task?" and she replied, "I don't know – perhaps he rescued you so you could testify to what you've experienced."

'I have not forgotten that, and never shall, and that is why I have written all of this down.'

THIRTY-ONE

A Man Who Simply Did His Duty

'How in the world did you pick that name?' he wanted to know, as I was leaving. So I told him how my mother had selected the name Maximiliane von Anders for her friend. Anders meant 'different' in German, and Irene was certainly taking on a different identity. The name Maximiliane was a joking reference to her fox terrier Maxi, but it also had an aristocratic ring to it.

For her papers we decided to make Frau Herz three years younger than she really was, but to keep her actual date and place of birth. We made her a head nurse in a lay nursing order, the Handmaidens of the Fatherland League in Berlin-Dahlem, whose records had been destroyed when the headquarters were bombed.

He listened in silence, and from his expression I could not tell whether, in retrospect, he found the story amusing, outrageous, or simply of no consequence.

But I suspected he could not be entirely indifferent to it, even twenty years later. For if he had known Sister Maximiliane's true identity at the time, he would have arrested her immediately and made her a part of the 'final solution'. He would have received a commendation, and perhaps his promotion would have come sooner. To complicate matters, Sister Maximiliane had helped look after his retarded daughter for almost a year. With great patience she taught the girl to speak a few words. While he greatly appreciated her kindness, he might have found himself in real trouble if the Jewish woman had been unmasked.

But retired Hauptkommissar Berger, whom I visited in 1962, seemed to give little thought either to the loving care his daughter had received at the hands of a Jewish woman in hiding or to the threat that had hung over his career without his knowledge. What troubled him most was his professional slip-up in this case. He muttered, more to himself than to me, 'Incredible . . . incredible. And right under my nose.'

He received me very cordially when I turned up without calling ahead. It happened to be almost exactly twenty years since our first meeting. When I arrived, he was busy pruning his roses.

'I've been retired for a couple of years now,' he told me, 'and I devote all my time to gardening. I feel terrific!'

That was clear. He must have been close to seventy, but he looked considerably younger, in spite of his white hair. As a Gestapo agent he had been pasty-faced and nervous but now he looked robust and glowing with health, with a deep tan and muscled arms.

He showed no reluctance to tell me about events in his life. In the autumn of 1942 he had finally been promoted to Kommissar and transferred to Düsseldorf. There he served at headquarters until the beginning of April 1945. Toward the end of the war he was drafted into the people's militia, where he commanded a unit of military police in the Ruhr Basin. When the troops in the Rhineland-Westphalian industrial area capitulated on 28 April 1945, Herr Berger found himself in British captivity. The British interrogated him and soon realised they had bagged a fairly high-ranking Gestapo agent. 'I was interned for eleven months,' he told me with a sigh. 'What an ordeal! At the beginning we suffered dreadfully from the cold and never had enough to eat, because there were shortages of everything. And they treated us wretchedly – especially the Poles who were sent in as guards. Some prisoners were even beaten!'

From the way he sighed, it was clear he viewed this period of imprisonment as a grim and undeserved injustice. As he continued his account, he noticed a rose that showed signs of powdery mildew, picked up a can of pesticide, and sprayed the plant thoroughly. 'Fortunately the Poles were pulled out, and we had a much better time of it with the Tommies. That's when I discovered my talent for gardening. I took care of the gardens at Major Wilkinson's villa, which had been shamefully neglected. I laid out the beds in perfect squares, trimmed the hedges till not a twig was out of place, and made the shrubs line up like soldiers.'

I glanced around his own garden, and saw that it was laid out with the same military precision.

'They released me early,' he went on, 'and for a while I had no job, but then I found a position with the police in Oberhausen, later in Krefeld and finally with the State Criminal Division as a Hauptkommissar.' He spoke with obvious pride. But he detected dubiousness in my expression. 'I always loved being a policeman,' he added, 'and it made sense to rehire experts like me. In fact anyone without blots on his record had a *right* to be employed again. After all, I had been with the police since 1921.'

He had first joined the police after the First World War, in which three of his older brothers had fallen. 'I came from a good Catholic family with a tradition of civil service. My years with the military counted toward my career in the police, so that by 1925 I had made sergeant and had permanent status. In 1929 I switched to the detective division and in 1931 became a junior detective in the fraud department.'

Until then Berger had belonged to no political party, but shortly after the seizure of power, in the spring of 1933, he joined the NSDAP, and two years later the SS. 'It was the temper of the times,' he commented. 'As a civil servant I didn't want to be on the outside.'

Toward the end of 1934 Berger was transferred to the Gestapo, where his first assignment involved combating 'communist subversion'. 'We had our hands full at that time. Almost every day our informants brought us illegal pamphlets which had been distributed in the factories, or they reported that seditious slogans had appeared overnight on walls and bridges. I was constantly shuttling between Krefeld and Düsseldorf, and my family life was affected by all the overtime I had to put in – the interrogations tended to drag on and on.'

What Berger neglected to mention was that in the Gestapo he developed into a brutal interrogator, whom all the prisoners feared. Early one morning in the winter of 1934–35, when Aunt Annie's husband was going to the bakery, he ran into a worker he knew. The man had blood streaming from his nose and mouth, and could barely stand on his feet. Greybeard Ney helped the man home and fetched a doctor. He stayed with the man while he was being bandaged up, and the sight horrified him so much that he could hardly sleep the next few nights: the man's back was a bloody pulp from his shoulders to his buttocks – the work of Berger, who had hauled him in for questioning the previous day.

'Berger worked him over for hours with a length of rigid rubber tubing,' Herr Ney told us later. 'He beat the man with the regularity of a machine, one blow every five seconds, exactly twelve blows per minute. He wanted to find out who had painted "Down with Hitler!" on the factory wall before the early shift. There were nine suspects, and Berger interrogated them one by one. He got nothing out of them, but the men were so badly injured it's doubtful any of them will recover . . .'

When I asked Herr Berger about the methods of interrogation he had used over twenty-five years earlier, he knew exactly what I was referring to. His reaction, however, surprised me.

'Yes, yes,' he said thoughtfully, and without a trace of shame. He even smiled. 'All kinds of stories made the rounds, and are still making the rounds, and much of what people say is exaggerated. But it's true we had to be pretty tough on the suspects when an 'intensive interrogation' was ordered. I often had to clench my teeth to make myself go through with it. I got many beatings as a child, especially from my godfather, who raised me. He tended to get angry. Anger is a bad thing – I always made a point of maintaining my self-control. After all, it was just part of our job. By the way, I never struck anyone unless I had written orders.' He paused, as though expecting praise.

By this time Herr Berger had finished rinsing and oiling his gardening tools and putting them away in the shed. He looked to make sure everything was in its place, straightened a hoe that was hanging a little crooked, then locked up the shed and strolled with me toward the house.

'Order must be maintained,' he said. 'That was also the original purpose of the concentration camps: to teach those people order and discipline. Later on, of course, excesses did occur, in violation of the guidelines.'

I asked him whether he had ever seen a concentration camp.

'I went to Esterwegen a couple of times in an official capacity, and later I had a three-week training course at Buchenwald. That was in the winter of 1939–40, soon after the end of the Polish campaign. At the time the camp was overcrowded, but nevertheless everything was in admirable order.'

'Really?' I asked.

He merely nodded. But this time we had reached the house, and he asked me to take a seat in the living room while he went to wash up and make tea. 'I'm alone today,' he said. 'My wife's gone to visit our daughter. After the war we found a place for her in an institution in the Eifel region.'

'Of course that wasn't possible before,' I said. He didn't respond. He knew as well as I did that during the Nazi period anyone institutionalised and considered incurable was killed.

While I waited for Herr Berger to return, I looked around the room, which was decorated in 'Old German' style. Everything was perfectly in its place, as if no one lived there. Even the books in the bookcase stood lined up like soldiers. Above the sofa hung two plaques, one for the Wartime Cross of Merit 2nd Class, conferred on Kommissar Peter Josef Berger in 1943; the other was the Federal Order of Merit conferred on Hauptkommissar Berger on the occasion of his thirty-fifth year of service with the Province Police. On the opposite wall hung various souvenir photographs, one of which particularly caught my attention: it showed about a dozen men in their thirties, some of them quite overweight, all in athletic shorts and shirts. I picked out Herr Berger without difficulty. They were standing on a wide bare space, posing for the picture and obviously enjoying themselves. In the background one could see a long, two-story building in the architectural style characteristic of SS headquarters buildings. When I examined the picture more closely, I saw it bore the caption 'Kommissars' Training Course, February 1940, Weimar-Buchenwald.'

From the kitchen I could hear the kettle whistling, and I knew that in a moment Herr Berger would return with the tea. I wanted to ask him about his impressions of Buchenwald, but I was sure I would only hear again how clean and orderly he had found the camp.

After he poured the tea, I inquired, 'When you were assigned to the Department for Jewish Affairs of the Gestapo office in Düsseldorf, was that something you had applied for? And how did you feel about what was called in those days the "Jewish question"?'

For the first time that day Herr Berger seemed unsure of himself. 'Yes, well, let me explain,' he began. 'You probably don't understand . . . You see, I came from a strict Catholic family. My father was a civil servant loyal to the Kaiser and active in the Catholic Men's Association. He had nothing in common with the *völkisch* groups and the anti-Semites, but when I was a child he forbade me to play with the Jewish children next door. I couldn't even accept a piece of candy from their mother.'

He went on to describe other experiences with Jews: a Jewish cattle dealer frequented his uncle's restaurant, an unpleasant character. In the army Berger had a Jewish drill sergeant who was such an exemplary soldier that Berger and his comrades joked that he couldn't really be a Jew – his mother must have had an affair with an officer.

After dredging up other such memories, he said, 'Well, I really can't say I felt hostile toward Jews. In fact – this you won't believe – I almost married one! Her name was Doris Rosenthal. Her father ran a successful fabric store. We really liked each other, and Doris said she would convert. I had just become a tenured civil servant, but old Rosenthal didn't want his daughter to become a Catholic and marry a policeman. Anyway, it was lucky nothing came of it. Later on I sometimes thought of that. I really felt sorry for some of the people when we had to evacuate them . . .'

I was amazed to hear him use the term 'evacuate' without the slightest irony, as if he still believed the Gestapo had merely been moving the Jews to safety!

'I suppose you went through special training before you began work in the Department for Jewish Affairs?'

Herr Berger laughed. 'And how! We had racial theory and ideological instruction, and also a special course on the "Legal Position of the Jews." Some of the instructors certainly put us through our paces. But I tell you, after the training and a few months on the job I could recognise a Jew thirty feet away, no matter how he tried to blend in or how blond and blue-eyed he was. I had an unfailing instinct when it came to picking them out!

'Of course,' he added hastily, 'I often closed one eye when I could do that without running foul of the guidelines. But I recognised every single one.'

His professional pride seemed to have gained the upper hand again, and I couldn't resist asking, 'Do you remember Sister von Anders – Sister Maxi?'

Of course he did. After all, she had taken care of his retarded daughter for almost a year. 'A splendid woman,' he said. 'I remember the first time our Gudrun said "Papa" to me – without Sister Maxi she might never have done that.'

'Do you remember Major von Elken?' I said quickly.

He thought for a moment, then said, 'Yes, I know who you're referring to: wasn't he the retired cavalry officer from Potsdam who was determined to go back on active duty? I met him a few times at Frau Ney's and we chatted a bit. A crusty old gentleman, a soldier of the old school, from the Kaiser's time.'

I mentioned several other men and women he had certainly encountered at the Neys' and later also at my mother's, but he shook his head.

'You must remember Monsignor Sprüngli,' I said. 'I mean the priest who arrived in 1940 from Switzerland to bring presents to the prisoners of war.' Aunt Annie had told me that when Herr Berger met Herr Sprüngli, the Gestapo agent had tried to kiss the monsignor's ring.

Herr Berger was beginning to understand why I was enquiring about all these people. 'Was the monsignor . . . Certainly he wasn't Jewish, was he?' he asked very hesitantly, and added quickly, 'To be quite truthful, I sensed at the time that the priest was not quite what he claimed to be. So he was a Jew? The man must have had damned good nerves!'

'That he did,' I replied, 'but *he* at least wasn't Jewish. He was a functionary of the Communist Party, serving as a courier for the underground Party leadership. But the others – Sister Maxi, Major von Elken, and the rest – they were Jews on the run, and fortunately your "infallible instinct" let you down in their case.'

It took some time before he regained his composure. Then he said, 'Listen here, I was simply doing my duty – no more and no less! I had nothing to be ashamed of, except that I let my superiors talk me into leaving the Church, and right after the war I rejoined. I'm happy to hear that those fine people managed to survive in the face of so many obstacles. I always said: a truly deserving person will come out on top, no matter how hard things are made for him. That goes for me too – or do you think it was easy to rise to the rank of Hauptkommissar with only an eighth-grade education?'

THIRTY-TWO

Plan 7

When I returned from leave, Krupa was waiting to pick me up at the station in Rouen. 'They've arrested Erwin,' he said, before I had a chance to say a word.

Five days earlier the Secret Military Police had appeared at Staff headquarters in Caudebec-en-Caux. Major Zobel, looking pale and distraught, had relieved Erwin of his post and put the double doctor in charge of our communications unit. Erwin had been seized by the police and searched. They had confiscated his possessions and driven off with him. As to the reasons for his arrest, no one had heard anything but rumours.

'Where is he now?' I asked.

'Here in Rouen, in jail. We've heard they're taking him to Paris tomorrow, to face a court-martial.'

The next morning I waited outside the prison, in a crowd of women with children, who were bringing their husbands clean clothes and cigarettes. With the help of an authorisation from our staff, signed by Major Zobel, I got as far as the central guardpost, a glass booth in the cell block that the Gestapo and the Secret Military Police had taken over for themselves. The 'watchdog' on duty, a noncommissioned officer, was not impressed by my stamped authorisation.

Not until I pulled out a photograph of a pretty blond girl and laid a pack of cigarettes next to his thermos, saying, 'She's expecting a child by him . . .' did the guard soften. He got up, beckoned to me, and unlocked Erwin's cell. It was lucky that Krupa had thought to lend me that picture.

Erwin was lying on his cot, looking much smaller than I remembered him. His entire head was bandaged with white gauze that left only one eye, his mouth, and his nostrils uncovered. When he saw who it was, he tried to sit up.

'That's all right, Erwin, stay where you are!' I said.

He could speak only with considerable difficulty. 'Those pigs – just like with my father. But they didn't get anything out of me – it was about Bruneval, you know.'

I was thunderstruck. What could Erwin have had to do with the British raid at Cap d'Antifer?

He saw how puzzled I was and whispered, 'Never mind, better for you not to know. Come on, give me a cigarette.'

I lit it for him and carefully inserted it between his swollen lips.

'You've got to do Plan 7 now,' he said quickly, as though he felt he had very little time. 'Promise!'

I promised.

Before I left, Erwin said, 'Take care of yourself. You'll get word about me. I'm not going to go like my father . . .'

The next day I did get word. In spite of the authorities' attempts to hush it up, the news spread like wildfire through the city and reached all the troops in the vicinity. As he was about to be taken off to Paris, Erwin had thrown himself in front of the train when it pulled into the station. He was handcuffed to the military police officer who had conducted his 'second-degree special interrogation', and he dragged the man with him under the train.

I never found out how Erwin had been implicated in 'aiding the enemy', but I will never forget his heroism: without any fuss he maintained his sense of humour and his humanity in the face of forces that could easily have crushed both. It was this heroism that gave him the strength in the end, despite his injuries, to make a protest, however small, that did not go unheard.

The following day I asked for an appointment with the colonel. Colonel Kessler displayed surprise and considerable dismay at my request. He paced the room, and then said, 'Have you really thought this through? Things have gone well up to now, and I've put in your name for a promotion to reserve officer – on April the 20th of next year you can be a lieutenant.'

At least he didn't say 'on the Führer's Birthday' – I was grateful for that. Then he added, 'The High Command was well disposed toward the request. In our group we have another case: an officer with years of good service – but of course his wife is partly non-Aryan . . .' He sighed, and I knew he was speaking of himself. It troubled him that he had not yet been promoted to general. 'Think it over again.'

'Yes, sir.'

With that, I had no choice but to inaugurate Plan 7, as I had promised Erwin. We had spent many hours working out ways to get released from the military. The seventh solution was one Erwin had worked out especially for me, and he was very proud of it. Like most experienced soldiers, he knew the regulations cold and took particular satisfaction in turning loopholes and fine distinctions in the military bureaucracy to our own benefit – to the consternation of our superiors.

'Your non-Aryan grandparents aren't enough,' Erwin had said. 'You've been in the service for three and a half years now; you'll just turn them against you if you bring up something they apparently want to forget. Of course, if you insist, they'll release you. But then you may find yourself under surveillance once you get home. And just asking to be released won't work. We know how the old man will react.'

After showing respect for Colonel Kessler's advice, I waited two weeks and then reported in sick.

'What's wrong with you?' the noncom in charge wanted to know.

'Headache, stabbing pains in the chest, fever . . .'

At the word 'fever' he did just what Erwin had predicted: he stuck a thermometer under my tongue and left it there for ten minutes. 'In the military they look down on such civilian practices as taking the pulse or putting a hand on your forehead,' Erwin had told me. 'They take your temperature, that's all. And if it's above normal they pack you off to sick bay.'

By rubbing the thermometer vigorously I had brought my temperature up a few degrees above normal. They sent me by ambulance to the Hôtel Dieu in Rouen, which they had transformed into a Luftwaffe hospital. By eleven that morning I was settled in bed in the isolation ward, and a French nursing sister of about seventy was asking me whether I needed the regular or the special diet.

The nursing order attached to the hospital had been careful to assign no nuns under sixty to the German soldiers. During the first two weeks of my stay, I gradually took Mère Thérèse, my nurse, into my confidence, in accordance with Erwin's Plan 7. She learned that I was not very sick, and that I wanted to attend Mass every day, which made her happy. She also learned that I loved France and had friends in the city, that there was really nothing wrong with me that couldn't be cured by the termination of this dreadful war, and that I would like to spend some time resting in the Hôtel Dieu but also wanted to make myself useful.

I caught a glimpse of the Luftwaffe staff doctor only once, when he appeared at the door to the ward and asked the patients whether they had anything special to report. We answered in chorus, 'No, nothing to report, Colonel, sir!' and before the words left our mouths he was gone. The young French resident who looked after us found my condition satisfactory, but suggested continued bed rest, even though the fever had subsided. After two weeks he gratefully accepted my suggestion that I help out in the laboratory. 'The third week is the crucial phase,' Erwin had said. 'Before that no one would dream of releasing you as cured, and by then you must have made yourself liked and indispensable – you'll find a way.'

In the lab I learned to do urinalysis and varioius other procedures. I received many compliments for being such a quick learner, and the doctor on the ward gave me permission to go out for a couple of hours every evening to 'gain strength'. I might have remained a patient at the Hôtel Dieu until the Allies captured Rouen if Plan 7 had not called for complete recovery in week 13.

'After hospitalisation of more than ninety days,' Erwin had quoted, pointing out that the regulation mentioned hospital stay, not the duration of the illness, 'the patient is to be released not to his troop division but to his home command. Ours is in Hanover.'

Before I set out for home, I took leave of my friends in Caudebec and reported once more to Colonel Kessler. 'You look much better,' he noted with satisfaction. 'Completely back on your feet? Good . . . I've approved your leave. In about two weeks you should even be able to take up your studies again – just in time for the winter term.'

After a brief recuperation leave I went to Hanover, where my release papers and my service record were waiting for me at the headquarters office. The noncom leafed through them once more before handing them over. 'What's this!' he exclaimed suddenly. 'You never took the oath!'

I thought again of Erwin, who had arranged things so I would not have to take the oath to the Führer, and gave the reply he had worked out for me: 'You know the guidelines – if you look at Luftwaffe regulation 2741-40, you'll see that my period of service takes precedence over such war-related bureaucratic omissions. I've been a soldier now for three years, eleven months, and twenty-seven days, more than half of which was spent at the front . . .'

'All right, all right, we'll let it go for now,' he said, and gave me my release papers. 'You're to come back in any case, so we'll take care of it then.'

But, of course, I wouldn't come back; that was the whole idea behind Plan 7.

On this particular day, 18 October 1942, the Wehrmacht bulletin announced that the last 'pockets of resistance' by the Soviets in Stalingrad had been wiped out, that in the Caucasus the enemy was still putting up 'embittered resistance', and that German positions in the north, outside Leningrad, and to the east of Orel had been further expanded. The Africa Corps under the command of Field Marshal

Rommel had advanced to within barely 100 kilometres of Cairo and was preparing for the last leg of the march on the Suez Canal. The 'campaign against partisans' in Yugoslavia was proving successful, according to the high command of the Wehrmacht.

Hitler's power seemed greater and more firmly established than ever before. Even Herr Desch, whom I went to see as soon as I returned from Hanover, appeared less confident than usual. 'We have to accept the fact that it may take years, and by that time . . .'

I knew what he was thinking. Just that month Düsseldorf had experienced a British 'thousand-bomber attack' for the first time. It had caused great destruction and took many lives. Then, too, the Gestapo was increasing its pressure everywhere. In Hamburg a special court had just sentenced a seventeen-year-old to death for secretly listening to the BBC and 'spreading enemy propaganda'. In Cologne, Essen, and Wuppertal, raids, house searches, and identification checks resulted in more than eighty arrests, and the Gestapo sent more than half of those arrested to concentration camps. The 'evacuation' of Jews had been under way for months; the only Jews spared were those with special privileges or with jobs in vital industries.

'We must find a new route,' Herr Desch told me. 'It's more urgent than ever. By the way, do you know Herr Wrobel? No? I'll introduce you to him tomorrow. I think he could use you in his office. The work he's doing is war-essential, and he's got authorisation numbers that would make your head spin!'

The system of authorisation numbers was new to me, and Herr Desch explained: organisations and companies doing work essential for the war effort received special numbers for telephone and telegraph hook-ups, train tickets, seat reservations, requisitions for equipment, spare parts, and raw materials, foreign currency, and permits of all kinds. The authorisation number itself revealed the degree of privilege to which its holder was entitled.

In all these areas Wrobel & Co. apparently occupied a top position. When I entered the office for the first time, Herr Wrobel, a stocky man in his mid-fifties with a tuft of reddish hair all around his bald pate, was on the telphone with Lisbon. He pointed to a chair. I picked up the newspaper lying there, and discovered to my amazement that it was a *London Times*, only two days old.

Besides Herr Wrobel, the owner and director of the business, I met Dr. Metzger, an expert on petroleum and also company spokesman; Fräulein Lachmann, his and Herr Wrobel's secretary; Frau Baum, in charge of finances, bookkeeping, personnel, and the kitchenette; and Fräulein Kasparek, the apprentice, who was responsible for running the duplicating machine, processing the mail, and fetching the newspapers from the main post office.

'You're just the man I need,' Herr Wrobel greeted me. 'Our Dr. Junghans had to go into the hospital. He's not well, and he's over seventy anyway. He was our coal and steel expert – you'll take that over, right?'

Before I could reply that I knew nothing about either coal or steel, he said, 'I know, I know, you're not familiar with the field, but you'll learn. The main thing is that you be able to translate quickly and accurately from French and English. Dr. Metzger takes care of Spanish and Portuguese, and for Swedish we get help from Consul Ekström, who lives on the second floor. As far as the analysis goes, I'll show you how that's done.'

He brushed aside my objections and continued, 'Don't worry – I'll take care of everything. Can you start at once? Splendid! We're way behind on coal and steel. I'll give you the authorisation numbers now – strictly confidential, of course, like everything else here. Dr. Metzger will fill you in on the rest. He's our office Nazi, but perfectly harmless. Just be careful not to chip away at his belief in the Führer and the final victory. There's a desk in his office for you. Make yourself comfortable.'

Dr. Metzger, a quiet, lean man whose age was difficult to guess, welcome me and handed me a stack of English and American newspapers.

'For now just start reading your way through – I'll tell you later what you're supposed to be looking for. You were a soldier up till now? Well, you've done your duty. Now you have another duty, equally important, and I can assure you that you won't be called up again before the final victory.'

'Are you sure?'

'Absolutely. Our authorisation numbers have the highest priority.'

As I sat down to study the *Economist* and a week-old *Wall Street Journal*, I thought of Erwin and his Plan 7, which had worked so well. If only he could have been there to enjoy its success!

THIRTY-THREE

The Supreme Effort

'That filthy pig! That criminal! That megalomaniac! And those cringing fools in their fancy-dress uniforms!' Herr Wrobel was shouting so loudly in the next room that I started in alarm.

'My God, what if someone hears him!' I exclaimed to Frau Baum.

'Well, the consul doesn't care,' Frau Baum remarked, and turned back to the papers she was getting ready for me. The Swedish consul, Herr Ekström, had the only apartment in the building besides Herr Wrobel's. Herr Desch had rented the basement – as a storeroom, and 'just in case'.

'What about Dr. Metzger?'

'He pretends he doesn't hear it,' Frau Baum said calmly. 'It bothers him that Herr Wrobel doesn't worship his beloved Führer, but that's about all. Here – I have your travel documents ready.'

I went in to get instructions from Herr Wrobel for my first business trip for the firm. He looked exhausted, sitting there limply with his collar open and his face flushed. 'Sometimes I just have to yell like that – otherwise I'd explode,' he explained.

It was February 1943, a few days after the catastrophe at Stalingrad. While the majority of Germans still knew little about what had happened there, the Swiss and Swedish papers had provided us with almost all the details. We knew that Hitler's insistence on holding Stalingrad at any cost had resulted in the total encirclement of the Sixth Army, and that attempts to break through the ring of Soviet troops or to supply the German forces from the air had failed miserably. On 2 February, Field Marshal General Paulus had surrendered, in defiance of Hitler's orders. The 91,000 surviving members of the 300,000-man Sixth Army, among them twenty-four generals and the field marshal, became Soviet prisoners of war. Only about 5,000 of them were ever to return home, and not until many years later.

On 3 February a special radio-bulletin from the Wehrmacht announced: 'The battle for Stalingrad is over. True to their oath to the last breath, the Sixth Army under the exemplary leadership of Field

Marshal General Paulus succumbed to the superior strength of the enemy and adverse conditions.' Then the second movement from Beethoven's Fifth Symphony was played, and a four-day period of national mourning was declared, during which all cinemas, theatres, and places of amusement remained closed.

We heard that Hitler had flown into a rage upon learning that Paulus and his generals had fallen into Soviet hands. Hitler felt sure the Russians would use them for anti-Nazi propaganda, and he turned out to be right. But many of his other prognoses proved less accurate, and his directives to the Wehrmacht had devastating effects in many places besides Stalingrad. In southern Russia the German armies positioned near the oilfields of Grosny managed to escape encirclement just in time and began the long march home. Their retreat meant the end of hopes of restoring Germany's depleted fuel supplies with Soviet oil.

In North Africa the British brought in fresh troops, and on 2 November 1942, they achieved the decisive breakthrough into Italian territory at El Alamein. Field Marshal Rommel, in danger of being encircled by the British, had asked permission to retreat. Although Rommel had gone for weeks without supplies or reinforcements, Hitler refused, insisting again that he 'hold out to the last man'. But on 4 November, Rommel took things into his own hands and ordered a retreat, to save the remains of his tank and motorised units. He left the entire infantry behind to be taken prisoner. In the following two weeks, Rommel's last units, amounting to barely 10,000 German soldiers with about 60 tanks, as well as 25,000 Italians, were chased along the Libyan coast in a westerly direction until all of Libya fell into British hands.

Meanwhile British and American troops had landed in the western part of North Africa, and with about 100,000 men occupied all of Morocco and Algeria. At that, Germany broke the cease-fire agreement, marching into the unoccupied regions of France: and Hitler dispatched 250,000 men to Tunisia to try to hold that last bit of African territory. But the move came too late; by the end of the spring the Wehrmacht lost all the soldiers, tanks, and weapons sent to Tunisia, as well as the remainder of the Africa Corps. In the end, more soldiers were taken prisoner in North Africa than at Stalingrad.

Aside from their strategic consequences, these reverses caused grave damage to the German war economy and strengthened the position of the Anglo-American armaments industry, because the Germans were now cut off from all their sources of raw materials in Africa and Asia Minor, while the Allies had regained access to them. No one in

Germany was in a better position to calculate the impact of Germany's losses than Wrobel & Co. We put together weekly reports for a very small, select group in government and industry. Using the information available to us, we provided accurate and unretouched accounts of American and British industrial production.

In addition to this vital work, Wrobel & Co. had its fingers in other pies. Just the night before Herr Wrobel's outburst, he, Frau Baum, Fräulein Lachmann, and I – Dr. Metzger and Fräulein Kasparek having gone home already – had discussed in detail the altered situation, particularly with respect to Turkey. The retreat of the Africa Corps from Libya, and of German Army Group A from the Caucasus and the eastern shores of the Black Sea, reduced German pressure on the government in Ankara. Herr Desch, who had joined us for the discussion, arranged with Herr Wrobel to see about setting up a new escape route through the Balkans.

Herr Wrobel had discovered that every day a neutral airline, SAS, operated a flight from Stockholm to Istanbul, with landings in Berlin, Vienna, Budapest, and Sofia. Between Berlin and Vienna, whenever seats were available passengers could use the plane without going through a passport check, for it was considered a domestic flight. And, the airline, as Consul Ekström told Herr Wrobel, had no objection to writing two separate tickets for any passengers who wished to travel from Berlin to Istanbul – one from Berlin to Vienna, the other for the rest of the route. The question was whether these passengers might not after all be checked by the German border police in Vienna or could simply remain on the plane, leaving German territory without the knowledge of the authorities. Herr Desch's friends would take care of Turkish entry visas if the rest could be worked out.

Herr Wrobel felt confident the ploy would succeed. 'In Berlin the only people who can get tickets are those with authorisation numbers. I'm fairly certain the Gestapo pays attention only to those who book beyond Vienna. Since they'll know nothing about the ticket to Istanbul, everything should go smoothly.'

Fräulein Lachmann was sent by train to Berlin to test the procedure. She would proceed to Vienna with a ticket for a domestic flight, and then on to Istanbul, returning two days later. Officially her assignment was to find a Turkish informant who could sent us regular reports on petroleum production in the Near and Middle East.

My own instructions were to take the train to Vienna, and there watch how Fräulein Lachmann's plane was handled. I would report to Herr Wrobel by telephone, and also obtain information about an additional escape route. 'You know how urgent it is, Herr Wrobel remarked. 'Herr Desch's "waiting list" is getting longer and longer.'

In the lobby of my hotel in Vienna I was to meet a gentleman with a magnificent moustache and a Hungarian accent. He would ask me about 'Renate', and in my reply I was to use the word 'welcome'. His other password would be 'married'.

By noon the next day I had called our office from my hotel to pass along the good news that 'the lady had a good trip' and was already 'on her way to meet our business associate'.

I had seen Fräulein Lachmann get off the plane and go to the transit area. Thirty minutes later she was airborne and heading for Budapest, along with the passengers who boarded in Vienna, and had gone through the passport control. But no one had checked *her* passport. The plane was painted luminescent orange to identify it as a neutral aircraft.

Twenty minutes before the appointed time I went downstairs to watch for the magnificent moustache. As I thought it over, two aspects of the SAS escape plan worried me. Herr Wrobel had felt that the agents issuing two tickets could be relied on, but I was not so sure. Then there was the problem that all passengers had to leave the plane in Vienna while the ground crews refuelled it; the Gestapo might have the passengers in the transit area under surveillance. Individuals who around their suspicion might be asked to show their papers, and then it would come out that they had valid tickets to Istanbul but neither German exit visas nor Turkish entry visas. The entire scheme seemed too risky to me, and I waited all the more eagerly for the appearance of the Hungarian with the alternative solution.

But where was he?

I had almost decided to call Herr Wrobel again, when a Hungarian major in uniform strode into the lobby, exactly two hours late. He looked around, rushed up to me, gave me a bear hug, kissed me on both cheeks, and exclaimed, 'What a pleasure! Was it a long wait? What news of Renate? Are you two married now?'

'Welcome, welcome,' I said, much relieved. No doubt about it: this was my man. He quickly came to the point. At the Budapest airport he had an absolutely safe way for passengers to get onto a plane for Istanbul without having their papers checked – a 'comrade' on his on duty would help. But his second piece of information sounded even more significant: on certain days our 'travellers' could board a train at Vienna's Eastern Station without being checked; they did not need a passport or even a ticket. The train went straight through without stopping at the border, and after a short stop at Hegyeshalom continued on to Budapest.

'It is a military train, and is under my command – every Tuesday and every Thursday,' he explained.

The travellers had only to purchase a platform ticket, go to the platform from which a train left for Pressburg, but then get onto the first-class car of the Hungarian military train waiting on the neighbouring track.

If it were especially urgent, he added, the whole thing could also be done on other days of the week, but he would have to be notified the previous day. On Tuesdays and Thursdays we could call him in the morning, using the direct line to Hegyeshalom from the Hungarian military mission at the Eastern Station. At the mission we had only to mention his name – the operator would know what to do. Either he himself or the station commandant would answer in Hegyeshalom; the latter was a 'good comrade'.

Much relieved, I returned that very evening to Düsseldorf. Herr Wrobel was delighted that we could start at once. The only thing he worried about was whether we could rely on the major.

'I hope so. Except for punctuality he seems solid as a rock,' I told him. 'The plan has the virtue of being very simple. So long as our travellers get into the first-class car of the right military train, they can go all the way to Istanbul without passing one checkpoint.'

On 18 February 1943, Reich Propaganda Minister Joseph Goebbels proclaimed the advent of 'total war' and called for 'the supreme effort'. Herr Desch remarked wryly that a supreme effort would be required of us as well. The new escape route through Vienna and Budapest, expensive though it was, would have to be put to heavy use, since we could not know how long it would remain safe. I received orders to set up a 'distribution warehouse' in Vienna, to which certain persons at high risk had to be brought immediately. With the Gestapo already on their trail, they could not get there by train, and plans had been laid for transporting groups of them by truck as 'extra freight' to Vienna.

Only one person at a time could use the military train on Tuesdays and Thursdays; the others had to be lodged in a safe place until their turn came. A little hotel by the Eastern Station had been recommended to Herr Desch by friends in Vienna. The owner, Frau Hacha, took excellent care of the fugitives, even accompanying them to the station and making sure they got safely onto the train.

The system worked very well until the end of July 1943. Then the flood of fugitives became so great that a new 'halfway warehouse' had to be found. Herr Wrobel dispatched me to Lower Bavaria to search for a suitable spot. 'Just tell them we have to move our machinery and lodge some of our workers injured in the bombing – for about four weeks,' Herr Wrobel instructed me. 'And of course we're willing to pay . . .'

But I crisscrossed Bavaria for a week, hearing the same story everywhere: they already had more than enough evacuees and victims of the bombing, and no space was to be had. Machines could be accommodated more easily, especially for good payment, but no one wanted to see more city folks.

After a few days I decided to try an area less congested with evacuees than Lower Bavaria. It was an area with which I was familiar, and besides, my mother had already established herself there. I arrived in the Fichtelgebirge on a hot August day and went to Mayor Arnold's farm, where my mother was staying. She got on well with the mayor's wife, and with her help she had gradually persuaded other farmers' wives to open up their homes to strangers. Most of the farmers and their sons were away in the army, and the women welcomed the opportunity to pick up a little extra cash by renting rooms to recommended summer – and later winter – guests.

One of the best-liked holiday makers was Major von Elken, retired, who had fixed up a room for himself in a cottage that housed the transformer for the local electricity supply. Uncle Erich, who no longer had any intention of fleeing the country, enjoyed great respect among the villagers – a real major, they said, yet always so outgoing and pleasant!

Another favourite guest was Sister von Anders, whom the local people always called when anyone got hurt. She was lodging with farmers on the hill across from the mayor's farm.

When I told my mother of my difficulties in Lower Bavaria, she was amazed that I had not come to her first. 'We have the perfect situation here,' she told me. 'There's a forest ranger's lodge in the woods, about an hour's walk from the railroad station. The forester was called up in 1940, and his family followed him to West Prussia. They left the key with the mayor, and gave him permission to rent it to orderly, reliable people.'

The place couldn't have been better. The only path led past the mayor's farm, and the lodge had a telephone link with the village inn. If one included the hayloft, the lodge could sleep two dozen people easily. A well supplied the house with water, and there was plenty of firewood. As for food, my mother assured me the Arnolds could provide bread, potatoes, and some bacon. 'You can also keep chickens there,' she said as we were returning from our inspection tour. 'The woods have mushrooms and berries – they'll be all right.'

After I telephoned the good news to Herr Wrobel, I sat in the inn for a while, waiting for him to call back to let me know when the truck with the fugitives would be arriving. The mayor and a few others had gathered in the taproom around Uncle Erich; they were waiting to hear the major's daily analysis of the war situation. Uncle Erich demonstrated that he had become not only a military expert but an authority on propaganda who could make sense of the confusing reports issuing from the various fronts and the government in Berlin.

On 2 August the Americans had bombarded the Rumanian oilfields for the first time. Major von Elken explained to his audience, 'This means Germany will soon run out of fuel. In Berlin they're already taking in the harvest with horses. Does that surprise you, Mayor Arnold, that they're growing wheat, potatoes, and cabbage right in the middle of the capital of the Reich? Well, look at this!' And he passed around a copy of the illustrated *Beobachter* that proved his assertion.

'Is the situation really that bad?' one of the men asked. 'We're still getting vegetables from Italy and wheat from Russia, aren't we?'

'Hardly anything is coming in from Italy,' Major von Elken replied. 'The entire country's in chaos. In Milan the workers broke into the prisons and freed all the political prisoners. Mussolini and his fascists are done for – the Duce's been thrown out of office and is being held on an island off Naples. The Americans and British have already taken Sicily. Soon they'll be on the mainland. Now the Wehrmacht high command will have to pull back from the Eastern Front, to try to hold Italy, just when the Russians have launched a counteroffensive.'

At that moment my telephone call came. 'The shipment will arrive in an hour and a half,' Herr Wrobel informed me. And that very night two women and seven men, two of whom had escaped while being taken to the Sachsenhausen concentration camp, moved into the forester's lodge.

The next day I returned to Düsseldorf and my activities vital to the war effort.

THIRTY-FOUR

A Messenger from Hell

As the summer drew to a close, it became clear that the 'supreme effort' would not be enough to save the Reich. On 18 August 1943, General Hans Jeschonnek, general chief of staff of the Luftwaffe, committed suicide. His interceptor aircraft had failed to prevent the British-American air attacks on the Wiener Neustadt industrial area, the ball bearing factories in Schweinfurt, the Messerschmidt aircraft plants in Regensburg, and the rocket-testing station in Peenemünde.

On the Eastern Front the Wehrmacht had to pull out of Charkow on 22 August, giving up the important Donets Basin industrial area. The troops were exhausted, and there could no longer be any thought of a German offensive on that front.

On 3 September the new Italian government concluded a cease-fire agreement with the Allies, whose troops had already landed in Calabria and near Salerno. In response, Hitler ordered the Wehrmacht to occupy Rome and all key positions in middle and northern Italy, and on 12 September an SS commando boldly freed Mussolini and swept him off to Germany. That same day the British captured Brindisi, and the following week the Wehrmacht had to pull back from Sardinia and then Corsica.

At the end of September the Russians launched a new offensive along a front 1,200 kilometres long. In the Crimea another German army was cut off after Hitler had forbidden it to retreat. On 1 November, Soviet troops landing in the Crimea took Perekop, and in the Ukraine the attack on the last German positions outside Kiev had begun.

That day, a Gestapo officer turned up at Wrobel & Co. for the first time. Fräulein Lachmann, looking rather pale, asked Dr. Metzger to speak with the visitor; Herr Wrobel was away. She threw me an anxious look. 'What can they be after?' she whispered. We tried to follow the conversation taking place in Herr Wrobel's office, but could not make it out.

Then the door flew open, and Dr. Metzger asked agitatedly, 'Does anyone have the key to the safe?'

We looked at him in dismay and remained speechless for a moment. Then Fräulein Lachmann pulled herself together and asked with feigned astonishment, 'To the *safe*? What do you mean, Dr. Metzger – we don't have that old thing any more!' She made gestures to him that the Gestapo man could not see.

Finally he got the point, 'Oh, of course,' he said somewhat hesitantly, 'how could I have forgotten! We left it in our old office after the bombing attack!'

If that was true, it must have been before my joining the staff. In any case, a safe stood in our air-raid cellar, and Herr Wrobel had donated it to the royal Swedish consulate, labelling it accordingly. The keys, however, had remained in Herr Wrobel's possession, and only Frau Baum had a duplicate pair.

'Well, there's nothing we can do at the moment,' we heard Dr. Metzger tell the visitor. 'But tomorrow our director, Herr Wrobel, will be back, around noon, and he can clear up any questions you still have. Thanks in any case for not initiating official proceedings yet. I can assure you, there is a proper explanation for everything. Again, many thanks! Heil Hitler!'

He accompanied him to the door, then came back and sank into his chair, groaning, 'What in the world have I got myself into! Lies are unworthy of a German!' We tried to comfort him, but we were also dying to learn what had brought the Gestapo agent to Wrobel & Co.

'Fräulein Kasparek!' Dr. Metzger told us, his voice trembling with indignation. 'She denounced us, that stool pigeon!'

Fräulein Kasparek had been caught buying black market goods. Hoping to avoid punishment she let it be known she could testify to something 'important': enemy propaganda was collected, duplicated, and disseminated at Wrobel & Co.!

Of course Wrobel & Co. had nothing to fear so far as its normal activity, blessed by those splendid authorisation numbers, was concerned. Herr Wrobel, as I now learned for the first time, worked closely with the armaments ministry and the high command of the Wehrmacht, and he had the backing of military intelligence. But precisely because a fierce rivalry existed between intelligence and the SD, which in turn was linked with the Gestapo, we had at all costs to prevent the agent from sticking his nose too deeply into our affairs – not to mention all our other activities.

The following day Herr Wrobel returned from his trip and blew his top when he heard the news. He dismissed Fräulein Kasparek on the spot and almost went storming off to the Gestapo office to protest against any and all interference, but Frau Baum calmed him down and persuaded him not to act in haste. And the following night the Royal Air Force neatly solved our problem: another 'thousand-bomber attack' on Düsseldorf caused extensive loss of life and property damage, including the destruction of the Gestapo office on Prinz-Georg-Strasse. The charges on which Herr Wrobel was expected to comment apparently got lost in the confusion, for in the months that followed we heard no more about them.

Wrobel & Co. did not escape unscathed from the heavy bombing. An aerial mine that exploded nearby shattered all the windows in the building. The attic caught fire, and Herr Wrobel's apartment just underneath suffered equally from the fire and the water used to fight it. He himself was uninjured, and moved in with Consul Ekström for the time being. Fräulein Lachmann and I finally found him there, sitting on the floor in the kitchen with one arm around the sleeping consul, the other beating time to a song he was singing:

> Oh, we'll go marching onwards,
> Till nothing's left but shards,
> Today we're lords of Germany,
> Tomorrow of all the world . . .

He fell silent as soon as he noticed us.

'How nice you're still around,' he assured us, his speech somewhat slurred. 'We're still around, too, my friend and I,' and he hugged the consul. Then something else occurred to him: 'Baum is still around, too – bombed out.' He looked around, glassy-eyed. 'She was just here – maybe she's getting something to drink.' He gestured vaguely in the direction of numerous empty bottles. 'Baum wanted to . . .'

Suddenly he seemed to remember something and tried to get up. We helped him up. The consul slumped sideways, having lost his support, but slept on.

After a cold shower and a cup of strong coffee Herr Wrobel was able to recall what had happened. Shortly after the air-raid sirens had sounded, as he and the consul were getting settled in the shelter, Frau Baum had come in with an unusual looking man: bald, hollow-cheeked, with a leather grey skin and deep-set, dull eyes. He was wearing an elegant suit, which didn't seem appropriate to his face or his large rough hands.

'A special case,' Frau Baum explained, 'he comes from Poland.'

The man said nothing, and Frau Baum took him to the cellar rented by Herr Desch 'just in case', where a cot was set up.

'It's the Golem,' Herr Wrobel whispered, still under the impression of the strange apparition.

'Herr Golem,' as we then called him, ended up staying in the rear cellar for two days. By that time Herr Desch had arranged a way for him to get to the Eastern Station in Vienna, escorted by Frau Baum, who was dressed all in black and wearing a dense veil. They arrived shortly before 5.00 P.M., and he was able to continue on immediately to Budapest, and arrived the following day in Istanbul. Unlike most of those whom we smuggled out, he was equipped with a valid Swedish passport, and Consul Ekström obtained a Turkish entry visa for him before he left.

I got a glimpse of him as he got into the special limousine, usually used only for funerals of important personages. He was dressed in a black overcoat and top hat. It was ghostly to see his dignified figure moving toward the car, looking neither to right nor left, and getting in. The blackened ruins of the buildings across the street provided a suitable backdrop.

I had suggested sending 'Herr Golem' to the Fichtelgebirge, where he would have been safe in the forester's lodge. But Herr Desch explained that in this case nothing would do but getting him to a neutral country immediately. I did not discover the reason until after the war.

Herr Golem was a *shaliach*, which is Hebrew for 'messenger'. In the summer of 1943 he had made his way somehow from Palestine to a town in eastern Poland, where he succeeded in locating two of the contacts to whom he was to deliver letters, money, and several other things. Perhaps he had been dropped by a parachute from an American plane somewhere over the Beskids, in the Carpathians; this was how thirty other death-defying messengers came in during 1943–44 to spark the courage of the Jewish communities faced with total destruction and assure them that they had not been forgotten.

He remained at his destination only a short time, for his second assignment was to try to return to Palestine with as much precise information as he could obtain about conditions in Hitler's realm. Like most of the messengers, he had not been able to fulfil this mission. He was seized and sent with many other Jews to the Treblinka concentration camp near Warsaw.

As he had learned in the meantime, almost 650,000 men, women, and children had already been murdered there, among them 310,000 Jews from Warsaw in the previous year alone.

When he arrived at Treblinka, the kapo who searched him for concealed valuables found the letter he was supposed to bring back to Palestine. It began with the words, 'At long last we received today with great joy your messenger and your letter . . .' and there followed a detailed report on the continuing liquidation of the Jews in Poland and Lithuania. It described in detail the desperate but heroic uprising in the Warsaw Ghetto, which began on 19 April 1943, and collapsed on 16 May. The SS had moved in with the artillery, tanks, and flamethrowers against the inadequately armed men and women, but had lost 800 men in the attack.

'When you shall have received this letter,' the missive ended, 'none of us will be alive. We are writing the letter in greatest haste, for the *shaliach* has no time . . . We herewith confirm the receipt of 50,000 Reichsmarks.'

The kapo was equally impressed by the fact that the messenger had put his life in total jeopardy by coming to Poland from a safe haven abroad and by the sum of money mentioned at the end of the letter. He helped get Herr Golem assigned to a special detachment, which enabled him to escape immediate extermination.

The special detachment to which he belonged for the next few weeks had the job of cremating the corpses of those who were murdered every day. The men who had this horrible task could not doubt, as many of their fellow inmates did, that the aim of their ruthless persecutors was to liquidate all of the Jews. These prisoners had managed to get their hands on a few submachine guns and hand grenades from the SS stock, and were determined to risk an uprising. When the theft of the weapons was discovered, they had to act sooner than they had planned: on 2 August they shot down their guards, set fire to the barracks and watchtowers, and with hand grenades destroyed the electrified barbed-wire fences. Those of the prisoners who still had the strength tried to flee. At least 200, possibly as many as 600 prisoners broke out of Treblinka, but most of them were recaptured by the SS in the next few hours and days, and shot. Only a few escaped – among them Herr Golem.

He was hidden by a crane operator who worked for the Todt Organisation, which was responsible for war-essential construction in the occupied territories. This crane operator, a Communist who had been in a concentration camp himself in 1936, later brought him in a lorry to Berlin, where he handed him over to comrades, who concealed the fugitive in their garden shed along the railway tracks in the Siemens-stadt housing development and fed him out of their own scanty rations.

When Frau Baum told me this story a few months after the end of the war, she ended with 'Herr Golem' hiding in the garden shed. 'You know the rest of what happened,' she said. 'He was determined to get out of Germany to fulfil his mission and spread the news as soon as possible about the liquidation of the Polish Jews, and he succeeded in doing that.'

'How did he find his way to you?' I asked.

She hesitated for a moment. 'Didn't you ever hear anything about the Baum Group?' she asked. 'You had some contacts in Berlin, and "the Baum" was known in resistance circles.'

Now I recalled what the three young Jews who had fled from Berlin said to me in Paris before they continued over the Pyrenees to Spain: 'If you ever want to link up with us, ask your Uncle Erich about "the Baum".'

As I now learned, they had been referring to Herbert Baum, the thirty-year-old electrician who was leader of the illegal Communist youth association for southeast Berlin. In 1941 the young Jew had been called up for compulsory labour service at the Siemens Company. Together with his wife Marianne and several reliable comrades and members of a socialist Zionists' group, all of whom worked at Siemens, he organised a resistance cell, which also attracted a number of students.

The Baum Group, to which about seventy young men and women belonged, began by printing flyers, which were secretly distributed in the Siemens plants and then also in the city; they urged resistance to the Nazis. In February 1942 Goebbels mounted an anti-Soviet propaganda exhibition called 'The Soviet Paradise', at which the Baum Group planned to distribute pamphlets. When that proved impossible, they decided to set fire to the exhibition. Staff members at the Kaiser Wilhelm Institute who belonged to the group procured the appropriate incendiary materials, and the day after the opening, 18 May 1942, Herbert and Marianne Baum and three other women and two men set the fire. Most of the exhibition was destroyed, and although part of it was saved by the fire department, the planned showing of the exhibition in all the major cities had to be cancelled. The attack on the exhibition, which could not be concealed from the public, caused quite a sensation. That brave deed strengthened the resistance in Berlin, and word of it spread throughout the Reich.

But meanwhile the Gestapo succeeded in identifying those responsible. Among the suspects who were first arrested at random was one conspirator who could not withstand the Gestapo's brutal methods of interrogation and betrayed the Baum Group. On 20 May, Herbert and Marianne Baum and all of those directly involved were arrested. Some of them, like Herbert Baum, died of the torture. The others were guillotined. Most of the other members of the group were executed or murdered in concentration camps. In addition, the

Gestapo arrested five hundred Berlin Jews who had had no part at all in the group's activities. They were taken to the former military academy in Lichterfelde, and that same evening every second one of these innocent people was shot. The rest were sent to the Sachsenhausen concentration camp, where they were killed in the autumn of 1942. One day after the mass arrest all the relatives of the hostages were seized, sent to Auschwitz, and murdered there.

'I was next door with some comrades when my brother and sister-in-law were picked up by Gestapo officers and pushed into a car,' Frau Baum said. 'The comrades hid me until Herr Desch and his friends brought me to Düsseldorf. They wanted to send me out of the country, but I insisted on staying here and doing something for the cause. After everything I had experienced in Berlin I could not have stood being abroad.'

'But why didn't you change your name? Wasn't that terribly risky?' I asked.

'I did change it. I was married and my husband was among those who were murdered. When Herr Desch got me new papers, I asked him to use my maiden name – it's not an uncommon name, and I wanted to have it back. But for safety's sake we changed the first name and the date of birth.'

THIRTY-FIVE

Aunt Martha is Buried

On 6 November 1943, Soviet troops recaptured Kiev. The Wehrmacht had lost the initiative all along the Eastern Front. Although it continued to put up stubborn resistance, it was being forced to retreat farther and farther.

In Italy, the British and Americans already held the lower third of the peninsula. On 3 December, they took up the struggle against the Germans for the heights around the monastery of Monte Cassino, 120 kilometres south of Rome.

But for Hitler the defensive fighting on the Eastern Front and in Italy was now of only secondary interest. His chief preoccupation was the 'Atlantic Wall', the German fortifications along the western coast of France, Belgium, Holland, and Denmark. He expected a major Allied invasion in the spring of 1944, if not earlier, and was keeping troops and armaments in reserve for it.

At Wrobel & Co., however, we had concluded that an invasion could not be expected before the summer. According to our calculations, the British and Americans would need at least half a year before they achieved the necessary superiority on land, at sea, and in the air, and solved all their logistical problems, including that of providing fuel to the armies. 'I'm afraid we'll have to resign ourselves to watching the war drag on for another year – provided, of course, our "greatest commander of all times" doesn't get his wonder weapon,' Herr Wrobel remarked.

The wonder weapon Herr Wrobel referred to was being developed at Peenemünde, the rockets later known as the V-1 and V-2 and actually deployed against England. The Swiss press already carried accounts of new German unmanned rockets with a range of 260 kilometres.

In December the Allies worked their way north in Italy, and the Russians recaptured more of their territory from the Germans. In order to cut off the supply of armaments and food supplies flowing along the northern Atlantic and Arctic route to Murmansk, and from there to the Soviet troops pressing westward, Hitler sent out the destroyer *Scharnhorst*. But on 26 December, the *Scharnhorst* was run down by the British navy, set afire with shelling, and sunk. Only 36 of the 1,600-man crew could be rescued.

Early in January 1944 units of the Red Army reached the former eastern border of Poland, and in mid-January others finally broke the blockade of Leningrad that had been in effect for three years. At the end of the month, thousands died in another series of devastating night air attacks on Berlin.

When the Red Army advanced to the Rumanian border, Hitler refused to grant his commanders' request for reinforcements; he expected the invasion in the west to occur at any moment. And because he needed a scapegoat for all the German reversals of recent months, he fired the head of military intelligence, Admiral Wilhelm Canaris. He claimed that Wehrmacht's intelligence operation had failed completely, and he turned the entire business of intelligence-gathering over to the Reichssicherheitshauptamt.

That was a harsh blow to Wrobel & Co. The company owed most of its privileges and latitude to its good relations with military intelligence and its director.

On the evening of 25 February, a few hours after Herr Wrobel had received the bad news, he, Frau Baum, Fräulein Lachmann, and I conferred on its implications for us. 'From today on we must be prepared for anything,' he said. 'Very soon now the SD will take another, closer look at us, and we must be ready, not only as an organisation but each of us individually.'

Then Herr Desch arrived with more sad tidings: he had learned of indications that Hitler meant to occupy Hungary and perhaps also Rumania, to prevent them from concluding a separate peace with his enemies. 'As soon as the SD takes over the Budapest airport, our Balkan route will be done for,' he said. 'We still have nine people in Vienna who must get out. My informant estimates the takeover of Hungary will occur in two weeks at most.'

Two days later I was the train, bound for Vienna, with the necessary papers for all nine. My job was to persuade the Hungarian major to move them out immediately. He was reluctant to alter his established routine, and when I gave him our reasons, he at first refused to believe the Germans would occupy Hungary; but finally he agreed to get all nine fugitives out by the following Sunday. We decided on three passwords to be used in an emergency, such as an earlier invasion by the Wehrmacht. Depending on whether he spoke of Aunt Martha's being injured, dying, or buried, different measures would have to be taken.

When I returned from Vienna, Herr Desch urged me to go to the Fichtelgebirge to inform our friends there of the changed situation. While I was away, Wrobel & Co. had completed calculations on British and American armaments production in the last two quarters of 1943. Statistics on Allied ships lost and ships being built had also become available. The Allies had gained clear superiority in all areas, besides which they could now ship across the Atlantic the arms and equipment they would need for the invasion; they no longer had to fear German U-boats.

'Tell the people in the Fichtelgebirge about all this,' Herr Desch urged me. 'They'll need something to keep their spirits up because it looks as though we may have quite a wait before the war is over.' I agreed to set out in three days.

The next day, on 1 March, Greybeard Ney celebrated his birthday with about twelve friends, among them Fräulein Bonse, who brought the latest news from the BBC.

As I was leaving, around ten-thirty, Herr Ney handed me an envelope and a small, heavy package. 'In case we don't see each other before you go to the Fichtelgebirge . . .'

The envelope contained a military passport for Uncle Erich, as well as ration stamps for sugar and soap, which the fugitives needed. And in the heavy package was a pistol for the people hiding out in the forest ranger's lodge.

As I took the last streetcar back to our apartment, where I was staying alone, I was wondering where I could hide these items until my departure.

Shortly after six the next morning I was awakened by the sound of a car stopping outside my building.

I jumped out of bed, checked quickly to make sure the radio was tuned to a German station, and peeked down at the street. A dark sedan had pulled up by the door, and standing beside it was a man in an ankle-length leather coat. I heard him say to a second man, who was out of my line of sight, 'I'll stay down here. Don't be long!'

The doorbell rang.

The military passport for Uncle Erich! I had stuck it into the side compartment of the suitcase I was planning to pack the next day, and the suitcase was on the high storage rack in the corridor. The pistol! I had unpacked it and stuck it into the pocket of my bathrobe, which hung on a hook in the bathroom.

The bell rang again.

I hurried to the door and pressed the buzzer, just as the bell rang a third time.

I heard him coming up the stairs.

He was alone, which meant he would probably not conduct a house search this time. But how could I get rid of the incriminating items? Of course Frau Kurz on the fourth floor had a key to the apartment.

He reached the door and rapped insistently. 'Open up! Secret Police!'

'*Who's* there?'

'Secret Police! Open the door!'

I was hoping Frau Kurz would hear him and call Wrobel & Co.

'What is it?' I asked through the door.

This time he shouted: 'Open up, will you! I have a warrant for your arrest!'

I let him in. He was a short, stocky man. He marched around the apartment with his hands in his pockets as if he owned the place.

'Get dressed, and make it snappy!' He looked all around, opening all the doors, glancing into the closets.

'Let me see your identification,' I said coolly.

He looked at me with surprise but then showed it to me.

I recalled Erwin's instructions, swallowed hard, and said, 'I am a member of the armed forces and fall under their jurisdiction. According to Luftwaffe regulations you are not allowed to . . .'

'Except *in flagrante delicto*!' He countered with a grin. 'Now get moving!'

As I was washing I had an idea. I took my bathrobe from its hook and left it in a heap on the bathroom floor. Frau Kurz would want to tidy up, would feel the weight of the pistol in the pocket and take care of that piece of evidence. I would leave the bathroom door ajar.

'Aren't you done yet?'

'Just one more minute! What deed am I supposed to have committed? Something in my sleep?'

'You'll find out soon enough. And don't get clever with me!'

He stayed with me while I dressed and kept urging me to hurry. When I closed the apartment door, he held out his hand for the key. 'We'll need that,' he said.

I gave it to him. I waited with bated breath to see whether he would put a seal on the door. If he did that, Frau Kurz would not dare to go in. But he was already on the stairs, jerking his head to indicate that I was to go on ahead of him. Before we left the building I glanced up and caught a glimpse of Frau Kurz's distraught face peering down over the banister.

During the twenty-minute drive neither agent said a word to me.

They chatted about overtime, about how their children were doing in school, and about the proper light and care for rubber plants.

When we reached our destination, they turned me over to a man in a faded grey-blue work jacket who hustled me down to the cellar and locked me into a tiny cell. I looked at my watch; it was exactly 6.30 A.M.

Shortly after nine, an older man in civilian clothes led me from my cell to a room on the second floor. As I went in, I caught a glimpse of the nameplate on the door: 'Councilm., Sturmbannführer'.

A bald man of about fifty was sitting behind a large desk piled high with documents. He dismissed my companion, glanced at me, and then buried himself in his papers again.

After a while he looked up and said matter-of-factly, 'Bad, very bad – might cost you your head. And for what? For a filthy louse of a Jew! Why would you do a thing like that – you, a German officer!' I hoped my astonishment did not show – to the end I had been a simple private, and I had been released as an N.C.O. Could I have become a lieutenant in the meantime, without knowing it? Or was this a case of mistaken identity?

'You're surprised, are you?' the bald-headed man said. 'We know everything – that's our job. All right, let's hear the rest! What was going on with that Jew Bernstein? How did you get mixed up with him, anyway?'

Now it all fell into place. Before 1933, Dr. Bernstein had been a prominent lawyer, hated by the Nazis. He had fled to Holland, and went underground when the Wehrmacht occupied that country in 1940. A few weeks ago he had to flee again. Herr Desch had arranged for him to escape by the Balkan route. I myself had brought him his new passport before he left for Vienna in a truck. I knew he had reached Vienna without incident. That meant he must have been caught at the Eastern Station – could the others have been nabbed too? What could I do? How much did the Gestapo know already?

'I'm waiting! Answer my questions, will you!' my interrogator snarled, but in the meantime I had regained my composure.

'Well, you are aware, sir, that I am allowed only to state my name, rank, and serial number. Those are the regulations. For any other information I would have to get permission from my command.'

I expected him to fly into a rage. Instead he smiled smugly and snapped my file shut.

'Just what I might have expected . . . But don't rejoice too soon! You're staying in custody, and soon you'll tell me the whole story – not just this business with the Jew Bernstein. You can count on it!'

I was taken back to my basement cell, and two hours later they transferred me to the remand prison on Ulmenstrasse. A genial guard who was in charge of new arrivals asked me, 'Have they given you anything to eat yet?'

By about 5.00 P.M. the admission procedures were completed. Outside my good-sized cell hung a sign that read: 'Solitary confinement. Gestapo. No visitors. RC.'

I was still puzzling over what 'RC' might signify when the door was unlocked and an elderly gentleman dressed all in black entered. 'You wish to confess, my son?' He nodded to the guard to leave us alone, sat down on my cot, waited until the guard's steps had died away in the distance, and then said, 'I'm the prison chaplain. I made sure you were registered as RC, Roman Catholic – otherwise I couldn't have got in to see you. A lady sends word that your Aunt Martha has been buried. She did not have to suffer, except for one sorrow, of which you know . . .'

A sense of great relief flooded me. All of our wards except Dr. Bernstein had reached safety; the operation was completed.

'The lady would like to know where you left the paper, and the little stamps,' he whispered, and I explained where I had hidden Uncle Erich's passbook and the ration stamps. He nodded with a gratified air, glanced at his watch, and said, 'We have only a little time before evening lock-up. The good woman wants you to know she found the packet. Herr Schneider will pick it up soon, along with the rest.' So Frau Kurz had discovered the pistol – I now had nothing to fear from a search.

'Is there anything you wanted to tell me?' he asked.

I quickly filled him in: so far I was under suspicion only for 'aiding and abetting' in Dr. Bernstein's escape; they thought I was an officer and apparently wanted to get at Wrobel & Co. through me. 'Perhaps one of my superiors could put in a word for me,' I concluded.

'Ah, yes,' he said, 'your boss sends greetings. I'm to tell you that winning time is the main thing. He said Spain and Portugal were all right for you, possibly also Sweden and Turkey. In about three weeks you could have Rumania – whatever that's supposed to mean.' He tucked away the slip of paper on which he had made a few notes, and in parting pressed cigarettes and chocolate on me: 'Your Aunt Annie sent these. She's praying that you may have not just one but three guardian angels . . .'

THIRTY-SIX

The Three Guardian Angels

March passed without the Gestapo's paying any attention to me. I remained in strict solitary confinement, forbidden to receive either mail or visitors, and waited with growing impatience for some change in this situation. My only source of information was the newspaper which my guard slipped to me when he had finished reading it.

From the daily Wehrmacht bulletins one could gather that the Red Army was pressing forward everywhere. Apparently Soviet forces had already entered Rumania. In mid-March, just a few days later than Herr Desch's informant had predicted, the Wehrmacht occupied Hungary, 'on the request of the Hungarian administrator, Admiral Miklós von Horthy', as Goebbels's Propaganda Ministry announced. Soon after that the American air force flew its first major bombing mission against Vienna. But all remained quiet along the Atlantic Wall.

At the beginning of April I was suddenly transferred to the little police prison in Ratingen, near the schoolhouse to which the Düsseldorf Gestapo office had been evacuated. Now I felt sure my interrogation would begin soon. But another two weeks passed before a Gestapo agent, whom my guards simply called 'Herr Kommissar', appeared and took me along for interrogation.

'We're going to walk. I don't want you to try anything funny on the way,' he told me. He showed me his pistol and put handcuffs on me. Once we were out on the street he said, to my surprise, 'Actually we're colleagues – I do domestic counterinteiligence – against sabotage and that sort of thing.'

'That's important stuff,' I said, feeling him out. 'They keep you pretty busy, I'll bet.'

He nodded.

'Especially with all the foreigners,' I added, to prevent the conversation from flagging. I knew that Germany had almost ten million foreigners working in the armaments industry and in agriculture; most of them were forced labourers from the occupied territories, but there were also some prisoners of war, in violation of the Geneva Convention.

'Yes,' he acknowledged, 'all those foreigners are quite a problem, especially from the security standpoint. They give us a lot of trouble. I wish I'd learned languages – then I wouldn't be stuck here but could be doing something interesting like you.'

'Like me?' I asked, and held out my handcuffed wrists.

He laughed. 'Don't worry, it won't be that bad,' he said. 'The main thing is for you to do plenty of talking and help us. Then they'll be willing to consider that business with the Jew a minor slip.'

'I hope so. You know as well as I do – you can't always pick your contact man. Or can you?'

He said nothing. Then he asked out of the blue, 'What do you think? Can we really win this war?'

'It would take a miracle.'

'Right,' he sighed, 'and *we'll* be the ones in hot water, while you guys have your alibis all set.'

I didn't want to respond to that, and he continued, 'It's all perfectly clear – you intelligence boys have your foreign contacts and your Jewish protégés, so nothing can happen to you. One hand washes the other. And meanwhile the little guys like me will really catch hell. They'll string us all up.'

'Well, if you want to look at it that way, you might be right,' I said, and then, pushing matters a little further, 'but right now I'm the one in trouble and you're still holding the cards. But if the situation happened to be reversed some day . . .'

'Yes, that's right, I'll give it some thought,' he said, and then added, 'In any case, thanks for the offer.'

Then he took me into the building where I had my previous interrogation.

The bald-headed Sturmbannführer did not seem to be in the mood for a chat. 'You've had plenty of time to think it over. Are you ready to talk?'

'If official authorisation has come, of course, sir.'

'It's come.' He tapped my file, which in the meantime had swollen to twice its size. 'Kommissar Richter,' he said, and nodded toward my escort, 'will show it to you. He'll get you the paper and pencils, or you can have a typewriter if you want. He'll tell you what issues we're interested in for the present. I want you to give me a comprehensive and thorough report – is that clear?'

'And when can I expect to be released?'

He put on a show of surprise and indignation. 'I must not have heard you right! If you're very lucky, you'll stay in protective custody and not have to appear before the People's High Court. That depends entirely on you – whether you tell us everything you know. And don't try to lead us along with fairy tales! Prisoners in protective custody can also do their time in a concentration camp, in case you were wondering!'

On the way back Kommissar Richter, who was lugging a heavy briefcase containing typing paper and my file, as well as the typewriter, trudged along in silence. Suddenly he asked, 'What sectors of the economy were you responsible for?'

'Coal, iron, steel . . .'

'And alloys, right? Where do we get our chrome from, do you know?'

He's feeling me out, I thought, and said, 'Mainly from Turkey and the Balkans, but . . .'

'Yes?'

'I've been totally out of touch for six weeks. For all I know, Turkey isn't delivering any more. The Allies were putting pressure on the Turks back in February.'

'And how long would our supplies last if they halted deliveries?'

I wondered what he was getting at. I pretended to do some quick calculations in my head, and then said, 'If we really stretch our stockpiles, till May or June, and maybe another few weeks after that.' I was fairly certain our supplies would last until the autumn, but I thought it would help to paint a bleaker picture. I added, 'Without chrome you can't produce tanks or artillery pieces, grenades, planes, trucks, or U-boats – but you know that.'

He nodded.

'Turkey has just stopped supplying us,' he said after a moment. 'According to what you say, our war production could grind to a halt in three months.'

We were passing a little café. He glanced in through the window, noted the place was empty, and said, 'I'll buy you a cup of coffee.' Then he removed my handcuffs, gave me the typewriter to carry, and let me enter ahead of him.

After the elderly waitress had brought us each a cup of ersatz coffee, Kommissar Richter resumed the discussion: 'What if the war were over and we were under Allied occupation. I'd be in jail, and you'd be at liberty. What could you do for me?'

'If that were the case,' I replied cautiously, 'I could certainly do something for you. For instance, I could testify that when I was in a really tight situation, Gestapo Kommissar Richter made himself enormously helpful to me. That would probably save your neck, provided of course you really had helped me and it could be proved.'

He nodded, drank a sip of the hot brew, grimacing at the taste. 'Your father is with the Australian army,' he said, as if he were speaking to himself. 'Your mother is registered in Düsseldorf, but she seems to have moved to the country because of the air raids, probably to Upper Bavaria. We haven't been able to trace her yet.'

'And it should be left at that,' I said, very much on my guard now. Might the whole thing be a trap?

'I have no problem with that,' he continued. 'But where will I find you when I need you?'

'Hm, where will you find me? That doesn't depend only on me, does it?'

He nodded, then suddenly drew my file out of his leather briefcase, laid it on the table, and leafed through it. I bent forward a little, trying to see upside down what was in it, but he held it in such a way that I couldn't make anything out.

'Oh, you're also non-Aryan!' He seemed to be pleased by the discovery, for he commented, 'All in all, not bad! If only I knew how we, I mean, how I could find you after the war.'

'The best thing would be to set up a "letter drop". Whoever gets there first will leave a note for the other or send it by a messenger. We'll find a way.'

'I think Düsseldorf would probably be best – how about a café?'

'That's a possibility,' I said, thinking of Aunt Annie.

'But what if the building's been bombed?' he wondered.

'Well, then you'd ask around the neighbourhood and find out where the owners had gone. We still have some time to pick a suitable place.'

'All right – or perhaps a country inn, on the left bank of the Rhine. And now take this down!' He handed me paper and a fountain pen, and I took down from his dictation: 'I hereby certify that Kommissar Richter from Moers helped me and my friends to the best of his ability and thereby saved my life.' Then he had me translate the text into English.

When he had carefully folded the piece of paper and put it away in an inner pocket, he shoved my file across the table to me. While I read it, he picked up a magazine from a nearby table and buried himself in it.

I now got a first-hand look at what the Gestapo had been able to gather on me: statements from Colonel Kessler and Major Zobel, both very complimentary; then an inquiry from Herr Wrobel as to when I would be returned to my 'extremely important work, crucial to the war effort'; a letter from Party Member Doctor Metzger stating that the absence of such an 'indisputably loyal and reliable member of the team' left an intolerable gap in the office; and various other items. The file contained only one piece of negative material: a Dr. Siegfried Segnitz, probably the SD spy assigned to us, attributed to me a 'hostile attitude toward National Socialism', but he could adduce no evidence.

I learned that I was a lieutenant in the reserves – 'Lieutenant Colonel' Wrobel had recommended me for the promotion to the Foreign Economic Section of military intelligence. And the reason for my being arrested also became clear: the file contained a report from the Vienna Gestapo to the effect that Dr. Bernstein's nervousness had aroused suspicion during a routine check of identification papers at the Eastern Station. He had betrayed himself by pulling out a passport, then stuffing it back into his pocket and presenting another one. They arrested him, but he committed suicide before he could be interrogated. In the lining of his jacket the Gestapo found a slip of paper on which Bernstein had jotted down my father's name and address and my first name – in spite of my insistence that he should memorise the address. So that explained everything!

Apparently, though, the Gestapo knew nothing about the Balkan route. They noted of Dr. Bernstein that he 'apparently intended to go to Pressburg'. They also had no proof that I had provided him with papers or had aided his escape.

From the other documents in the file I discovered what measures they had undertaken so far and what they planned to do with me. The Reichssicherheitshauptamt, Foreign Intelligence Division, had instructed the Düsseldorf office to withdraw me from circulation for the present – putting me in solitary confinement without mail or visitors. Then inquiries about my father had been set in motion. Wrobel & Co. had also come under scrutiny, and the Gestapo had concluded that our office represented an 'important link in the military intelligence-gathering service' with 'particularly interesting foreign contacts.' I had to laugh at that; we derived almost all of our information from foreign newspapers, and even our informants in neutral countries rarely reported anything to us that could not be found in the English, American, Swedish, and Swiss press.

The last paper in the file was an order from the RSHA to keep me strictly isolated. A member of 'Group D of the SD office for Foreign and Domestic Intelligence' would interrogate me shortly. In the meantime I should supply detailed information on our 'important foreign contacts', particularly in light of 'possible political advantage', and in addition I should describe precisely my activities at Wrobel & Co.

'That will be hard to do without my files,' I said.

Herr Richter laid aside the magazine and gathered up the file. 'That's up to you – didn't anything else strike you?'

'You mean the "political advantage" part?'

He nodded.

'That can only mean,' I said, 'that those fellows in the RSHA want to negotiate with the other side on their own – or am I mistaken?'

'That's how I see it.' He got up, and we left, I in handcuffs again. When we reached the police prison, a clerk hurried out to receive us. 'You just had a call, Kommissar Richter. The prisoner is supposed to be transferred today – to Anrath.'

At Anrath I spent four and a half months in strict isolation. In the same section of the old prison near Krefeld were eighteen prisoners from Holland. We saw each other only during our daily 'walk', which involved fifteen minutes of shuffling around in a circle, in a special courtyard to which the other prisoners had no access. We were strictly forbidden to speak, but of course we whispered to each other. I found out that they were all prisoners of the SD; some of them had been there for eighteen months already. They had lost a great deal of weight because they were not supposed to be put to work and therefore were receiving meagre 'lazy-bones rations'. Since their arrests they had had no contact with their families – they were 'NF' prisoners. NF stood for 'night and fog', and was derived from an executive order the Führer had issued in December 1941, which stipulated: 'No word of these civilians must be brought back to their homelands. The population must be left in total uncertainty as to their fate.'

The man in the cell next to mine, Marinus, a welder from Rotterdam, had been walking his dog one evening fourteen months earlier. A German patrol came by, and the dog barked at them. They shot the dog and took the man with them then and there. The family had no idea what had happened to him.

That was NF.

At the beginning of May, I was fetched from my cell and taken to the interrogation room.

'Are the reports done?' Kommissar Richter wanted to know.

'I'm not making very good progress. It's difficult without files or records. And I can concentrate for at most an hour or two – with so little to eat . . .'

'You're playing for time,' he remarked. 'I'd probably do the same in your position. But don't push it too far.'

Then he brought some sandwiches out of his briefcase. While I ate, he read over what I had written. When he reached the passage that read, 'Production from the ore quarries of Nikopol guarantees the Reich's manganese supply for years to come,' he remarked dryly, 'That may have been true at one time, but the Russians have had Nikopol back for quite a while. By the beginning of April they had already recaptured Odessa, 300 kilometres to the west. And right now the Wehrmacht is clearing out of its last bases in the Crimea.'

'You see,' I said, 'I can't write anything useful without current information.'

'How about the story on the "politically advantageous" foreign contacts? They're really eager to hear about those.'

'Well, I could suggest a rendezvous in Lisbon. An English business-man who was still there in February is a brother-in-law of Lord Palmer, the armaments minister. Something might be arranged . . .'

'That sounds all right. I don't know much about it, but that's the sort of thing they're likely to go for. But you haven't written anything about it –' he pointed to my typed pages.

'I wanted to hear your opinion first. I could make other suggestions, too, but the problem with all of them is that then I wouldn't be needed, you understand? And we do want to see each other alive after the war, don't we?'

'Yes, there's some truth to that. That has to be kept in mind. Oh well, you still have time – something will occur to you, I'm sure. By the way, I've been thinking about our rendezvous – the best thing would be a café on the left bank of the Rhine. After all, I live in Moers. Can you think of a place in Upper Kassel?'

I hesitated a moment, trying to be sure I wouldn't get Aunt Annie and Greybeard Ney into any difficulties. Finally I said, 'On the way here, we drove past a café . . .' I described its location.

'Oh I know that one – it's the Ney Café. It's right by the streetcar stop on the line to Moers. That's perfect!'

During our next walk in the courtyard I passed on to the other prisoners some details about the war situation. In April Odessa and now the Crimea had been won back by the Soviets. Half of Italy had already fallen into the hands of the Allies. Only in the west were things still quiet.

One of the Dutchmen wanted to know how I had obtained my

information. 'From the agent who interrogated me – they're getting cold feet now, and suddenly they're willing to talk.'

'That's interesting,' said the Dutchman.

At the end of May, I was again summoned to the interrogation room, but this time I found not Kommissar Richter but an SD officer from Berlin, a youngish man in civilian clothes. He seemed well disposed toward me, read my various reports with interest, and suddenly looked up and asked me, 'Are you sure you understand what we're after?'

I tried to avoid answering this tricky question, but that proved unnecessary, for he launched into a long monologue about how urgent it was to convince the Western powers that they should *join with* Germany to defend Europe against bolshevism; that it was sheer *madness* for them to destroy Germany . . . In conclusion he remarked, 'Two of your proposals strike me as quite interesting. I'll have them looked into. Keep thinking about it – perhaps you'll come up with something more. If you do, the Kommissar can let me know.'

A week later, early on the morning of 6 June, word spread through the prison that the Allied invasion had finally begun. That afternoon Kommissar Richter turned up and confirmed the rumour. 'How long do you think it will take before they get here?' he asked.

'Not long, I hope,' I replied.

'You won't go back on our agreement, will you?'

I assured him I would not. But the breakthrough of the Allied troops was not to come so soon. The Wehrmacht had been preparing for an invasion for months and was ready to put up fierce resistance. Unfortunately for the German troops, however, Hitler was convinced the landing in Normandy was a deceptive manoeuvre; he expected the real invasion to come at Calais, aimed at the heavily industrialised Ruhr area. For almost a week he refused to dispatch reinforcements or replacements to the embattled troops. When he finally authorised sending in the tank groups that had been held in reserve, it was too late. The counterattack collapsed under a hail of Allied bombs and shells. Nevertheless, the British and American armies remained stuck near the coast all through June and July. Although the Soviets had reached the outskirts of Warsaw and had advanced deep into Finland and Rumania, and Allied troops were in Genoa, Florence, and Rimini, we were still waiting for an Allied breakthrough in France.

On 21 July we heard rumours that an attempt had been made on Hitler's life the previous day. It filled us with despair to learn it had failed.

At the beginning of August, Kommissar Richter called me in again. He seemed downcast. The British had finally broken through in Normandy, but it would be weeks before they reached the Rhine. 'They have us working day and night,' he told me. 'In the last few days more people have been arrested than in all of last year.'

'Because of the 20th July?'

'That too, of course – anybody in any way involved, and all those who were under suspicion earlier. But that's not half of it. All hell has broken loose in France. Suddenly there are armed opposition groups, strikes, revolts – they're even attacking the Wehrmacht! In Yugoslavia the partisans have gone on the offensive, and in Warsaw the SS had to put down a major revolt. Besides, these daily air raids are slowly but surely doing us in. The foreign workers are getting more and more rebellious – one case of sabotage after another; and then the deserters and their collaborators . . .'

Now I understood why he seemed so depressed and frightened. 'How do things stand with my case?' I asked. 'Have you heard anything from Berlin?'

'They don't want any more reports. I'll take the typewriter with me.'

'What does that mean?' I asked in alarm.

He merely shrugged.

Suddenly things moved very quickly in France. The Allies swept through the country, capturing everything but a couple of ports in the north and south. On 26 August de Gaulle entered Paris.

In the east the Red Army crossed the Vistula on 2 August and also made great headway in the southeast. On 30 August the Ploesti oilfields fell into Russian hands, and the day after that, Bucharest. A week earlier the new Rumanian government declared itself independent of Germany. This switch by Rumania ripped such a large hole in Germany's line of defence that the Wehrmacht had to abandon the entire Balkan peninsula.

American troops had reached northern Italy, and were advancing steadily in France and Belgium.

On 1 September, I was told I would be transferred the following day. I was shown the warrant for my 'protective custody'. The form, printed on pink paper, bore the signature of Ernst Kaltenbrunner, Heydrich's successor as head of the Security Police, the SD, and the RSHA. The reason given for my imprisonment was 'abetting Jews', and the form indicated I was to be sent to the Flossenbürg concentration camp, 'for the duration of the war'.

'Where's Flossenbürg?' I asked the guard.

'I haven't the faintest,' he replied. 'But tomorrow morning they're taking you to Düsseldorf for the time being.'

On 5 September, I was still in Düsseldorf, having been shifted from the Ulmenstrasse prison to the police prison on Kavalleriestrasse. Brussels had just been captured by the Allies, and the train that was supposed to transport prisoners was needed for troops being rushed to the Aachen area to defend the border.

We prisoners began to feel somewhat hopeful.

On 6 September they took about eight of us, all chained together, to the station. In our group were men and women, Germans and foreigners, criminals and political prisoners, some destined for prisons, others for concentration camps. Guards and railway policemen with dogs kept a close eye on us.

This time the specially equipped prison train arrived. I was able to read the metal signs hung on the outside of the cars: TRIER via Cologne – Koblenz – Cochem. They locked us into tiny individual cages, but the prospect of being taken in the very direction I had hoped for made the trip bearable.

In Cologne most of the group was taken off the train. My cage was also opened for a moment, but then the guard looked at his list, muttered something, and locked me in again.

At noon in Koblenz the train stopped for some time. The prisoners received a bowl of soup and a piece of bread. The guard came by and asked, 'Where's Flossenbürg?'

'Someone told me it was near Trier,' I said.

In Trier he had some difficulty getting rid of me, but he succeeded. That evening I found myself in the 'new arrivals' section of the Trier penitentiary. A grouchy guard fumed, 'This is the second one they've sent us, the idiots! What are we supposed to do with them? I've never *heard* of a Flossenbürg concentration camp!'

I was hoping to stay put, but the next day they shipped me off again. Four days later, on 11 September, the Americans reached the German border at Trier.

Our return trip ended in Cologne. There I was handcuffed to the other man destined for Flossenbürg, a taciturn farmer who had been drafted into the Reichswehr and as a Jehovah's Witness had refused to take the oath to the Führer. That night we two were crowded with three others into a one-person cell. The next day our odyssey continued, this time to Hanover. Along the way fellow prisoners told us they were being evacuated because heavy fighting was under way around Aachen and Düren.

When we reached Hanover, we were almost sent back to the

Rhineland, but then they decided to take us off the train, and we were kept in Hanover until 11 September. 'There'll be a transport train leaving for Magdeburg and Leipzig then,' the guard informed us.

But our wanderings had not yet ended. From 13 to 18 September we stayed in Leipzig. Then we were sent to Kassel, from there to Würzburg, on to Nuremberg, then to Hof, Bayreuth, and Weiden in the Upper Palatinate. On the morning of 24 September an SS truck came to pick us up. After glancing at the farmer's warrant for protective custody, the driver commented, 'Ten days in the quarry, and you'll be off to join your Jehovah.' We drove through the Upper Palatine Forest, through countryside that became increasingly wild and desolate. After we reached the village of Flossenbürg the road climbed steeply. High on a barren cliff we could see watchtowers, barbed wire, and the camp gate.

'Two new ones – one of them Witnesses and a political.'

I saw SS men with machine guns, and prisoners in tattered black-and-white striped prison garb, hollow-eyed, emaciated. A well-fed kapo, wearing the green patch for criminals, was carrying a stout stick. Then I heard his command: 'Out! In there for clothes!'

The kapo in charge of the clothing depot looked at us with scorn. 'A waste of good clothes – you're probably going to the quarry tomorrow.'

Another kapo came into the clothing storeroom. He was small and wiry and wore a red patch. He looked at Fritz, the farmer, first, then turned to me and we recognised each other almost simultaneously.

'My God, what are you . . . I thought . . .'

He paused for a minute, then burst out, 'You've got to get out of here – as quickly as possible. Don't you know languages?'

I nodded, at a loss for words.

'There's a shipment leaving for the new camp at Hersbruck. They desperately need an interpreter. You can do that. I'll put your name on the list right now – then you'll be all right.'

I jerked my head toward Fritz.

He understood. 'Sure, him too. I'll come to your barracks later. Then we can talk.'

And with that he disappeared, the third guardian angel Aunt Annie had been praying for – along with the chaplain and the Kommissar – a Communist from Düsseldorf.

THIRTY-SEVEN

Waiting for Liberation

'*Fous le camp, salaud, vas te promener!*' the professor shouted from the corner.

'What's he saying?' the SS Scharführer asked me. He had just stepped into the barracks.

'He says you should be careful, Scharführer! This is the contagious disease barracks – typhoid, spotted fever, maybe the plague . . .'

He was already gone. From outside he called to me, 'You come out here, but don't get too close!'

I told the professor what I was doing and went outside. 'How many prisoners in this block?' the Scharführer asked, holding his handkerchief over his nose and mouth.

'Two hundred and seventeen, Scharführer,' I replied at random.

'How many of them can still walk?'

I was alarmed. 'That depends, Scharführer, on how far . . .'

'As far as the ramp – the camp has to be cleared out! There's a train leaving for Dachau in an hour.'

We knew about it already and had discussed all night what would be the best course of action: to stay here, waiting for the Americans and running the risk that the SS might blow up or set fire to the barracks and the remaining prisoners; or to let ourselves be moved, not knowing what awaited us?

Except for the professor and me, all those still able to participate in the discussion had been in favour of staying.

'None of those prisoners inside is capable of walking or being transported,' I told the Scharführer.

'But you're coming along?'

'Yes, and the Frenchman too.'

'All right – we leave in thirty minutes. Take your blanket with you!'

That was on 20 March 1945. We had stuck it out for five months at Hersbruck, the auxiliary facility of the Flossenbürg concentration camp, twenty kilometres east of Nuremberg. Except for Fritz, the Jehovah's Witness, who had died in January of spotted fever, and a few kapos, I was the only German among the prisoners. The others came from all over Europe: France, Belgium, Holland, Poland, and so on. There were Jews from Hungary, deportees from Yugoslavia and Greece, Czechs, Italian officers, Spaniards who had fought against Franco, Gypsies, Norwegians, Canadian and Soviet pilots who had been shot down.

I had been transferred to Hersbruck the previous October, along with twelve hundred other prisoners. The camp was still under construction, and some of us were assigned to build underground production and storage facilities for the armaments industry. Others were sent to work in factories in the surrounding towns.

In November and December, when the Red Army was already marching into East Prussia, Hungary, and eastern Czechoslovakia, and the Allies had occupied Aachen and the Saar Valley, shipments of prisoners arrived from the camps at Auschwitz and Gross-Rosen, which had been vacated by the SS. The exhausted and starving prisoners were put into hastily erected new barracks, known as the 'convalescent section'. A Jewish doctor from Cracow was assigned to Convalescent Section 1, with a physical therapist from Paris as block superintendent. Because the doctor spoke German but no French, I was sent in to act as interpreter. Until then I had been using my translating skills only on the side; during the day I had to work on the construction of the underground facilities.

I was relieved to get away from the work detail; the work crews suffered constant harassment because the tunnels kept collapsing. Among the prisoners were some very skilled at causing cave-inns without its appearing to be sabotage. A further advantage of being in the convalescent section was that the SS guards were terrified of catching something from the prisoners, who suffered from tuberculosis and many other diseases, and were crawling with lice. Their fears were fully justified; after Fritz, the doctor himself was the next to die of spotted fever. From then on the French therapist assumed responsibility for caring for the prisoners. We jokingly called him the 'professor'. We had no medications; the most he could do was try to bring down the prisoners' fever with cold compresses, and cheer them up. His indestructible optimism turned out to be the best medicine.

He got us through January by portraying the Allies' situation, about which he knew as little as we, in the most rosy colours imaginable: they had already taken dozens of major German cities – Cologne, Frankfurt, Hamburg (he didn't know the names of any others) . . . In three, or perhaps even in two, weeks the Americans would have fought their way through to Nuremberg, the Soviets to the Czech border, and then it would be just a matter of days or even hours before they would liberate us, and we would get all the food, medicine, and red wine we wanted.

Around the middle of the month I managed to get my hands on a three-day-old newspaper, brought into the camp by a member of the factory detail. The Wehrmacht bulletin mentioned an air raid on Frankfurt by the Americans, and boasted of the success of the German offensive in the Ardennes. Retaliatory blows had been launched against England with the V-1 and V-2 rockets, and fighting was going on in northern Italy and along the borders of East Prussia. We were bitterly disappointed.

On my twenty-fourth birthday, at the end of January, I developed chills and fever.

'It'll pass soon,' the professor comforted me. 'The Americans will be here in a few days, and they'll cure you in a wink.'

The next day my fever was higher, and I was in such pain I could hardly breathe. 'Please go and see whether any mail has come for me,' I begged the professor. Just before Christmas I had finally obtained a form on which prisoners could write letters, and wrote to my mother that I was well but urgently needed medicine for my fellow prisoners. The doctor from Cracow had given me the names of a few medicines and had also mentioned various items that would be very helpful as food supplements.

When the professor went to enquire, it turned out that my mother had in fact come in person to the camp and delivered a small crate a few days earlier. Now we had salt, onions, grape sugar, garlic, pills, and medications for injecting, along with a hypodermic. The professor gave me a 10 cc injection that would have knocked over a horse. By the next day the pain vanished, and the fever began to recede.

By the time I was back on my feet, the Allies had taken up positions along the Rhine, and the Russians had cut off East Prussia and were pressing on into Pomerania.

'They've crossed the Rhine! They'll be here in ten or twelve days!' the professor asserted. He had been stealing garbage from the SS kitchen, and eavesdropped on the cooks' conversation.

'Is it really true?'

'*Pas de blague – c'est vrai!* This time it's true!'

But two weeks passed, and the Americans were still 80 kilometres from Hersbruck when word arrived that the camp had to be evacuated.

Some of the prisoners had already been moved, sent on foot over the mountains into Czechoslovakia. Now the SS wanted to move the rest of us south to Dachau. We arrived in Dachau the next day, a procession of a couple of hundred wretched figures. Twelve had died along the way and two had been killed when our group was strafed. We dragged ourselves to our barracks. I was one of those in better shape – weighing about ninety pounds.

'Hey, you, you're a German, aren't you?' One of the officers in charge of the camp had picked me out. 'Tomorrow you're reporting to fight for the Fatherland!'

That was all I needed!

The professor comforted me: 'Don't worry, he didn't take your name.' But just in case, he made sure I got the jacket of a Frenchman who had died the day before, with a black F on a red patch and a different number. 'Now you'll be all right! Imagine having to go and fight, when the Americans will be here tomorrow or the day after at the latest!'

But weeks passed, and nothing happened. The Ruhr area had long since been occupied, and Berlin encircled by the Red Army. The British had reached the Elbe in the north, and the Americans had pushed forward to the border of Czechoslovakia and liberated Hersbruck.

If only we had stayed there! For days we had no food. Fellow prisoners were dying all around me. I had abscesses on my legs, and hunger oedema. Even the professor couldn't help; he was almost done for himself. We lay there in a stupor, no longer believing rumours that the SS had fled.

Suddenly we heard wild shouting outside, and our first thought was, 'Now they're coming in to shoot us all.'

The door to the barracks flew open. A soldier in battle dress filled the doorway. 'Anyone in here speak English?' he called, and groped for a cigarette.

Zero Hour

The complete collapse of the German Reich was now unavoidable. On 30 April 1945, Hitler committed suicide in the bunker of his heavily fortified Reich Chancellery in the centre of Berlin. The city was extensively destroyed, and almost entirely surrounded by the Red Army.

On May 1, Admiral Karl Dönitz, named by Hitler as his successor, ordered that combat against the Western powers be stopped. On 2 May, the last defenders of Berlin surrendered to the Red Army. On 7 May 1945, Radio Flensburg, the last station of the Greater German Broadcasting Corporation, which for so many years had announced the triumphs of the German forces to fanfares of trumpets, and which, to the very end, had exhorted the population to 'hold out to the final victory', announced the 'unconditional surrender of all German troops'. At midnight on 8 May, a cease-fire took effect on nearly all fronts. The last battles occurred in Czechoslovakia on 9 May, and in the Courland area in the northeast on 10 May 1945.

General Alfred Jodl, Hitler's closest military adviser and chief of the Wehrmacht operations staff since the beginning of the war, signed the capitulation at Rheims. Afterwards, he rose and declared in English, 'With this signature the German people and the German Armed Forces are, for better or worse, delivered into the hands of the victors . . . In this hour I can only express the hope that the victor will treat them with generosity.'

If the general expected approval from the representatives of the victorious powers, he was mistaken. In October 1946, he was sentenced to death and hanged by the International Military Tribunal at Nuremberg.

At that time the Allies were still determined to demonstrate no generosity at all toward the defeated Germans.

Allied officers governed every city and rural district in the occupied zones and made dictatorial use of their nearly unlimited power. Yet despite all the regulations – in some places pedestrian and bicycle traffic was permitted only with written authorisation, and unauthorised picking of grass from roadsides and embankments by Germans was punishable by law – chaos, epidemics, and famine could not be prevented. British Foreign Secretary Ernest Bevin, who represented England at the Potsdam Conference in July 1945, complained later before the House of Commons that the unconditional surrender and the resulting vacuum of power left the occupying forces with an ungovernable monster, 'a Germany without laws, without a constitution, without a single person with whom we could negotiate, without a single institution with which we could master the situation. We had to rebuild from the ground up with absolutely nothing as a basis.'

Great heaps of rubble lay everywhere in the cities. In many places the gas and electricity services had broken down, and often even the water supply and the sewer system had been destroyed. Postal service was at a standstill. The entire communication and transportation system was paralysed. Streets, bridges, and railway lines were largely unusable. In the British zone, which included Hamburg, Hanover and the whole Ruhr area as well as Cologne, of 13,000 kilometres of railway track barely a thousand were negotiable. There were only a few makeshift bridges over the Rhine, and food supplies in the overcrowded areas were running out. In Frankfurt am Main, the hub of the American zone, conditions were similar. Robert T. Pell, who later became press officer at American headquarters, noted at the time: '. . . a city of the dead. After the seven o'clock curfew, the sound of the GIs' boots echoes like footsteps in a crypt. You hear no dogs barking, and not a sound from any other animals.'

The moral state of the defeated Germans was just as desperate: 'In a society where ninety percent of the population is hungry,' commented Alfred Andersch, 'shoplifting is no longer considered a crime'. Prostitution, despite the curfews and orders against fraternisation with the enemy, had also become commonplace and was considered no more degrading than the black marketeering by which even out-of-work lawyers, discharged officers, and university professors now attempted to keep their heads above water. 'What passes through our consultation room every day and what we see on every street and square in Germany is not to be described with words,' Provost Heinrich Gruber, former concentration camp inmate and director of the Evangelical Relief Organization in Berlin, reported to his fellow clergymen in England. 'Men take their own lives out of despair. Thousands of corpses float down the Oder and Elbe into the sea; no one pays attention to it any more. Thousands of corpses hang from trees in the forests surrounding Berlin; no one cuts them down any more . . . tens of thousands are on the roads, dying of hunger and exhaustion. Thousands haven't known for weeks, for months, if they'll ever find a home again.'

Many cities were menaced by epidemics, particularly those places where the water supply had collapsed and the sewer system no longer functioned. In Kassel during the final bombing attacks, typhoid patients had fled the isolation wards of destroyed hospitals; some of the prisoners released from concentration and prisoner of war camps had eluded the strict quarantine and brought infectious diseases into the cities.

Into this chaos poured the stream of refugees from the east. At first the new arrivals were gathered in temporary camps or in open fields. But soon they were shunted to less war-torn areas, where they were often a thorn in the side of the local people. For the most part, the farmers regarded those who had been billeted with them as intruders; 'refugee' became a term of abuse, especially in places like Schleswig-Holstein, where the homeless from the east comprised nearly one half of the total population. In the occupied Zones the number of refugees climbed to almost 23 per cent by 1948.

What remained of the German armed forces, from adolescent anti-aircraft auxiliaries to old Volkssturm soldiers, were prisoners of war – altogether about twelve million men. They were interned in camps situated all the way from the Arctic Circle to Egypt, from Great Britain to eastern Siberia. In the detention camps in Germany, sheer famine prevailed.

Initially the Allies planned to keep all the German prisoners of war behind barbed wire until the conclusion of a peace treaty, and to use them as forced labourers in the reconstruction of areas that had been laid waste by German troops. But then they decided on a policy of gradual release, and by early 1947 nearly four-fifths of all the prisoners had returned home.

Still, many were detained by the victors beyond this point: approximately 31,000 in the United States, and 435,000 in Great Britain and the Commonwealth. Of the 700,000 German soldiers the Americans turned over to the French for forced labour, 630,000 were still in French custody in the spring of 1947. According to official records, almost 900,000 prisoners were still being held in Soviet camps, and at least 300,000 in Poland, Yugoslavia, Belgium, and other places. All told, about 2.4 million men still had not returned home two years after the surrender.

In spite of this and other sufferings that the German people had to endure, they truly could not complain about their treatment by the victors. 'On the contrary,' says Hagen Rudolph in a study of the situation at the war's end, 'at least for those born after the war who, stunned and horrified, hear about the atrocities and the millions of murders committed by the Nazis, it remains inexplicable that large-scale acts of violence and rioting inspired by revenge did not occur in Germany after the war. Instead, in 1945 civilisation resumed pretty much without interruption.' Indeed, given the war's grim horrors, the postwar Germans incurred at the hands of their conquerors only a fraction of the violence which they had earlier inflicted on those who had been in their power.

Yet it would be a mistake to assume that the defeated dwelt on such comparisons for long and then exhibited suitable shame and repentance. On the contrary: as soon as the first shock was over, the Germans allowed their recent past to sink quickly into oblivion. At first, forgetting was a matter of self-preservation. One could not have gone on living in constant awareness of a guilt of such incomprehensible proportions. And eventually, one simply got used to acting as if certain things – from the first murders and tortures in the cellars of SA taverns in February 1933, to the brutal, bloody pogrom against the Jews in November 1938, the countless atrocities in the conquered lands, and the hanging of war-weary soldiers and civilians in early May of 1945 – had not happened at all.

The external circumstances of the early postwar period afforded ideal conditions for such suppression of the truth: most of the men, who had certainly witnessed the barbarism far more frequently than their wives and children, were still in POW camps; in 1946 the population of the four occupied zones consisted of 44 per cent adult women and 23 per cent children. Survival was at stake; hectic activity was required; there was no time for brooding over the past. Survival meant standing on line every day in front of nearly empty stores to get what little rations were being distributed. At the end of May 1945 the average consumer received tin weekly rations of 140 grams of meat or sausage, 50 grams of fat, 200 grams of cereal and 100 grams of sugar or sugar beet syrup, as well as monthly rations of 400 grams of salt, 25 grams of real coffee, 100 grams of ersatz coffee, 12 kilos of potatoes and 9 kilos of bread. But one had to keep one's eyes open constantly to be sure to get these allotments, and not miss an opportunity to get hold of some extra food. It took a lot of time and bother just to get some milk, a few eggs, or some vegetables now and then. Survival also meant keeping a look-out for boards and planks, nails and window glass to make at least temporary and urgent repairs; every sort of shelter had to be restored or improvised, an enterprise which demanded one's entire strength. Contrary to the original expectation, the food ration decreased from month to month. Most Germans were far better off nutritionally during the war than in the postwar period, for now they no longer had the imports from the occupied countries. In October 1945 the daily average intake in Germany had sunk to 1,500 calories, and in some places to 1,350. Still, even these figures are deceptive because they refer to a diet consisting almost entirely of carbohydrates; there were such tiny quantities of fat and protein that it resulted in serous nutritional deficiencies.

By the beginning of winter, the Allied authorities feared that hunger would make the Germans rebellious. On 31 October 1945, General Eisenhower notified Washington that there were indications of an imminent armed uprising. That was, however, a complete misjudgment of the situation. Even in their dreams no one in defeated Germany thought about resisting the Allies, much less open revolt. The Germans had had enough of politics: men and women, old and young, those who had just recently been fanatical Nazis and those who had remained uncommitted – all dreamed of nothing else but a 'healed world' in which one had enough to eat, didn't freeze, was decently clothed, had a comfortable home, earned good money for hard work, and, with that money, once again achieved standing and respect. Nothing else mattered. 'Forget the past, only the future counts' – that was the leitmotif of the German postwar reconstruction.

I saw my cousin Gudrun again in 1949, more than seven years after our last meeting in Berlin. She had become somewhat plumper, but was no less gay or effervescent than I remembered her. Now in her late twenties, she was an elegant, well-groomed woman, and judging by the expensive jewellery she wore, was apparently quite well off.

I visited her at her house on the fringe of the Alps in Bad Tölz, an hour's drive south from Munich. Uncle Karl had given me the address and begged me to look her up when I was in the area.

Gudrun welcomed me with tremendous warmth, and talking nonstop the entire time, showed me around – as she had done once before, long ago – the lovely country home in which she lived alone.

As we sat down to coffee, she began to tell me of her life at the end of the war, and during the occupation.

Gudrun was living in Bad Tölz when the war ended. 'You know, I was expecting a child, but I had a miscarriage . . . In any case, Horst-Eberhard wanted me to stay here because of the air raids. I had visited him a few times – in the Government General and later in the Warthegau. It was terribly boring there. And the food was too fatty – I put on three or four kilos every visit! And then all those executions – that wasn't for me. Of course, I knew there was no other way. Drastic measures had to be taken, especially as the front moved closer. The last time I saw Horst-Eberhard was at Christmas in '44 – the Americans had broken through the West Wall in the Saar, and the Russians were already in Tarnow – that's when I left on the double. It was high time!'

Then she endured, as she put it, 'the horror': at the Oder bridge her car was trapped in a throng of refugees. 'A depressing sight,' she said, one that made her aware for the first time how serious the situation had become. 'Those poor, harried people with their last few belongings, in little pony-carts, and sometimes with only wheelbarrows, or on bicycles, stumbling along just ahead of the Red Army. Everyone was crowding over the bridge to the west bank, and I almost missed my train. And then that horrible train ride! We were constantly rerouted in the area around Berlin because of an air raid – in broad daylight! And in the afternoon, in Thuringia, we suddenly stopped on an open stretch of track because planes were strafing the train. Everyone rushed out and threw themselves into the ditches and furrows on either side of the track! I was the only one who stayed in my compartment, or else by the time it was over all my bags would have been stolen – and I had food, valuables, furs . . . At night in Munich we had another bad bombing. In the rear part of the train people had been killed and seriously injured. Then some cars were uncoupled, and the locomotive left Munich for Weilheim with only the first-class carriage. I was terribly afraid: what would I do with seven heavy suitcases and boxes if our chauffeur didn't show up? But luckily he was there – the change had been announced over the loudspeaker . . . I had a migraine for days after that horrible trip.'

I asked Gudrun what had become of Horst-Eberhard, and found out that a Polish court had sentenced him to death. He was executed in 1946. 'I didn't find out about his death until a month later,' Gudrun said, 'and even though I figured it had happened, it was still pretty much of a shock. The American major who brought me the news was very nice. "You must be brave," he said, "You mustn't cry. Just say to yourself that your husband, the general, died for the Fatherland, like so many others . . ." After that we saw each other more frequently and became good friends. He was from General Patton's staff, but his sympathies were completely on our side. He hated the Jews and the Bolsheviks, and he was decidedly against making trouble for the

National Socialists. Unfortunately, he was relieved of his duties and his successor wasn't half as friendly.'

Nonetheless, Gudrun had no 'trouble' whatsoever. True, a part of her country home was requisitioned by the military government and a few young officers were billeted with her. But that was, she explained, laughing, 'very amusing,' especially since at that time she would have been 'quite alone otherwise.'

'My goodness!' she said. 'What parties we threw here then, in April of 1945. It was like an endless party. Bryan – that was the lieutenant whom I was closest to – was only twenty-three years old, just a year older than me. He came from New Hampshire. You should have seen all the things he brought me, just so I wouldn't lack for anything! Nylon stockings, and the newest records, perfume, and two refrigerators, and of course loads of cigarettes and alcohol and gas for the car . . .'

'You even had a car?!'

'Of course. Horst-Eberhard's old Horch – it had almost been requisitioned. You know, the Polish women my husband sent me ran to the military government immediately and denounced me. That was really something, considering how well I treated them – I never hit them, and they got fed almost the same food as we Germans . . . Oh well, nothing happened to me – the Amis didn't pay much attention to denunciations, and Bryan saw to everything for me. He was a nice guy; he would've married me and taken me back to New Hampshire. But at that time I was in love with someone else, a captain from Texas, and I just laughed at him. Two years later Bryan came back and tried for two days and two nights to persuade me to become his wife. But at the time I was having a relationship with that nice major; and besides that, I was already receiving my pension as a general's widow. A buddy of Horst's had arranged it, someone who had cooperated with the Amis from very early on. Not one of my American friends would have been able to offer me so much money – certainly not Bryan, who had gone directly from college into the army, and had no profession yet. Still, he was a really nice young man, and at the time, in April of 1945, we were unbelievably happy together. We had come through the war unscathed, and no sooner had become aware of it than we couldn't stop celebrating our luck. It was a wild time – the champagne flowed in streams, and when we weren't totally drunk, we made love . . .'

Gudrun indulged in her memories a while longer before she noticed my quietness and stopped. Then she politely asked, 'You had trouble then, didn't you? Or was that already over? Where were you then in April of '45, when the Amis entered Munich?'

'Not very far from here at all,' I said, 'but unfortunately a little too far.'

'Really? Strange, isn't it, what a difference a couple of kilometres can sometimes make.'